OFFICIAL ROAD MAP OF NEW MEXICO

ISSUED BY NEW MEXICO STATE HIGHWAY DEPARTMENT

1947

NOTE: *This map is being distributed temporarily until our 1947 road map in color is available.*

SCALE IN MILES
0   5   10   20   30   40   50

Plotted on this 1947 New Mexico road map are these important Roswell incident sites:

1 The Brazel/Foster Ranch debris field

2 The "conventional wisdom"/original Frank Kaufmann crash site, a location probably inspired by comments to the press by ufologist Stanton Friedman in 1987

3 The Jim Ragsdale/International UFO Museum crash site and the tiny hamlet of Arabela, near which the classified-research device that became the Roswell crashed saucer was last seen in flight

4 The "revisionist" Randle-Schmitt/first Ragsdale/"true" Kaufmann crash site

5 Roswell Army Air Field

6 Alamogordo Army Air Base, base of operations and launch site for the New York University Constant-Level Balloon Project/Mogul teams

7 The town of Tularosa, where rancher Mack Brazel's family home was located

8 The Barney Barnett/Gerald Anderson crash site

9 Kirtland Army Air Field.

(State of New Mexico; annotations, Mary Martinek)

ROSWELL

ROSWELL

Inconvenient Facts
and the
Will to Believe

KARL T. PFLOCK

Foreword by Dr. Jerry Pournelle

 **Prometheus Books**

59 John Glenn Drive
Amherst, New York 14228-2197

Published 2001 by Prometheus Books

Inquiries should be addressed to
Prometheus Books
59 John Glenn Drive
Amherst, New York 14228–2197
VOICE: 716–691–0133, ext. 207
FAX: 716–564–2711
WWW.PROMETHEUSBOOKS.COM

05 04 03 02 01   5 4 3 2 1

Library of Congress Cataloging-in-Publication Data

Pflock, Karl T.
    Roswell : inconvenient facts and the will to believe / Karl T. Pflock ; foreword by Jerry Pournelle.
        p. cm.
    Includes bibliographical references and index.
    ISBN 1–57392–894–1 (cloth : alk. paper)
    1. Unidentified flying objects—Sightings and encounters—New Mexico—Roswell.
I. Title.

TL789.5.N6 P48 2001
001.942'09789'43—dc21   00–054864

Printed in the United States of America on acid-free paper

For
M^2
who makes everything I do worth doing
and
S^2
who didn't duck when he could have and who is sorely missed

With special thanks to my friend
Fred Whiting
who stood by me when others had doubts

Contents

APPENDICES

Acknowledgments

So many people have been remarkably helpful to me as I have pursued my research and writing, it is difficult to know where to begin in acknowledging their kindness and contributions. So let me do so "before the beginning" with thanks to Stan Friedman and Bill Moore, who were the first ufologists to suggest there was more to Roswell than a mere weather balloon. (They were correct, but for the wrong reasons.)

Above all in the before-the-beginning category, thanks to the "difficult" Bob Todd, who got there first and without whose tireless questioning and archival digging, document analysis, and continual raising of inconvenient facts the truth about Roswell and many of those involved may never have been established. Even when we have been at significant odds—a frequent occurrence—Bob has generously shared key fruits of his labors with me, and I greatly appreciate it. Bob, you deserve far better than you have gotten at the hands of ufology.

I am deeply grateful to Professor C. B. Moore for the hours he spent searching his files and memory, recontacting old associates, and analyzing data, and for the many hours he has spent in correspondence and conversation with me, sharing his results and views. Getting to know Charlie Moore has been one of the major pluses of my Roswell investigation.

Particular thanks to Bob Pratt for insights into some of the more obscure and shadowy aspects of the case and related matters and, especially, his generosity in sharing his very important and enlightening interview with Jesse Marcel Sr., and permitting me to make it publicly available. Thanks, too, to Mark Rodeghier, scientific director of the Center for UFO Studies, for arranging my access to the center's Roswell files and sharing other important source material with me, and to the Fund for UFO Research for its early support of my work and publication of my interim report, *Roswell in Perspective*.

Many other people went out of their way to be helpful, assisting me with research, volunteering important leads and materials, suggesting lines of investigation, offering "reality checks," and giving of their time for interviews and reinterviews and, in some cases, re-reinterviews. In neither any particular order nor by any means all inclusively, my thanks to: Kent Jeffrey and his father, Col. Arthur Jeffrey, USAF (Ret.); Vic Golubic; Kevin Randle; Gene Nieri; Jim Winchell; Mary Cavitt and her late husband, "Cav"; Herb Taylor (who kept after me—and *after* me—to write this book); Jean LaPaz; Arthur Exon; Doyle Rees; Chuck Shaw; Jud Dixon; Ed Bethart; Al Trakowski; Bob Shirkey; Mike Cook; Rhian Jones; Walter Haut; Bob Sheeran; Jim Marion; Joe Stefula; Rick Biskynis; Dave Thomas; Linda Corley; James McAndrew; Jennifer Dalton; Brad Sparks; Phil Klass; Earl Zimmerman; both John Eichelmanns; the late Dave Skeen; Bud Payne; Miller Johnson; Frank Joyce; Dr. Jesse Marcel; Clair Miller; the late Bob Goforth; Martha Proctor; Kal Korff; John Locke; Troy Wilson; William O'Brien; Pat Flanary; the late Walt Whitmore; Mrs. Karl Lambertz; Dan McDonald; Jim Canan; Michelle Van Cleave; Lesley Gosling; Juanita Sultemeier; Hans Mark; Jack Krings; Bob Slusher; the late Daniel Graham; Bob Richardson; Louis Schiavo; Don Berliner; Walter Unrath; Jake Castellano; Manuel Melendez; Max Stanley; David Wagnon; E. T. Wooldridge; Duke Gildenberg; Terry Isaacs; Merle Tucker; Frank Carlucci; Bill LaParl; Jason Rail; Jack Rodden; Christopher Allan; Paul Sewell and his father, Col. Virgil Sewell, USAF (Ret.); Al Putnam; Wolfgang Elston; Klaus Keil; Jim Moseley; William Cassidy; Lucius Free; John Stahl; Ernest Hubbard; John Frampton; Bob Durant; and Mrs. Anton Hansen.

Finally, very special thank yous to my agent, Cherry Weiner, who never gives up, and to my editors, Steven Mitchell and Meghann French, not the least for their patience with my chronic inability to meet deadlines and my charming crotchetiness.

Foreword

Dr. Jerry Pournelle

This is a courageous and important book, and I use neither word lightly. It will take me a bit to explain, and a bit more to show that I've got some right to make such pronouncements. Bear with me.

Karl Pflock opens his book with the bald statement that he is a "pro-UFOlogist." This means that on the balance of evidence he believes there is something there: that when you consider the data in detail, you will find events that cannot be explained by any explanation employing accepted and generally known science and technology. This doesn't mean he is naive. He knows that most cases do have such explanations. Of those, most are misinterpretations of real and explicable events.

Some of those events can be extraordinary. For example, there were the Peruvian and Chilean sightings: big objects in the sky leaving fiery trails as they fell to earth. They were seen by thousands, perhaps tens of thousands, and were certainly "real." They were accompanied by well-articulated stories of alien spacecraft and actual alien sightings. Those stories sprang up everywhere after the sightings in the sky.

They were UFOs all right, in the sense of being unidentified flying objects, but they had a rational—if not easily discovered—explanation.

There was even a government conspiracy.

During the Cold War treaties forbade putting weapons in orbit and building and testing orbital bombardment systems. This was interpreted to include FOBS, Fractional Orbital Bombardment Systems, in which a weapon is placed into earth orbit, but de-orbited to reenter before it makes a complete orbit around the planet. In other words, it depends on what the meaning of the word *orbital* is. The leaders of the USSR, for what seemed to them good, strategic reasons—with a FOBS system they could attack the United States from the south, and thus avoid our early warning systems—decided to develop and test orbital weapons. In order to avoid detection, the weapons were launched southward and made to reenter the atmosphere over South America.

The reentering dummy warheads were seen by far too many people to be simply dismissed as hallucinations. An explanation was needed, and the KGB provided one. It spread UFO stories, including stories of sightings of aliens. Meanwhile, the United States didn't want the USSR to know just how much we knew about their experiments, so the CIA did nothing to counter the rumors. In a word, there was a cover-up in which the leading intelligence services of the world pursued different ends to accomplish the same result. People believed they had seen "real" UFOs, and neither side was interested in debunking the stories.

This interplay between real events and official lies is not uncommon. Often there's another factor: people make statements they later wish they hadn't made but are embarrassed by the prospect of being caught out, so they stick to their stories and embellish them. Then come the commercial hype artists who make money writing up those stories.

All of this makes it very difficult for me to sum up my position as sharply and succinctly as Pflock has done his, but I think I ought to try.

My first introduction to "serious" UFO investigations came when I was in charge of special projects at Aerospace Corporation, Ballistic Systems Division, which was headquartered in San Bernardino, California. Aerospace provided technical support to the U.S. Air Force Systems Command. One of the jobs the air force had in those days was investigation of UFO reports. The sole mission of those investigations was to determine if there was a threat to the United States. This was a "George job," assigned to the junior officer on the base, which meant frequent changes of personnel but sometimes brought in a young enthusiast who took the position seriously. I watched perhaps five investigations and noted that, while they always found a plausible explanation for the reports, it generally took a lot longer and cost a lot more when the investigation was done by a "believer"—but always with the same result, misinterpretation of something real followed by confusion, embellishment, and often outright fraud.

My major task at Aerospace Corporation was to edit a compilation of missile and rocket technologies, Project 75, which was supposed to put together everything we could do in 1964, and everything we would be able to do ten years later (in 1975). For obvious reasons, this was a highly classified project. It also gave me official access to everything officially known, certainly by the ballistic systems and foreign technology divisions of the air force. General Bernard Schriever of systems command created Project 75 and took a personal interest in it. He directed that Dr. Dorrance, the Project 75 director, and I, the editor, be given access to everything affecting rockets, guidance, targeting, reentry, weapons, and spaceflight. No one but a damn fool would assume he knows everything, but if anyone did know everything about space technology at that time I was one of them. I suppose it is possible that somewhere in the air force there was a store of technology derived from study of recovered alien spacecraft and carefully kept secret from the people responsible for restructuring our strategic offensive forces (SOF)—that was the point of Project 75—but I seriously doubt it. What would be the point? What would it be kept secret for? Rebuilding the SOF was the most important task the air force had; certainly all the generals thought so.

Years later I became the science editor of *Galaxy Science Fiction* magazine. Unsurprisingly, I got a lot of "flying saucer" stories. Most of them were hogwash, but once in a while I'd get one that I couldn't figure out. In those days I met a lot of UFO enthusiasts. They didn't seem sufficiently skeptical. On the other hand, I met and interviewed a lot of people, including some of the leading figures—pro and con—in the UFO world of the 1970s, and I got pretty familiar with the evidence.

I was also president of the Science Fiction Writers of America and was often on book tours promoting my books, so I got asked about the subject a lot. As it happened, I was on one television show—I think David Susskind's—with Isaac Asimov, and when the subject of UFOs inevitably came up, Isaac said, "They can't exist. If they were real, they'd come to the government and say, 'Here we are,' unless of course they have some reason to be secret, but if they do want to be secret, any technology that would let them be here at all would be enough to let them *be* secret. There's no possible explanation of those sightings! If they want to be secret, they'll be secret."

That irritated me, and I shot back, "Isaac, you don't work much with students, do you? Suppose the Alpha Centauri University Department of Xenothropology wants to study us and forbids the students to contaminate us with knowledge of their existence. Do you really think seniors and grad students might not get drunk and play some tricks?" Isaac had no answer, but he remained convinced: there were no such things, there never were, and that's that. If the standard UFO investigators seemed to me insufficiently skeptical, Isaac seemed overly so.

So eventually I wrote my own take on the subject, which was pretty close to Karl Pflock's today. I hadn't found any single case that convinced me, but there was just so much there! And I said in my article that we have convicted people of murder on less evidence than we have for the existence of "real" UFOs.

All of which is the long way around to answer the question, do I believe in UFOs, and what do I think of people who do? To this, I would have to say that over the years I have become less inclined to be a "pro-UFOlogist" than Karl.

Which brings me to this book and why I call it both important and courageous. It's important because the subject is important. The subject is important because it opens the possibility of data unexplainable by our current knowledge—and there's very little more important than that.

Years ago I was charged by a major aerospace firm to investigate the "Dean Drive," a gadget that theoretically could convert angular acceleration to linear acceleration—in other words, a "spacedrive." Such a thing is totally impossible within physics as we know it, but if one existed and worked, then clearly we needed new theory, and the company that owned such technology would be in line to make a lot of money, not to mention Nobel prizes for some of the scientific staff. I won't go into details, but I didn't buy the Dean Drive. Later I discovered that another major company had a team in Washington at the same time I was there. Boeing wasn't the only outfit smart enough to see how important such a thing would be it in the highly unlikely event that it worked.

In the course of chasing down the Dean Drive I came across some pretty respectable people who thought they had seen it work. Unfortunately, they had never been given the chance to do extensive tests, and the demonstrations they had seen left plenty of room for misinterpretation or outright fraud. One person who took Dean seriously was Col. William Davis, Ph.D., USAF, who developed a series of equations called Davis Mechanics that seemed to open the possibility of a spacedrive. Most physicists didn't agree. They called him Willy "Spacedrive" Davis.

Twenty years later I was given a small grant to put together a meeting of people who had once taken Davis Mechanics seriously. I also brought in the last of those who had actually seen the Dean Drive, and Dr. Robert Forward, a Hughes physicist open to new ideas. Nothing much came of the meeting, but in the course of it Dr. Forward said something I never forgot: "Get a result. A contrary result is worth more than all the theory you'll ever develop."

And of course he was right. Most scientific progress comes from experimental results that aren't in line with what you expected. And clearly, if UFOs are real in the sense of being unexplainable by contemporary theory, then that fact is one of the most important things we'll ever learn.

Secondly, this book is important because it is thorough and complete, and definitive. When you finish it, you will know about as much as we will ever know about "Roswell": what happened, what didn't happen, and why we believed so much that ultimately turned out not to be true. This is as thorough and definitive a case investigation as I have ever seen.

Finally, we come to courageous. This book is courageous because it honestly examines what has become the best-known UFO incident in history. Ask anyone what they know about UFOs and, unless they are of that small group that takes the subject quite seriously, they will begin to talk about the Roswell incident—and some of the major UFO experts will do so as well. In that sense, Roswell is the most important UFO incident of all time.

Years ago, science-fiction author Ted Sturgeon was asked what it would take to get him to believe in "flying saucers." His reply was, "Wreckage and bodies." Ted died before Roswell became famous, but he would have been highly interested. Wreckage and bodies. For most people that's what Roswell promises.

When you finish this book you will know everything you need to know about Roswell. You may not like the conclusions Pflock draws, but it's hard to quarrel with them. They aren't the conclusions that he and perhaps most of his readers hoped to come to. Seeking the truth means taking the truth seriously and following the facts where the lead, no matter what you want to believe. That takes courage.

As I said, an important and courageous book.

Studio City, California
August 2000

Man's most valuable trait is a judicious sense of what not to believe.

—Euripides

ONE

"THE MOST IMPORTANT CASE IN UFO HISTORY"

I am a "pro-UFOlogist."

This is what my friendly ufological antagonist–colleague Philip J. Klass calls those of us who are convinced by the data that there is something more to UFOs than mistakes, hoaxes, delusions, weather balloons, and tub-thumping by hucksters to keep the book, television, and lecture-circuit pelf flowing.

I am also an "anti-Roswellian."

These two facts confound both pro- and "anti-UFOlogists." How is it possible someone who takes UFOs seriously, even thinks some of them were vehicles from another planet, can also be convinced the event that leading ufologists and thousands of UFO buffs have considered and continue to consider "the most important case in UFO history" is bunk?[1] This is a question I hope to answer to everyone's satisfaction in this book.

I began my inquiry into Roswell an agnostic, with no ax to grind, no vested interest in one theory or another, no allegiance to anything but a commitment to uncover and make public the truth about this remarkable case. I began with no conclusions about what was found in the remote reaches of south-central New Mexico in July 1947, nor about official actions taken with respect to it. I began only with the strong suspicion that whatever was discovered was *not* the remains of a mere weather balloon and its radar target—the official "explanation"—and that military authorities who acted on the discovery apparently felt constrained to cover up the true nature of what was found.

I was wrong—about myself, that is. My odyssey through the tangled Roswell incident maze revealed to me I was not as objective as I believed myself to be. All too often, my personal hopes and preconceptions blinkered my thinking, and it was only after some rude awakenings and subsequent and sometimes painful reconsideration that I realized this. Thus this book is not only about the Roswell case itself, but also my own inner journey of discovery, a trek I believe has made me a better researcher—and, yes, a better ufologist.

That said, there is *no doubt* what fell to earth and was recovered by the U.S. Army Air Forces was not just a weather balloon and associated equipment. So, too, there is no doubt the military concocted the weather balloon yarn to squelch press and public interest in the matter and took other actions to keep the truth about it under wraps.

There are several highly credible witnesses who have given remarkable and mutually corroborative accounts of what was found, where it came from, and what was done about it—and what was not found and how it came to be a part of the Roswell story. There is substantial documentary and other evidence that supports what these witnesses have recounted. There is still more that tends to support or in important ways is not inconsistent with their stories.

This body of testimony and evidence establishes beyond a reasonable doubt that alien voyagers were *not* shipwrecked here over a half century ago.

There are also other witnesses—and "witnesses"—whose stories, along with seemingly supporting documentary and other evidence, have fueled the furor over Roswell and captured the public imagination as has no other UFO case before or since. This more titillating side of the story has dominated the debate and persuaded thousands that a flying saucer crashed, killing its crew, with the lot being swept up and spirited away into secrecy by the United States government. This remains the prevailing ufological and popular view, despite the fact that the weight of evidence is overwhelmingly on the other side of the scales.

SPECULATION AND JOURNALISTIC LICENSE

A good deal of what has been accepted as fact about this case—both pro and con, though mostly the former—is unacknowledged speculation; or comes to us from less than credible witnesses; or is the result of a troubling mixture of faulty analysis, conclusion jumping, and failure to address "inconvenient" facts and contradictions because of an overwhelming will to believe. In some instances, all or several of these factors are involved. The melancholy truth is that much of what has been advanced as fact is little more—and all too often, nothing more—than speculation, armchair theorizing, unacknowledged taking of journalistic license, and uncritical presentation of purportedly factual testimony and evidence.

I do not ask the reader to accept the above assertions on faith. In the pages that follow, my findings and supporting sources and documentation are set forth for all to judge. I ask only that judgment be suspended until everything I offer has been considered with care and objectivity.

VALLÉE'S LAW

Much of the difficulty of sorting out the truth about Roswell is a consequence of what I think of as Vallée's Law. In *Confrontations*, veteran ufologist and computer scientist Jacques Vallée observes that the excitement and sometimes circuslike atmosphere surrounding highly publicized UFO cases almost invariably interferes with getting at the truth about what happened. He writes, "Here we must assume that some of the data is misleading. The cases that receive a high level of media publicity are especially suspect."[2] To this I would add that, even when the truth is ferreted out, the hype frequently makes it all but impossible to make it known and accepted. The legend become reality is all but unchallengeable.

Roswell is such a case, in spades. Moreover, the investigator's job is made still more difficult by the need to penetrate the mists of time and fallible memory. More than fifty-three years have rolled by since the original events unfolded, and there was an almost thirty-one-year hiatus before UFO researcher Stanton T. Friedman interviewed former air force intelligence officer Jesse Marcel and ufology realized Roswell might be something other than just another hoax or mistake—or weather balloon.[3]

Further, the Roswell "mystery" now sustains a virtual mini-industry, paralleling in almost every respect that spawned by the assassination of President John F. Kennedy, with a colorful and voluble cast of True Believers and True Unbelievers and, of late, the New Witness of the Month Parade. After a slow start, the town of Roswell has joined in, raking in tourists and their money by the thousands and millions with annual saucer crash-and-burn festivals and year-round promotion keying on a UFO Capital of the World theme.

The principal surviving witnesses find themselves having—or wanting—to be "on" almost constantly. Other individuals have gained seats on the Roswell bandwagon with tales of their alleged involvement in or knowledge of the incident and/or its aftermath, while still others have embellished their genuine roles in a sometimes unconscious attempt to keep up with the "more interesting" accounts of the Johnny- and Janey-come-latelies. In the ranks of ufology, the atmosphere of the case remains highly charged, with all the elements, positive and negative, of a competitive treasure hunt.

With all this implies, it is no wonder a Roswell mythos has taken firm root and bitter rivalries have flared among researchers, reminiscent of the nineteenth-century "dinosaur wars" waged by pioneer paleontologists Edward Drinker Cope and Othniel Marsh. Like that famous fossil feud, the Roswell treasure hunt has inspired a tremendous and often uncritical gathering of material and a rush to often equally uncritical interpretations of that material, pro and con. As a result, Roswell has become a curious ufological contradiction. It has given the field what almost certainly is the largest body of data ever collected on a single UFO case, while at the same time saddling it with the ufological equivalent of the brontosaurus.

Roswell and related matters, along with the UFO abductions obsession, have taken center stage in ufology and the public perception of the field and its subject matter. Far too many of the field's very limited resources have been poured into investigation—and exploitation—of the case, to the detriment of study of others that offer real potential for advancing our knowledge and understanding of the phenomena labeled *UFO*. In *Roswell in Perspective*, my 1994 interim report on my research and findings, I wrote, "It may be no exaggeration to say, as Roswell goes, so goes ufology."[4] And so it has gone.

THE RESEARCH THAT GOT ME HERE

At its outset in mid-1992, my investigation was an entirely self-funded effort. Nine months and a research trip to New Mexico later, the Fund for UFO Research (FUFOR) approved a substantial grant to support my work, including another field investigation visit to New Mexico, where I have resided since December 1993. On my second trip, I spent two and a half weeks interviewing and reinterviewing about two dozen witnesses and sources and conducting archival and on-site research, including a visit to the location at which rancher William W. "Mack" Brazel made his at first surprising discovery.

After relocating to the Land of Enchantment, I made many additional trips to Lincoln and Chaves counties and conducted interviews with additional witnesses and knowledgeable sources, plus follow-up interviews with others. I visited the ranch house where Mack Brazel, Jesse Marcel, and U.S. Army Counter Intelligence Corps Capt. Sheridan Cavitt are said to have spent the night before investigating Brazel's find, and have trekked to two of the several locations identified as the "true" site where a crashed flying saucer and the bodies of its crew are alleged to have been found.

I also have spent uncounted hours digging into the files of and consulting with researchers at the Center for UFO Studies, the National Archives, the Library of Congress, the University of New Mexico's Institute of Meteoritics, the U.S. Naval Observatory, the Smithsonian Institution, the Center for Air Force History, the National Personnel Records Center, the New Mexico Institute of Mining and Technology, the International UFO Museum and Research Center at Roswell, the Roswell Public Library, and so on.

Even greater time has been devoted to in-person and telephone interviews with witnesses and sources; viewing and reviewing the unedited videotape "depositions" taken under the auspices of the Fund for UFO Research; listening to audiotaped interviews conducted and kindly provided to me by others; and study and analysis of and follow-up research based upon affidavits executed by more than thirty witnesses, other original source material, and the books, published papers, and other materials of my fellow Roswell investigators and the pertinent work of other researchers.

My Washington and intelligence community experience and associations were helpful on a number of fronts. I sought to learn what former high-level officials, whom it is reasonable to assume well could have been "in the know," knew and remembered. I also explored certain aspects of the case with members and key staff of the U.S. Congress. I tracked down, invited, and gained assistance from retired and other former agents of the Counter Intelligence Corps and its air force successor, the Office of Special Investigations, who had been involved in or had knowledge of Roswell and related matters.

I also have compared notes, shared information, and debated theories, facts, and issues with fellow ufologists across the spectrum of belief about the case and UFOs in general. I am grateful to all of them for their insights and generous sharing of time and the fruits of their work. Of course, I alone am responsible for what is set down here.

PUTTING ROSWELL IN PERSPECTIVE

My colleague Jerome Clark's judgment that Roswell is the most important case in UFO history may well be right on the mark, but not in the sense he meant. What Clark had in mind was what it would mean for mankind if the wreckage of an alien craft and the bodies of its crew had been recovered on New Mexico's high desert in 1947.

Less earthshaking to say the least, but very important to those of us concerned to restore a measure of balance and perspective to ufology, is how the field deals with the far more mundane but nonetheless fascinating reality of Roswell. So far, it has not done well. Ufology has gotten well out on the Roswell limb, a branch overburdened with questionable claims and conclusions, and faulty analysis. It is high time ufologists set aside their will to believe (and *dis*believe) and faced up to the facts—including and especially the inconvenient ones—consistently, truthfully, and objectively, and that fantasy, exaggeration, and fraud are rooted out and exposed, not only with respect to Roswell but across the board.

I hope that by recounting here what I have discovered in more than eight years of investigating Roswell and, through this work, what I have learned about ufology and my own thinking and approach to UFO research, I may contribute some small measure to a new and productive direction in ufology. Skeptics and "pro-UFOlogists" who are sincere and critically thoughtful in their pursuit of the facts and the truths they embody share a good deal of common ground. If we come to recognize this and deal with each other as colleagues, who knows what might come of it?

NOTES

1. For example, see Jerome Clark in the *International UFO Reporter* (July–August 1993): 14.

2. Jacques Vallée, *Confrontations* (New York: Ballantine, 1990), p. 15.

3. Stanton T. Friedman and Don Berliner, *Crash at Corona* (New York: Paragon House, 1992), pp. 8–11; Ted Bloecher, *Report on the UFO Wave of 1947* (Washington, D.C.: self-published, 1967), pp. I–13, 14.

4. Karl T. Pflock, *Roswell in Perspective* (Washington, D.C.: Fund for UFO Research, 1994), p. 3. An aside: On p. 130 of his book *The Real Roswell Crashed-Saucer Coverup* (Amherst, N.Y.: Prometheus, 1997), Phil Klass makes a point of noting that the cover of *RiP* carries this disclaimer: "The conclusions, opinions, and ideas expressed herein are those of the author and do not necessarily represent the views of the Fund for UFO Research, its officers, or its board members." Klass implies this was something unique and indicated fund concerns about my findings. In fact, until recently, the fund included this disclaimer on *all* of its publications, including those written by its own board members. I prepared the cover for *RiP* myself and lifted the disclaimer word for word from an earlier fund publication.

TWO

THE "CONVENTIONAL WISDOM"

Not including the government's cover story—and there *was* a cover story—two comprehensive versions of the Roswell incident have been advanced and continuously "improved upon." The first encompasses what Roswell author Kevin Randle has labeled the "conventional wisdom"—Roswell as we first came to know and, at least some of us, love it. The other is "revisionist," with Randle and his former partner Donald Schmitt and Schmitt's new sidekick Thomas Carey its principal proponents. Blending new material, interpretations, and speculations with elements of the conventional wisdom, it is Roswell as some would have us know and love it.

In order to assess these interpretations of the complicated and convoluted Roswell story, the true state of knowledge about the facts and the fiction, and discern the truths they embody, it is important to have a firm grasp of the salient elements of each version and how they relate to each other and to new and some not so new but previously unpublished or ignored information, as well as the many Roswell outriders that keep surfacing. So this is where I shall begin, presenting first the conventional Roswell story and then the revisionist.

July 2, 1947. The day had been a very hot one throughout the American southwest, perhaps nowhere hotter than in the small southeastern New Mexico city of Roswell. Shortly before ten o'clock that evening, Mr. and Mrs. Dan Wilmot were relaxing on the front porch of their home near the center of the town of about fifteen thousand, hoping to catch a cool breeze. Suddenly, a large oval object, "like two inverted saucers faced mouth-to-mouth" appeared in the sky, streaking in from the southeast. Glowing "as though light were showing through from inside," the UFO sped rapidly and silently northwest, toward Corona, about eighty-five air miles distant. When Wilmot, a respected local businessman, reported the sighting to the *Roswell Daily Record* about a week later, he said the object appeared to be fifteen to twenty feet in diameter, flew at high speed, "between 400 and 500 miles per hour," and passed over the city at about fifteen hundred feet.[1] How Wilmot estimated the size, speed, and altitude of the UFO is not recorded, but without references to objects of known size and other benchmarks, these could not have been anything more than guesses.

At about the same time that evening, quite possibly the same phenomenon was observed by William Woody and his father from their farm southeast of Roswell and due east of Roswell Army Air Field. However, the Woodys' interpretation was quite different from Dan Wilmot's. In a May 1993 interview, the younger Woody told me he and his father were startled to see a large, very bright object appear out of the southwest, moving at very great speed. Displaying a long red tail and glowing intensely white, so bright objects on the ground cast shadows, it sped across the night sky and quickly passed from sight beyond the northern horizon. Woody says his father was certain it was a very large meteorite, which he thought surely had struck the earth about forty miles north of Roswell.[2]

Also about the same time, about twice that distance northwest of the Woody farm, a violent thunderstorm reportedly raged over neighboring Lincoln County, an early harbinger of New Mexico's monsoon season. William W. "Mack" Brazel watched the storm with interest from the tiny ranch house on the J. B. Foster Ranch, about thirty miles southeast of Corona. As ranch manager, the prospect of rain for the thirsty land was always important to him. According to his son Bill, speaking years later, Mack Brazel thought the storm unusual. Bill quoted his father as saying, "The lightning kept wanting to strike the same spots time and again." Bill also claimed his father heard a strange explosion, louder that the storm's violent thunderclaps. When interviewed in 1991, one of Brazel's neighbors, the late Marian Strickland, also said she recalled the storm and a loud explosion.[3]

THE DISCOVERY

Early the next morning, July 3, Brazel, possibly accompanied by seven-year-old neighbor William "Dee" Proctor, rode out across the ranch to assess the rainfall resulting from the storm of the night before and check on the well-being of some of the livestock. A couple of miles from the ranch house, Brazel was surprised to discover a large amount of unfamiliar debris strewn over an area his son Bill recalls as being about a quarter mile long and several hundred feet wide, with a gouge four to five hundred feet long down the middle on its long axis, oriented roughly north-south.[4]

According to contemporary news reports of a July 8 interview with Mack Brazel and the much later accounts of Bill Brazel, Bill's younger sister Bessie Schreiber, Mack's sister Lorraine Ferguson, and some of the Foster Ranch area neighbors, the debris was peculiar but not something they considered at the time to be out of this world. It included a grayish-silver metallic foil, in pieces ranging from a few inches to two, three, or more feet across; many small, lightweight "beams" the color and texture of balsa wood, one-half to three-eighths of an inch thick and ranging from a few inches to a couple of feet in length; a quantity of tough, parchmentlike paper; pieces of hard, black or blackish-brown plastic; and lengths of something resembling monofilament fishing line. Some of the beams were attached to fragments of the foil-like material with wide, "whitish" or clear tape imprinted with pastel designs resembling flowers or, as Lorraine Ferguson said her brother Mack put it, "like the kind of stuff you find all over Japanese or Chinese firecrackers; not really writing, just wiggles and such."[5]

Later the same day, Brazel visited neighbors Floyd and Loretta Proctor, showing them a small piece of the material he had found, from Mrs. Proctor's description, apparently a piece of one of the balsalike beams. When I interviewed her in 1992, she remembered it being "a little sliver of a wood-looking stuff . . . kind of a brownish tan . . . about the size of a pencil and about three or four inches long." Mrs. Proctor told me she thought Brazel and her husband, Floyd, attempted unsuccessfully to cut and burn the woodlike material. She also recalled that Brazel talked about finding other very lightweight material, which looked like aluminum foil. According to her, he said this foil would "fold out" after being "crinkled up." Brazel also described "tape that had some sort of figures on it" and said these figures were "a kind of purple" color. From her neighbor's description, Mrs. Proctor had the impression these markings "resembled hieroglyphics [sic]." The Proctors suggested Brazel report his find to officials in Roswell. They thought it might be something belonging to or of interest to the government, and he might get a reward if he took it in.[6]

On Saturday evening, July 5, Mack Brazel went into the small railroad town of Corona, the nearest settlement of any size. While in the town's bar, he ran into a relative, Hollis Wilson, and an acquaintance. When Brazel mentioned his discovery, the two men excitedly told him about the flying saucer reports streaming in from all over New Mexico and other western states, hundreds of them during that Fourth of July weekend alone. Flying saucers had been in the papers and on the radio for a couple of weeks, since a private pilot named Kenneth Arnold had reported seeing a formation of nine unidentified, strange, and high-performance flying machines near Mount Rainier in Washington State on June 24. Rewards were even being offered for proof of their reality.

Working out on his remote ranch with no radio or newspapers, Brazel had been completely unaware of these reports and the excitement and concern they had generated. Thinking Mack may have found parts of a downed saucer, Wilson seconded the Proctors' suggestion that he report his discovery to the authorities.[7]

BRAZEL REPORTS HIS FIND

The following morning, Sunday, July 6, Brazel made the long drive to Roswell, taking some samples of what he had found and characterized to his daughter Bessie as "just a bunch of garbage." According to his son Bill, when Brazel got to town, he first called the United States Weather Bureau office. Someone there suggested he take his find to the Chaves County sheriff.[8]

While Brazel was telling County Sheriff George Wilcox about the discovery and showing him the collection of odd material, a call came in from Frank Joyce, an announcer and news reporter at KGFL, one of Roswell's two radio stations. Joyce was making his regular morning "who got drunk last night" local news call, and the sheriff put Brazel on the line to tell his story. When I first interviewed him, in 1992, Joyce told me that, at the time, he did not think much of the rancher's story, but nonetheless, he suggested Brazel or Wilcox call Roswell Army Air Field, home of the 509th Bomb Group, then the only unit in the world equipped to deliver nuclear weapons. His notion was that, since the thing probably fell out of the sky, the army air forces ought to be told about it.[9]

Sheriff Wilcox then called Roswell AAF and was put through to the 509th's intelligence officer, Maj. Jesse A. Marcel, who in the late 1970s recalled he was just sitting down to lunch in the base officers' club. As soon as he finished his lunch, Marcel went into town, talked with Brazel and the sheriff, and looked over what Brazel had brought in. He arranged to meet Brazel at the sheriff's office later that afternoon and, taking some or all of the debris with him, returned to the base to report to base and bomb group commander Col. William H. "Butch" Blanchard.[10]

THE ARMY SWINGS INTO ACTION

According to Marcel, he and Blanchard decided some unusual type of aircraft may have crashed, and Blanchard ordered his chief intelligence officer to "take whatever . . . [he] needed" and get out to the ranch right away. More than thirty years later, in several interviews with a number of different investigators and reporters, Marcel claimed he and the late Sheridan W. Cavitt, the officer in charge of the Roswell AAF Counter Intelligence Corps (CIC) detachment, followed Brazel back to the Foster place, each driving his own vehicle. He said they arrived at the primitive ranch house near dusk, and as it would soon be too dark to do anything effective on the debris site, they stayed overnight.[11]

As reported by Roswell authors Randle and Schmitt, Brazel is alleged to have brought some of the debris, including a piece about ten feet in diameter, from the field and stored it in a shed adjacent to the house. During the night's stay, according to Randle and Schmitt, Marcel checked the large piece with a Geiger counter and found no radioactivity.[12]

While Marcel, Cavitt, and Brazel were on their way to the Foster Ranch, Blanchard apparently contacted his superiors at Eighth Air Force headquarters at Fort Worth Army Air Field (later Carswell Air Force Base), Texas. The matter quickly was passed up the chain of command to Strategic Air Command headquarters at Andrews Army Air Field, outside Washington, D.C. This led to orders from SAC's deputy commander, Maj. Gen. Clements McMullen, for the material Brazel had brought in to be flown to him via Fort Worth. Early that evening, an aircraft, probably the 509th's command B-25, a twin-engine bomber used as an executive and courier transport, arrived at Fort Worth AAF, carrying a sealed bag filled with the debris.

The aircraft was met by Eighth Air Force Chief of Staff Col. Thomas J. DuBose and Col. Alan Clark, soon to be the Fort Worth base commander. According to DuBose, the bag immediately was turned over to Clark, who then boarded the Eighth Air Force command B-26, another type of twin-engine bomber serving as an executive transport, which then departed for Andrews AAF. In a 1991 interview, DuBose recalled that McMullen intended to forward the material to Brig. Gen. Benjamin

Chidlaw, deputy commander of Air Material Command at Wright Army Air Field (now part of Wright-Patterson Air Force Base), Ohio.[13]

According to Marcel, early the next morning, Monday, July 7, Marcel, Cavitt, and Brazel trekked overland to the debris site, a stretch of dry, rolling prairie about two miles from the ranch house. Cavitt and Brazel rode horses, and Marcel followed in one of the vehicles he and Cavitt had driven to the ranch.[14] Decades later, Marcel claimed what they found there was totally unfamiliar to him, yet in most respects, his descriptions of the material are closely similar to those attributed to Mack Brazel—odd but hardly unearthly.[15] The two army officers collected as much of the material as they could handle and, well after dark, headed back to Roswell AAF, traveling separately.[16]

Marcel did not go directly to the base. He first stopped at his home in town, waking his wife, Viaud, and eleven-year-old son, Jesse Jr., to tell them about the strange discovery. He brought some of debris into the house, where he and his son spread it out on the kitchen floor as Mrs. Marcel watched.

Now a medical doctor, the younger Marcel told me in 1993 what he excitedly examined that night included "a thick foil-like metallic gray substance; a brittle brownish-black plastic-like material, like Bakelite; and . . . fragments of what appeared to be I-beams." Dr. Marcel recalled that some of the I-beam fragments were "embossed" with "pink or purplish-pink" characters which, in a general way, reminded him of Egyptian hieroglyphs, and said that his father "may have mentioned the words 'flying saucer' in connection with the material." In a 1981 interview, Viaud Marcel said it was she who first noticed these markings, which she recalled as being very faint, and brought them to the attention of her husband and son.[17]

THE PRESS ANNOUNCEMENT

Very early on the morning of Tuesday, July 8, Major Marcel, possibly joined by Captain Cavitt, conferred with Colonel Blanchard, showing him at least some of the debris they had collected. Blanchard then convened his regular morning staff meeting an hour and a half earlier than usual. After this meeting, at which the strange debris was discussed, Blanchard apparently telephoned 1st Lt. Walter G. Haut, the base public relations officer, and dictated this now famous press announcement:

> The many rumors regarding the flying disc became a reality yesterday when the intelligence office of the 509th Bomb Group of the Eighth Air Force, Roswell Army Air Field, was fortunate enough to gain possession of a disc through the cooperation of one of the local ranchers and the sheriff's office of Chaves county.
>
> The flying object landed on a ranch near Roswell sometime last week. Not having phone facilities, the rancher stored the disc until such time as he was able to contact the Sheriff's office, who in turn notified Major Jesse A. Marcel of the 509th Bomb Group Intelligence office.
>
> Action was immediately taken and the disc was picked up at the rancher's home. It was inspected at the Roswell Army Air Field and subsequently loaned [sic] by Major Marcel to higher headquarters.[18]

About noon, Haut contacted Roswell's two radio stations and two newspapers, KSWS, KGFL, the *Roswell Daily Record*, and the *Roswell Morning Dispatch*. Station KSWS program director George Walsh broke the story after Haut read it to him over the telephone. He immediately put it on the air and then phoned it in to the Associated Press bureau in Albuquerque. Soon after, KGFL's Frank Joyce, in his capacity as a United Press Association stringer, filed the story with UP by Western Union telegram.[19]

National and international media interest was massive and built rapidly. Soon the Roswell AAF public relations office, the local papers, the sheriff's office, and KSWS were swamped with calls.[20] The Associated Press directed its Albuquerque bureau to pursue the story as a top priority. Wasting no time, the bureau chief sent reporter Jason Kellahin and wire-photo technician and photographer R. D. "Robin" Adair to Roswell.[21]

George Walsh remembers the furor well. As he told me in an April 1993 interview,

> All afternoon, I tried to call Sheriff Wilcox for more information, but could never get through to him. . . . Media people called me from all over the world. . . . [T]hat same afternoon, Haut called for the second time. He was quite indignant. "What the hell did you do?" he asked. I told him. He then said he had not been able to make a call out of his office since his initial conversation with me. He also said, "I got a call from the War Department that told me to shut up." This was very unusual, so I asked if the department had given him a correction or another contact to provide the media. He told me his orders were to, quote, shut up, unquote.[22]

SECURING THE DEBRIS FIELD

While the world press pursued the story, CIC Captain Cavitt and his senior agent, M.Sgt. Lewis "Bill" Rickett, who died in November 1992, drove to the Foster Ranch to inspect the debris field. In interviews with several ufologists and authors, Rickett claimed a number of military policemen and base provost marshall Maj. Edwin D. Easley were on the site, controlling access to it.[23] Rickett said he remembered seeing only some of the foil-like debris and asserted that it possessed unusual lightness and strength. He also said, "There wasn't very much of it, maybe forty or fifty small pieces," and attributed cryptic but pointed comments to Cavitt and one of the MPs which he said made clear to him this was a hush-hush matter.[24]

Possibly the same afternoon, July 8, William Woody and his father, in the hope of finding the huge meteorite they were certain they had seen fall to earth a few days before, headed north from Roswell, driving up U.S. Highway 285. William Woody told me he and his father were surprised to discover armed soldiers blocking all access off 285 from about twenty miles north of Roswell to the general store and gas station at Ramon, about sixty miles north of town. At Ramon, the Woodys turned around and headed home.[25]

THE SAUCER AND ITS CREW

Glenn Dennis, a key player in the Roswell saga, claims he first became involved on that same fateful day. Dennis, then twenty-two and fresh out of the San Francisco College of

Mortuary Science, was an embalmer and hearse-ambulance driver at the Ballard Funeral Home in Roswell. He alleges that, at about one-thirty in the afternoon, he began receiving a number of odd telephone inquiries from the Roswell AAF "mortuary officer."

The funeral home had a contract with the army to provide mortuary and ambulance services, so it was not unusual to receive telephone calls from the air base. However, Dennis told me in our first of many interviews, these calls involved specific questions about preparation and preservation of bodies that had been exposed to the elements for some time. They also included inquiries about the size and availability of the smallest hermetically sealed caskets Ballard stocked.[26] Dennis said he assumed there had been a military plane crash and offered to be of assistance, but he was told the information was needed "in case something comes up in the future."[27]

According to Frank J. Kaufmann, apparently not long before Dennis received his first call from the mortuary officer, the army's search activities on the Foster Ranch led to the discovery of a second site about two and a half miles east-southeast of the debris field. Kaufmann, who had served as an army enlisted man at Roswell AAF during and for a time after World War II and in July 1947 was a civilian personnel clerk on the base headquarters staff, claims to have still been on active duty in an intelligence capacity and a key player in the army's saucer recovery and cover-up efforts. In 1990, he told authors Randle and Schmitt it was at this second site a damaged but nearly intact disk-shaped craft about thirty feet in diameter was discovered. It appeared the debris found by Mack Brazel had fallen from the stricken saucer as it plunged toward the earth. Then he added this startling claim: The alien craft had carried its crew to its death. Near the crashed saucer, he said, the bodies of three or four small, slightly built beings with large heads and eyes were discovered, sprawled on the harsh desert soil.[28]

According to Kaufmann, army teams continued to collect the debris at both sites and transport it to Roswell AAF throughout the afternoon. Allegedly, this was carried out under the direction of "Warrant Officer" Robert Thomas, who, said Kaufmann, flew in from Washington, D.C., on special assignment. Late in the day, the bodies were trucked to the base. (I enclose Thomas's rank in quotation marks because Kaufmann has alluded that it was merely a cover, that Thomas had a much higher rank and status.)[29]

During one of his early interviews with Randle and Schmitt, Kaufmann sketched the crashed vehicle as he said it appeared at the site where it was discovered. He refused to give the authors the original drawing, which he tore up, but Schmitt, a skilled artist, redrew it from memory immediately after the interview.[30]

"DEBRIS LIFT"

About the same time Glenn Dennis says he received the first telephone call from the Roswell AAF mortuary officer, a B-29 bomber was readied for a flight to Fort Worth, on orders from Colonel Blanchard. Allegedly, at least the senior members of the crew for this special flight were hand-picked by Blanchard. These are reported to have included lieutenant colonels Payne Jennings, Roswell AAF and 509th deputy commander, and Robert I. Barrowclough, base executive officer.[31]

Robert R. Porter, by interesting coincidence one of Loretta Proctor's brothers, was the bomber's flight engineer. He has related that he helped load a number of very lightweight, brown-paper-wrapped packages delivered to the aircraft in a staff car. Porter has testified that Capt. William E. Anderson, a Roswell AAF engineering officer, said the packages contained parts of a flying saucer.[32]

In a 1992 interview, Robert Shirkey, in 1947 a first lieutenant and an assistant bomb group operations officer, told me he helped make out the flight plan for this trip on Blanchard's orders. Soon after this was completed, Blanchard arrived in the base operations building. Shirkey said he stood in the operations office doorway with Blanchard, watching Major Marcel and several others quickly pass down the hallway and through the building to the waiting B-29. According to Shirkey, Marcel and another member of the group carried open cardboard boxes filled with debris, including what appeared to be pieces of metal, "brushed stainless steel in color," and a small "beam" about two feet long with peculiar markings on it. One of the other men carried a piece of the metallic sheet material, measuring about eighteen by twenty-four inches. Shirkey also said he recalled seeing packages wrapped in brown paper being loaded from a staff car directly into the aircraft on the ramp. Shirkey alleged he later heard all the material was from a crashed flying saucer.[33]

Marcel and the material he and the other man carried to the aircraft were put aboard the B-29, and the bomber departed on a nonstop flight to Fort Worth Army Air Field in Texas. Shirkey told me Blanchard waited until the airplane lifted off and then left the operations building, according to some, to visit the debris field under a cover story that he was going on leave.[34]

The flight carrying Marcel was probably the second in a "debris lift" that has been claimed to eventually total as many as eight flights. It was preceded by the B-25 courier mission ordered by McMullen and, allegedly, was followed the next day, Wednesday, July 9, by the departures of three fully loaded C-54s, four-engine transports with average payloads of more than twelve thousand pounds, which carried their cargo to destinations purportedly including Wright Army Air Field, Ohio, Kirtland Army Air Field, near Albuquerque, and the then-closed city of Los Alamos, where the atomic bomb had been developed. It also has been claimed that another B-29, bearing a mysterious sealed crate, also flew out of Roswell that day.[35]

The late Robert E. Smith was an enlisted member of the 1st Air Transport Unit, based at Roswell AAF in July 1947. Smith came forward after the Roswell crashed-saucer story was featured on the popular television show *Unsolved Mysteries* in late September 1989 (rebroadcast in January 1990). Among other things, he testified that, under conditions of high security, he helped load crates aboard some of the 1st ATU's C-54s. He said the members of his detail were told the contents were from a plane crash, but they heard from an unnamed someone in Roswell they actually were from "a strange object." Smith claimed a sergeant in his unit showed him a small piece of what he said was the unusual material being loaded. It was jagged and about two to three inches square. "When you crumpled it up, it then laid back out; and when it did, it kind of crackled, making a sound like cellophane. . . . There were no creases."[36]

The conventional wisdom has it that one of the aircraft Smith may have helped load was a 1st ATU C-54 allegedly piloted by Capt. Oliver "Pappy" Henderson. Henderson's widow, Sappho, claimed he told her he delivered his cargo to Wright Field, Ohio, home of the Air Materiel Command and the Air Technical Intelligence Center, and that it included several strange bodies, not of this earth, which were packed in dry ice.[37]

THE AUTOPSY AND THE NURSE

While Marcel and some of the debris he collected on the Foster Ranch were winging toward Fort Worth the afternoon of July 8, at least three of the alien bodies lay in the Roswell AAF hospital, according to what Glenn Dennis told me and other Roswell researchers he learned from a friend who was an army nurse stationed there at the time.

About 5 P.M., Dennis pulled the Ballard Cadillac combination hearse-ambulance around to the rear of the base infirmary, stopping next to one of three (in some of Dennis's tellings, two) military field ambulances parked at the entrance ramp and near which two military policemen stood. Dennis told me he was bringing in a soldier who had been injured in a motorcycle accident in town. As he and his patient walked up the ramp, he noticed that the back doors of two of the army vehicles were open. Inside he saw some unusual wreckage. "There were several pieces which looked like the bottom of a canoe, about three feet in length," he said. "It resembled stainless steel with a purple hue, as if it had been exposed to high temperature. There was some strange-looking writing on the material resembling Egyptian hieroglyphics [sic]."

After signing in the injured soldier, Dennis headed for the staff lounge, intending to find his nurse friend and "have a Coke" with her. As he walked down the hall, she emerged from one of the examining rooms "with a cloth over her mouth. She said, 'My gosh, get out of here or you're going to be in a lot of trouble.' " She then rushed through another door, near which an army captain stood, a man Dennis did not recognize. This officer asked Dennis what he was doing there. Dennis told him and asked if they had a plane crash and would be needing his services. The captain told him to wait where he was. Moments later, two military policemen took charge of Dennis and began escorting him from the hospital, saying they had orders to make sure he left the airfield and returned to the funeral home.

The three had not gotten far when they were halted by another officer, a captain or a colonel, depending upon which of Dennis's tellings we rely upon. This fellow was a redhead "with the meanest-looking eyes I had ever seen." This menacing man told Dennis, "You did not see anything, there was no crash here, and if you say anything you could get into a lot of trouble." After an exchange of words, with a black sergeant chiming in with, "He would make good dog food for our dogs," the military policemen whisked Dennis out and back to the apartment he and his first wife shared behind the funeral home.

Dennis told me that early the next day, Wednesday, July 9, Sheriff George Wilcox made an urgent visit to Glenn's father. Wilcox, a close friend, warned, "I don't know what kind of trouble Glenn's in, but you tell your son that he doesn't know anything and hasn't seen anything at the base." Wilcox also said the military asked him for Dennis family names and addresses. Glenn's father immediately drove to the funeral home. He woke Glenn, took him outdoors where Glenn's wife would not overhear the conversation, asked what had happened, and passed on the sheriff's warning and the implied threat to family members.

At about eleven o'clock that same eventful morning, after several unsuccessful attempts to reach the nurse, Dennis received a call from her. She was terribly upset. They agreed to meet at the base officers' club. There, the nurse told Dennis she had helped two doctors with preliminary autopsies of three very strange bodies, two of which were badly mangled. All three showed signs of exposure to the elements and the ravages of scavenging animals. An all but overpowering stench emanated from them. The nurse drew sketches of parts of the bodies, which she gave to Dennis.

According to Dennis, the nurse described the bodies as being three and a half to four feet tall, with heads disproportionately large. Dennis recalled, "The eyes were deeply set; the skulls were flexible; the nose was concave, with only two orifices; the mouth was a fine slit, and the doctors said there was heavy cartilage instead of teeth. The ears were only small orifices with flaps. They had no hair, and the skin was black—perhaps due to exposure in the sun."

This meeting was the last time Dennis was to see his friend. After trying to reach her for several days, he claims, he was told by another nurse at the base hospital that she had been transferred out. About two weeks later, he got a letter or postcard with an armed forces overseas post office (APO) number, indicating she was now stationed out of the country. Dennis told me he wrote a letter in response. Some time later this was returned, the envelope marked "Return to Sender—DECEASED." When he tried to learn more, he was told by another Roswell AAF nurse that rumor had it his friend had been killed in a plane crash.[38]

THE "CRATE FLIGHT"

According to the remarkably knowledgeable Frank Kaufmann, on the night of July 8, all the weird cadavers were sealed in body bags, placed in a single closed wooden crate, and removed to a deserted hangar, where the container was illuminated by a spotlight and kept under armed guard, in true Hollywood tradition with respect to such events. The late Sgt. Melvin E. Brown, a cook stationed at Roswell AAF in July 1947, claimed to have been posted as a guard that day at both the recovery site and the hangar, according to his daughter, Beverly Bean. She claims Brown told her and other family members he saw strange bodies under a tarpaulin on a truck at the ranch. That night, when Brown and his squadron commander looked into the hangar, all they saw was the sealed crate.[39]

Late the next afternoon, July 9, the crate was moved to a bomb-loading pit, still under armed guard. There it and its guards were loaded into the forward bomb bay of a B-29, which then departed for Fort Worth AAF. In 1993, Robert Slusher, a member of the bomber's crew, told me the flight was unusual on several counts. It was ordered hastily. The outbound leg was flown very low and with the crew-space pressurization off. They returned immediately after delivering their cargo and passengers.

When the flight arrived in Fort Worth, Slusher recalled, it was met by six men, including three military policemen and an undertaker. The latter had been a classmate of the B-29's bombardier, the conveniently late 1st Lt. Felix Martucci. Slusher also told me they had Major Marcel as a passenger on the return leg, and that, when they landed at Roswell, Martucci declared, "We made history."[40]

"YOU WILL IMMEDIATELY CEASE ALL COMMUNICATION"

Lydia Sleppy, who in July 1947 was administrative assistant to Merle Tucker, owner of Albuquerque's radio station KOAT, claimed to have been one of the first to encounter efforts allegedly taken by federal authorities to contain public disclosure of the discoveries on the Foster Ranch. In a 1993 interview, Sleppy told me that, shortly before noon on a weekday ("I never worked weekends") in early July ("almost certainly after the Fourth"), she received an excited phone call from John McBoyle, part owner and general manager of Roswell radio station KSWS, which was associated with KOAT. McBoyle said he wanted to dictate a story for Sleppy to put on the Teletype to ABC News headquarters in Hollywood (KSWS could receive wire stories but not transmit them).[41]

McBoyle told Sleppy he had been on a break in a Roswell coffee shop when Mack Brazel came in. The rancher told McBoyle about his strange discovery. Sleppy recalls McBoyle saying, "There's been one of those flying saucer things crash down here north of Roswell." As McBoyle dictated, Sleppy typed his words directly onto the wire. She told me she had barely begun when the warning bell rang on her machine and she was preempted by an incoming message, which she remembers as: "THIS IS THE FBI. YOU WILL IMMEDIATELY CEASE ALL COMMUNICATION." Sleppy told me she took the rest of McBoyle's story down in shorthand, "but we never put it on the wire because we had been scooped by the papers"—not to mention George Walsh, program manager at McBoyle's radio station, who, as we have seen, had already broken the story on the air and telephoned it to the Associated Press.[42]

Early on the evening of July 8, the B-29 carrying Marcel and some of the debris arrived at Fort Worth AAF. In a 1979 interview with *National Enquirer* reporter Bob Pratt, Marcel said, "They had a lot of news reporters and a slew of microphones that wanted to interview me, but I couldn't say anything. I couldn't say anything at all until I talked to the general [Brig. Gen. Roger M. Ramey, commanding general of the Eighth Air Force]."[43]

Marcel said he met with Ramey in the general's office and showed him some of the material he had brought from New Mexico. Purportedly, this material was then removed from Ramey's office and pieces of a ruptured neoprene weather balloon and a battered aluminum foil and balsa wood radar reflector were substituted. Later, Marcel, Ramey, and Col. Thomas DuBose, Ramey's chief of staff, were posed with this material for photographs taken by *Fort Worth Star-Telegram* photographer J. Bond Johnson and Fort Worth AAF public information officer Maj. Charles Cashon.[44]

Soon after, WO Irving Newton, a base weather officer, was summoned to Ramey's office, where he told the press the debris spread out on the floor—on brown wrapping paper like that recalled by Robert Porter—unquestionably was the remains of a balloon and a radar target of a type he had launched many times.[45] Newton also was posed and photographed with part of the battered radar reflector. Ramey then issued a statement to the press, declaring the Roswell "saucer" had been positively identified as the fragments of a weather balloon and its radar target. For this reason, he had canceled the special flight that was to have taken the debris to Wright Field for further examination. Later that evening, Ramey made a similar statement in an interview aired on Fort Worth radio station WBAP.[46]

More than four decades later, retired Brigadier General DuBose straightforwardly explained what was behind Ramey's statements: "The weather balloon explanation for the material was a cover story to divert the attention of the press."[47] DuBose did not offer any explanation of the purpose of this diversionary story, noting only that all involved were military professionals and did their duty without questioning their orders.

At about the same time Ramey was issuing the cover story, Mack Brazel was at the *Roswell Daily Record* office being interviewed by Associated Press reporter Jason Kellahin and a *Record* reporter named Skeritt. Also present were Walter E. Whitmore Sr., majority owner of radio station KGFL, and AP wire-photo technician Robin Adair.[48] As reported by Kellahin and Skeritt in stories that appeared the following day, July 9, Brazel said he had made his find more than three weeks earlier, rather than the week before, as stated in the Roswell AAF press announcement. He described it as mundane scraps of foil, wood, "rather tough paper," and rubber, as well as "some tape with flowers printed upon it." Brazel's low-key approach to presenting his account may have been suggested by military authorities, but if it was, Brazel seems to have had the last laugh, because he is quoted as telling the reporters, "I am sure what I found was not any weather observation balloon."[49]

Following the interview at the *Daily Record* office, Brazel may have gone or been taken to see KGFL announcer Frank Joyce at the radio station. According to what Joyce has told me and others, Brazel began by giving him a story substantially the same as that he had given the newspaper and wire-service reporters, a somewhat more elaborate version of what he had related to Joyce in their telephone conversation on Sunday, July 6. Joyce claimed Brazel made it clear he had been "persuaded" to play things down, but then added "the part about the little green men." According to Joyce, after relating the routine story, Brazel hesitated a moment then said something like, "You know what they say about little green men," then adding, "only they weren't green."[50] So now Joyce was asserting Brazel had seen the saucer crew and had cryptically let him in on the secret.

George "Jud" Roberts, in 1947 Whitmore's partner in KGFL, and Walter E. Whitmore Jr., both now deceased, told me the senior Whitmore managed to spirit Brazel away and wire-record an interview with him. Radio KGFL had been scooped on the crashed-saucer story by its rival KSWS, and Whitmore planned to recoup by broadcasting the exclusive interview the next day, July 9. According to his son, before he could do so, he received a telephone call from T. J. Slowie, executive secretary of the Federal Communications Commission. For national security reasons, Slowie said, KGFL should not broadcast anything further, threatening the station with the loss of its license if this order were violated. Whitmore Jr. said his father told him Slowie, whom I have confirmed was the FCC's executive secretary at the time of the incident, followed up with a telegram conveying the same message.[51]

Jud Roberts told me of another call from Washington, which he claimed he took at the radio station. Roberts remembered this as a friendly warning and, although he was unsure after the passage of so many years, he felt it had come from the office of either Agriculture Secretary and former New Mexico congressman Clinton Anderson or New Mexico's junior U.S. senator, Dennis Chavez: "We understand you have some information, and we want to assure you that if you release it, it's very possible that your station's license will be in jeopardy, so we suggest you not do it."[52] The interview was not aired and, according to Whitmore, the wire recording and the recorder on which it was made have long since been discarded.[53]

According to the uncertain recollections of Merle Tucker and Art McQuiddy, former editor of the *Roswell Morning Dispatch*, and the highly questionable claims of Frank Joyce, on July 8 or 9, officers from Roswell AAF *may* have visited the newspaper offices and radio stations in Roswell and recovered copies of the original "flying disc" press release. George Walsh of radio station KSWS remembers nothing like this. He told me the only word KSWS got of the "corrected" official story came in on the AP wire, and he stated quite emphatically that he never was given a written press release on the incident. McQuiddy says he remembers someone at the base other than Haut telephoning him about the "error," and he is uncertain about the fate of the written release he thinks Haut may have brought to him.[54]

As we have seen, other claims have been made about attempts to hush up the story. Glenn Dennis says not very subtle direct and implied threats were made against his family and him at the hospital and conveyed the next day through Sheriff George Wilcox. According to Wilcox's granddaughter, Barbara Dugger, the sheriff and his family also were threatened. Dugger has said that many years later her grandmother, Wilcox's wife Inez, told her "'the military police came to the jailhouse and told George and I [sic] that if we ever told anything about the incident, not only would we be killed, but our entire family would be killed.'"[55] Then, of course, there is the alleged disappearance and untimely death of the army nurse befriended by Glenn Dennis.[56]

According to Mack Brazel's son Bill and the late Marian Strickland, one of Brazel's neighbors, the cover-up included detaining Brazel at Roswell AAF for several days. Bill Brazel says his father told him he was questioned repeatedly about his find and sworn to secrecy, and Marian Strickland said Mack complained bitterly of being "held in jail." They and others have said the senior Brazel said virtually nothing about the matter for the rest of his life, and it has been suggested he may have been paid for his silence.[57]

ENTER LINCOLN LAPAZ

On September 18, 1947, a bit over two months after the Roswell case had been laid quietly to rest as far as the public was concerned, the U.S. Air Force came into being as an independent service. According to former CIC agent Lewis Rickett, at about this same time he was ordered to work on a follow-up investigation with Dr. Lincoln LaPaz, founder and director of the University of New Mexico's Institute of Meteoritics and a scientific consultant to the air force. Rickett said their assignment was to attempt to determine the speed and trajectory of the crashed vehicle found on the Foster Ranch, applying the techniques which LaPaz had perfected and used to find numerous meteorites.[58]

Rickett claimed he and LaPaz were on the road all over central and southeastern New Mexico for about three weeks, interviewing many witnesses and discovering a "touchdown" site not far from the debris field. There they found some of the unusual foil-like material, and the soil seemed to have been subjected to intense heat. Rickett said LaPaz's fluency in Spanish was very helpful in dealing with the Spanish and Mexican ranchers and hands in the area.[59]

Rickett said that, upon completing their field investigation, he and LaPaz each filed written reports, his an informal one through channels and LaPaz's formal and perhaps submitted directly to air force officials in Washington. Rickett asserted LaPaz told him he had concluded the craft was extraterrestrial and repeated this conclusion when they met at a restaurant on a highway east of Albuquerque about a year later.[60]

TAKING CARE OF LOOSE ENDS

Mack Brazel's son Bill testified he found out the air force continued to keep an eye on things for some time after the excitement over the incident had passed. Bill reported he occasionally came across bits of material the military missed in its cleanup of the debris field, and his father confirmed they were probably "some of the contraption" he found. Brazel kept the pieces in a cigar box and one summer evening in 1949 mentioned this while in the bar in Corona. He said he was visited the next day by an officer and several enlisted men from Roswell AAF (by then, Walker Air Force Base). They persuaded him to turn over the material and suggested it would be wise if he did not talk about what he found and what happened to it.[61]

AFTERMATH

It is *certain* at least some of the debris collected on the Foster Ranch was flown to Fort Worth Army Air Field—probably that brought in by Mack Brazel and certainly at least a portion of that recovered by Marcel and Cavitt. Contemporary press reports and an FBI telex message dated July 8, 1947, and other information leave little doubt this material and perhaps additional debris eventually was taken to Wright Field.[62] We also have some sensational claims that alien bodies were recovered and flown to Fort Worth and ultimately elsewhere, perhaps Wright Field, the first of which did not surface until three decades had passed and original Roswell investigators Stanton T. Friedman and William L. Moore were conducting their inquiries.

For more than twenty years the late Leonard H. Stringfield gathered much interesting if unsubstantiated testimony about alleged retrievals of crashed flying saucers and their crews and the scientific, technical, and medical research carried out on the recovered materials and cadavers.[63] Several of Stringfield's sources told him about seeing and working on alien bodies and flying saucer crash debris at Wright-Patterson Air Force Base—the merged Wright and Patterson fields—and elsewhere, the descriptions of which seem consistent with what is said to have been recovered in the Roswell area in July 1947. However, nothing Stringfield ever made public indicated any of these sources have claimed certain knowledge that what they saw was connected with the Roswell incident. Moreover, Stringfield never made public any information that would permit objective evaluation of these claims.

In 1989, Roswell authors Randle and Schmitt located retired Air Force Brig. Gen. Arthur E. Exon. The general was stationed at Wright Field in July 1947 as a lieutenant colonel and student at the Air Force Institute of Technology, following an assignment on the staff of the Air Materiel Command, also at Wright Field. According to Randle and Schmitt, Exon was aware alien bodies and debris from Roswell were on the base and knew of research being conducted on the debris. Randle and Schmitt also reported Exon told them he flew over what may have been the debris field and crash site and knew of a high-level group established to control "access to the wreckage, bodies, and information about the crash."[64] As we will see, General Exon has quite a different take on what he actually said and intended to convey.

Until relatively recently, the only person to claim certain knowledge of a possible transfer of Roswell debris and bodies to Wright Field was John G. Tiffany, who was interviewed in 1990 by Schmitt and Stanton Friedman. Tiffany said that in 1947 his father had been assigned to an army air forces unit at Wright Field that supported Roswell AAF's 509th Bomb Group. According to Tiffany, sometime in summer 1947 his father was a crew member on a flight to a destination in Texas. The mission was to pick up some strange debris and a large Thermos-like cask and fly them back to Wright Field. After delivering the unusual cargo, the flight crew was told by a "high-ranking official" never to discuss the flight—"It didn't happen." Tiffany also is reported to have claimed his father told him about three strange bodies, which he either saw or heard about from others.[65]

In its essentials, this is the original, conventional-wisdom Roswell story. Now we must consider the revisionist version championed by Kevin Randle and his erstwhile partner Don Schmitt, with a little help from some remarkable "witnesses."

NOTES

1. "RAAF Captures Flying Saucer in Roswell Region," *Roswell Daily Record*, July 8, 1947.

2. Personal interview with William M. Woody, May 22, 1993; Woody affidavit, app. H.

3. Bill Brazel as quoted in Charles Berlitz and William L. Moore, *The Roswell Incident* (New York: Berkley, 1988), p. 85; Marian Strickland, videotaped interview, September 27, 1991 (edited version appears in *Recollections of Roswell—Part II*, available from the Fund for UFO Research).

4. Bill Brazel in Berlitz and Moore, *Roswell Incident*, p. 86, and Kevin D. Randle and Donald R. Schmitt, *UFO Crash at Roswell* (New York: Avon, 1991), p. 52.

5. See, for example, "Harassed Rancher who Located 'Saucer' Sorry He Told About It," *Roswell Daily Record*, July 9, 1947; Bill Brazel in Berlitz and Moore, *Roswell Incident*, and Randle and Schmitt, *UFO Crash*; Lorraine Ferguson in Berlitz and Moore, *Roswell Incident*; and

app. H, affidavits of Jason Kellahin, Loretta Proctor, Bessie Brazel Schreiber (who is misidentified as "Betty" in the *Daily Record* story), and Sallye Strickland Tadolini, with all of whom I have conducted audiotaped interviews.

6. Audiotaped personal interview with Loretta Proctor, October 31, 1992; Proctor affidavit, app. H.

7. Bill Brazel in Berlitz and Moore, *Roswell Incident,* p. 86; Bessie Brazel Schreiber affidavit, app. H.

8. Bill Brazel in Berlitz and Moore, *Roswell Incident,* p. 91.

9. Audiotaped personal interview with Frank Joyce, November 3, 1992. See also, for example, videotaped Joyce interview in "Recollections" and Joyce as quoted in Randle and Schmitt, *UFO Crash.*

10. See app. A, complete transcript of Jesse A. Marcel Sr. interview conducted by Bob Pratt, December 8, 1979.

11. Ibid.

12. Randle and Schmitt, *UFO Crash,* p. 49.

13. DuBose affidavit, app. H; DuBose interview, "Recollections."

14. App. A.

15. See, for example, ibid.; Stanton T. Friedman and Don Berliner, *Crash at Corona* (New York: Paragon House, 1992); Randle and Schmitt, *UFO Crash*; and Marcel interview, "Recollections."

16. App. A.

17. Audiotaped telephone interview with Dr. Jesse Marcel Jr., September 23, 1993; Marcel Jr. affidavit, app. H; Marcel Jr. in "Recollections"; Viaud Marcel, audiotaped interview, May 5, 1981, with Linda Corley (audiotape courtesy Stanton T. Friedman).

18. "Disc Solution Collapses," *San Francisco Chronicle,* July 9, 1947; Walter G. Haut, audiotaped personal interview, November 2, 1992, affidavit in app. H, and interview in "Recollections."

19. Walsh's recollections were the first indication that no written press release was distributed. The peculiar use of the word *loaned* in the announcement text as published in many newspapers seems to have been a consequence of Walsh mistaking it for *flown* as Walter Haut dictated the announcement to him over the telephone. Audiotaped telephone interview with George R. Walsh, April 15, 1993; Walsh affidavit, app. H; "Army Announces Finding 'Saucer,'" Associated Press wire story in the *Rapid City (S.D.) Daily Journal,* July 8, 1947; "Flying Disc Transforms Sheriff's Office to International Newsroom," *Roswell Morning Dispatch,* July 9, 1947; Frank Joyce, November 3, 1992, and "Recollections"; Haut, November 2, 1992, and "Recollections." Despite the fact it was spelled out in the cited newspaper articles and probably many others, Walsh's role as the newsman who broke the story had been overlooked by Roswell researchers until 1994, when I reported it in *Roswell in Perspective,* after which it seems to have been ignored as an "inconvenient" fact by those who were committed to Frank Joyce's account.

20. Haut, November 2, 1992; audiotaped personal interview, Arthur R. McQuiddy, May 19, 1993, and affidavit, app. H; George Walsh, April 15, 1993, and affidavit, app. H; articles in both Roswell papers, July 9, 1947.

21. Audiotaped personal interview with Jason Kellahin, May 11, 1993; Kellahin affidavit, app. H; "Harassed Rancher," *Roswell Daily Record,* July 9, 1947. The *Record* story incorrectly identified R. D. Adair as R. A. Adair.

22. George Walsh, April 15, 1993; Walsh affidavit, app. H. Haut says he does not remember either call (various personal conversations, 1993, and letter to the author, September 27, 1993).

23. See, for example, Randle and Schmitt, *UFO Crash*, pp. 61ff. In several interviews (e.g., with Mark Rodeghier, January 1990, and in "Recollections") Rickett misidentified the provost marshall as "Darden." The Roswell AAF provost marshall at the time of the incident was Maj. Edwin D. Easley.

24. For example, audiotaped interview conducted by Mark Rodeghier, January 1990; Rickett as quoted in Randle and Schmitt, *UFO Crash*, pp. 62–63.

25. William Woody, May 22, 1993; Woody affidavit, app. H.

26. L. M. Hall, in 1993 a member of the Roswell City Council and former Roswell chief of police, provided the first and only independent testimony which seemed to support Dennis's claims about these calls. See Hall affidavit, app. H.

27. Audiotaped personal interview with Glenn Dennis, November 2, 1992; Dennis affidavit, app. H; Dennis in "Recollections"; Friedman and Berliner, *Crash at Corona* (pp. 114ff) includes lengthy excerpts from the first interview with Dennis, conducted by Stan Friedman on August 5, 1989; Karl T. Pflock, "Star Witness" (interview with Glenn Dennis), *Omni*, fall 1995, pp. 100–105, 132.

28. Randle and Schmitt, *UFO Crash*, pp. 89 and 181, and crashed saucer sketch and caption, illustration section between pp. 144 and 145; Donald R. Schmitt and Kevin D. Randle, "Second Thoughts on the Barney Barnett Story," *International UFO Reporter* (May–June 1992): 4. The source of this information is not identified by Randle and Schmitt, but I have established with certainty it was Frank J. Kaufmann (called "Joseph Osborne" in the cited *IUR* article), a significant and troublesome figure in the Roswell story. Concerning the alleged appearance of the bodies, see Dennis affidavit, app. H; Henn-Dennis sketches in the photo insert; Dennis in "Recollections"; Randle and Schmitt, *UFO Crash*, pp. 91–93; Pflock, "Star Witness," p. 104.

29. Randle and Schmitt, *UFO Crash*, pp. 63–67, 90, 166, 205. That the bodies were trucked to the base is attributed to the late Sgt. Melvin E. Brown by his daughter Beverly Bean; see ibid., pp. 90–91, 96, and Bean in "Recollections."

30. Randle and Schmitt, *UFO Crash*, sketch between pp. 144 and 145.

31. Robert R. Porter, affidavit, app. H, "Recollections"; Robert J. Shirkey, audiotaped personal interview, November 2, 1992, affidavit, app. H, letter to Donald R. Schmitt, July 18, 1991 (courtesy Robert Shirkey), "Recollections." Porter is the source of the named crew members. Researcher Joseph J. Stefula obtained copies of the 509th Bomb Group headquarters morning reports for the period July 1–16, 1947, which he has been kind enough to share with me. An entry in the July 9 morning report (app. F) indicates Barrowclough returned to duty from thirty days leave on that date, calling into question his participation in the July 8 flight. In a 1994 audiotaped telephone interview with Barrowclough, which I have listened to, Barrowclough told Roswell case researcher Kent Jeffrey that he did not make the flight. He recalled seeing some of the material in a base headquarters office and that it was remnants "some damn' balloon" from "some secret project." The retired colonel added that a UFO researcher whose name he could not remember had contacted him some years before. Barrowclough told him what he remembered, and, the colonel related, "He all but called me a liar."

32. Porter affidavit, app. H, "Recollections"; Shirkey, November 2, 1992, "Recollections," letter to Schmitt. Captain Anderson appears in the *Roswell Army Air Field Yearbook* (Roswell, N.M.: RAAF Public Relations Department, 1947) as a member of Squadron "A" (base administration); in his photograph, he is wearing the collar insignia of the Army Corps of Engineers.

33. Shirkey, November 2, 1992; affidavit, app. H; letter to Schmitt; "Recollections." Shirkey's remembrance of seeing the wrapped packages was the first independent testimony supporting Porter's description of the material carried on the flight.

34. Randle and Schmitt, *UFO Crash*, pp. 32 and 65ff, re Blanchard's leave.

35. Robert E. Smith, affidavit, app. H; "Recollections." Robert A. Slusher, affidavit, app. H.

36. Smith affidavit, app. H, "Recollections."

37. Sappho Henderson, affidavit, app. H, "Recollections." It has been reported that Henderson's flight preceded Marcel's departure and that Robert Shirkey watched the loading of Henderson's C-54 (Randle and Schmitt, *UFO Crash*, p. 207). According to Shirkey, however, it was Marcel's B-29 flight he watched being loading and that Henderson's flight went out later, probably on Wednesday, July 9. Shirkey, November 2, 1992; personal conversation with the author, May 15, 1993; letter to Schmitt cited above.

38. Dennis, November 2, 1992, and numerous personal conversations, 1992–94; Dennis affidavit, app. H; "Recollections"; Friedman and Berliner, *Crash at Corona*, p. 119 (re search for crash records); Pflock, *Omni* interview cited above.

39. Kaufmann and Bean, as attributed in Randle and Schmitt, *UFO Crash*, pp. 95–96, 166–67.

40. Personal interview with Robert A. Slusher, May 23, 1993; Slusher affidavit, app. H.

41. Audiotaped telephone interview with Lydia A. Sleppy, May 3, 1993; Sleppy affidavit, app. H; Sleppy in "Recollections"; audiotaped personal interview with Merle Tucker, May 27, 1993. This is the first time it has been established Sleppy would not have been at KOAT on a weekend. This is significant because the "revisionist" scenario (chap. 3) has McBoyle speaking with Sleppy on Saturday, July 5.

42. Sleppy, May 3, 1993; affidavit, app. H; "Recollections."

43. App. A.

44. Donald R. Schmitt and Kevin D. Randle, "Fort Worth, July 8, 1947: The Cover-Up Begins" and "The Fort Worth Press Conference: The J. Bond Johnson Connection," in *The Roswell Report: A Historical Perspective*, ed. George M. Eberhart (Chicago: Center for UFO Studies, 1991), pp. 56–70.

45. Ibid.

46. "Finds 'Flying Saucer,' Says Lt.; Only Weather Balloon, Says General," *Portland (Maine) Press Herald*, July 9, 1947.

47. DuBose affidavit, app. H, "Recollections."

48. "Harassed Rancher"; Kellahin affidavit, app. H. Although it has been reported previously that military personnel were present at this interview, Kellahin recalled them waiting outside on the street.

49. Ibid., "Harassed Rancher."

50. Joyce, November 3, 1992; "Recollections." This exchange has been reported previously with Brazel saying as he was leaving, "Frank, you know how they talk about little green men? Well, they weren't green" (*UFO Crash*, p. 79).

51. Audiotaped personal interviews with Walter E. Whitmore Jr., October 31, 1992, and May 16, 1993. Audiotaped personal interview with George "Jud" Roberts, May 19, 1993; Roberts affidavit, app. H. T. J. Slowie is listed as executive secretary of the FCC in all editions of the *United States Government Manual* for the period December 1, 1946 through June 30, 1948 (telephone conversation, March 11, 1993, Tab Lewis, Civil Reference Branch, National Archives and Records Administration, Washington, D.C.).

52. Roberts, May 19, 1993; Roberts affidavit, app. H. Walter E. Whitmore Sr. was a prominent New Mexico Democrat and very close to both Anderson and Chavez, so it would not have been unusual for one or both of them to contact him about something like this (Roberts, May 19, 1993; Whitmore Jr., October 31, 1992).

53. Whitmore Jr., October 31, 1992. It has been suggested that the wire recording was confiscated by the military, but Whitmore told me this is not true, that he personally disposed of the recorder, wire spools, and associated equipment when KGFL acquired tape recorders in the early 1950s.

54. Joyce, November 3, 1992; Tucker, May 27, 1993; McQuiddy, May 19, 1993, and affidavit, app. H; Walsh, April, 15, 1993, and affidavit, app. H.

55. Dennis, November 2, 1992, affidavit, app. H, "Recollections." Barbara Dugger in "Recollections" and Dugger affidavit on file with the Fund for UFO Research.

56. Dennis, November 2, 1992, affidavit, app. H, "Recollections." See also, for example, Friedman and Berliner, *Crash at Corona*, and Randle and Schmitt, *UFO Crash*. Robert Shirkey was abruptly transferred soon after the incident. However, although as he remembers it, there are some unusual aspects to his transfer to the Philippines, nothing has been found linking it to his involvement in preparing the flight plan for and watching the loading of the aircraft that took Major Marcel to Fort Worth.

57. Strickland, "Recollections"; Brazel as attributed in Randle and Schmitt, *UFO Crash*, and Berlitz and Moore, *Roswell Incident*. The testimony of Kellahin and Schreiber tends to contradict this (affidavits, app. H), and Haut says he remembers talk about Walter Whitmore Sr. hiding Brazel out in the hope of getting a scoop on the crashed saucer story (Randle and Schmitt, *UFO Crash*, pp. 142–43). The testimony of Whitmore Jr. (October 31, 1992, and May 16, 1993) tends to support Haut's recollections. Concerning the alleged bribe, see Loretta and Norris Proctor as attributed in Randle and Schmitt, *UFO Crash*, p. 226.

58. Rickett, audiotaped interview with Rodeghier, January 1990, interview with Donald R. Schmitt, October 29, 1989 (transcript), "Recollections."

59. With reference to LaPaz's alleged fluency in Spanish, see chap. 10.

60. See n. 58 above. Internal evidence in the January 1990 interview suggests Clines Corners as the site of the meeting.

61. Bill Brazel as quoted in Berlitz and Moore, *Roswell Incident* (p. 89) and Randle and Schmitt, *UFO Crash* (pp. 130–31). See also videotaped interview in "Recollections."

62. The FBI telex is reproduced as app. C.

63. See Stringfield's "Status Reports," I through VII.

64. Arthur E. Exon, as attributed in Randle and Schmitt, *UFO Crash*, pp. 108–12, 231–34.

65. John G. Tiffany, as attributed in Randle and Schmitt, *UFO Crash*, pp. 103–104.

THREE

ROSWELL AS SOME WOULD
HAVE US KNOW AND LOVE IT

This account of the revisionist case is based upon my personal research and investigation, including my lengthy and quite revealing May 17, 1993, interview of Frank Kaufmann, as well as numerous other sources. Most important among the latter are the public remarks of and articles by the three leading revisionists, Kevin Randle, Don Schmitt, and Tom Carey; personal communications from Randle and Schmitt to me and others; and Randle and Schmitt's curiously titled 1994 retake on the case, *The Truth About the UFO Crash at Roswell*. In addition, regrettably, as all too often in ufology, I have had to rely on a limited amount information, leads, and other material provided by a number of sources who prefer to remain anonymous, most of which I have verified independently.[1]

BOGEY!

Under the revisionist scenario, the Roswell affair actually began to unfold on Tuesday, July 1, 1947, when army radars at three locations in New Mexico—White Sands Proving Ground, about 120 air miles southwest of Roswell, Kirtland Army Air Field, more than 160 air miles northwest of Roswell at Albuquerque, and at Roswell AAF itself—detected a strangely behaving "bogey," or UFO. It was first picked up in the restricted air space over the White Sands reservation and was sporadically tracked for almost four days as it "flitted around from one place to another" over southern New Mexico.[2]

Frank Kaufmann told me he received direct orders from a General (Martin F. "Mike") Scanlon to hot foot it from Roswell to White Sands, "which had the best radar contacts," to see what was going on. Kaufmann says he and others watched the UFO's blip move erratically on the White Sands radarscopes for many hours, then returned to Roswell AAF. Between 11:00 and 11:30 P.M. on Friday, July 4, the unknown's blip "flared up," flooding the scopes at White Sands, Kirtland, and Roswell with blinding light. Referring to the same event, Don Schmitt said there was a "burst on the screen at Roswell. It appeared as though something had exploded. It appeared as though something went down just north of Roswell." When the "flare" faded, the unknown had dropped off the radars, and Kaufmann told me, "We knew it was down."[3]

THE "CAMPERS"

According to the late Jim Ragsdale, he and a married lady friend, "Trudy Truelove," also deceased, saw the mysterious bogey fall from the sky.[4] In the first version of his story, Ragsdale claimed he and Truelove were taking advantage of the rare three-day weekend, as well as the absence of Truelove's husband, an enlisted man stationed at Roswell AAF. They were lounging "buck naked" and drinking beer in the bed of Ragsdale's pickup truck at a remote spot about forty road miles north of Roswell. Their trysting place was a location he said he knew about because of his work as part of a team surveying the route for a soon to be constructed El Paso Natural Gas Company pipeline.[5]

In a 1993 interview with Schmitt, Ragsdale said, "On a night during July, 1947, . . . during a severe lightning storm . . . [we] observed a bright flash and what appeared to be a bright light source moving toward the southeast."[6] Randle and Schmitt reported that Ragsdale, while unsure of the exact date, was certain this event took place during the long Fourth of July weekend.[7]

Ragsdale and Truelove watched and heard the object roar overhead and apparently strike the ground "a mile or two" from their location.[8] "Later, at sunrise, driving in that direction, . . . [we] came upon a ravine near a bluff that was covered with pieces of unusual wreckage, remains of a damaged craft and a number of smaller bodied beings outside the craft." Ragsdale collected some of the strange debris, which by his description was similar to that found by Mack Brazel. He began putting the material in his vehicle, but Truelove, frightened and anxious to leave, threw it out almost as fast as he loaded it.[9]

According to Ragsdale, the lady seems to have had good reason to be concerned. He claimed "a military convoy arrived and secured the scene. As a result of the convoy's appearance we quickly fled the area."[10]

FARMER AND SON, CORPORAL, AND NUNS

Randle and Schmitt suggest William Woody and his father, on their farm south of Roswell, observed the same object seen by the campers rather than that seen by the Wilmots on July 2. According to them, the younger Woody reports seeing a flaming object "coming from the northwest and going down about due north of Roswell," that is, exactly opposite the direction and track reported by the Wilmots, but consistent with Ragsdale's alleged recollections.[11] Moreover, they assert, Woody's description of the object he and his father saw much more closely matches what Ragsdale claimed to have seen—a flaming something streaking across the sky—than it does the Wilmot UFO.[12]

Then there is the account of E. L. Pyles who, as an army air forces corporal in 1947, was assigned to a radio-range facility some miles southwest of Roswell AAF. According to Randle and Schmitt, on a night "early in July of 1947," Pyles was at the radio range facility when he saw "an object flash across the night sky to his north, going down toward the ground." They further relate that Pyles believes this occurred on a weekend because "he was awake after the main lights had been turned out at eleven," and it was "before midnight, when he normally went to bed."[13]

Another visual sighting of what Randle and Schmitt suggest was the same object— and, they conclude, probably that tracked by army radars—purportedly was recorded by Franciscan nuns who served as nurses at Saint Mary's Hospital at what was then the southern outskirts of Roswell. Randle and Schmitt report these nuns "made routine observations of the night sky, and their log records the appearance of a fiery object on July 4, 1947, sometime between 11:15 and 11:30 P.M."[14] The entry describes "a flaming object, arcing downward north of Roswell," according to Schmitt.[15]

Coupled with Kaufmann's account of the radar observations and subsequent military activities, these sightings led Randle and Schmitt to conclude the Roswell object crashed between 11:00 and 11:30 P.M. on Friday, July 4, rather than about 10 P.M. on Wednesday, July 2, as they previously had thought.[16] From this they extrapolate that Brazel, about thirty-five air miles northwest of the crash or what they call "impact" site, heard the odd explosion late on the Fourth rather than two nights earlier.[17]

THE ARMY MOVES IN AND FINDS...?

According to Frank Kaufmann, sometime during the electronic cat-and-mouse game between army radars and the UFO, members of a special team were flown in from Washington and perhaps elsewhere. The team was directed by one Robert Thomas, who came in from Washington and held the nominal army rank of warrant officer (as I have previously noted, Kaufmann slyly implies Thomas's actual rank and status were much higher). The roughly triangulated coordinates provided by the three radar sites indicated the UFO had fallen not far north of Roswell. As soon as this was determined, the special team began organizing a convoy of experts, military police, and equipment to recover it.[18]

Before dawn on Saturday, July 5, the group, including Kaufmann, headed north on U.S. Highway 285. About thirty-five miles north of town they turned off the blacktop, heading west on an unpaved ranch road and eventually continuing over open, roadless country. There was considerable concern because, Kaufmann claims, he had been alerted "there were civilians on the site" (how this was known we are not told). Shortly after sunup, the recovery convoy came upon the crashed craft "in an arroyo." The special detail immediately set about securing the area and, say Randle and Schmitt, unwittingly frightening off Ragsdale and Truelove.[19]

The claims of an anonymous source, whom Randle and Carey tell us telephoned Randle out of the blue sometime in February 1990 and whom I will call "New Mexico Jones," suggest according to the revisionist scenario that the "civilians on the site" may have been a group of archaeologists, Jones among them. According to Jones, they had stumbled upon the site not long before the army arrived. "About a half mile away in the arroyo below," they saw "something that looked like a fat aircraft fuselage without wings. . . . They drove down toward it and stopped. There was another man already there . . . who was standing close to something lying on the ground." Jones said that, in addition to the "badly damaged" craft, which appeared to have no dome, ports, hatches, or markings, he saw three strange bodies, at least one in a silvery flight suit.[20]

According to Jones, the army arrived soon after—"a jeep . . . carrying soldiers." The officer in charge ordered Jones and his colleagues "not to tell anyone what they had seen—it was a matter of national security." After their names and other pertinent information were taken and they had been threatened with the loss of government grants and other funds if they talked, the archaeologists were escorted from the site and told to drive east out of the area via a nearby ranch road, which under the new scenario would have taken them to U.S. 285. Jones told Randle that, as they drove eastward, they passed two soldiers standing by an army vehicle parked on the roadside.[21]

Revisionist proponent Tom Carey reports vertebrate paleontologist C. Bertrand Schultz claims to have discussed this incident with archaeologist W. Curry Holden sometime in 1947. Holden "told him the entire story of the Roswell UFO crash/retrieval, because he had been there! . . . [He] told him that everyone at first thought that it was a Russian device, but that it wasn't."[22] Following up on this lead, Kevin Randle interviewed the ninety-six-year-old, ailing Holden in November 1992. While Randle tells us the elderly archaeologist had no memory of the details of the alleged event or who was with him at the time, he reports Holden responded the same way to three separate questions about Roswell: "I was involved . . . I was there and I saw everything." Holden died in April 1993.[23]

SECURING THE SITE AND INVESTIGATING THE FIND

Once the archaeologists had been sent on their way with the fear of Big Brother instilled in their hearts, the special team set about its investigation. According to Kaufmann, this work was carried out with the assistance of and under on-site security provided by special groups of military policemen brought in from Kirtland AAF. Kaufmann told me there were five such groups of about twenty MPs each, and they were rotated through in order to prevent their members from seeing too much, an odd procedure that would have dramatically increased the number of those in the know, thus compounding the security problem rather than making it more manageable.[24]

Randle and Schmitt are convinced the soldiers whom William Woody says he and his father saw posted along both sides of Highway 285 very likely were part of the security arrangements for the impact site. They also suggest paleontologist Schultz probably saw the same soldiers. Schultz says he remembers seeing "military personnel standing by certain roads which were cordoned off" as he drove south on Highway 285 on a trip to Roswell sometime in the summer of 1947.[25]

Kaufmann related that members of the special team, some working in protective clothing, inspected the craft and examined the bodies. According to Randle, the craft, rather than being "a classic disk" as Kaufmann had at first claimed and drawn, was wing- or lifting-body-like. It was not very large, about twenty-five to thirty feet in length and spanning only twelve to fifteen feet, and was imbedded in the side of the arroyo.[26]

Allegedly, five bodies were found. A "firsthand witness"—whom we now know to be Frank Kaufmann—told Randle two bodies were outside the vehicle, one on the ground beside the craft, the other resting against a wall of the arroyo, above the crash site. Two of the three within the craft were visible from the outside. Randle reports Kaufmann told him the beings were four and a half to five feet tall, had "normal" five-digit hands, and wore close-fitting silvery flight suits. He says they were "very human looking," but lacked hair and were "more finely featured"—their skin and eye color reminding Kaufmann of the *Star Trek* character Data. Accordingly to Randle, Kaufmann was struck by the "serene" look on the face of the being whose body rested against the cliff, "like he was at peace with the world."[27]

The craft and bodies were removed from the site and taken to Roswell AAF before the day was out. Kaufmann alleges the bodies were transported in lead-lined body bags and stored briefly in Hangar 84 (P-3 in 1947) before being moved to the base hospital for the preliminary examination in which Glenn Dennis's friend the nurse was required to assist, which under the new scenario would thus have taken place on Saturday, July 5 (as would Dennis's hallway confrontation with military authorities). However, because the previously described stench emanating from the bodies was so terrible, they were again encased in their bags, placed in a closed wooden crate, and returned to the hangar.[28]

It is unclear how long they are alleged to have remained there, but according to what Randle says he was told by Kaufmann, they were flown out of Roswell AAF at about 3 A.M.—presumably on Sunday, July 6, or Monday, July 7—aboard two aircraft, with an eventual destination of Wright Field. Continuing to rely on Kaufmann, Randle now contends the July 9 flight carrying a mysterious crate to Fort Worth AAF was a diversion, providing cover for the actual flights transporting the bodies out of Roswell AAF.[29]

MACK BRAZEL, THE FLY IN THE OINTMENT

Jim Ragsdale and Trudy Truelove had escaped detection at the impact site. Thus, as far as the army knew, Glenn Dennis and the archaeologists were the only civilians aware of the crash/retrieval. Both of those problems seemed to have been dealt with effectively, so by the early afternoon of Sunday, July 6, military authorities had reason to be confident the secret of their extraordinary discoveries was secure.

Then Mack Brazel arrived at the Chaves County sheriff's office to report his find, which according to the new chronology, he would have made the day before, Saturday, July 5. The army quickly learned from Sheriff Wilcox that he and Brazel had spoken with Frank Joyce at Radio KGFL and soon discovered Brazel had talked with neighbors and perhaps others about his find. The threat to the secret of the saucer crash/retrieval was obvious. Something had to be done, and done fast.[30]

THE PRESS ANNOUNCEMENT "EXPLAINED"

According to Randle and Schmitt, who got their information from none other than Frank Kaufmann, "someone in the military had the clever idea of issuing a press release that admitted the recovery of a flying disc, then retracting the claim a few hours later." This variation on the purloined letter trick would allow the army to hide the truth behind the blush of its own "embarrassment." Randle and Schmitt further contend "the press release was carefully crafted to divert attention away from the site where the main body of the object came to rest" by referring only to something being "found on the Foster ranch."[31]

The alleged scheme was initiated on Tuesday, July 8, when Walter Haut contacted the Roswell media with the "true" story. It was brought to fruition with General Ramey's weather balloon announcement a few hours later. The payoff came with the next day's "Ramey Empties Roswell Saucer" headlines.[32] The lid was on the saucer, and those directing the Roswell cover-up and exploitation breathed a sigh of relief and got on with their clandestine activities.

FRANKIE ROWE

Frankie Rowe first appeared on the Roswell incident scene in 1991, about the time Randle and Schmitt's *UFO Crash at Roswell* was published. Rowe has since told various versions of her remarkable tale to Roswell researchers and numerous producers of television "documentaries" about the case. In July 1947, when Rowe was twelve, her father, Dan Dwyer, was a firefighter with the Roswell Fire Department. According to Rowe, one night in early July 1947, "Daddy came home from work . . . [and] said he had been out to what they initially thought to be a plane crash."[33]

It seems, she said, a Roswell Fire Department truck with her father aboard had been sent to a location about thirty miles north of Roswell early that morning. In a 1993 telephone interview, Rowe told me her father

> said it was a crash of something that was not from the earth. He said this crash had left a lot of pieces of small material around, and two small bodies and one person walking around. He said it was from another planet . . . that they did not look like us. He said they were very small, and the one that was walking around was about the size of a ten-year-old child, and it didn't have any hair, and it had very small ears and rather large dark eyes. They had on a one-piece suit that covered the whole body. The two that had been killed had been put in body bags. It [the survivor] seemed so scared and lost and afraid, and he felt sorry for it.[34]

According to Rowe, not long after her father told this story to his family, he added a postscript. She said he told them of a friend, a painting contractor who was working at the Roswell AAF hospital the day her father had been called out to the crash site. This man claimed to have seen the surviving being walk into the hospital under guard.

Three or four days later, Rowe told me, she was at the fire station, waiting for her father to finish his shift and take her home. She had recently had her tonsils removed and had been to see her doctor, whose office was nearby. As she waited, a state police officer came in and said he wanted to show the firemen something. "He took his hand out of his pocket," Rowe said, "and he dropped what he had in his fist on a table. He said it was something he picked up out at the crash site. It looked like quicksilver when it was on the table, but you could wad it up."[35]

The material was "a little bit larger than . . . [the state trooper's] hand. It had jagged edges" and was a dull grayish-silver color. Rowe said she touched it, although she had been told she was not supposed to. "You couldn't feel it in your hand," she said. "It was so thin that it felt like holding a hair. . . . It wasn't anything you'd ever seen before." She told me it "flowed like quicksilver when you laid it on the table," and the firemen and the trooper "tried to tear it, cut it and burn it. It wadded up into nothing. The state cop said he'd gotten away with just this one small piece, and he said he didn't know how long he'd be able to keep it, if the military found out."[36]

Rowe claims that, several days after this incident, something transpired that made clear the military did get wind of the trooper's indiscretion. When her father was out of the house, four army men came to the Rowe home.

> They were MPs [military policemen]—three of them—and one that wasn't an MP, the biggest of the three. He said he wanted to talk to the person that was at the fire station. Mother sent the rest of the kids outside.
>
> [This man] . . . was extremely dark complexioned and he had a heavy . . . [New York or Brooklyn] accent and a loud, booming voice. He asked me what I'd seen at the fire station. He said I had no business being there. He said I hadn't seen anything, and I said I had seen a piece of material. He kept saying I didn't see anything and . . . that I would be responsible if they killed everybody, if I talked about it. He said, "There are choices—we can take your mother and father either to Orchard Park [a former World War II POW camp] or down at Artesia, down at the Japanese internment camp," and we [Frankie and the other children] might go to the other one or we might be sent back east and adopted out, or if he found out that any of us had talked, they might just take us out to the middle of the desert and shoot all of us and nobody would ever find us.[37]

As Rowe tells her story, it simply does not fit what is known and alleged about the timing of events, the nature of what (and who) was found, and the army's actions. Nonetheless, Randle and Schmitt and others promoting the revisionist scenario include Rowe's account as part of the "truth," and there is yet another such tale that the revisionists have bolted onto the basic story.

LITTLE MEN AND JIM BEAM

In early January 1993, ufologist Stanton Friedman called to tell me he had been approached by someone when he was in Roswell the previous November for a book-signing and research visit. The man claimed a prominent New Mexico politician, now deceased, had been directly involved in the Roswell incident. Stan thought my political connections in New Mexico would facilitate an investigation of this potentially very important story. The source's name was Ruben Anaya, and the politician was Joseph Montoya. In 1947, Montoya was New Mexico's lieutenant governor. Later he served the state in the United States Congress, first as a congressman (1957–64) and then as a senator (1964–77).[38]

In early April 1993, I had a long, audio-taped telephone conversation with Ruben Anaya.[39] He told me he and his brother Pete were very politically active in 1947, as they still were when he and I spoke. They were good friends and supporters of Montoya's, in New Mexico political parlance, *Montoyistas*.

Anaya told me that, one evening in early July 1947, he, Pete, and two friends, Moses Burrola and Ralph Chaes, were relaxing at the Anaya home when the telephone rang. Ruben Anaya answered. The caller was a "real excited, panicky sounding" Joseph Montoya. "Ruben," he said, "I'm at the base. I've gotta get out of here! Get your car and come after me here at the base." Anaya asked Montoya exactly where he was and was told, "I'm at the big hangar. I'll meet you here. Hurry!"

The four men piled into Ruben's car and drove to the base. Ruben, recently out of the army, was a member of the noncommissioned officers' club and had a base pass for his car, so they were waved through the gate. They pulled up by the big hangar and tried to go in. "But nobody would let us in," Anaya told me. "They had MPs . . . and city police . . . there. Then he [Montoya] came out. That man was as white as a sheet, really shook up. He said, 'Come on. Let's get out of here.' I asked him if he wanted us to take him to his hotel, but he said, 'No. Just take me to your house. I need a drink bad.' "

After they arrived at the Anaya home, Montoya "sat on the couch and drank down a quart bottle of Jim Beam, three-quarters full. We said, 'Take it easy!' He said, 'No. I've got to calm myself down.' "

The four men demanded to know what had happened. Anaya told me Montoya replied,

> "You're not going to believe it. There was a flying saucer—*un plato muy grande con una machina en la media* [a big saucer with a machine in the middle]—that came down by Corona. There were four little men not from this world. One was alive!" He said they were little, came up only to his chest—and Montoya was a little guy [he was known as Little Joe]. . . . He described them, wearing silvery suits, with big eyes and a very little mouth. . . . We thought, this guy, he's out of whack. . . .
>
> Then he called his wife, talked with her about it, and then called the Nickson Hotel [where he was staying] and got a friend and his brother Tom Montoya . . . to come and get him. . . .
>
> About ten-thirty the next morning we went to the hotel and talked to him. He told us, "Confidentially, they shipped everything to Texas, and those guys are in the hospital. . . . Look, if any of you guys say I talked about this, I'm going to say you're a bunch of liars."

Anaya added that, some time later, New Mexico's then-junior U.S. Senator Dennis Chavez was in Roswell and summoned his brother, Barrola, and Chaes, and him to the Nickson Hotel. There he told them, "Joe Montoya was a damn' liar. He didn't see anything. . . . It was a very, very secret project, it could hurt us with Russia and Germany [if it came out]."

I asked Anaya how Montoya happened to see the saucer and the little men. He told me the lieutenant governor was "at the base all day. They had a special program for elected officials, they were going to christen one of those big planes. It was a special day here in Roswell."

REVISIONIST RECAP

Under the revisionist timetable, events begin to unfold a day earlier than originally thought, with the strange, multisite radar contacts on Tuesday, July 1. The crash took place on Friday, July 4, rather than Wednesday, July 2, and the main body of the craft slammed to earth much closer to Roswell than previously believed.

The army located the craft and its crew at the impact site on Saturday, July 5, rather than Tuesday, July 8, and did so before rather than after learning of the debris field. While the army was dealing with the impact site, Mack Brazel discovered the debris field, on Saturday, July 5, rather than Thursday, July 3.

Beginning with Sunday, July 6, the revisionist scenario starts to reconverge with the conventional wisdom. Key differences are the timing and means of the airlift of the bodies, the crate flight as a cover operation, the motivation behind the press announcement of July 8, and the major inconsistencies introduced by the inclusion of the Frankie Rowe and Ruben Anaya accounts.

Clearly, there is a problem. Both scenarios cannot be correct, and the revisionist scenario must be at least partially false. In truth, of course, both are false, though the conventional wisdom, not having the benefit of as much "creative thinking" and opportunities to build upon well-publicized earlier accounts incorporates more of what we now know to be the real Roswell story.

NOTES

1. See chap. 5 for Kaufmann interview; Kevin D. Randle and Donald R. Schmitt, *The Truth About the UFO Crash at Roswell* (New York: Evans, 1994).
2. Audiotape, Kevin D. Randle and Donald R. Schmitt, lecture, Portland, Oregon, March 28, 1993; personal interview with Frank J. Kaufmann, May 17, 1993.
3. Audiotape, Donald R. Schmitt, lecture, Albuquerque, New Mexico, November 14, 1993; Kaufmann, May 17, 1993.
4. Trudy Truelove is the pseudonym used by Randle and Schmitt; *Truth*, pp. 3ff.
5. Schmitt, Albuquerque; Kevin D. Randle and Donald R. Schmitt, "When and Where Did the Roswell Object Crash?" *International UFO Reporter* (January–February 1994): 13–16.
6. Jim Ragsdale, affidavit, app. H.
7. Randle and Schmitt, "When and Where?" p. 14.
8. Ibid.; Ragsdale affidavit, app. H; Schmitt, Albuquerque.
9. Schmitt, Albuquerque.
10. Ragsdale affidavit, app. H.
11. Randle and Schmitt, "When and Where?" p. 14.
12. Woody, May 22, 1993, and affidavit, app. H.
13. Randle and Schmitt, "When and Where?" p. 14.
14. Ibid.
15. Schmitt, Albuquerque.
16. Randle and Schmitt, Portland, and "When and Where?"
17. Randle and Schmitt, "When and Where?"
18. Kaufmann, May 17, 1993; Randle and Schmitt, Portland; Schmitt, Albuquerque.

19. Randle and Schmitt, Portland; audiotape, Kevin D. Randle, lecture and workshop, Phoenix, Arizona, September 1993; Schmitt, Albuquerque.

20. Kevin D. Randle and Donald R. Schmitt, *UFO Crash at Roswell* (New York: Avon, 1991), pp, 115–17; Thomas J. Carey, "The Continuing Search for the Archaeologists: Closing the Circle," *International UFO Reporter* (January–February 1994): 4–12. Carey notes Randle *did not* audiotape the conversation. In *Truth* (p. 109) Randle and Schmitt report that Carey eventually learned the name of the anonymous caller from anthropologist George A. Agogino, who claimed to have been told the same story and named an allegedly corroborating source.

21. See n. 20 above.

22. Carey, "The Continuing Search," p. 10.

23. Ibid., p. 12. Carey reports Randle *did not* audiotape his conversation with Holden.

24. Kaufmann, May 17, 1993.

25. Woody, May 22, 1993, and affidavit, app. H.; Carey, "The Continuing Search," p. 10.

26. Randle, Phoenix; Randle and Schmitt, Portland.

27. Randle and Schmitt, Portland; Schmitt, Albuquerque. See also chap. 5.

28. Randle and Schmitt, Portland.

29. Ibid.; Randle, Phoenix.

30. Randle and Schmitt, "When and Where?" p. 16; Kevin Randle and Donald Schmitt, "The UFO Crash at Roswell," *MUFON UFO Journal* (March 1994): 8–10.

31. Randle and Schmitt, "When and Where?" p. 16.

32. *Roswell Daily Record,* July 9, 1947.

33. Summary transcript of videotaped interview of Frankie Rowe conducted by Kevin D. Randle and Donald R. Schmitt. Transcript prepared by Frederic L. Whiting, then secretary-treasurer of the Fund for UFO Research. I have studied the entire unedited videotape, and the words I quote are Rowe's, verbatim.

34. Telephone interview with Rowe, May 12, 1993; summary transcript, see n. 33 above.

35. Telephone interview with Frankie Rowe, May 12, 1993, ibid.

36. Ibid.

37. Summary transcript, see n. 33 above.

38. United States Senate, *Biographical Directory of the United States Congress, 1774–1989* (Washington, D.C.: Government Printing Office, 1989).

39. Audiotaped telephone interview with Ruben Anaya, April 3, 1993.

FOUR

THE REVISIONIST VISION
Less Than Meets the Eye

Roswell continues to grip the imagination of the general public and still is taken and debated seriously in ufological circles. However, the focus of interest has shifted away from "Did it happen?" and "If so, what happened and where, and who was involved and why?"

Now the emphasis is, on one hand, certain technical specifics and, on the other, disputation over the authenticity of documents allegedly confirming the saucer crash tale. This plays out against the backdrop of a generally accepted consensus story, with inconvenient facts central to that story conveniently ignored: "A saucer *did* crash and it and its dead crew were grabbed by the government. Don't sweat the inconsistencies and other problems."

I often wonder to what degree the transparent absurdity of the revisionist Roswell has contributed to this "don't confuse me with the facts" attitude. There seems to be an unacknowledged sense of embarrassment about it, a feeling that things were pushed too far. And indeed they were.

THE ADVENTURES OF JIM AND TRUDY

In May 1993, during one of my investigative visits to Roswell, I learned there may have been a civilian witness at the alleged impact site, someone other than the elusive archaeologists. It was said he and a lady friend had been camping nearby at the time of the crash/retrieval. A bit of checking led me to Kevin Randle and Don Schmitt, who had been introduced to this person a few months before by Max Littell who, with Roswell affair principals Glenn Dennis and Walter Haut founded Roswell's International UFO Museum and Research Center, the town's second, premier, and ultimately sole surviving UFO "museum."

I sought an opportunity to talk with the man while I was in town, but Schmitt told me he was unwilling to grant an interview at that time. However, the fellow did authorize Randle and Schmitt to give me a redacted copy of his sworn affidavit, with his and his lady friend's names deleted. I found this waiting for me when I returned home about two weeks later.[1]

It was not long before I discovered the camper was Jim Ragsdale, but in deference to Randle and Schmitt, I held off contacting him. Instead, I did some discreet background investigation on their new witness. What I learned was ambiguous and raised some serious questions about Ragsdale's credibility.

In November 1993, I telephoned Jim Ragsdale. He answered, and I told him I was doing some historical research on military activities in the Roswell area during the immediate post–World War II years. He responded, "I don't hear well on the telephone. Please talk with my wife."

When Mrs. Ragsdale came on the line, I explained I was doing historical research concerning events in and around Roswell and involving Roswell Army Air Field. I said I understood her husband may have witnessed something in 1947 north of Roswell which was relevant to my research. "I don't think he can help you," she replied. "He didn't live here then."

I asked when her husband moved to Roswell. "In nineteen fifty-nine," she replied. "I think you have the wrong Ragsdale." That ended the conversation, but not my interest in Mrs. Ragsdale's husband, who indeed was the correct Ragsdale and whom she would divorce about a year later.[2]

The same day, I followed up the telephone contact with a letter to Ragsdale explaining my serious and sincere interest in his story, assuring him of my concern for his and his wife's welfare and privacy, and outlining my informal role in support of the inquiry Congressman Steven H. Schiff (R-N.M.) was conducting into the Roswell case. I asked him to get in touch, inviting him to telephone me collect (I was then still residing in the Washington, D.C., area).

More than three weeks later, having heard nothing from Ragsdale, I followed up with another letter.[3] Ragsdale never replied. On September 9, 1994, I finally was able to arrange a meeting with Ragsdale through Max Littell, a cofounder of Roswell's International UFO Museum, who had been in regular contact with Ragsdale since he first surfaced. Littell was present during the interview, where we both heard an excitingly "enhanced" version of Ragsdale's story, which, when it became more widely known, significantly undermined his contribution to the revisionist scenario.

Ragsdale had told Randle and Schmitt he had managed to hold onto some of the strange debris he picked up on the impact site, despite the desperate efforts of his companion Trudy Truelove.[4] He confirmed this to me during our 1994 interview. He said he kept it hidden in the trunk of his car, and according to Schmitt, about three years after the event, he and Truelove "display[ed] some of the material in one of the local pubs—the Blue Moon Tavern, at that time located south of Roswell. [I]t's quite possible the word got out he was the proud owner of some of the material." An indeterminate time after this indiscretion, according to Schmitt, Ragsdale was on "an extended trip" when "not only was the car stolen, but the horse trailer behind it."[5] Schmitt's implication was that the target of the theft was the material hidden in Ragsdale's automobile.

During my September 1994 interview with him, Ragsdale said the theft took place during a burglary of his home. He claimed the perpetrator ignored a coin collection and other valuables, taking only the saucer debris, which he had transferred from his car to a hiding place in his bedroom. In addition, the burglar knew just where to look for the contraband, as there was no rifling of drawers and the like. This is more than a slight variation on a theme.

So, too, was what Ragsdale told me about the location of his and Truelove's rudely interrupted tryst. Instead of being about thirty miles north of Roswell a few miles west of U.S. Highway 285, it was more than fifty miles west-northwest of Roswell in the Capitan Mountains near the tiny hamlet of Arabella. Unlike the sun-baked prairie of the original location, this was a high, cool, forested area popular with the locals in the summer for camping and partying. It made much more sense than the original site as a place for Ragsdale and Truelove to make whoopee, but for the revisionist partisans, it had a major drawback: it was many miles away from the spot Frank Kaufmann claimed he and the special team had located the downed UFO.

In addition, the saucer had crashed much nearer the lovebirds' campsite, almost landing on top of them. When they rushed over to inspect the wreckage, Ragsdale boldly climbed where no human had gone before, into the strange, disk-shaped craft. There, he told me, he discovered several lifeless humanoid creatures. He even attempted to remove a helmet from one of the bodies. "Liked to tore his head off," he said.

Ragsdale also told me Trudy Truelove had been killed when her speeding car crashed into a bridge not long after the two of them had shown the odd material around at the Blue Moon. She had some of the debris in the car with her, but when he went through the wreckage after it had been towed in from the scene of the accident, it had disappeared. This is repeated in an affidavit Ragsdale executed seven months later (see appendix H). It struck me as more than a little bit curious that, given her fears at the crash site, Truelove would have publicly associated herself with the debris and carried some of it in her car, but I kept this to myself as Ragsdale continued with his story.

He also told me of a similar incident involving his brother, a truck driver who had some of the debris with him when he was involved in a serious road accident in which he was rendered unconscious. When the young man came to, the alien material was gone. Curiously, this incident is not mentioned in Ragsdale's new affidavit, and in *The Jim Ragsdale Story*, published by a company in which Max Littell and two of his family members are principals, it is denied that Ragsdale's brother was in any way involved in the crashed-saucer incident, even in this after-the-fact fashion. Moreover, Max Littell asserts he does not recall Ragsdale saying anything about his brother during our interview.[6]

The Ragsdale clan and friends seem terribly prone to traffic accidents. In 1992, forty-two years after the aforementioned car-and-trailer rustling/house burglary, Ragsdale and his wife were involved in a near-fatal collision just outside the main gate of Cannon Air Force Base, near Clovis, New Mexico. According to Schmitt, and confirmed to me by Ragsdale in our 1994 chat, the young son of an officer stationed at the base sped out of the gate and hit the Ragsdales' motor home broadside, rolling it. The Ragsdales were severely injured. Schmitt told me Ragsdale believes this frightening accident may somehow be linked with his knowledge of events at the so-called impact site in 1947.[7]

Perhaps I lack imagination, but I find it impossible to credit the notion that the latter incident had anything to do with Roswell. It took place months before Ragsdale revealed his story to any Roswell investigator and decades after the alleged crashed-saucer incident. There is nothing to suggest it was more than a tragic consequence of reckless driving. To be coldly pragmatic about it, the risk-benefit ratio of murdering Ragsdale—not to mention the prospect of success by the chosen means—is outrageously negative. What did he know, what could he have proven that so threatened the Roswell secret that it could warrant such high-stakes thuggery? Further, where are the attempts on the lives of others who have revealed information far more significant than Ragsdale's?

As for the 1950 automobile-trailer theft/house burglary (which in a later telling Ragsdale moved back in time to the same day as the crash incident), if Ragsdale did show and tell too much in public so soon after the Roswell events, and just up the road from Walker Air Force Base (née Roswell AAF) to boot, it is certainly possible, even likely, this would have come to the attention of the air force. It also makes sense that the military would attempt to relieve Ragsdale of his "stash." Why, however, resort to the risky business of trailing him on "an extended trip" and stealing his car and horse trailer (or breaking into his house)? Why not do what was reported to have been done only the year before, after Bill Brazel talked too much in a Corona bar? Why not simply pay Ragsdale a visit, make his "patriotic duty" clear, and relieve him of his souvenirs?

The odds of success would be very high, the associated risk very low. And speaking of Bill Brazel, the similarity of this alleged Ragsdale episode to Brazel's well-known confiscation account, first publicized in 1980, is too close to be dismissed lightly.[8]

Ragsdale claims he and Trudy saw the flaming craft drop out of the sky during a violent thunderstorm. Yet local newspaper weather forecasts and reports for the Fourth of July say nothing about thunderstorms in the greater Roswell vicinity.

Some have suggested it is possible there was a highly localized storm in the area of the alleged impact site that went unpredicted and unreported in such a sparsely populated region. Unfortunately for those who favor this notion, official National Weather Service records have established beyond any doubt that the only thunderstorm activity anywhere in all of southeastern and south-central New Mexico from July 2 through July 7 was at Alamogordo the afternoon of July 2, with a trace of rain reported at Cloudcroft on the same date, both locations far distant from the site north of Roswell.[9] Clearly, as the alert reader will have realized, these weather data raise storm warnings not only for the Ragsdale-Truelove tale but also other accounts central to both versions of the Roswell story.

Ragsdale's account includes nothing that suggests he and his lady friend saw anyone other than army personnel on the impact site. Nor do they seem to have seen any vehicles other than their own and those in the army convoy. But even this changed.

A rather detailed description of the army detachment, its vehicles, and activities attributed to Ragsdale appears in Randle and Schmitt's *The Truth About the UFO Crash at Roswell*, published in 1994, which account also has the lovebirds driving a jeep rather than a pickup.[10] However, the affidavit Ragsdale executed in April 1995 has the duo departing the scene—in a pickup—at the sound of the approaching military convoy and before it came into view. This document also significantly alters other elements of Ragsdale's story, clearly a work in progress until its author's death.

So what of the account of anonymous alleged archaeologist "New Mexico Jones"? Does it include anything about Ragsdale and Truelove? According to Tom Carey, his story places "another man already there" on the site, but says nothing about what became of the fellow. Neither does Jones make mention of a woman nor of any vehicle other than those in which he and his colleagues and, soon after, army personnel arrived.

It hardly seems likely Ragsdale would have forgotten to mention seeing a group of civilians appearing at the site shortly before the military rumbled over the horizon. Nor does it seem possible Jones would have failed to mention seeing a woman had he done so.

However, although Carey has unearthed interesting information and leads on and from archaeologists whom he thinks may have been present at the saucer crash site, Jones remains anonymous. Moreover, his reported characterization of the army's arrival ("a jeep arrived carrying soldiers") and what then took place bears a too-close-for-comfort resemblance to the *Unsolved Mysteries* dramatization that had been rebroadcast the month before Jones telephoned Kevin Randle. Should Carey's leads be fruitful and back up Jones's story, then the question would be, Is Ragsdale Jones's mystery man? But this assumes the question will remain to be asked when that time comes.

According to Randle and Schmitt's original accounts, Ragsdale was familiar with the impact site area where he claimed to have been camping with Truelove because he had been working nearby as a member of a survey team blazing the route for a new El Paso Natural Gas Company pipeline slated to be built soon north of Roswell.[11]

Pursuing the matter, I took care to make no reference to the Roswell incident, telling those I contacted only that I was doing historical research. I called the headquarters of El Paso Natural Gas and was referred to John F. Eichelmann Sr., who had joined the company in 1931 and became chief engineer in 1937, eventually retiring as senior vice president.[12] Eichelmann was a principal in the pipeline's conception, development, and design. He supervised its construction, and his son told me he "can remember every spade of dirt turned" on the project.[13]

The senior Eichelmann told me the pipeline—the Permian–San Juan Cross-Over Line, running diagonally northwest across New Mexico from Plains, Texas, to Gallup and on to Kingman, Arizona—was built in 1953, with construction starting in late spring or early summer. Oklahoma Pipe Line Constructors laid 150 miles of the thirty-inch pipe from Plains to a point near Corona, not far from the debris field site on the Foster Ranch, and the R. H. Fulton company took it from there to Gallup.[14]

Next, I asked when the route survey was conducted. Eichelmann said the work was carried out in late 1952, more than five years after the Roswell incident. I asked him if it was possible any preliminary work had been done in 1947. He replied succinctly: "We didn't start *thinking* about the line until 1952." These recollections are confirmed in a history of El Paso Natural Gas and a contemporaneous article in the company magazine.[15]

When he learned of the results of my pipeline project research, Schmitt told me his and Randle's understanding of what Ragsdale had said was in error. It seems Schmitt misunderstood Ragsdale during their first interview. Ragsdale suffered from severe respiratory problems for which he was on oxygen and which affected his ability to speak clearly. This was still the case when I interviewed him in September 1994. Even so, why did Randle and Schmitt go public with this information as supportive of Ragsdale's claims without first doing a little checking?[16]

Jim Ragsdale's movable tryst shifted to the Capitan Mountains at about the same time he struck a deal with the International UFO Museum and Max Littell. Kevin Randle reports that, while on a visit to Roswell in September 1994, he gained access to a letter from Littell to Ragsdale, dated September 10—the day following my interview with Ragsdale—to which was attached the new Ragsdale affidavit. Littell wrote,

> This letter constitutes a letter of understanding as relates to the International UFO Museum and Research Center and the information prepared by the Museum staff after a series of interviews that have occur[r]ed during the past few weeks. You have verified the total information being put into print as being totally yours, and not from any secondary source. . . .
>
> . . . From this date, any net proceeds realized by the Museum will be divided with you, for your lifetime, on the basis of 25% of any gross amount to Jim Ragsdale, and 75% to the Museum.
>
> In exchange the Museum will own the rights to do this on a permanent basis and any designation of the impact site, and all material relating thereto will be designated as "The Jim Ragsdale" . . . site. As evidence of good faith of the Museum, an initial check is attached hereto as an advance against proceeds.

This arrangement was latter modified when Littell set up Jim Ragsdale Productions, Inc., to market Ragsdale's story in print and on videotape, with Ragsdale's percentage of the take to go into a trust fund for his grandchildren. Ragsdale Productions is a Littell family enterprise, with Max Littell's son-in-law Danny Boswell its president, his daughter Lana Boswell its secretary, and Littell himself its vice president. Jim Ragsdale's daughter Judy Lott sits on the company's board of directors.[17]

Randle has made it clear he is convinced, and I agree, that Ragdale's "improved" memory of the alleged crash site's location was prompted by his business arrangement with Littell, a notary public, who, interestingly enough, witnessed Ragsdale's signature on the affidavit setting down the first version of his account. However, according to what Randle told me when both of us were in Roswell for the fiftieth anniversary celebration of the non-UFO crash, he also remains certain Ragsdale's original story (exactly which version?) is true—although he admits the man's accommodating ways have completely destroyed any value that story had to the revisionist case.[18]

FIRE—OR FIZZLE?—IN THE SKY

Several persons have reported seeing a spectacular flaming or glowing object flash through the night sky near Roswell in the early summer of 1947. Advocates of the revisionist version of the Roswell incident have seized on these reports as proof that, whatever the Roswell object was, it fell to earth between 11:00 and 11:30 P.M. on Friday, July 4.

Randle and Schmitt correlate sightings made by William Woody and his father, army air forces Cpl. E. L. Pyles, vaguely identified Franciscan nuns, and Jim Ragsdale and Trudy Truelove. They say all these witnesses report seeing a flaming object following a *southeasterly course* and then disappearing below or near the horizon (in Ragsdale's case, crashing to the ground) at about the same location north of Roswell. Further, they tell us documentary evidence shows the nuns' sighting took place between 11:00 and 11:15 P.M. on the Fourth. This, Randle and Schmitt assert, when considered together with other information they attribute to some of the witnesses, gives good reason to believe all the sightings occurred about the same time on the same date, July 4. Finally, since two of those witnesses, Ragsdale and Truelove, were very near the impact site where Ragsdale claims they later found a strange craft and bodies, Randle and Schmitt conclude that what was seen by all was the stricken craft plunging to its doom.[19] Not so fast, Roswell fans!

William Woody joined me for breakfast at the Roswell Inn on May 22, 1993. As we ate, he told me he was fourteen in July 1947, living with his family on their farm south of Roswell and east of Roswell AAF. He said it was on this farm "one night during the summer of 1947, probably in early July," that he and his father saw "a large, very bright object in the *southwestern sky, moving rapidly northward*" (emphasis added). They "watched the object travel all the way across the sky until it disappeared below the northern horizon." Woody's description of the object closely matches that of a very large, bright meteor or bolide, but it did not seem to him to move as fast as a meteor, "and it definitely went out of sight below the horizon, rather than winking out like a meteor does."[20]

According to Randle and Schmitt's initial accounts, "Woody and his father reported an object *coming from the northwest* [moving on a southeasterly track] and going down about due north of Roswell" (emphasis added).[21] Clearly, this is not consistent with what Woody told me and later confirmed in a signed affidavit. It is interesting that references to the Woodys' sighting in Randle and Schmitt's *Truth About the UFO Crash at Roswell* include no mention of the object's direction of flight and where it first appeared in the sky, only that it fell "toward the ground north of Roswell."[22]

In a telephone interview on January 24, 1994, E. L. Pyles, told me he was an army air forces corporal in July 1947, assigned to the 101st Airways and Air Communications Service Squadron. He was stationed at the army radio range facility about twelve miles southwest of Roswell Army Air Field, but visited the main base frequently, on duty and to visit the post exchange, the noncommissioned officers' club, and other facilities.

Concerning his sighting, Pyles said, "What I saw one night was *just a streak across the sky. I couldn't tell you what direction it was going* now" (emphasis added). Neither did he recall where in the sky he saw it. "If I was at the base, I could probably pick my direction and tell you then. But it's just been too long ago, and it would just be almost impossible to say anything about that." He went on to say, "I thought it was just a meteorite. . . . It was in a downward motion, had a long streak back of it, kind of a tail. . . . It looked like it went past the horizon, and then it just disappeared out of sight." Pyles added that what he saw was larger and more spectacular than an ordinary meteor. "That's what brought my attention to it."

I asked Pyles when this took place. He replied, "It was in forty-seven. *I don't remember the month or the date I saw it.* . . . It seems to me like it was summertime" (emphasis added). I then asked him if he was on the main base, Roswell AAF, when he saw the "streak." He said, *"Yes, I was.* . . . I was walking across a drill field . . . there on the base . . . [with a] friend of mine [another member of the 101st AACS, whose name Pyles does not recall]. [emphasis added] We both saw it."

Next, I pursued the time of night the sighting occurred. Pyles said, "Well, it had to have been between, say, eight o'clock, probably, . . . [and] eleven. . . . [I couldn't] pinpoint the time, but it was before midnight. I think we had been to the club, NCO club." A "few days later," he saw the "RAAF Captures Flying Saucer" story in the *Roswell Daily Record*, and he wondered if what he and his friend had seen had anything to do with it.[23]

First note that Randle and Schmitt place Pyles at the radio range, not Roswell AAF, when he had his sighting. Now compare Pyles's own words above with what is attributed to him by Randle and Schmitt: "He told us that in early July 1947 he had seen an *object* flash across the night sky *to his north*, going down toward the ground [emphasis added]. Although he doesn't remember the exact date or time, he did say that he believed it was a weekend because he was awake after the main lights [at the radio range where Pyles was billeted] had been turned out at eleven."[24] As with William Woody, this account is in significant conflict with what Pyles told me personally, which itself clearly contains so little pertinent information as to be useless in any attempt to establish that a mysterious craft crashed somewhere north of Roswell on July 4 or, for that matter, any other night in early July 1947.

According to Randle and Schmitt, Franciscan nuns Mother Superior Mary Bernadette and Sister Capistrano, while making their rounds at Roswell's Saint Mary's Hospital on the southern outskirts of town, saw a "fiery object on July 4, 1947, *sometime between 11:15 and 11:30 P.M.*" (emphasis added). Randle and Schmitt tell us the nuns left a written record of their sighting in the hospital log. Allegedly, the entry states the object was "arcing downward north of Roswell."[25] According to Schmitt, these nuns were "avid astronomers" and routinely made observations of the night sky.[26]

To date, the actual log entry has not been made public, and Randle and Schmitt have been cryptic in their references to it, stating only that it is in "records held by the Franciscan Catholic nuns."[27] Their characterization of what is set down there suggest it does not offer much. First, the description of the object is vague, but it has the earmarks of a meteor and nothing more interesting.[28] Second, the time of the sighting is remarkably imprecise for "avid astronomers," for whom precise recording of observational data is, dare I say it, almost a religion.

Once again, there appears to be less here than some would wish.

Jim Ragsdale's account includes his seeing "a bright light source" streak overhead on a southeasterly course and crash about two miles from his campsite.[29] As we have seen, however, grave problems with other elements of Ragsdale's tale(s) make anything he said about what he claims to have seen in the sky useless in making a case for a Roswell crash date of July 4.

So with what are we left with? We have three sightings, all of which it seems reasonable to believe took place given the apparent credibility of the witnesses.[30] One of these purportedly was logged by the observers. It is the only one tied in any way other than speculation with a definite date, July 4, but as I have already noted, the log entry has never been produced by Randle and Schmitt to confirm this.

All three accounts suggest rather spectacular meteors but, with the exception of William Woody's, nothing out of the ordinary.[31] Each description, two of which I have heard personally from the witnesses, differs significantly from the others as to the appearance of the phenomenon, where it was first seen, and the course it was following.

From their vantage point *southeast* of Roswell, Woody and his father first saw their object in the *southwestern* sky, and it followed a *northerly* track. Pyles does not remember in which direction he first saw his object nor in which direction it was going as he watched it from Roswell AAF. As reported, the nuns' log entry gives no indication of where they first saw their object or the course it followed.

With respect to where whatever was seen by the witnesses was lost from view, William Woody says he remembers the object he and his father saw as disappearing beyond the horizon north of Roswell. The nuns, too, are reported to have seen theirs on an earthward track north of town. Pyles recalls his sighting ending when the object dropped below the horizon, but he does not remember the direction he was looking.

While it is certainly possible all three sightings were of the same object, the connection is far from clear-cut. None of the sightings suggests a vehicle of any sort, but rather an eye-catching natural phenomenon. Moreover, none reflects an object or craft on a southeasterly course and proceeding from a quadrant of the sky northwest of Roswell. Under the revisionist scenario, such a track would be required if an object were to spew debris over the Foster Ranch before grounding at the impact site thirty-five miles to the southeast and about the same distance north by northwest of Roswell. Only Ragsdale's account incorporates something flying on a northwest to southeast course, and even he, apparently always willing to accommodate his listeners, said he was not sure of the date of his alleged experience.

Finally, as mentioned above, official National Weather Service records have established there were no thunderstorms or rain of any kind in the area during the Fourth of July weekend. However, stipulating that, if there were such activity on the Fourth at the time of the alleged crash, would it not have been difficult for the Woodys, Corporal Pyles and his friend, and the Franciscan nuns to see the object? Even if the storm were north of town and the sky at least relatively clear over Roswell proper, is it likely Pyles and the younger Woody would not remember the object as disappearing into or behind storm clouds rather than below the horizon? Is it likely the nuns—"avid astronomers"—would not have noted this in their log entry?

SPARSE SHARDS AND BARE BONES

Tom Carey's success in tracking down archaeologists who may have been on the impact site is a tribute to his hard work and diligence in the face of long odds. However, it seems clear a great deal more digging will be necessary before anything conclusive can be determined about whether and when they were there—not to mention where "there" was and if it has any relevance at all to the Roswell crashed-saucer affair.

The recollections of paleontologist C. Betrand Schultz and the late W. Curry Holden, the archaeologist whom Schultz says told him of being on the site, are sketchy at best. Apart from his lead to Holden, Schultz's most important recollection is of seeing soldiers stationed along U.S. 285 north of Roswell sometime in the summer of 1947. This is far from chronologically precise, but suggests he may have seen the same activity reported by William Woody and the possibility the impact site may have been much closer to Roswell than previously thought.[32] However, if the military wanted to keep the incident quiet, sentries would not have been posted in full view of passers by on a relatively busy highway. They would have been stationed some distance back on side and ranch roads, where they could deal quietly with any intruders. If Woody and Schultz are relatively accurate in their recollections, then it seems more probable the soldiers were involved in something not involving security concerns, perhaps a training exercise.[33]

Kevin Randle reports all the "fading" ninety-six-year-old Holden could tell him a few months before his death in April 1993 was, "I was involved . . . I was there [where?] and I saw everything [what?]."[34] New Mexico Jones, the anonymous archaeologist, is reported to have told Randle in February 1990 that he and his colleagues "had been driving on back roads and across open country . . . in *Lincoln County*" searching for signs of early Indian occupation "in the area *north* of the Capitan Mountains" when they came upon a strange grounded craft (emphasis added). In other words, Jones's account suggests that he and his associates made their alleged discovery in the vicinity of the Foster Ranch and the debris field near Corona rather than significantly further southeast in Chaves County, where the revisionist impact site is said to have been. Jones's account does not seem to include a precise date for the discovery, wherever it may have been.[35]

In his 1997 book *The Randle Report*, Randle relates that in his continuing investigations, Carey talked with Dr. George Agogino, an anthropologist at Eastern New Mexico University and longtime member of the scientific and technical consultants panel of the Committee for Scientific Investigation of Claims of the Paranormal. According to Randle, Carey read Randle's notes of his conversation with Jones to Agogino, who responded, "That's what he told me." Reportedly, Agogino also supplied Jones's true name, and Randle writes, "I spoke to him again when I saw him at his place of business. The tale gained a great deal of importance now that I know who he is."[36] While that may be true for Randle on a personal basis, it is not yet true in an objective sense. Jones remains anonymous to the ufological community. This, together with the fact that the above is all Randle tells us about his in-person interview with the man, leaves us no further along than we were before.

In an attempt to remedy this, I telephoned Professor Agogino on August 10, 2000. I spoke with Mrs. Agogino, who said her husband was quite ill, had just returned home from the hospital, and could not come to the telephone. After I explained who I was and what I was calling about, Mrs. Agogino agreed to discuss what she knew about the matter. She told me, "We're not sure who that person was. Somebody told us that they were there a long time ago. This was many, many years ago, in the fifties or early sixties, and we didn't pay much attention to it." She repeated that she and her husband still were uncertain who the person was, adding, "What I was told was that they said they saw the people who had crashed, and that they were human but old and bald." She went on to relate that, after being approached by Carey, they tried to assist him in identifying their source, but "every time we asked somebody [and said] that we thought it was them, they said, 'No.' "

Clearly, the "archaeological record" remains far too fragmentary and questionable to depend upon in any evidentiary way. Still, perhaps Jones and other anthropologists did stumble onto something unusual. There were many peculiar things falling out of the New Mexico skies in the 1940s, 1950s, and 1960s, some of them resembling old, bald humans (see chapter 13).

MOST OF THE TRUTH ABOUT THE PRESS ANNOUNCEMENT

Why the authorities at Roswell AAF issued the famous "We've got one!" press release has been a mystery since UFO researchers began to take this case seriously in the late 1970s. According to the conventional wisdom, the announcement was an innocent, shoot-from-the-hip mistake, without which the world would never have known about the strange discovery. According to the revisionist scenario, it was a diabolically clever ploy designed to head off media attention engendered by Mack Brazel's untimely visit to Sheriff Wilcox. The former is much closer to the likely truth.

There are several problems with the revisionist interpretation of the "why" of the press announcement. First and most obvious, if the revisionist scenario is correct, such a high-profile, high-risk tactic was far out of proportion to the problem it was intended to address, and it carried with it the seeds of potentially far more serious difficulties. Only a handful of people knew about Brazel's find, all of them local, several of them law-enforcement officials with whom the military had close working relationships, and only one, KGFL's Frank Joyce, a media person. Quiet discussions with all of them, appealing to their patriotic duty, perhaps suggesting what was found was from a classified government project and hinting at dire consequences for talking too much would have spiked the story at the outset. There simply was no need to wave a red flag that inevitably would draw global press attention given the then rampant international excitement about flying saucers. In fact, to do so would be foolish in the extreme.

Second, there were the archaeologists. They had been threatened into silence. What might they think and do when they saw headlines announcing the army's capture of a flying saucer? Would they not think the lid was off and start talking about what they had seen? Certainly there was a substantial risk one or more of their number would see an opportunity for fame and fortune and take it.

Third, Brazel is supposed to have driven to Roswell on Sunday, July 6, stopping by the sheriff's office in the early afternoon. Sheriff Wilcox alerted the army at Roswell AAF soon after, and it would not have been long before the full story of who knew what was known. Yet Walter Haut did not give his media contacts the first phase of the "cover story," the captured "disc" announcement, until midday Tuesday, July 8, two full days after the army knew it had a problem on its hands.

Finally, Randle and Schmitt have suggested the release was cleverly crafted to divert attention away from the impact site near Roswell. They claim it referred to something being "found on the Foster ranch," and "the impact site close to Roswell is not mentioned whatsoever."[37] In fact, what was actually said in the announcement as crafted by the army is uncertain. No copies of the release Haut used in getting the story out have been found, and there is very good reason to believe a written release was never given to the media.[38]

However, George Walsh of Roswell's Radio KSWS remembers very clearly and without any doubt in his mind that Haut telephoned him with the release, and he wrote down what Haut dictated to him. Walsh told me he then called in those exact words to the Associated Press bureau in Albuquerque, which in turn put them on the AP wire.[39] It is this wire story representation of the army's statement as reproduced in several newspapers, apparently in its entirety, to which we must refer when analyzing the press release.[40]

This statement makes no reference whatever to the Foster place or Lincoln County, and it does not mention Mack Brazel by name. However, it does say, "The flying object landed on a ranch *near Roswell* sometime last week" (emphasis added). It also refers to the assistance of "the Sheriff's office of Chaves county." Both Roswell and the putative impact site are located in Chaves County. Clever crafting, indeed.

My assessment of what really was behind the press announcement is presented in chapter 7.

FRANKIE AND RUBEN MEET REALITY

I turn now to the accounts of Frankie Rowe and Ruben Anaya, which seem to be included as part of a throw everything at the wall and see what sticks approach on the part of the Roswell revisionists. They do not mesh with the revisionist story, nor for that matter, do they fit the conventional wisdom scenario. When the Roswell puzzle is assembled, they are leftover pieces. Yet the revisionists cling to them. Perhaps the following considerations may give them pause.

There are numerous problems with Frankie Rowe's tale. Most obvious is the basic account of the fire call to the crash site which her father and other Roswell firemen answered. Since Dan Dwyer reportedly saw two beings in body bags (or at least two body bags with something in them), it would appear the army was already there with security in place. How did Dwyer and his fellow firefighters get so close? If they did manage to get through the military cordon somehow, why were they not detained and sworn to secrecy on the spot, precluding Rowe from ever hearing the story? And who called in the town fire department in the first place? The military certainly would not have done so.

There is another difficulty on this point. As part of my investigation of Rowe's story, I interviewed three retired members of the Roswell Fire Department who served with Rowe's father at the time of the incident. I also discussed the matter with a former member of the Roswell City Council who served on the council committee responsible for public safety policies. None of the former firefighters remembered the department making such a run. Moreover, they and the former councilman said it was standing department policy not to respond to calls outside the city limits, even if they were close in—let alone thirty or thirty-five miles out—because of concerns about not being able to respond to in-city calls if the department's equipment was committed elsewhere (the department had only two trucks in July 1947). The department chief— in July 1947, Rue Crissman—had the authority to make exceptions in extreme emergencies, but this was only rarely exercised. No official record of this alleged exception has been found, although Kevin Randle reports finding a record of another in June 1947, the month before.[41]

Next, there are the horrendous threats. The same overkill argument applies here as it does to the alleged press release roundup.

Then there is the painter, a civilian contractor who allegedly saw a hurt but living alien walk into the Roswell air base hospital. According to the revisionist scenario, the incident took place on Saturday, July 5. It is highly unlikely a civilian painting contractor would have been working on the base on a Saturday, especially on a long holiday weekend.

Further, Rowe's description of the material she says she saw at the fire station differs considerably from those of all others who claim to have seen the saucer wreckage. No one else has described anything that behaved like quicksilver or that could be "wadded up into nothing." Moreover, it hardly seems likely a state trooper worried about the army discovering he had palmed a piece of debris would have stopped by the firehouse and so casually shown it around. And if he did so, is it likely he would have permitted his friends to attempt to cut, tear, or burn his souvenir?

Rowe says her tonsils were removed at what was then Saint Mary's Hospital. In 1993, my colleague Stanton Friedman made inquiries at the hospital, then Eastern New Mexico Medical Center South, and learned it had no record of this procedure or of Rowe being hospitalized for any reason at any time during the period in question.[42] Stan also attempted to locate records of the attending physicians, but these are no longer available.[43]

Rowe claims the terrifying threats of the big army man with the Brooklyn accent traumatized her, which she at first said caused her not to talk about her experience and her father's story with anyone until 1991, when she was interviewed for the first time by Kevin Randle. She also told me her father "never talked about" the case with anyone after this threat to his family, that the subject was taboo. Yet according to Roswell photographer Jack Rodden, Rowe told him about it some years ago, and it was he who brought her to Randle's attention. Further, Rowe herself told me her sister, Helen Cahill, remembers Rowe first told her about the threatening visit in the early 1960s, although Rowe said she did not remember this conversation.[44]

Although the internal difficulties of Ruben Anaya's story and its inconsistency with other, credible Roswell accounts were obvious and made even more difficult to credit than Frankie Rowe's, the possibility that a prominent public figure may have been caught up in the case made it worth pursuing and easy to check. One has to wonder why the revisionists did not bother to do so.

Anaya claimed Joseph Montoya, then New Mexico's lieutenant governor, the state's second-ranking elected official, was in Roswell for a public ceremony at Roswell AAF on a "special day." Walter Haut, the base public relations officer in July 1947, could remember no such event, and he volunteered to help me with research into the matter. He and I independently combed through the Roswell newspapers for the two-week period July 1 through July 14, 1947. I also checked both Albuquerque papers for the same dates. Other than community Fourth of July festivities, no special ceremony of any kind took place in Roswell or at the base, and Montoya was not mentioned in connection with the Independence Day activities. There was nothing in any of the papers about Montoya being present in Roswell during that period for any reason. Further inquiries at the New Mexico State Library also turned up nothing.

I discussed Anaya's story with two very close family-political friends of the Montoyas. On my behalf, one of them approached Montoya's widow, Della Montoya. She told him she did not remember her husband being in Roswell for anything at that time, and she most certainly did not remember a hysterical telephone call from him about a flying saucer and little men from outer space. Similarly, both family friends, one of whom has known the Montoyas for more than fifty years, had never heard anything about Joseph Montoya being involved in the Roswell incident before I told them of Anaya's story.

As with Frankie Rowe's story, there is an outside chance Anaya's is based on something real, but once again, whatever it was, it had nothing to do with crashed saucers somewhere near Roswell.

Next I turn to consideration of the man whose claims form the bedrock of the revisionist Roswell as well as contributing key elements to the foundation of the conventional wisdom—the versatile, imaginative, and nimble Frank J. Kaufmann.

NOTES

1. Telephone conversation with Donald R. Schmitt, May 17, 1993. The unredacted affidavit is reproduced in app. H of this report.

2. Telephone conversation with Jim Ragsdale and his wife, November 14, 1993.

3. Copies of both letters are in my files.

4. Kevin D. Randle and Donald R. Schmitt, *The Truth About the UFO Crash at Roswell* (New York: Evans, 1994), pp. 7–8.

5. Audiotape, Donald R. Schmitt, lecture, Albuquerque, New Mexico, November 14, 1993. In an April 15, 1995, affidavit attesting to his revised story, Ragsdale claimed the visit to the Blue Moon took place later on the day he and Truelove had taken the debris and run for it.

6. Ragsdale Productions, *The Jim Ragsdale Story: A Closer Look at the Roswell Incident* (Roswell, N.M.: Ragsdale Productions, 1996).

7. Schmitt, May 17, 1993.

8. See Charles Berlitz and William L. Moore, *The Roswell Incident* (New York: Berkley, 1988), p. 89; Kevin D. Randle and Donald R. Schmitt, *UFO Crash at Roswell* (New York: Avon, 1991), pp. 130–31; videotaped interview with Brazel in *Recollections of Roswell—Part II*, available from the Fund for UFO Research.

9. Hourly observation records, daily precipitation, U.S. Weather Bureau, June and July, 1947, from the archives of the National Climatic Data Center, Asheville, N.C.; copies in my files. I am grateful to Professor C. B. Moore for providing me with this information.

10. Randle and Schmitt, *Truth*, pp. 7–8. This account also includes some significant departures from what is set down in the affidavit Ragsdale signed for Randle and Schmitt.

11. Schmitt, Albuquerque; Kevin D. Randle and Donald R. Schmitt, "When and Where Did the Roswell Object Crash?," *International UFO Reporter* (January–February 1994): 14.

12. Telephone conversation, Lesley J. Gosling, President, El Paso Natural Gas Foundation; Frank Mangan, *The Pipeliners: The Story of El Paso Natural Gas* (El Paso, Texas: El Paso Natural Gas Company, 1977), p. 85.

13. Telephone conversation, John F. Eichelmann Jr., February 14, 1994.

14. Telephone conversation, John F. Eichelmann Sr., February 14, 1994. Mr. Eichelmann at first remembered the years as being 1951 and 1952, but he quickly corrected this.

15. Mangan, *Pipeliners*, pp. 164–65, 195–97; "The Big Expansion," *The Pipeliner* (El Paso Natural Gas employee magazine), autumn 1953, pp. 2–7.

16. Kevin D. Randle, *Roswell UFO Crash Update: Exposing the Military Cover-Up of the Century* (New Brunswick, N.J.: Global Communications, 1995), pp. 24–25. Here Randle suggests the impression that Ragsdale claimed to have known and picked his campsite because he was working on the El Paso pipeline resulted from "poor communication on our [Randle and Schmitt's] part rather than anything said by Ragsdale." Much of *Crash Update* is devoted to attempts to refute material in my *Roswell in Perspective*.

17. Kevin D. Randle, *The Randle Report: UFOs in the '90s* (New York: Evans, 1997), pp. 167–68.

18. For the evolution of Randle's thinking on Ragsdale, see his Roswell *UFO Crash Update*, pp. 26–29, and *Randle Report*, pp. 163–77.

19. Randle and Schmitt, "When and Where?" pp. 13–16.

20. William M. Woody affidavit, app. H.

21. Randle and Schmitt, "When and Where?" pp. 13–14.

22. Randle and Schmitt, *Truth*, pp. 3, 136, 160, 164.

23. Audiotaped telephone interview with E. L. Pyles, January 24, 1994; follow-up telephone conversation on March 8, 1994, to confirm Pyles's location at the time of his sighting.

24. Randle and Schmitt, "When and Where?" p. 14.

25. Ibid.; Schmitt, Albuquerque; Randle and Schmitt, *Truth*, pp. 4, 137.

26. Schmitt, Albuquerque.

27. Randle and Schmitt, *Truth*, p. 217, fn. 4 to chap. 1.

28. Since it was the Fourth of July, it is also possible the sisters saw part of a fireworks display.

29. Jim Ragsdale January 27, 1993, affidavit, app. H.

30. It should be taken into consideration that, to date, no other comparable sightings are known to have been made in the Roswell area at that time.

31. The moon was just past full on July 4, 1947, so any meteor or other such phenomenon would have to have been very bright and/or very large to have been noticed (source: James E. McDonald, astronomical data tables compiled from annual volumes of the *American Ephemeris and Nautical Almanac*, February 1969). James Winchell, a former associate of both Lincoln LaPaz and C. B. Moore, and I independently checked the major New Mexico newspapers for the period June 23 through July 15, 1947, for sightings of large meteors and other spectacular aerial phenomena. Although there were numerous flying saucer reports, we found nothing similar to these observations. My inquiries to the University of New Mexico's Institute of Meteoritics, the U.S. Naval Observatory, and the Smithsonian Institution were equally unproductive.

32. Thomas J. Carey, "The Continuing Search for the Roswell Archaeologists," *International UFO Reporter* (January–February 1994): 10.

33. Newspapers from the period and official records contain no reports of either civilian or military aircraft accidents in the area during the period in question.

34. Carey, "The Continuing Search," p. 12.

35. Ibid., pp. 6–7; Randle and Schmitt, *UFO Crash*, p. 116.

36. Randle, *Randle Report*, p. 199.

37. Randle and Schmitt, "When and Where?" p. 16.

38. George R. Walsh affidavit, app. H.

39. Walsh affidavit, app. H; "Army Announces Finding 'Saucer,'" *Rapid City (S.D.) Daily Journal*, Rapid City, July 8, 1947; "Flying Disc Transforms Sheriff's Office to International Newsroom," *Roswell Morning Dispatch*, July 9, 1947; Arthur R. McQuiddy affidavit, app. H.

40. See for example "Disc Solution Collapses," *San Francisco Chronicle*, July 9, 1947.

41. Audiotaped personal interview with George Daniels, former chief of the Roswell Fire Department, May 20, 1993; personal interview with Bob Thomas, retired Roswell firefighter, May 20, 1993; telephone interview with J. C. Smith, retired Roswell firefighter who was on the department 1941–1984, October 18, 1993; personal conversation with Max Littell, former Roswell city councilman, May 1993. Others whom I asked about this and related issues are L. M. Hall, former Roswell city councilman and chief of police (audiotaped personal interview, May 17, 1993) and Tommy Thompson, former Roswell chief of police and chief deputy to Sheriff Wilcox in July 1947 (audiotaped personal interview, May 21, 1993).

42. Rowe told me Kevin Randle said she should not be surprised her records are missing, that those behind the cover-up are very thorough. Telephone conversation with Frankie Rowe, December 10, 1993.

43. Telephone conversations with Stanton T. Friedman, April 22 and 23, 1993.

44. Personal interview with Jack Rodden, May 18, 1993; telephone conversation with Rowe, December 10, 1993.

FIVE

TALES OF KAUFMANN

Frank J. Kaufmann looms large in the Roswell stories. He first came on the scene as the source for an abundance of remarkably diverse and sensational key information presented in Randle and Schmitt's 1991 book, *UFO Crash at Roswell*, wherein he is identified as "Frank Kaufman" (no middle initial, only one *n*) and associated by name with several important revelations ("Frank 1a") and, anonymously, with a number of others ("Frank 1b"). It is also now solidly established that Frank 1b was the sole or principal source for unattributed accounts of what took place on, around, and over the debris and conventional-wisdom crash sites as presented by Randle and Schmitt in *UFO Crash*.

Kaufmann later surfaced as a critically knowledgeable source in the debate about the Barney Barnett/Plains of San Agustin flying saucer crash report, identified as "Mr. X" and "Joseph Osborne" ("Frank 2").[1] In his next incarnation he emerged as the "witness" whose testimony forms the backbone of the revisionist scenario as presented in various articles by Randle and Schmitt and in their second book-length Roswell collaboration, *The Truth About the UFO Crash at Roswell* ("Frank 3"), wherein he is given yet another pseudonym, "Steve MacKenzie."

FRANK 1A

In January 1990, Randle and Schmitt interviewed Kaufmann twice, first on the telephone and then in person. Randle "tracked down" this hot new witness and made the initial telephone contact, but it is not clear how or from whom the duo got their lead in the first place. On the phone, Kaufmann was reluctant to tell Randle much, but he did "admit" having firsthand knowledge of the incident and mentioned a special flight from Washington, D.C., which came into Roswell AAF on July 8 (revisionist date, July 4). He volunteered to Randle that "no one talked about the crash after the special flight from Washington came in."[2]

When Randle and Schmitt spoke with Kaufmann in person, he was somewhat more forthcoming. He claimed he was "on the outside of most of it," but one of the men aboard the special flight, Army Counter Intelligence Corps WO Robert Thomas, was a friend of his. Kaufmann related that, on the afternoon Thomas arrived, he told Kaufmann of the debris field and reconnaissance flights over the area, saying, "We don't know if there are bodies, but we're looking for them." He also said he thought Thomas was now dead (January 1990).[3]

Kaufmann also told his interviewers, "I know that one crate was taken to a hangar and left there overnight. There were spotlights on it and it was in the center of the floor with MPs around the walls, guarding it." He mentioned there were many rumors of bodies being found and of "finding some of them alive," but said the only thing he was sure of was the crate. Later, he apparently opened up still further, telling Randle and Schmitt the crate contained the strange bodies examined at the Roswell AAF hospital.[4]

Although he repeatedly said "he didn't know that much," Kaufmann claims he was sworn to secrecy. Randle and Schmitt report he and others "were taken into a room in small groups and told that the recovery was a highly classified event. No one was to talk about it to anyone. They were to forget it happened."[5]

FRANK IB

In March 1991, Randle and Schmitt interviewed "one of the intelligence operatives who had been assigned to the Roswell Army Air Field in 1947," a person whom they had interviewed before, in January 1990. This source was not identified with this interview by name, but internal evidence in *UFO Crash at Roswell*, which I confirmed independently in 1993, established with no room for doubt we are once again dealing with Frank J. Kaufmann.[6]

Kaufmann repeated his story of being taken aside with others in small groups, debriefed, and sworn to secrecy. Then, "in a roundabout fashion," he added new information. According to Randle and Schmitt, he told them "the news release issued by Walter Haut was damage control," written "to end the rumors circulating around Roswell."[7] (It is important to note that no one other than Kaufmann has ever claimed there were rumors of the crash "circulating around Roswell" before the Roswell AAF press announcement was issued on July 8.)

Kaufmann introduced his next revelation by making a sketch of "the object found at the second site on the Brazel [Foster] ranch. The *disc-shaped* object was seemingly squared off at its visible end[,] which might have been a result of the impact. It had a slight dome on top and was tipped up at an angle."[8] In a dramatic gesture, Kaufmann immediately shredded his drawing, but Schmitt redrew it from memory as soon as the interview was concluded. This drawing appears in *UFO Crash at Roswell* with this caption: "One of the few witnesses to see the impact point (second crash site) provided eyewitness testimony about its location and the object seen there."[9]

Randle and Schmitt say Kaufmann cryptically discussed the scene at the crash site: "Very few were allowed close to the impact . . . ," and "[g]uards were posted and men were organized to clean up the debris[,] but they were kept away from the object." This "major witness" then told Randle and Schmitt "flatly that they would never find anyone from the military who would provide firsthand testimony about the bodies."[10]

FRANK 2

Sometimes labeled "Joseph Osborne" and sometimes "Mr. X," Frank Kaufmann figured importantly in the debate over Grady L. "Barney" Barnett's reported claim to have seen a crashed flying saucer and the bodies of its crew on the Plains of San Agustin in July 1947, a secondhand account that led pioneer Roswell researchers William L. Moore and Stanton Friedman to conclude *two* saucers may have crashed in New Mexico on the same day, perhaps after colliding with each other in midair. In the May–June 1992 *International UFO Reporter*, Randle and Schmitt report Kaufmann— identified as Joseph Osborne—"saw an object about 30 feet in diameter [a *disk*]" at a crash scene "away from the debris field, at a separate site where bodies were located." When "asked specifically about the Plains and the Barnett story, he characterized them as a diversion."[11]

While other Roswell authors discounted the Barnett–Plains of San Agustin tale, Friedman, and, later, Fund for UFO Research board member and Friedman Roswell book collaborator Don Berliner became convinced of the second saucer crash when Gerald Anderson, a man with a remarkable and creative memory, came forward after *Unsolved Mysteries* rebroadcast its Roswell episode in January 1990. Anderson claimed to have been at the Plains site as a boy of five, where he saw not only the downed saucer, but also members of its crew, one of them still alive. More about Anderson anon.

During a February 1992 conference on the Plains controversy, Randle and Schmitt are said to have informed Roswell research colleagues that a Joseph Osborne, identified in the conference proceedings as Mr. X, claimed Barney Barnett

> had indeed told everyone that he had seen a crashed saucer and alien bodies on the PSA [Plains of San Agustin], but that he had been directed by the government to do so. . . . X had supposedly been at the Corona site, seen the bodies, had access to all information and had said there was no crash in the PSA. But the government had become quite concerned that the Roswell story would be exposed as a result of the publication of Frank Scully's 1950 book, *Behind the Flying Saucers*, and articles in *Newsweek* and *Time* in 1950.
>
> Therefore, according to X, Barney had been instructed to divert attention from the Roswell story. . . . It was claimed X was talking to . . . [Randle and Schmitt] because he liked them.[12]

As I established in 1993, there is absolutely no doubt Osborne/X and Frank J. Kaufmann are one and the same person.

FRANK 3

When I made my second investigative trip to New Mexico in May 1993, one of my priorities was to interview Frank Kaufmann. By that time, I had established to my satisfaction Frank 1a and Frank 1b were one and the same and, thus, that the conventional wisdom account of the alleged impact site and certain elements of the cover-up were principally, and perhaps entirely, based upon his testimony. I was virtually certain Kaufmann was also Osborne/X, and I knew he was a key source for the revisionist "interpretation" of Roswell that was beginning to emerge. I also had heard varying degrees of skepticism about his claimed role in and knowledge of the Roswell incident voiced by several prominent Roswell area residents who had known him for many years.

Under the circumstances, I thought it best not to follow my usual practice of first introducing myself to sources in writing and then making interview appointments. Shortly before noon on May 17, I called Kaufmann "cold" from the office at the original location of the International UFO Museum in downtown Roswell. Fully expecting to be put off, I identified myself, said I would be in town for several days, and expressed my hope for an interview opportunity. Kaufmann said he knew who I was— "I had you checked out." To my surprise he then said, "Why don't you come out now." About twenty minutes later, Kaufmann and I were seated at a table on his patio in south Roswell, drinking Cokes and enjoying the beautiful spring weather.[13]

Kaufmann told me he was in the army air forces and stationed at Roswell AAF in July 1947 as a member of the "Western Training Flying Command" (actually, the Western Flying Training Command), headquartered at Santa Ana, California, and commanded by "Lieutenant General Scanlon." He said he was at Roswell in some capacity associated with the Norden bombsight, at the time still a very sensitive and highly classified piece of technology. He explained Roswell AAF was the Strategic Air Command's central depot for the sight, and all SAC bombers had to go there to have it installed, calibrated, and so on.

(An aside: Martin F. Scanlon's official biography on file at the U.S. Army Military History Institute, Carlisle Barracks, Pennsylvania, reveals his highest attained rank and the rank he held upon his retirement from military service on February 29, 1948, was brigadier general, two grades below lieutenant general. He served at Roswell during World War II, first commanding the First Provisional Flying Training Wing and later the 38th Flying Training Wing. Although Scanlon had also been commanding general of the Western Flying Training Command during the war, at the time of the Roswell incident he was assigned to the Air Defense Command—not SAC—and stationed at Mitchell Field, New York, as deputy chief of staff and command public relations officer.[14])

Kaufmann was very vague and cryptic about his rank and duties at Roswell. At one point in our more than two-and-a-half-hour conversation, he said he had been the NCOIC (noncommissioned officer in charge) of something unspecified but implicitly very sensitive. He also stated he had "various ranks." I asked him if he had been a pilot. He responded, "Well, I did a lot of things." Taking a slightly different tack, I asked if he had been a rated commissioned officer or NCO. He replied, "Well, you know, I had my Boy Scout rating and I had my Cub Scout rating."

Kaufmann told me he left the service in December 1947, after which he stayed in Roswell, where he has lived since. In January 1948 he took a position with the Roswell Chamber of Commerce, ultimately becoming executive vice president. He retired from the chamber in 1972, worked for a while as an industrial and economic development consultant in association with a Dallas, Texas, firm, later returning to the

Roswell chamber for about two years to assist with local industrial and economic development initiatives.[15]

Kaufmann opened the conversation by asking about my research and my relationship with other researchers. I explained my independent investigation, my informal support to Congressman Steve Schiff's inquiry into the case, and my continuing effort to work as closely and cooperatively as possible with other Roswell case researchers. He then said, "Do you believe in UFOs? Do you believe in aliens?" I told him I had no doubt about the existence of UFOs and was convinced that some of them were alien craft, extraterrestrial or otherwise. He followed up by asking if I believed alien bodies had been recovered, making no specific reference to Roswell. I said I was impressed by some of the testimony to that effect, but in my opinion, there was no proof of this yet in hand.

These preliminaries out of the way, Kaufmann said, "I was in [509th Bomb Group and Roswell AAF commander Col. William H.] Blanchard's office when the decisions were made and Walter Haut came in to get that press release he put out." Startled, I said, "Oh, really? You were in the office when Walter came in?" He responded, "Yes, Walter came in and got the press release. He was given the press release.

"See, there were about fifteen of us in this meeting where these decisions were made," Kaufmann continued, "including General Scanlon and General Ramey and me, and the provost marshal . . . I can't remember his name." I volunteered, "Easley? Maj. Edwin Easley?" He said, "Yeah. And others," this last delivered rather slyly and with a smirk.

(Later in the conversation I attempted to learn more about the "others." Because of the testimony of another witness at that time known only to me, I asked Kaufmann if he had ever heard anything about Charles Lindbergh being involved. After a long pause, he replied, "Yeah, yeah. He was one of the group. He was there.")

Also in the meeting was Robert Thomas, who, according to Kaufmann, was in charge. I asked if this was the same Thomas referred to and identified as an army warrant officer in *UFO Crash at Roswell*. He agreed, but implied Thomas's rank was considerably higher than warrant officer and hinted he had some very special status. When I asked if Thomas was a Counter Intelligence Corps agent, Kaufmann said, "I can't go into that."[16]

Kaufmann said the meeting had been going on since the night before, with no clear reference to dates despite my asking specifically, queries Kaufmann chose not to hear. They were trying to decide what to do, what to tell people. "See, we had all these reporters there." A press conference had been called and was about to begin in the conference room adjacent to Blanchard's office. They had to come up with something and finally decided, "Let's just tell the truth."

This "revelation" stunned me, as it was completely inconsistent with the established facts, but I tried not to show my surprise and pressed on. I asked if this was really a decision to come clean or, rather, with the Machiavellian thought that the truth was so bizarre it would not be believed. Kaufmann never explicitly addressed this, but implied the latter was the case.

It was decided that Thomas, known as "Mr. Glib Mouth," would be the press conference spokesman. Thomas went into the conference room, where about ten reporters —including two women—waited. He got right to the point: "Ladies and gentlemen, we wish to announce that we have recovered an alien spaceship and five bodies." This provoked laughter and competition for the nearest exit. Thomas tried to control things, saying, "No, no. This is what really happened."

Not one news story appeared concerning this incredible press event and Thomas's announcement, truly an all-time, world-class first in the history of journalism.

At this point in his account, Kaufmann headed off on another tangent. I had some success steering things back to the press issue by asking if the Haut press release was part of the cover story. He said, "Oh, yeah. This was the slickest cover operation you've ever seen. It was absolutely the slickest thing that's ever been done." After this comment, I was unable to get him to discuss press matters any further. Considering Kaufmann's new tangent, I am certain the reader will appreciate my lapse.

Kaufmann told me he was one of three surviving members of a nine-member "special team," the only ones allowed to "go out to the site" (note this assertion well). The other two are Thomas (whom, as we have seen, Kaufmann had implied to Randle and Schmitt was dead) and a man named Fletcher, whom Kaufmann repeatedly referred to as "Fletch" (identified in Randle and Schmitt's *Truth About the UFO Crash at Roswell* as Howard Fletcher). He implied but did not state explicitly that Scanlon, Ramey, and Lindbergh were members of what I have come to think of as "Team Nine," and what Kaufmann has taken to calling The Nine.[17]

Kaufmann's story that day implied this mysterious group existed before the Roswell affair, with its members available to be called in from their normal pursuits as needed. At the time he never clearly stated the exact mission of the team, but dealing with "extraordinary" anomalous events like Roswell seemed to be central. Recently, Robert Shirkey, the assistant operations officer who drew up the flight plan for the B-29 that took Major Marcel and the Foster Ranch debris to Fort Worth, self-published *Roswell 1947: "I Was There."* The book includes an amusingly melodramatic chapter devoted to Kaufmann and The Nine, based upon what Kaufmann "revealed" to Shirkey "as a peer." Among other things, we learn that Team Nine/The Nine, all members with the rank of major and under the command of Maj. Robert Thomas, was a spooky outfit among other things responsible for vetting everyone considered for selection to form the original 509th Provisional Bomb Group, organized to carry out atomic bomb missions during World War II.[18]

Returning to May 1993, Kaufmann told me Team Nine was alerted when "radars at White Sands" picked up "strange blips. See, it was the blips, see? The blips were really strange. There was a blip here, and then all of a sudden, there was a blip there. The blip even went from one screen to the other." They could not track it "like a normal aircraft." This went on for "three or four days," beginning about Monday, June 30, or perhaps Tuesday, July 1. Kaufmann was not precise about this, but at some point during the blips' performance, Team Nine was called in.

Radar at Roswell AAF also picked up the strange target or targets, but "they weren't getting it as good, so we went down to White Sands." (Except that, of course, Kaufmann was one of them, exactly who "we" were is uncertain.) At the army proving ground about 120 air miles west of Roswell, beyond an intervening mountain range, Kaufmann and his colleagues watched the erratically behaving blips, "jump[ing] from one screen to the other."

During a "violent thunderstorm [unrecorded by the U.S. Weather Bureau]," Kaufmann said, the "craft was hovering." All of a sudden, "the radar screen lit up with a tremendous flash," and they "knew" their target had been hit by lightning and crashed. It seems the lightning bolt struck the vehicle "in the belly" where "cells" of some sort were located. This had disabled the craft and brought it down.

(An aside: Kaufmann had at hand some blank sheets of paper on an aluminum clipboard. As he talked, he made a rough sketch of the craft being hit by lightning, as he would do of other things throughout our conversation. I copied these quite closely in my own notebook while at Kaufmann's, and they are reproduced herein as appendix D.)

I asked Kaufmann if Mack Brazel had found pieces of the shattered cells. He said, "No. The lightning just disabled them," and went on to add that the debris field "was just a diversion" (presumably like the Barnett story). There was only one real site, the impact site north of Roswell where the craft and bodies were recovered.

Surprised yet again, I asked him about the conventional wisdom scenario, in which the impact site was said to be only about two and a half miles from the debris field. Kaufmann was visibly disturbed by this question, clearly unsure about how to deal with it. He opted to change the subject.

Kaufmann made a fast cut in his account, moving the scene back to Roswell AAF, where Team Nine had determined from the radar plots where the craft probably crashed. Taking two army vehicles, at least one equipped with "powerful spotlights," the team drove north from the base, through town, and out into the country on U.S. Highway 285. At a point about thirty-five miles beyond Roswell's northern city limit, they turned west onto an "old ranch road." Kaufmann said they saw "a glow over the horizon," and that is how they were "sure" they were on the right track.[19]

After some time bouncing over rough country and cutting ranch fences(!), the little convoy drew up to an arroyo. Clambering out of their vehicles, the team gazed down into the shallow ravine at a "shocking" sight: the crashed craft, "split open," a "body" thrown up against the arroyo wall, another hanging from the craft, legs dangling from the rent in the hull. The stunned group approached to within "about twenty-five feet" and then, overwhelmed by the weird tableau, "backed off."

They then brought the spotlights to bear. With the better illumination, they discovered three other bodies inside the downed craft, a total of five. Kaufmann said all were clad in "very, very close fitting one-piece" uniforms, "like wet suits," which were "silvery" in color. Each wore a belt which had a "clear thing" where a belt buckle normally would be.

Without any prompting from me and with some indignation, Kaufmann announced that the standard alien–Gray description—big black eyes set in a disproportionately large head perched upon a short, spindly body—"is all wrong. See, these people were just like us. Well, just like us only better."

I asked him what he meant. "More perfectly formed," Kaufmann said, while sketching what he spoke of as he talked. They had proportionately smaller noses, eyes, and ears, no hair, but generally "normal" human form. They were very slender, trimly built, all on the order of "five-foot-three." Their hands were "normal," with four fingers and a thumb.

The principal difference from human appearance was the color of the skin, which was "paler, grayish." I asked him if he could think of a comparison, and wondered aloud if he watched the then-current television science-fiction series *Star Trek: The Next Generation*. After a bit of hemming and hawing, he replied, "Well, not very often." I then said, "There's a character on there, uh, what's his name? . . ." Pause. "Oh, Data?" Kaufmann offered. I agreed. He then said the skin of the beings bore a strong resemblance to television's favorite android.[20]

The team was "constantly monitored" on radio by Roswell AAF. Despite his earlier statement that Team Nine members were the only ones permitted on the site, he now told me they quickly called in "additional equipment and support." This included "four medical MPs [military policemen] in protective clothing and lead-lined body bags." I asked what the bags were for, had they detected radiation? Kaufmann replied, "No, no, no. We saw some deterioration. It was like the bodies had begun to deteriorate, so we wanted to prevent that." (With lead-lined body bags?)

The "medical MPs" recovered the three cadavers from the craft and sealed all five sets of remains in the body bags. The beings were then removed from the impact site—"the first things to go out"—and taken to Roswell AAF, where they were "laid out" in "Hangar 84" (P-3 in 1947) with a "bright spotlight" shining on them (and, presumably, continuing to deteriorate). Kaufmann noted the hangar had been "cleared out in thirty minutes" on orders from Team Nine.

The added support also included about one hundred "special-duty" MPs brought in from Kirtland AAF, near Albuquerque. These troops were used to provide security and help recover the craft and impact-site debris. They worked in twenty-man details, each detail rotating out after completing a particular job. This was to prevent any of them from seeing and learning too much (but added significantly to the number of persons in the know and, thus, to the security problem. Brilliant tactics).

According to Kaufmann, while this activity was underway, the bodies were being dealt with at the air base. He said a "Major Sanford, pathologist, was brought in from Beaumont General [Hospital at Fort Bliss, Texas]." Sanford worked with another doctor, "Major Sullivan, brought in from Chicago." Kaufmann told me both doctors were, of course, now dead.

"*One* body was taken to the base hospital" for examination, Kaufmann said (emphasis added).[21] I asked if Sanford and Sullivan were the examining physicians. Kaufmann replied, "Yes. I asked about that." I inquired about Glenn Dennis's friend, the army nurse, being involved. After taking pains to point out Dennis did not see any bodies, Kaufmann said, "That might have happened. I don't know."

At some point the bodies were flown out of Roswell. Kaufmann said two aircraft were used to guard against loss of all the bodies in an accident. The first such "body lift" was in a B-25 twin-engine bomber, flown by Captain Pappy Henderson and, yes, Frank Kaufmann. They went from Roswell Army Air Field to Fort Worth AAF, on to Andrews AAF, Maryland, just outside Washington, D.C., and, ultimately, to Wright Field, Ohio.

They remained at Andrews for an unspecified time so "some people there who wanted to see the bodies" could view them. I asked who these people were, was President Harry S Truman among them? Kaufmann replied, "Well, I don't know. I don't think so. Maybe." So I asked him where he was while the VIPs were filing past the bodies. "I was right there," he said.

I did not press the point that he probably would have recognized Truman. Instead, I asked if then Army Chief of Staff Dwight Eisenhower was there. Kaufmann smiled slyly, saying, "He might have taken a peek."

After the VIP viewing, Kaufmann said, he and Henderson flew to Wright Field, outside Dayton. On arrival, they pulled their aircraft into a hangar, where they were immediately ushered aboard another B-25. This ship was identical to their own right down to the tail number. They departed immediately on the return flight to Roswell. Kaufmann offered no explanation for the switch.

Kaufmann said the second body-lift flight was also a B-25 with Wright Field as its ultimate destination. Kaufmann did not detail the route this flight followed (although I got the impression it included a stop at Fort Worth), but he did say there were at least eight flights out of Roswell, most of which were "diversions." Such as the crate flight to Fort Worth? "Yeah, that one, too."

I asked why the bodies were taken to Wright Field, and he replied, "Well, that's where they do R&D [research and development] and things." I pointed out it was not a biomedical facility and asked if he ever had any indication Lovelace Medical Center in Albuquerque had been involved. Kaufmann seemed somewhat taken aback by this question, and after a bit of verbal fumbling, said, "Well, no, I suppose that makes sense. I just don't remember anything like that."

Meanwhile, back at the impact site, the rotating "nuts-and-bolts" details were finishing up their work and readying the main body of the craft to be taken from the site. The vehicle was hoisted onto a flatbed truck and driven to Roswell AAF, where it and the other debris were loaded on transports and flown out, presumably to Wright Field. I asked Kaufmann what type of airplane was used to transport the craft, which he said was twenty-two to twenty-five feet long, about fifteen feet across at its widest point, about five feet deep at its thickest, and seemed not to have a powerplant or any fuel aboard ("just the cells"). He did not answer this question, instead turning to other matters.

Kaufmann made a rough planform sketch of the craft on his clipboard, an elongated diamond with a thick black bar down the center and aligned with and on the craft's long axis ("kind of a dome"). As he finished his drawing, he said, "You look at that, that looks just like— You know the stealth bomber? Well, that's what came from this. See, the technology for the stealth bomber, the design of the stealth bomber came from this." Oh. "Also, it being light and thin and hard to detect by radar and all that?" Yes . . . ? "That's the same thing here, and if you touch it with the human hand, it loses its effectiveness, just like with the stealth aircraft." Okay.

Further, Kaufmann said, all our advances in night-vision technology derived from the "special prismatic glass" in the craft's viewport, a sort of panoramic window through which Team Nine discovered the three alien bodies inside. He said the "zigzag" arrangement of the "crystals" in the glass "extracted the energy frequencies" which were too faint to be seen and "concentrated" them, bringing forth daylight from darkness, making everything as bright as noonday, "just like here, now." Oh. And presumably on a two-way basis as well.

Kaufmann said these are just two examples of why "this thing" is being held so closely. It is being kept secret because what was learned has been so vital to development of our advanced defense technologies, and "the group" controlling matters does not want this known.

Kaufmann went on to say the mysterious control group—which is "totally independent" and "reports to no one, even the president"—manages things such that, as new applications of alien knowledge and technologies are learned, they are transferred into "less secret" projects, so-called Black programs like the B-2 stealth bomber. This is accomplished without revealing the source to anyone and without any of the usual budgetary and program review oversight. Okay.

Following a bathroom break, I returned to the patio to find Kaufmann gone. He soon emerged from his house carrying a large manila envelope, saying, "I'm going to show you something really strange." With that, he withdrew from the envelope a five-by-eight, black-and-white photograph with names written on the back—Team Nine at one of its periodic secret meetings, he said, this one in 1965, Houston. Kaufmann handed the photo to me for a quick look, then took it back.

With one exception, all were wearing dark blazers, light slacks, and striped ties. The exception was a naval officer in the U.S. Navy summer-white uniform. Most of the others were wearing light-colored baseball caps with a logo emblazoned on them, which resembled a Navy command or unit insignia. On the breast pockets of all the blazers was a different logo, shieldlike in shape with a scroll curled around the bottom, very much like the style favored by the U.S. Air Force. The men appeared to range in age from early twenties to midforties.

Kaufmann pointed out himself, Thomas, who was standing next to him, "Fletch," and "the admiral," the officer in whites. Earlier in our conversation, he told me one of the team was an admiral who had been assigned to White Sands. The naval officer in the photograph to whom Kaufmann pointed and referred to as the admiral looked to be about twenty-five, far too young to be an admiral. On his shoulder boards he was wearing the single gold stripe of an ensign, the U.S. Navy's lowest commissioned rank and consistent with his apparent age.

To the extent I have been able to make sense of what Kaufmann told me, it seems that, following the Roswell crash/retrieval, Team Nine managed the cover-up and technology exploitation efforts ("it wasn't MJ-12 or the Unholy Thirteen, it was us"). It appears that at some point these jobs were handed off to the control group now directing things, and Team Nine became a kind of advisory body and institutional memory. They—now reduced by the Grim Reaper to three—are still called together periodically, briefed on all the latest developments, and asked for their advice ("we know more than the members of the control group"). The 1965 meeting was one such gathering. Kaufmann said another was due "soon," for which "military planes [will] be sent to pick us up wherever we are." He said the first stop would be Dallas, and from there they would go to a "secret site" for the meeting.

Kaufmann returned the photo to the envelope and withdrew another item. This was a letter-size envelope with preprinted U.S. postage of three cents. The postmark was Roswell, with a smudged date—July something, 19-something-7. Secured to the envelope with yellowed cellophane tape was a photograph of a thirtyish Frank Kaufmann, which appeared to have been clipped from some publication. There was no mailing or return address on the envelope, even under the photograph. Inside this envelope was a sheet of heavy white but graying tissue paper folded origami fashion, then folded over to fit within the envelope.

Kaufmann removed the paper and unfurled it to reveal a folded-paper, wing-like craft, roughly diamond shaped in planform, with turned up wing tips and "tail," and a turned-down, "droop snoot" nose. On the top left side of the wing was written (in pencil?) what appeared to be a formula of some sort, the only elements of which I remember being "J 89." Next to this was drawn a stylized shooting star, similar to a NASA astronaut's rating pin. On the top right side of the wing was this cryptic three-line inscription: "$7 + 7 = 4$ / SAME TODAY / AS BEFORE."

I asked Kaufmann what the inscription meant. "I don't know." I asked where he got the envelope and its strange contents. "It came to me in the mail. The Post Office delivered it—without an address or anything, just as you see it here." I asked if he heard anything further or received anything else connected with the peculiar communication. "No, no, no."

Following up, I suggested that, being in a very sensitive security situation, he must have turned it over to his security people for them to study. He replied, "Oh, yes, of course." I asked what they came up with. Answering "Nothing," Kaufmann tucked the origami craft back into its envelope and returned them to the larger envelope containing the Team Nine photograph. I did not voice what I was thinking: "Security returned the stuff to you . . . ?"

We went on. I asked Kaufmann if he had returned to the impact site in the years since the event. He said, "Oh, yes. Once, about twenty-five years ago, I drove out there, and I had this terrible feeling, this funny feeling, this very odd feeling—and I had to leave. I just couldn't stay." After a long pause, he added, "See, I can't forget the expressions on the faces of the beings. They were so peaceful and so serene. It seemed as though they would never do harm to us. It was clear when you saw them they would never do anything to hurt us."

I asked if he had tried to return to the site after this first attempt. He replied, "I tried to find it again . . ." trailing off without completing his sentence. I tried again, asking if he had been out there more recently. "No, I have not." Of course, in recent years Kaufmann has had no apparent difficulty visiting the site numerous times with various television crews, although I have been told he managed to get one of these thoroughly lost.

As we approached the end of our conversation, Kaufmann mentioned having a copy of an issue of the *Congressional Record* in which his name appeared with reference to testimony he, Charles Lindbergh, and rocket scientist Wernher von Braun gave before a congressional committee. I asked him the subject of the hearings, which precipitated a series of long pauses, "ums," and "uhs," finally leading to: "It wasn't about flying saucers. It was about extraterrestrial . . ." trailing off again. Then, "It was because of this incident."

I wondered out loud which committee held the hearings. "It was a special committee." Oh, a select committee. "Yeah." Although I said I was very interested in seeing the *Record*, he never offered to show it to me.[22]

Kaufmann said that, as a result of this hearing, many people had come to him and tried to get him to "talk." People in Congress tried to "strong-arm" him. They "weren't very professional, didn't know how the game was played," threatening him with subpoenas and jail. People from Hollywood offered him as much as "fifty thousand dollars" for his "full story." He asked them if they believed in UFOs, and they said they "were going to do this investigation, then we'll see." So, "that was it," he refused to cooperate because they did not believe and "wouldn't handle it right." There were many others, too, but he has brushed them off.

As discussed above, Kaufmann told me he, (the late?) Robert Thomas, and Fletcher were the remaining survivors of the original Team Nine. They still serve as advisers to the Roswell control group. Kaufmann never mentioned what Fletcher does these days, but Thomas is "one of the top UFO investigators" for the group. As a matter of fact, currently he was deeply involved in an investigation of a major recent Australian sighting, with video tape, a "major scientist" witness, and so on. This was to be the subject of the upcoming Team Nine meeting. Moreover, according to Kaufmann, of the many thousands of UFO cases, only three—this one, another somewhere in Russia, and, of course, Roswell—are "real." I asked what he meant. He replied, "I mean solid, where we've got something on them."

I reminded Kaufmann of the congressional inquiry into Roswell being pursued by Congressman Schiff, intending to ask him if he would be willing to offer what he knows. Before I could ask, he said, "Oh, well, they'll never find anything, you know. They'll never learn anything. See, all the codes have been changed, and all this material [presumably the physical evidence] has been reclassified and coded in special ways—some of it's furniture, some of it's light bulbs, some of it's canned food." Further, he said, serial numbers of Team Niners were changed "numerous times," and their ranks and "other things" were changed as part of the cover-up (yet, a couple of hours before, Kaufmann had suggested I could "probably get" his military records to review).

I asked if he would be willing to talk with congressional investigators who were properly cleared and so on, and if so, under what circumstances. "Well, what would I tell them?" Why not what you just told me? "What's that going to prove? There's no way they're going to prove it. There's no way they're going to be able to get the information they need to back that up. So I'll just come across as some kind of a nut, and that will be the cover for this."

Okay, how about—"I won't talk to Congress or testify in any kind of a hearing unless I have a complete and total release." Presumably, he meant a release from his security oath. I asked him how we could secure this. "Well, I'd have to get it from my people." Would you be willing to approach them and ask if this would be possible? "Nah, there's not any point in that. I know that I can't be released from that. They won't release me from it." You asked them about this before? "They don't have to tell us that. We know that. They'll tell us if they want us to say anything. When the day comes, then we'll be free to do this. We have to maintain this oath of *total* silence until that time" (emphasis added). Okay.

I tried another tack. Suppose you were approached by properly authorized congressional staff and asked whom they should contact to get you the permission you need to tell them you story? "Well, I can't tell them that." Why not? "Because, see, that would be giving [them] the keys to the barn door." In other words, if Kaufmann gave congressional staff the names of the people who would have to approve his talking, that would unveil the whole Roswell scheme.

Catch-22.

Kaufmann cannot talk unless given a full and complete release to do so. For that release to be granted, someone has to approach "Control Central." Kaufmann cannot approach CC on his own initiative, and he is bound by oath not to reveal who or what CC is, because to do so would reveal the secrets the investigators need the release to learn.

Given this, Kaufmann reiterated, there would be no point in his talking to anyone, because there is no way he can prove his story. I pointed out he had told Randle, Schmitt, and me. "Yeah, right," he replied. "But who's going to believe it?"

GOOD QUESTION, FRANK

Good question, indeed. To which the answer seems to be, the many people who *want* to believe you, Frank. This seems particularly true of those who are the principal advocates of the revisionist Roswell, such as Kevin Randle, who have come to realize that, as the credibility of "witness" after "witness" falls by the wayside, without Kaufmann, they have no case.

This acceptance continues, even after it has been established by official records, some provided by Kaufmann himself, that in July 1947 Kaufmann had been out of uniform almost two years, since late 1945, and was employed as a civilian at the Roswell base in the singularly routine job of personnel clerk, the same work he did in uniform. It is sustained even with Kaufmann's elaborations on his tales and his dropping of discredited elements of them as necessary, not to mention his willingness to talk and be identified by name and face on one television "documentary" after another. His standing as a revisionist Roswell witness seems quite secure, with few seeming to notice that this required major changes from and contradictions of the yarn he spun that made him a witness essential to the conventional wisdom scenario.

Of course, Kaufmann has had more than a little help walking the credibility tightrope. Consider for example a move he made apparently to counter the vigorous challenges to his story by myself and others. Despite an obvious "candor gap," it seemingly has not caused Randle and others like him to have substantial doubts about their star witness.

Under the gun, Kaufmann came up with a copy of what he claims is his Top Secret official report on the Roswell incident, dated July 26, 1947, the first page of which appeared to be on 1947-vintage Roswell AAF letterhead. This document, which Kaufmann has "allowed" to be shown on television, included his sketches of the craft (which look nothing like the one he made during our May 1993 conversation) and the aliens (the faces of which bear a substantial resemblance to the face he sketched in 1993). Unfortunately, if unsurprisingly, Kaufmann has produced only a photocopy of this alleged report, so no forensic analysis can be performed to determine its authenticity. Moreover, as Philip Klass has pointed out, the fact that Kaufmann has a photocopy of the *original* document is telling, since the photocopier was not yet on the market in 1947.[23] But when you are out of carbon paper, I suppose you have to do what you have to do.

Recently, Kaufmann teamed up with Robert Shirkley. Kaufmann has contributed a foreword, his "Top Secret" sketches of the alien craft, and, as noted above, an interesting new twist on the Team Nine tale to Shirkey's book *Roswell 1947: "I Was There."* He and Shirkey also have made a video tape in which they star, telling their "I was there" stories.

And still the revisionists cleave to Kaufmann.

So what is going on here? Perhaps Kaufmann got clearance from his "people" to spill everything, since, after all, "Who's going to believe it?"

The tales of Kaufmann and their evolution speak eloquently for themselves. However, there are a number of points which deserve special mention.

First, what Kaufmann claims appeared on the radars when the craft was struck by lightning is strictly in the science-fiction special effects category. One expert with whom I spoke characterized it as "very creative." If a target being tracked by a radar of the types then in use by the army in New Mexico, members of the long-wave (ten centimeters plus) SCR-270 and -584 families, were hit by lightning, the result on the radarscope, if any at all, would be no more than a slight, momentary brightening of the target blip or a tiny segment of the cursor line that sweeps around the circular scope at the same rate the radar's antenna rotates. Which of these minimal and fleeting pulses might be seen would depend on the particular type and model radar set involved. Moreover, something would be seen *only* if the lightning struck precisely at the same instant the radar beam swept across the target. Otherwise, the scope would show *no* evidence of the strike. Of course, if the target were destroyed, it would disappear from the screen, but the radar would not reveal why it did so. It is also worth noting that, because of simple physics, lightning strikes on airborne objects are exceedingly rare.[24]

Second, mountains ranging in elevation from seven thousand to twelve thousand feet lie between White Sands and the debris field and the alleged impact site. The elevation of the White Sands area is between four thousand and forty-five hundred feet. A similar mountain barrier exists between the sites and Kirtland Air Force Base (nee Army Air Field), which lies at about fifty-three hundred feet. Anything flying at an altitude putting it behind the mountains as seen from these locations would be invisible to their radars. Anything flying only slightly higher than the mountains would be lost to the Lloyd's Mirror effect, in which the radar signal return from the aerial target and that from the ground (mountains) cancel each other out. This means only the Roswell radar would have been in a position to track the craft, and even it only on a limited basis, as Roswell's elevation is about thirty-six hundred feet, while the alleged impact site and the debris field lie at approximately forty-one hundred and fifty-eight hundred feet, respectively.[25]

As for Kaufmann's claim that triangulated radar plots were used to determine where the craft crashed, it merely exposes his woeful ignorance of radar. Data from more than one radar is not required to determine the direction and distance of a target that has gone down. The crash location can be calculated quickly from the last azimuth (directional) reading and slant range (straight-line distance from the radar antenna to the object in flight) from a single radar. The name radar, after all, is a contraction of the phrase "radio detection and ranging."[26]

Third, there is Kaufmann's claim the damaged but intact craft was transported out of Roswell by air without being dismantled. According to Kaufmann, the alien vehicle spanned fifteen feet and was twenty-two to twenty-five feet long and five feet thick. In July 1947 and for years after, there was no aircraft in the world, let alone the American military inventory, capable of accommodating a object of those dimensions.[27]

Fourth, with respect to the claims of a crashed flying saucer being found on the Plains of San Agustin, over 200 air miles from Roswell, the notion that Barney Barnett's story was a government-concocted diversion because of concerns inspired in 1950 by Frank Scully's book and articles in national news magazines is ludicrous. As Stan Friedman has pointed out, Scully's tale of a 1948 saucer crash near Aztec, New Mexico, almost 300 air miles from the alleged impact site, would itself have constituted a fine, if inadvertent, diversion from Roswell.[28] Further, there is no evidence whatsoever that Barnett ever told his story even semipublicly. To the contrary, it seems virtually certain that before his death in 1969 he related it to very few people, all but one close family members and friends. Finally, Barnett's alleged involvement with a crash on the Plains surfaced publicly for the first time in 1980, when second-hand reports of his account were related in *The Roswell Incident*.[29]

Fifth, there is *nothing* mysterious about the development of so-called stealth and night-vision technologies and applications. They are the products of straightforward— if often highly classified and very imaginative—scientific and technical research and engineering development in composite materials, airfoil and airframe design, electronics, optics, computerized control systems, and so on. Nothing about these capabilities or in the scientific and technical literature in the fields bearing on them even hints at anything more than steady progress from one concept and application to another, no quantum leap or mysterious introduction of something new.

Moreover, although this sort of "trust me" observation does not constitute proof, I know from firsthand experience in government and industry that, while these technologies are marvelous and truly amazing, they are quite clearly the fruit of *Homo sapiens sapiens* intelligence and "skull sweat."[30]

Finally, if the alien vehicle Kaufmann says was recovered at the impact site had "stealthy" properties, how would it have been possible for the radars at White Sands, Roswell, and Kirtland to detect it? In any case, it would not have needed such properties to snoop around undetected. In July 1947 Roswell and Kirtland had only very short-range air traffic approach-control radars utterly incapable of performing the search-and-tracking tasks described by Kaufmann. White Sands Proving Ground had no radars with such capabilities, either, only a trailer-housed antiaircraft SCR-584 being used for and turned on only during and oriented specifically for launches of captured German V-2 rockets and, on occasion, in support of the highly classified project that inadvertently spawned the whole Roswell saga. Moreover, this radar had a maximum search range of less than forty miles and a maximum tracking range of just over eighteen, so even if search-and-tracking radars had been located at Roswell and Kirtland AAFs, it would have been impossible for the White Sands radar to be used in conjunction with them at their respective distances of about 120 and 160 miles.[31]

FLAWED VISION

The evidence offered in support of the revisionist Roswell is fatally flawed. Most significant in this respect is the testimony and "documentation" provided by Frank J. Kaufmann, the person who contributes not only the cornerstone but the framing, bricks, and mortar of the scenario. Kaufmann is an energetic, hale-fellow-well-met sort of guy with a lot of chutzpah. The same was true of Silas Newton, the clever and charming confidence man behind the Aztec saucer noncrash made famous by Frank Scully.[32]

NOTES

1. Stanton T. Friedman and Don Berliner, "Yes, There Was a Saucer Crash in the Plains in 1947," in *The Plains of San Agustin Controversy, July 1947: Gerald Anderson, Barney Barnett, and the Archaeologists*, ed. George M. Eberhart (Chicago and Washington, D.C.: Center for UFO Studies and Fund for UFO Research, 1992), pp. 6–12; Donald R. Schmitt and Kevin D. Randle, "Second Thoughts on the Barney Barnett Story," *International UFO Reporter* (May–June 1992): 4.

2. Kevin D. Randle and Donald R. Schmitt, *UFO Crash at Roswell* (New York: Avon, 1991), p. 161.

3. Randle and Schmitt, *UFO Crash*, p. 224.

4. Ibid., pp. 95, 167.

5. Ibid., pp. 166, 215.

6. Ibid., p. 181.

7. Ibid.

8. Ibid. Mark Rodeghier, scientific director of the Center for UFO Studies, identified the source of the crashed-saucer sketch to me in a conversation at the Center on May 9, 1993. This was subsequently confirmed to me by both Randle and Schmitt.

9. Ibid., illustration section between pp. 144 and 145.

10. Ibid., p. 181.

11. Schmitt and Randle, "Second Thoughts." Re the Barnett claims, see for example Stanton T. Friedman and Don Berliner, *Crash at Corona* (New York: Paragon House, 1992).

12. Friedman and Berliner, "Yes, There Was," in *The Plains of San Agustin Controversy*.

13. Except as otherwise noted, everything in this section, "Frank 3," is derived from my written notes taken at this meeting and my audiotaped notes dictated immediately after the meeting. Although I had my tape recorder on the table during the interview, I did not ask to record our discussion because I sensed it would inhibit Kaufmann. The material attributed to him inside quotation marks is exactly as I noted it and as I remembered and dictated it into my recorder the day of our conversation, immediately afterward. Kaufmann is a rather colorful speaker, so his particular turns of phrase, inflection, etc., are not difficult to recall. Where there was any doubt about the accuracy of my recollections of Kaufmann's exact words, I have paraphrased and not used quotation marks.

14. Famed aviator and World War II hero James H. Doolittle made reference to Scanlon in his autobiography, citing an incident which makes one wonder if Scanlon would have been much concerned about flying saucers zipping around near an atomic-bomber base. In 1937, Doolittle had visited Nazi Germany, where he had seen how the German air force was developing and had a close look at many of its new combat aircraft. On his way back to the United

States, Doolittle stopped in at the American embassy in London, where he reported what he had seen to the American air attaché, Maj. Martin Scanlon. "To my surprise," Doolittle wrote, "Scanlon seemed completely uninterested. He said, disdainfully, 'You know "Hap" Arnold [the U.S. Army Air Corps commanding general]. Go back and tell him what you saw. There's nothing I can do about it.' " James H. Doolittle with Carroll V. Glines, *I Could Never Be So Lucky Again* (New York: Bantam, 1991), p. 211.

15. Kaufmann, telephone conversation, September 28, 1993, and other sources.

16. See n. 3 above.

17. Ibid.

18. Robert J. Shirkey, *Roswell 1947: I Was There* (Roswell, N.M.: Movin' On Press, 1999), pp. 121–25.

19. It is interesting to note a United Press broadcast wire story filed on July 8, 1947, said "residents near the ranch [the Foster Ranch in Lincoln County] reported seeing a strange blue light" (see app. E). I do not know if Kaufmann was aware of this report before I spoke with him, but Randle and Schmitt had a copy of the UP wire report.

20. I asked this question because Kevin Randle, speaking in Portland, Oregon, on March 28, 1993, said the first impact-site witness he and Don Schmitt had located said the beings resembled Data. Audiotape, Kevin D. Randle and Donald R. Schmitt, lecture, Portland, Oregon, March 28, 1993.

21. The nurse whom Glenn Dennis claimed told him she had participated in an examination of strange bodies at the Roswell AAF hospital allegedly saw three bodies. Dennis affidavit, app. H.

22. Proceedings of congressional hearings do not appear in the *Congressional Record.* They are published as separate documents by the committees conducting the hearings.

23. Philip J. Klass, *The Real Roswell Crashed-Saucer Coverup* (Amherst, N.Y.: Prometheus Books, 1997), pp. 200–201.

24. C. B. Moore, "An Assessment of Steve MacKenzie's [Frank Kaufmann's] Account of the Radar Tracking of an Unidentified Object over Southern New Mexico During Early July 1947" [online], www.project1947.com/roswell/cbm.htm [September 1995]; Daniel N. Lapedes, ed., *McGraw-Hill Dictionary of Scientific and Technical Terms,* 2d ed. (New York: McGraw-Hill, 1978); Tom Compere, *The Army Blue Book, 1961* (New York: Military Publishing Institute, 1960); Robert W. Marks, *The New Physics and Chemistry Dictionary and Handbook* (New York: Bantam, 1967); David Halliday and Robert Resnick, *Fundamentals of Physics* (New York: Wiley, 1970); telephone interview with C. B. Moore, New Mexico Institute of Mining and Technology (emeritus), October 18, 1993; audiotaped telephone interview with Albert C. Trakowski, March 21, 1994.

25. Various topographical, road, and other maps of New Mexico; Moore, October 18, 1993.

26. Moore, "An Assessment of Steve MacKenzie's. . . ."

27. Leonard Bridgman, *Jane's All the World's Aircraft, 1949–1950* (New York: McGraw-Hill, 1949); James C. Fahey, ed., *U.S. Army Aircraft, 1908–1946* (New York: Ships and Aircraft, 1946) and *United States Air Force and United States Army Aircraft, 1947–1956* (Falls Church, Va.: Ships and Aircraft, 1956); William Green and Gerald Pollinger, *The Aircraft of the World* (New York: Hanover, 1956); Joseph P. Juptner, *U.S. Civil Aircraft Series,* vols. 1–9 (Blue Ridge Summit, Penn.: TAB Books, 1993, 1994).

28. Friedman and Berliner, "Yes, There Was," in *The Plains of San Agustin Controversy,* p. 8.

29. Ibid.; William D. Leed, III affidavit on file with the Fund for UFO Research; see also Stanton T. Friedman and Don Berliner, *Crash at Corona* (New York: Paragon, 1992), p. 88. Leed interviewed Barnett very briefly in the early 1960s.

30. Phil Klass has some interesting observations on this point based upon long experience as a reporter for *Aviation Week and Space Technology* and, before that, working on defense programs. See Klass, *Real Roswell Crash*, pp. 226–31.

31. United States Air Force, *Aerospace Defense Command Statistical Data Book, Radar*, vol. 3 (ADCHO 73-8-12), originally classified Secret, declassified September 6, 1985; Kenneth Schaffel, *The Emerging Shield: The Air Force and the Evolution of Continental Air Defense 1945–1960* (Washington, D.C.: Office of Air Force History, 1991); Joseph T. Jockel, *No Boundaries Upstairs—Canada, the U.S., and the Origins of North American Air Defense* (Vancouver: University of British Columbia Press, 1987); personal files and recollections of C. B. Moore and Albert C. Trakowski; Moore, "An Assessment of Steve MacKenzie's Account...."

32. Frank Scully, *Behind the Flying Saucers* (New York: Holt, 1950); Karl T. Pflock, "What's Really Behind the Flying Saucers?: A New Twist on Aztec," *The Anomalist* (spring 2000): 137–61.

SIX

WHAT WE <u>REALLY</u> KNOW
AND WHAT IT TELLS US

As we have seen, the revisionist Roswell is for the most part a mirage, Roswell as we had come to know it viewed through the distorting lens of creative storytelling abetted by wishful thinking and credulity. What, then, of the conventional wisdom version of the case?

On finishing my deconstruction in this and the six chapters that follow, the reader may think "What We *Don't* Know" might have been a more appropriate lead-off chapter title, since my principal focus is on important elements of the Roswell story that have seemed so certain but which careful examination reveals to be otherwise. However, "What We *Really* Know" captures my intent, which is to address selected key issues in light of my research, show that the received wisdom is neither necessarily correct nor as sensational as we had thought, and demonstrate that, even shorn of its crashed-saucer trappings, Roswell remains an important and interesting case, both ufologically and in a more conventional historical sense.

THE WILMOTS' FLYING SAUCER AND OTHER AERIAL SIGHTINGS

To begin at the beginning, let us consider the Wilmot sighting on the night of July 2. The Wilmots reported seeing a classic flying saucer, "like two inverted saucers faced mouth-to-mouth." Dan Wilmot told the *Roswell Daily Record* he and his wife last saw the UFO heading northwest in the general direction of Corona, and that it appeared to be flying low, at an estimated 1,500 feet. Of all the apparently credible aerial object sightings reported in the region during the days before Mack Brazel turned up at Sheriff Wilcox's office and connected by various investigators with Brazel's find and other alleged discoveries, this is the only one that entails an object described as a vehicle, a structured mechanical contrivance. All of these points seemed to suggest the Wilmots' saucer as a good candidate for the role of Roswell's doomed craft.

However, there is virtually nothing on record to lend substantive support to this, and there are important elements of testimony that militate against it. Not the least important in this regard is William Woody's account, which I address below.

Seemingly supporting if indirect testimony was provided by Lydia Sleppy, who claimed Radio KSWS co-owner and general manager John McBoyle telephoned a report to her in Albuquerque in which he described a crashed vehicle like "a big crumpled dishpan."[1] Other reports have suggested Brazel used his pickup truck to tow a large circular piece of debris under a stock and fodder shelter.[2] Frank Kaufmann's descriptions of the craft alleged to have been found on a crash site removed some two and a half air miles—in his revisionist version, approximately thirty-five air miles—from the debris field are at significant variance with each other, in the first instance a classic saucer, in the second a fat bat. All of these reports are highly questionable.

Finally, although descriptions of the alignment of the debris field discovered on the Foster Ranch by Mack Brazel are contradictory, it has been generally accepted—but as we shall see *not* in agreement with objective fact—that the debris lay along a northwest-southeast line in an elongated, roughly fan-shaped pattern, with the broad end to the southeast and the debris progressively thinning out in that direction. This has been interpreted to mean the stricken object was flying on a southeasterly course, although it is equally reasonable to assume the reverse. Clearly, if the vehicle that littered Brazel's pasture was flying southeast at the time, it is unlikely to have been the Wilmots' saucer. If the reverse, it *could* have been, although it is now certain it was not.

The Woodys' object, glowing bright white and streaking rapidly northward over and beyond Roswell could well have been the same phenomenon seen by the Wilmots. The ufological literature includes numerous instances in which spectacular meteors were interpreted by startled witnesses as structured, low-flying oval or disk-shaped craft.[3] The date of the Woodys' sighting is uncertain, although their subsequent trip "two or three days later (definitely not the next day)" in search of what they hoped would be a large meteorite suggests it was before Brazel's discovery and, thus, that it could well have been July 2.[4]

The other reports of aerial object sightings so hopefully linked with the debris and crashed spaceship accounts suffer essentially the same difficulties discussed above. As I have already discussed, the credible witnesses have but vague recollections or, reportedly, contemporaneously set down only a sketchy outline of what they saw, with no certainty of important factors such as direction of flight, date, time, and so on. In addition, their descriptions are not only consistent with meteor sightings, but include specific interpretation of the observed phenomena as meteors. It is only certain Roswell sleuths who have attempted to make more of them.

So, in reality, the alleged link between anything reportedly seen in the sky and what was found by Mack Brazel and, supposedly, elsewhere by the military is at best highly tenuous and more a product of speculation than factual evidence. Only the Wilmot and Woody sightings offered any reasonable, credible basis for considering such a connection, but on examination these both appear likely to have been independent sightings of the same very large, very bright meteor. Until the evidence establishing the source of the odd collection of debris recovered from the Foster Ranch became known, the responsible if far less exciting choice would have been to suspend judgment about any connection between things flashing through the sky and junk found on the ground.

MACK BRAZEL'S DISCOVERY

When Brazel actually made his discovery has been a matter of considerable debate, fueling speculations of cover-up and intimidation.

Contemporaneous written accounts that refer to a date for the find, specific or approximate, are contradictory. An article in the July 9, 1947, *Roswell Daily Record* and an Associated Press story by Jason Kellahin datelined "Roswell, July 9" in the July 9 *Albuquerque Tribune* both report Brazel told the authors of the stories that he discovered the debris on June 14, ten days before Kenneth Arnold's sighting launched the first UFO flap. A United Press wire story filed by the UP Santa Fe bureau on the afternoon of July 8 tends to support this date, reporting that Sheriff Wilcox "[s]ays that the disc was found about three weeks ago." Similarly, an Associated Press wire story run in many papers on July 9 and datelined the day before, July 8, stated the debris "had been found three weeks previously." On the other hand, another AP story date-lined the following day, July 9, and run in several papers of the same date said it had been "found several days ago."[5]

For a long while, I thought there was at least some reason to doubt the mid-June date. Both Brazel and Sheriff Wilcox had been questioned by the army before talking with wire service and *Daily Record* reporters. The late Jason Kellahin, the former Associated Press reporter who interviewed Brazel, a prominent Santa Fe attorney, and a native of Roswell who knew Wilcox well, told me the sheriff claimed "the military indicated to him it would be best if he did not say anything." Brazel made his statement in an interview during which military personnel either were present or, more likely, waiting outside. Moreover, his description of the amount, extent of the distribution, and, to some degree, nature of the debris varied from that of other firsthand witnesses, such as his daughter Bessie Brazel Schreiber and Maj. Jesse Marcel.[6] When I still thought it possible flying saucer wreckage may have been discovered, it seemed reasonable Brazel could have been directed to use a cover story that included June 14 rather than the correct date, and that Sheriff Wilcox had been given similar "guidance."

Other testimony, including that of Brazel's daughter Bessie—who, contrary to the conventional wisdom, was at the ranch at the time of the incident and helped her father collect some of the material—his neighbors Loretta and Floyd Proctor and J. O. "Bud" Payne, and AP reporter Kellahin, suggested the discovery was made during the first week of July.[7] In addition, the army press announcement of July 8 as reported by the AP states "the disc landed on a ranch near Roswell sometime last week," that is, during the period June 30 through July 5.[8]

In retrospect, with the benefit of knowing beyond a reasonable doubt what actually was involved and what Brazel really stumbled upon, June 14, give or take a day or two, seems most likely to be correct. A rule of thumb in historical ufological research is—or should be—unless there is strong reason not to, give the most weight to the facts reported and set down at the time of the event under investigation. June 14 is the date personally given to journalists by Brazel during a face-to-face interview on July 8, 1947, not thirty, forty, fifty, or more years later.[9]

Moreover, until he was told about flying saucer reports by a relative and another man on or about July 5, Brazel seems not to have considered what he found to be much more than a nuisance.[10] This is an attitude consistent with a discovery made well before flying saucer reports hit the newspapers, exciting public interest and giving reason to consider anything strange that seemed likely to have fallen from the sky as having something to do with the mysterious disks.

Most probably, Brazel essentially ignored the debris until learning of the flying saucer reports and the rewards being offered for proof of saucer reality. According to statements made by Maj. Jesse Marcel while he was at Fort Worth Army Air Field and attributed to him in a July 9, 1947, article in the *Fort Worth Star-Telegram*, this indeed is what happened. The article notes that the debris had "been found three weeks previously [i.e., on or about June 14]." It goes on to say Brazel

> bundled the tinfoil and broken wooden beams of the kite [radar target] and the torn synthetic rubber remains of the balloon together and rolled it [*sic*] under some brush.
> . . . On a trip to town at Corona, N.M., Saturday night [July 5], Brazel [*sic*] heard the first references to the "silver flying disks," Major Marcel related.
>   Brazell hurried home, dug up the remnants of the kites and balloon on Sunday and Monday [July 7] headed for Roswell to report his find to the sheriff's office.

When first approached by ufologists in 1979, Loretta Proctor and her late husband Floyd had no certain recollection of when their friend Mack dropped by with a piece of the debris. Ten years later, Mrs. Proctor told Kevin Randle she could not remember the chronology of events, saying, "I don't, really. I'm getting old myself, and forgetful."[11] According to the Proctors, Brazel was excited and talkative, not at all his usual easygoing, taciturn self. This suggests he probably visited them after having been to Corona, rather than before, as previously thought.

But what about Brazel and the sheriff being asked by the military to say nothing or play things down? It was not until the evening of July 8 that Brazel was interviewed at the office of the *Roswell Daily Record* and Jason Kellahin spoke with Sheriff Wilcox. By that time, senior army air forces authorities all but certainly had a good idea what they had on their hands. It is highly likely their subordinates in Roswell had been told to do some damage control. Under the circumstances, telling the sheriff "it would be best if he did not say anything" and asking Brazel to avoid any sensational speculation would have been quite appropriate.

The conventional wisdom has it that Brazel's family was not with him on the ranch when he supposedly heard a strange explosion and the next day, when he made his surprising find. It has been reported he may have been accompanied on his morning ride of discovery by a seven-year-old neighbor, William D. "Dee" Proctor.

According to Dee's mother, Loretta Proctor, Dee often spent time with Brazel, staying over for a day or two, riding and helping with chores. She told me that the day Mack showed some of the debris to her and her husband Floyd, she thinks he was also bringing Dee home from one of these visits, although she is not certain of this. She added that Dee, now sixty, does not remember anything about the debris or related events.[12]

Dee Proctor has assiduously avoided being interviewed about the incident. However, I have interviewed Mack Brazel's daughter, Bessie Brazel Schreiber (misidentified as "Betty" in the July 9 *Roswell Daily Record* story). Schreiber, who was fourteen in July 1947, told me her mother, her brother Vernon, and she were on the Foster Ranch when her father found the debris field. "Our family had a home in Tularosa," she said, "where my mother, my younger brother Vernon, and I lived during the school year. The three of us spent summers on the Foster place with dad." She does not recall Dee Proctor being with them or with their father on his fateful ride. She told me it was possible, but "it was a long time ago" and she simply did not remember.[13]

The story in the July 9 *Roswell Daily Record* reporting the interview given by Mack Brazel the night before states that "on June 14 he [Brazel] and an 8-year-old son, Vernon, were about 7 or 8 miles from the ranch house . . . when they came upon a large area of bright wreckage." There is no mention of Dee Proctor. Unfortunately, Vernon Brazel went missing as a young man and has long been presumed dead.[14]

In a 1979 interview, Bessie Schreiber's older brother Bill recalled other members of his family being on the ranch with his father at the time the debris fell there. "Dad," he said, "was in the ranch house with two of the younger kids [presumably Bessie and Vernon] late one evening when a terrible lightning storm came up. . . . [T]he next morning while riding out over the pasture to check on some sheep, he came across this collection of wreckage." Bill also mentioned specifically that, on the way to Roswell with some of the debris, his father dropped off the children with their mother in Tularosa.[15]

Jason Kellahin provided testimony which lends support to these recollections of Bill Brazel and his sister. Kellahin told me that, while on assignment to cover the crashed disk story, he visited the Foster Ranch on July 8, *before* going on to Roswell. There he found "Brazel, his wife, and his small son," as well as several military men.[16]

So it would seem the conventional wisdom about the "who" of Mack Brazel's discovery is not correct. At least two of Brazel's children were with him on the ranch at the time, and it is likely his wife was there soon after. This is not merely a bit of trivia, as will be demonstrated in my consideration of the "what" of Brazel's find.

Like so much about the Roswell affair, the timing and sequence of events surrounding Brazel's report of his discovery are uncertain to some degree. The conventional wisdom has it that Brazel drove to Roswell on Sunday, July 6, taking some of the debris with him and going directly to the Chaves County sheriff's office. While he was there, Brazel had a telephone conversation with KGFL announcer Frank Joyce, and Sheriff George Wilcox contacted 509th Bomb Group intelligence officer Maj. Jesse Marcel at Roswell AAF, beginning the chain of events which came to be known as the Roswell incident. How certain can we be that this took place that sleepy Sunday afternoon?

Contemporary press accounts say Brazel made his report while in Roswell to arrange for the sale of wool. His daughter Bessie recalls he did so while in town to order winter feed.[17] In either case, it is highly unlikely Brazel would have made the long trek to Roswell on a Sunday—a Sunday of a rare three-day weekend at that—when such businesses were closed. Moreover, Brazel's son Bill emphatically dismisses the wool-selling claim, pointing out wool buyers went to the ranchers, not the other way around—a practice that continues today. Bill's recollection was that his father's real primary purpose for the trip was "about trading his pickup," but this, too, would make a Sunday trip unlikely, as would Bill's recollection that his father contacted the Roswell office of the U.S. Weather Bureau before visiting the sheriff. In addition, in a 1979 interview, Jesse Marcel recalled that when he met with Brazel at the sheriff's office, "I wanted Brazel to accompany me back to the base with his truck, but he said he had some things to do first and could he meet me somewhere in an hour or so."[18] This, too, points to Monday rather than Sunday.

A United Press wire story filed the afternoon of Tuesday, July 8, seems to confirm Brazel visited the sheriff two days before. According to this account, Sheriff Wilcox said Brazel reported his find "day before yesterday [Sunday, July 6]."[19]

Talking with reporter Bob Pratt in 1979, Jesse Marcel said, "I don't remember the exact date. It was in July 1947." He continued, "I was in my office. I went to the officers' club for lunch and was sitting having lunch when I got a call from the sheriff from Roswell."[20] In *The Roswell Incident*, Charles Berlitz and William L. Moore attribute possibly contradictory statements to Marcel, quoting from 1979 interviews conducted by Moore and Stanton Friedman: "We heard about it on July 7 [Monday] when we got a call from the county sheriff's office at Roswell. I was eating lunch at the officers' club when the call came through. . . ." And, "On Sunday, July 6, Brazel decided he had better go into town and report this to someone. When he got there, . . . he told the story to the sheriff. It was the sheriff, George Wilcox, who called me at the base. I was eating lunch at the time. . . ."[21]

The Roswell AAF announcement released to the press by Walter Haut on Tuesday, July 8, said "the many rumors regarding the flying disc became a reality yesterday [Monday, July 7] when the intelligence office of the 509th Bomb Group . . . [gained] possession of a disc. . . ." The announcement goes on to state that when the army learned of Brazel's discovery from the sheriff, "action was *immediately* taken" to recover the "disc" (emphasis added).[22]

The late Walter E. Whitmore Jr., whose father founded and was majority partner in radio station KGFL, told me he came home from college in Denver for the Fourth of July holiday break, only to find Mack Brazel sleeping in his room. His father was "hiding" Brazel in an attempt to score a scoop on his story. Whitmore did not remember the day or date of his arrival at home, but he thought "it was probably a day or two before the Fourth," and he recalled Brazel staying "at our house three or four days; I remember having breakfast with him at least twice."[23] Whitmore's memory of finding Brazel at his father's home before the Fourth clearly was faulty, but there appears to be little reason to doubt his recollection of Brazel's presence.

It seems most unlikely Major Marcel, a family man who lived off base, would have been on duty on a Sunday, especially on a long holiday weekend, unless something extraordinary were taking place. In the numerous interviews he granted to researchers, newsmen, and others over the years between the day Friedman found him in February 1978 and his death in 1986, Marcel said not a word about anything out of the ordinary happening *before* Sheriff Wilcox contacted him. His son, Dr. Jesse Marcel, has told me he recalls nothing about his father being required to report to the base or being called out for anything special that weekend. Similarly, others with whom I have spoken who were stationed at Roswell AAF at the time have no memory of any alert or unusual activity disrupting the slow holiday routine. In addition, we now know that most of the aircraft based at the Roswell field and their crews and support personnel were out of the area that weekend, participating in Fourth of July events all over the country.[24] Things were even quieter than usual on the base that weekend.

Adding further to the confusion, the late Brig. Gen. Thomas J. DuBose, a colonel and chief of staff of the Eighth Air Force at the time of the incident, testified a small amount of debris in a sealed bag was flown at his direction from Roswell to Eighth Air Force headquarters in Fort Worth and then immediately on to Strategic Air Command headquarters near Washington, D.C. DuBose said he thought this took place "two or three days" before the Roswell AAF press announcement was made on Tuesday, July 8.[25] If DuBose's remembrance of the approximate timing of the delivery flight was correct and the debris it bore was that brought to the sheriff's office by Brazel, it is *possible* Brazel arrived in Roswell on Sunday, July 6.

Once again, something that seemed certain is not so certain after all. However, the weight of the evidence is very much against the conventional wisdom. It is quite strongly suggestive of Monday, July 7, being the day on which Brazel innocently arrived in town, perhaps hoping for a reward. Significantly, we have the contemporaneous account of Major Marcel himself, speaking to a reporter at Fort Worth Army Air Field on July 8, 1947, and published on July 9 in the *Fort Worth Star-Telegram:* "Brazell [*sic*] hurried home, dug up the remnants of the kites and balloon on Sunday *and Monday [July 7] headed for Roswell* to report his find to the sheriff's office" (emphasis added). This would appear to resolve both the date of Brazel's appearance in Roswell and the seeming contradiction in what Marcel told Moore and Friedman in 1979.

MARCEL AND CAVITT ON THE DEBRIS FIELD

Not long after Mack Brazel moseyed into Sheriff Wilcox's office, he was leading Maj. Jesse Marcel and another army officer, the late Counter Intelligence Corps Capt. Sheridan Cavitt, out to the ranch he managed. According to Marcel, they arrived too late in the day to go directly to the debris field, so they stayed overnight in the small ranch house nearby. Soon after sunup the next morning, they covered the remaining few miles to the discovery site, Brazel and Cavitt on horseback and Marcel at the wheel of the jeep carryall Cavitt had driven from the base.[26] Certain significant elements of this part of the Roswell incident story as incorporated into the conventional wisdom are questionable or in direct conflict with Marcel's firsthand account.

According to Randle and Schmitt in their *UFO Crash at Roswell*, Brazel had stored some of the debris in a stock shelter or hay shed adjacent to the ranch house. During their night's sojourn, Marcel and Cavitt examined this material, which allegedly included the "largest chunk . . . [Brazel had] found, a piece about ten feet in diameter," checking it for radiation.[27]

The source cited for the "largest chunk" and radiation-check claims is Steve Tom and Leonard Stringfield's April 7, 1978, telephone interview with Marcel as reported in Stringfield's *UFO Crash/Retrieval Syndrome*. While Stringfield's report does state Marcel checked the *debris field* for radiation, it makes no mention of an overnight stay, no mention of *any* material being hauled off the site by Brazel, and no mention of any off-site check of debris for radioactivity. Moreover, with one exception, in none of many interviews did Marcel himself mention anything about checking for radiation *anywhere*. The exception was the interview conducted by Stringfield and Tom.[28]

With respect to Marcel's claim that he, Cavitt, and Brazel stayed on the ranch overnight, in a 1995 interview, Cavitt told me this was not true. The year before, in a sworn statement made before a U.S. Air Force investigator and relieved by a letter from the secretary of the air force of any relevant secrecy obligation, he had said the same thing.[29] It is important to note that the only way an overnight sojourn can be accommodated by the timing of known events (e.g., the date and time of the Roswell AAF press announcement, released by Walter Haut about noon on Tuesday, July 8) is if Brazel had arrived in town on Sunday, July 6. However, as we have seen, this is unlikely—and we have Marcel's own contemporaneous account setting the day and date he met Brazel at the sheriff's office and later trekked with him and Cavitt out to the ranch as Monday, July 7.

In addition, we have the recollections of the entire Marcel family that the intelligence officer arrived at his home "in the middle of the night," awakening his wife and son for show-and-tell. Moreover, the younger Jesse told me he has no certain memory of his father being away overnight, this despite the fact he does have clear memories of both the dramatic night in the family kitchen and his father's quick trip to Fort Worth—although significantly, when he spoke with me, he candidly admitted having no definite recollection of which came first. These memories are more consistent with a round-trip to the ranch on a single day than one involving an overnight stay.[30]

Randle and Schmitt report that, when Marcel and Cavitt got to the site, they found the "debris field was oriented *northwest to southeast*," and that "*Marcel said* it . . . [had] a gouge at the top end of it that was about five hundred feet long and ten feet wide" (emphasis added).[31] However, in December 1979, Marcel told Bob Pratt, "One thing I was impressed with was that it was obvious you could just about determine which direction it [the source of the debris] came from and which direction it was heading. It was traveling from *northeast to southwest*. . . . I could tell that it [the debris] was thicker where we first started looking and it was thinning out as we went *southwest*" (emphasis added). He also told Pratt "nothing actually hit the ground, bounced on the ground. It was something that must have exploded above ground and fell. . . ." Further, Stringfield reported Marcel told him in April 1978 "the area was thoroughly checked, . . . but *no fresh impact depressions were found in the sand*" (emphasis added). It is worth noting that before World War II Marcel was a cartographic draftsman with Shell Oil Company.[32]

Again, things are not quite what they were thought to have been. The dramatic touch of an overnight stay at the ranch all but certainly never happened. The alleged orientation of the debris field seems to be off more than a few crucial degrees, and the great scar on the land has faded like the Cheshire Cat. These are important matters. If, as Marcel reported it to Pratt and now seems highly likely, the field of scattered debris ran northeast to southwest, it is unlikely for a related site to have been located southeast of the Foster Ranch location. Similarly, the lack of any signs of heavy impact raises materially important questions about the nature of the debris source, the answers to which I will discuss in due course. All of this also calls into question the credibility and thoroughness of certain witnesses and investigators.

NOTES

1. Lydia A. Sleppy affidavit, app. H.
2. Kevin D. Randle and Donald R. Schmitt, *UFO Crash at Roswell* (New York: Avon, 1991), p. 49.
3. See, for example, Allan Hendry, *The UFO Handbook* (New York: Doubleday/Dolphin, 1979); Philip J. Klass, *UFOs: The Public Deceived* (Amherst, N.Y.: Prometheus Books, 1983).
4. William M. Woody, affidavit, app. H.
5. See app. E. An example of the AP story is "Mystery of Discs Deepens As Texas Find Proves Dud," *Boston American*, July 9, 1947.
6. Jason Kellahin affidavit, app. H; Bessie Brazel Schreiber affidavit, app. H; app. A, Bob Pratt interview with Jesse A. Marcel Sr., December 8, 1979.
7. Kellahin, Schreiber, Proctor, and Payne, affidavits, app. H.
8. "Disc Solution Collapses," *San Francisco Chronicle*, July 9, 1947.
9. "Harassed Rancher Who Located 'Saucer' Sorry He Told About It," *Roswell Daily Record*, July 9, 1947.
10. Bessie Brazel Schreiber and Sallye Strickland Tadolini affidavits, app. H.
11. Transcript of April 20, 1989, interview with Kevin Randle in Kevin D. Randle, *Roswell UFO Crash Update: Exposing the Military Cover-Up of the Century* (New Brunswick, N.J.: Global Communications, 1995), p. 163.
12. See for example, Randle and Schmitt, *UFO Crash*, pp. 37–38. Audiotaped personal interview with Loretta Proctor, October 31, 1992.
13. Audiotaped telephone interviews with Schreiber, August 26 and 27, 1993; Schreiber affidavit, app. H.
14. Schreiber interview, August 27, 1993.
15. Bill Brazel as attributed in Charles Berlitz and William L. Moore, *The Roswell Incident* (New York: Berkley, 1988), pp. 85–86.
16. Kellahin affidavit, app. H.
17. "Harassed Rancher," *Roswell Daily Record*, July 9, 1947; Schreiber affidavit, app. H.
18. Berlitz and Moore, *Roswell Incident*, pp. 69–70, 86–87, 91.
19. See app. E.
20. App. A.
21. Berlitz and Moore, *Roswell Incident*, pp. 69, 71–72.
22. "Disc Solution," *San Francisco Chronicle*, July 9, 1947.
23. Audiotaped personal interview with Walter E. Whitmore Jr., October 31, 1992.

24. Audiotaped telephone interview with Dr. Jesse A. Marcel Jr., September 23, 1993. Audiotaped telephone interviews with David N. Wagnon, September 17, 1993, and E. L. Pyles, January 24, 1994; telephone conversations with Walter G. Haut and Robert J. Shirkey, February 10, and March 21, 1994, respectively; telephone conversation with Capt. James McAndrew, USAFR, January 1995.

25. Thomas J. DuBose, affidavit, app. H; see also videotaped interview in *Recollections of Roswell—Part II*, available from the Fund for UFO Research.

26. App. A. Apparently, the staff car Marcel drove to the Foster place was left at the ranch house during this first visit to the debris field.

27. Randle and Schmitt, *UFO Crash*, p. 49.

28. Leonard H. Stringfield, *The UFO Crash/Retrieval Syndrome, Status Report II* (Seguin, Tex.: Mutual UFO Network, 1980), case A-10, pp. 16–17. Nor do earlier versions of this paper include such references.

29. Personal interview with Sheridan W. and Mary Cavitt, July 7, 1995; United States Air Force, *The Roswell Report: Fact versus Fiction in the New Mexico Desert* (Washington, D.C.: U.S. Government Printing Office, 1995), attachment 17 to "Report of Air Force Research Regarding the 'Roswell Incident.' "

30. Audiotaped telephone interview with Dr. Jesse A. Marcel Jr., September 23, 1993; Marcel affidavit, app. H.

31. Randle and Schmitt, *UFO Crash*, p. 50. The sources cited are Stringfield, *Status Report II*, re the gouge and, oddly, Bill Brazel re orientation of the debris field (see *UFO Crash* nn. 2 and 3 to chap. 5, p. 291).

32. App. A; Stringfield, *Status Report II*, p. 17. Bill Brazel has been quoted as saying his father told him "that from the way this wreckage was scattered, you could tell it was traveling 'an airline route to Socorro,' " which is almost due west of the debris field. See Berlitz and Moore, *Roswell Incident*, p. 86.

SEVEN

THE REST OF THE TRUTH ABOUT THE PRESS ANNOUNCEMENT

Contrary to the Frank Kaufmann–inspired potboiler-thriller version of things, the startling announcement Walter Haut issued to the Roswell news media was not the first chapter of a too-clever-by-half cover story. Instead, it seems very likely to have been a mistake born of hubris.

THE "BLANCHARD FACTOR"

According to a number of those who served with and under him, Col. William H. Blanchard, commander of the 509th Bomb Group and Roswell Army Air Field at the time of the Roswell incident, was a remarkable man. A veteran of the air war against Japan, he was a West Point graduate and an outstanding pilot, highly skilled, steel nerved, something of a risk taker—a "natural." He was an inspirational leader who expected nothing but the best and nothing short of all-out effort from those he commanded, and got it by giving what he expected. In short, he had the "right stuff" and was always "pushing the envelope."[1]

Unsurprisingly, Blanchard lacked neither ego nor ambition, and sometimes these traits led him to do more than just push the envelope. All too frequently, he tore it. This tendency to let eagerness overpower prudence created detractors among his military colleagues, got him into scrapes and tight spots, some of them potential career stoppers, earned him his nickname, "Butch," and, according to a general officer who knew him very well, a reputation as a "loose cannon."[2]

Fortunately for Blanchard, he had a very powerful, influential patron, the legendary Gen. Curtis E. LeMay, himself "an experimenter by nature."[3] LeMay was the daring and outspoken architect of the strategic bombing campaign against Japan; effectively the creator of the Strategic Air Command, which he led for nine years (1948–1957); and, ultimately, chief of staff of the Air Force. At the time of the Roswell excitement, LeMay was a major general and assistant chief of the army air staff for research and development. LeMay's assistance in getting his fair-haired boy Blanchard out of hot water now and then gave the latter the opportunity to use his natural leadership and other outstanding professional attributes to become a four-star general, inspector general of the air force, and vice chief of staff of the Air Force before his untimely death in 1965.[4] In the absence of any proof or reasonable theory to the contrary, it is my considered opinion that the "flying disc" press announcement was an example of Blanchard tearing the envelope.

The discovery of the debris field on the Foster Ranch came in the midst of tremendous international excitement and official and public concern about flying saucers. Kenneth Arnold's headline-making sighting had occurred less than two weeks before Mack Brazel walked into the Chaves County sheriff's office. During the days following Arnold's sighting, reports of at least five hundred sightings of the elusive objects had poured into police, military, and news offices, more than three hundred of them during the Fourth of July weekend and the lion's share from the western United States. On July 3, U.S. Army Air Forces Chief of Staff Carl Spaatz directed the air research and development section of the Air Materiel Command "to check on the reports and try to ascertain what the discs are."[5] During the holiday weekend, West Coast–based army and national guard fighter planes had been put on alert to follow up UFO reports with attempts to intercept and identify the strange disks and capture them on gun-camera film. Rewards totaling about $3,000 were offered for physical proof of the saucers' existence, and speculation as to the objects' origin ran rampant, most focusing on the Soviet Union.

The Roswell object fell through this highly charged atmosphere into the lap of Butch Blanchard. Arthur R. McQuiddy and the late Maj. Gen. Woodrow P. Swancutt, both good friends of Blanchard, told me Blanchard had confided to them he was sure his men had retrieved something very unusual and significant. McQuiddy, editor of the *Roswell Morning Dispatch* in July 1947, said that three or four months after the event, "reluctantly admitt[ing] he had authorized the press release," Blanchard told him, "The stuff I saw, I've never seen anyplace else in my life." Swancutt, who was assistant Roswell AAF operations officer in July 1947 and flew combat missions with Blanchard in World War II, said Blanchard "was convinced he had something very important *at first* [emphasis added]." Similarly, Blanchard's first wife, Ethel Simms, told Roswell researcher William Moore her husband first "thought it might be Russian because of the strange symbols on it. Later on, he realized it wasn't Russian either."[6]

Given the circumstances, Blanchard's ambition and "take charge" style, the unusual nature of what had been found, and the fact that flying saucer matters were not yet classified, it is both consistent with Occam's razor and entirely reasonable to conclude Blanchard decided to run with what he had, claiming credit for reeling in the proof everyone was seeking. He took a chance in the hope of becoming hero of the hour. In short order, he was himself reeled in by his superiors and, implicitly, made the goat instead of a hero. It seems likely he was helped through this episode by LeMay, who became commander-in-chief of the Strategic Air Command in October 1948, about the same time Blanchard was transferred to Fort Worth to take over as director of operations and plans for SAC's Eighth Air Force.[7]

WHERE'S THE PAPER?

Walter Haut told me he "thinks" he distributed copies of a written "flying disc" press release on July 8, but he is not absolutely sure of this. Art McQuiddy says it is possible he got such a release, but he is far from certain of it. Frank Joyce told me he is quite certain Haut brought him one at Radio KGFL. George Walsh, who broke the story, was equally emphatic when he told me he never received a written release, that Haut telephoned the story to him at Radio KSWS.[8]

No copy of the release has ever been found, and although there are claims the reason for this is that the army rounded up and destroyed all copies (and, now, also the wire-recorded KGFL interview of Mack Brazel), it seems more likely that, except perhaps for the copy Haut read from, there never was a written release. Walsh's recollection of how he and, probably, his counterparts received the story is backed up by contemporaneous press and wire service accounts. An example is this succinct United Press broadcast wire exchange between the UP bureaus in Denver and Santa Fe at 3:17 P.M. local time, July 8, made available by Frank Joyce:

> Denver (DX) to Santa Fe (FR): "Let's have text Army announcement fastest. Just put on as te[x]t an[d] let roll in quotes."
> Santa Fe (FR) to Denver (DX): *"Army gave verbal ann[oun]c[e]ment. No text."* [Emphasis added][9]

Further, Walsh remembers nothing of an army press release "sweep." He told me the only indication of the reversal of the "flying disc" story he recalls KSWS getting was the Associated Press wire report of Ramey's weather balloon cover-up announcement. McQuiddy is certain only about receiving a telephone call from Roswell AAF advising him of the "error" and is quite unsure about whether there was any other official follow-up of any kind to Haut's announcement.[10]

Frank Joyce claims KGFL was swept clean of "every scrap of paper that had anything about the event on it." Joyce also claims Jud Dixon, the UP man in Santa Fe in July 1947, "reported the same thing. . . . Dixon's files on the Roswell event had vanished."[11] Yet Joyce has supplied Kevin Randle, Don Schmitt, and me with copies of the UP wire printouts of the Roswell stories which came in on the Teletype receiver at KGFL, one of which is quoted from above. As for Jud Dixon, he told me in 1993 that, not only does he not remember any such action by the army, he does not recall anything at all about the Roswell incident. He said it is clear from his initials on some of the Santa Fe bureau wire stories that he was involved, but he had completely forgotten about the incident and Frank Joyce until recently, when Joyce contacted him. To Dixon it was just another flash-in-the-pan story among many hundreds during a very long career in journalism.[12]

It is very difficult to credit the idea that professional newsmen and press and public relations specialists such as George Walsh, Art McQuiddy, and Jud Dixon would not have a vivid memory of the army taking storm-trooper-style action against them. It is even more difficult to believe the army would be so unwise as to make such a move against the press, a virtual guarantee of further publicity and outcry, when all that was needed was Ramey's weather balloon announcement and a few "Oops!" telephone calls. As for Haut's office copy of the release, he remembers nothing out of the ordinary about it and assumes it went the way of most of the file copies of press releases his office generated, eventually landing in "file 13."[13]

Once again, an article of the conventional wisdom turns out to be less certain and sensational than previously thought.

NOTES

1. Audiotaped telephone interview with Maj. Gen. Woodrow P. Swancutt, USAF (ret.), March 21, 1993; telephone interview with Robert J. Shirkey, March 21, 1994; audiotaped personal interview with Walter G. Haut, November 2, 1992; telephone interview with Col. Virgil Sewell, USAF (ret.), September 12, 1993; audiotaped telephone interview with Col. Arthur Jeffrey, USAF (ret.), October 17, 1993.

2. For example, a retired Air Force general officer who prefers to remain anonymous and who knew Blanchard well, both in 1947 and the years following, still thinks of him as a "loose cannon" and remembers kidding Blanchard about the 1947 incident when both were serving in very senior positions in the Pentagon in the early 1960s.

3. Alfred Goldberg, ed., *A History of the United States Air Force, 1907–1957* (Princeton, New Jersey: Van Nostrand, 1957), p. 86.

4. See n. 1.

5. Berliner, Don, "A Historical Perspective," in Fred Whiting, "The Roswell Events," a limited distribution congressional briefing paper (Washington, D.C.: Fund for UFO Research, December 1993), p. 46. See also Ted Bloecher, *Report on the UFO Wave of 1947* (Washington, D.C.: self-published, 1967); Loren E. Gross, *UFOs: A History—1947* (Port St. Lucie, Fla.: Arcturus Books, 1991); and Jan L. Aldrich, *Project 1947: A Preliminary Report on the 1947 UFO Sighting Wave* (Washington, D.C.: UFO Research Coalition, 1997).

6. William L. Moore, "Crashed Saucers: Evidence in Search of Proof," in *MUFON Symposium Proceedings* (Seguin, Tex.: Mutual UFO Network, 1985), p. 160; Swancutt telephone interview, March 21, 1993; audiotaped personal interview with Arthur R. McQuiddy, May 19, 1993; McQuiddy affidavit, app. H.

7. See nn. 1 and 3 above.

8. George R. Walsh affidavit, app. H; audiotaped personal interview with Walter Haut, November 2, 1992; McQuiddy interview, May 19, 1993.

9. See app. E.

10. Walsh affidavit, app. H; McQuiddy interview, May 19, 1993; McQuiddy affidavit, app. H.

11. Audiotaped personal interview with Frank Joyce, November 3, 1992; Joyce as attributed in Randle and Schmitt, *UFO Crash*, pp. 136–37 (United Press is misidentified here as the Associated Press).

12. Judson J. Dixon in letters to the author, April 13 and 29, 1993. I am indebted to Mr. Dixon for his assistance in interpreting the 1947 UP wire codes and techniques.

13. Haut interview, November 2, 1992.

EIGHT

RECOVERY OPERATIONS

Although much has been asserted with certainty and in some detail about the army's activities on and over the Foster Ranch after Marcel and Cavitt reported in, the basis for this detail and certainty is, to be polite about it, tenuous at best.

SECURING THE DEBRIS FIELD

It seems likely that at some point the army moved to secure the debris site to keep out the curious. A number of reports attest to this, among them that of J. O. "Bud" Payne, at that time a rancher and neighbor of Mack Brazel's. Payne told me that, upon hearing

> about the flying saucer coming down on the Foster ranch a few days after it happened in early July 1947, I decided to see if I could get a piece of the thing. . . . I drove over there in a pickup truck. . . .
>
> Before I reached the site, I was stopped by two soldiers sitting in an Army truck parked beside the ranch road I was on. . . . There were more vehicles and soldiers on higher ground beyond where I had been stopped.
>
> I told the two soldiers who had stopped me I was going to where the flying saucer had come down. They said, "We know where you're going, but you can't go in there. . . ." They did not threaten me, but they had their instructions to turn everybody back.[1]

Counter Intelligence Corps agent Sgt. Lewis Rickett also testified that military policemen and the base provost marshall were at the debris field when he and his commanding officer, Sheridan Cavitt, visited it the afternoon of July 8. Moreover, he said Cavitt and others on the site made cryptic remarks clearly indicating this was a sensitive matter not to be talked about or even admitted to.[2] Based on known exaggerations and significant errors of fact in Rickett's testimony, as well as what Cavitt told me personally, it seems likely Rickett embellished a bit concerning the hush-hush huggermugger. However, I see no reason to doubt that he did visit the site and that a certain amount of security was in place when he did.

It is far from clear *when* the army decided it was necessary to put things under wraps. When I met with him in his Santa Fe home, former Associated Press reporter Jason Kellahin clearly remembered visiting the Foster Ranch with AP wire technician and photographer Robin Adair on the afternoon of July 8. He told me Brazel

> took Adair and me to the pasture where he made his discovery. When we arrived, there were three or four uniformed Army officers searching some higher ground about a quarter to a half mile away. . . .
>
> After looking at the material, I walked over to the military men. They said they were from RAAF and were just looking around to see what they could find. . . . They had a very casual attitude and did not seem at all disturbed that the press was there. They made no attempt to run us off.[3]

Perhaps the security clamp was imposed when Colonel Blanchard arrived on site, as some have asserted he did. Randle and Schmitt report that then Lt. Col. Joe Briley told them he was "sure" Blanchard had gone to the site, although Briley also denied "he had any firsthand knowledge of the crash," having at the time been in command of one of the 509th's bomb squadrons rather than serving in group headquarters as he did later in the year. Randle and Schmitt place Blanchard's visit to the Foster Ranch on the afternoon of July 8, after he left instructions with his staff to tell anyone who inquired that he had gone on leave.[4]

According to information sourced by Randle and Schmitt to the late Edwin Easley, provost marshal ("chief of police") of Roswell AAF in July 1947 and reportedly in charge of on-site security at the debris field, when Blanchard arrived at the Foster Ranch location, he told Easley "everything there was now classified top secret." Further, "nothing had been given to . . . [Easley] in writing and he wrote nothing down. According to him, Blanchard didn't want anything in writing."[5]

Is it possible Blanchard went to the debris field to survey the situation personally? Reliable testimony, press reports, and an official document strongly suggests he did not. First, Robert Shirkey told me that about midafternoon that day he was with Blanchard in the Roswell AAF operations building, where the colonel personally was overseeing the dispatch of the B-29 that took Jesse Marcel and some of the debris to Fort Worth. Second, Walter Haut vividly recalls Blanchard colorfully complaining to him that same afternoon about not being able to place outside telephone calls because the base switchboard was tied up with inquiries about the flying saucer.[6]

If Blanchard did indeed visit the debris field, he did so on the evening of July 8 or, more likely, very early on Wednesday, July 9. According to the 509th's headquarters morning report and a tiny Associated Press story in the July 10, 1947, *Albuquerque Journal*, the ninth (not the eighth) was the day he began "a three weeks leave in Santa Fe and Colorado."[7] The AP's Kellahin and Adair were on the site the afternoon of July 8, and no security was in place. Bud Payne heard about the crash and tried to get to the site "a few days after it happened," only to be turned back by soldiers on perimeter watch. It is reported Easley got his "top security" instructions from Blanchard on the site.

In 1991, Robert Todd located a teletype message in U.S. Army Air Forces headquarters files from Roswell AAF, dated July 9, 1947. It was sent from Roswell about 8 A.M. and advised that "Colonel William H. Blanchard . . . [has] an appointment with Governor Mabry for Nine July to request his proclaiming of Air Force Day." So it is clear that Blanchard intended to be in Santa Fe later that day. As it turned out, the governor was out of town, and it was necessary for Blanchard to schedule a July 14 appointment with Lt. Gov. Joseph A. Montoya, who evidently had recovered sufficiently from his traumatic experience in Roswell just a few days before to handle his duties as acting governor in Mabry's absence. An article in the July 15, 1947, *Albuquerque Journal* reported on the proclamation ceremony, and the July 25, 1947, edition of the Roswell AAF base newspaper, the *Atomic Blast*, carried a photograph of Montoya signing the proclamation as Blanchard looked on.

Taken together, these fragmentary and in some part questionable bits of testimony and considerably more substantial documentation point to a delay before the 509th was instructed to treat the Brazel discovery as a sensitive matter. They also suggest Blanchard *could* have personally conveyed this guidance to those in the field, perhaps as he was on his way north on a long-planned vacation—although some have contended he headed somewhere else entirely.[9]

Both the reported security and the delay in putting it in place are consistent with what is now known to have been the source of the debris discovered by Brazel, a highly classified project being conducted for the army air forces from a location near the White Sands Proving Ground, about ninety air miles southwest of Roswell. This project was outside the scope of the responsibilities and "need to know" of those stationed at Roswell AAF. It took some time for higher headquarters to get a fix on what actually had been discovered, after which it is reasonable to expect they would want to have as much of the debris recovered as possible and minimize intrusions by souvenir-seeking civilians. Given Blanchard's role in stirring up the storm of unwanted press and public attention, he may have decided to be certain everything was being taken care of appropriately before beginning his leave. We will never know for certain.

CRASH SITE?

A central element of the Roswell stories, conventional wisdom and revisionist, is the alleged discovery of a nearly intact crashed flying saucer and the bodies of its crew. Ostensibly, the craft and bodies were found by aerial reconnaissance employing the assistance of Mack Brazel.[8] In the conventional wisdom version of things, the site of this amazing discovery is said to have been about two and a half miles east-southeast of the debris field. Here, according to Frank Kaufmann, a disk-shaped craft about thirty feet in diameter was found, imbedded at an angle in the rocky soil, where it had come to rest apparently after caroming off a nearby cliff. A short distance away, the bodies of three or four large-headed, large-eyed, slightly built beings were located, sprawled on the ground.

Reportedly, this crash site was located while Blanchard was on the debris field, the news radioed to him from one of the several small reconnaissance aircraft that Kaufmann claims had been searching the area for some time. Upon receiving this electrifying message, Blanchard, "a small number of MPs, and one or two of his top officers left the debris field, disappearing to the east as they crossed one of the ridgelines and then vanishing into one of the many canyons," following radioed directions from the recon plane, which, with Mack Brazel aboard, continued to circle the new discovery.[10]

According to an account attributed by his daughter, Beverly Bean, to the late Sgt. Melvin E. Brown, the strange bodies found at the crash site were placed on ice and trucked back to the base late the same afternoon. Bean claims her father was a member of the recovery detail on the crash site. She says he rode back to the base in the back of a truck with the bodies, which he saw when, against orders, he lifted the tarpaulin covering them. At the base, Bean says, her father was posted as a member of the guard detail at the hangar where the bodies were stored temporarily.[11]

According to Randle and Schmitt, Blanchard is reported to have kept the recovery teams in the field overnight, staying on the ranch himself, allegedly in the same house used by Marcel, Cavitt, and Brazel. Blanchard did not want to call attention to the army's activities, so no fires were allowed and everyone ate cold C rations. The next day, the men carefully swept the sites. Blanchard "wanted no signs of anything left behind."[12]

To date, apart from the Brown-Bean story and a few rather tenuously associated references, *everything* about the discovery of the crash site, what was found there, and army actions taken with respect to it comes from Frank Kaufmann, without attribution or attributed to him by name or identified as "one of the intelligence operatives who had been assigned to the Roswell Army Air Field in 1947," "Joseph Osborne," Joseph Osborne/"Mr. X," or "Steve MacKenzie." Despite my best efforts and those of several other researchers, to my knowledge no other credible testimony or record in support of these accounts has surfaced so far.

The Brown-Bean story presents a number of difficulties. First, it is secondhand. Unfortunately, the late Sergeant Brown left no written or other record of his experience, and all we have are the recollections of what his daughter Beverly says he told her. His widow and oldest daughter refuse to discuss the matter, and despite concerted efforts by myself and others, Beverly has never responded to requests that she sign an affidavit attesting to her account.

Second, key elements of the description of the bodies attributed to Brown (yellowish-orange skin with a lizardlike texture) are inconsistent with what Glenn Dennis was told by the nurse who allegedly assisted in the examination of strange bodies at the Roswell AAF hospital.[13]

Finally, Brown was a cook, assigned to Squadron "K" of the 509th, not a military policeman or any other sort of security or intelligence/counterintelligence specialist. Given the highly sensitive nature of the recovery operations, it seems most unlikely cooks would be detailed to such duty. Moreover, standard military procedure is that mess and medical personnel are the last to be taken from their primary duties for other assignments, and then only in extreme situations. Roswell AAF was a huge base with thousands of personnel assigned, many of them in redundant staff positions (e.g., squadron clerks), so if there was a need for extra hands on the Lincoln County sites, there was a substantial pool from which to draw before resorting to a raid on the mess hall kitchens.[14]

As for the unattributed information (e.g., Blanchard's trek to the crash site and his overnight stay on the Foster place), it may be pure speculation or "creative journalism." However, my May 1993 conversation with Frank Kaufmann and the claims with respect to aerial reconnaissance activities and what was found on the crash site sourced to Kaufmann by name and as an "intelligence operative" lead me to have no doubt this, too, is based on his accounts.

I have asked Loretta Proctor, Juanita Sultemeier, and Sallye Strickland Tadolini, all neighbors of Mack Brazel in July 1947, if they remembered any unusual aircraft activity in the days following Brazel's discovery. All have vivid memories of Brazel's brush with history. All made a point of telling me how very conscious ranchers and their families were of airplanes overflying the area. None—not one—remembers any unusual air activity during the summer of 1947.[15]

It has been suggested that Proctor recalls Brazel being flown to or over the area in an army aircraft and activity at a second site removed from the debris field.[16] I asked her about both claims. She emphatically denied any knowledge of a second site and said she first heard about it "only a few years ago." In 1993, she also told me she had no firsthand knowledge of Brazel being flown anywhere by the army, but "someone," a Roswell researcher (Schmitt?), had mentioned it to her recently. She said she remembers no airplane other than her brother's landing anywhere near her place in the 1940s. I also raised both questions with Sultemeier, and she, too, remembered nothing of the kind.[17]

Of course, these recollections are not conclusive. These ladies may simply have missed all the army observation planes buzzing about low over their heads in a part of the country where one can "see forever."

RECOVERY RECAP

It is certain the army acted with some dispatch to recover what fell on the Foster place at what is now known as the debris field site. The testimony of several credible witnesses to these activities and apparently related events has established this beyond any reasonable doubt.

However, the testimony so far available with respect to a nearby crash site where a nearly intact craft and unusual bodies were found is slight, sketchy, highly questionable, uncorroborated, and in significant degree secondhand. The accounts of the principal source of testimony about this site, Frank Kaufmann, have "evolved" dramatically, leaving what has been attributed to him on this count as part of the conventional wisdom in a state as tattered as the debris discovered by a surprised and somewhat annoyed Mack Brazel. Yet again, what was thought of as given has been found for all practical purposes to be unsubstantiated in any credible way.

NOTES

1. J. O. "Bud" Payne affidavit, app. H.

2. As attributed in Kevin D. Randle and Donald R. Schmitt, *UFO Crash at Roswell* (New York: Avon, 1991), pp. 61–63.

3. Audotaped personal interview with Jason Kellahin, May 11, 1993; Kellahin affidavit, app. H. I also interviewed the late Robin Adair (audiotaped personal interview, May 25, 1993). He spun an interesting yarn which was so wildly at odds with known facts (including his position and status at AP in 1947) that it must be discounted entirely.

4. Randle and Schmitt, *UFO Crash*, pp. 158–59.

5. Ibid., p. 66.

6. Robert J. Shirkey affidavit, app. H; audiotaped personal interview with Walter Haut, November 2, 1992.

7. App. F; "Commander on Leave," *Albuquerque Journal*, July 10, 1947.

8. Robert G. Todd, "Roswell Record Found," *Cowflop Quarterly*, July 5, 1996, pp. 1–2.

9. Randle and Schmitt, *UFO Crash*, p. 66.

10. Ibid., pp. 66 and 181.

11. Bean as attributed in ibid., pp. 95–96; Bean in *Recollections of Roswell—Part II*, available from the Fund for UFO Research.

12. Randle and Schmitt, *UFO Crash*, p. 67.

13. Glenn Dennis affidavit, app. H.

14. *Roswell Army Air Field Yearbook* (Roswell, N.M.: RAAF Public Relations Department, 1947); telephone conversations with Walter Haut and Robert Shirkey, February 10 and March 21, 1994, respectively; my personal experience.

15. Audiotaped telephone interview with Loretta Proctor, September 23, 1993; personal interview with Juanita Sultemeier, May 19, 1993; audiotaped telephone interview with Sallye Strickland Tadolini, September 18, 1993.

16. Personal conversation with Donald R. Schmitt, Chicago, May 8, 1993.

17. Proctor, September 23, 1993; Sultemeier, May 19, 1993.

NINE

WHAT WE ARE TOLD WENT WHERE

There is no doubt at least some of the debris recovered on the Foster Ranch was flown to Eighth Air Force headquarters at Fort Worth Army Air Field. This is one of the few things about the case on which both skeptics and believers agree.

Most of the material, in the custody of Maj. Jesse Marcel, left Roswell aboard a B-29 on the afternoon of July 8. Although others who have looked into the Roswell affair do not share my view on this, I am convinced there is good reason to believe a small amount, probably that brought in by Mack Brazel, was flown to Fort Worth the day before. According to Gen. Thomas DuBose, the latter was transferred to another aircraft, flown directly to Washington, D.C., and later apparently turned over to Air Materiel Command deputy commander Gen. Benjamin Chidlaw at Wright Field, Ohio. Despite claims to the contrary, it seems likely the material Marcel delivered also went on to Wright Field aboard a transport aircraft.[1]

Was more flown out? And where did the bodies go?

THE DEBRIS

Once again, the evidence is sketchy and in very large degree highly questionable. All that can be said with any measure of confidence is that two additional "debris flights" *may* have followed the first two.

The first of these follow-on flights may have been a First Air Transport Unit C-54 transport piloted by Capt. Oliver Wendell "Pappy" Henderson to Patterson or Wright AAF near Dayton, Ohio. Just when this flight took place, if it did, is in doubt, but given the recollections of Robert Shirkey and others, the time required to recover the debris from the Foster Ranch, transport it to Roswell AAF, prepare and load it for flight, and so on, it now seems most likely to have departed Roswell on or within a few days after Wednesday, July 9.[2]

While several persons have claimed knowledge of Henderson's alleged flight, including the late Pappy Henderson himself, only one person has offered testimony concerning the other possible follow-on flight. According to CIC agent Lewis Rickett,

Marcel signed over a sealed package of debris to Rickett's commanding officer, CIC Capt. Sheridan Cavitt. In turn, Rickett was given the package to put aboard an aircraft which had come in to Roswell AAF from another location, either Kirtland AAF or Washington, D.C., Rickett thought. He testified he knew the copilot. He also said he asked where the flight was going and recalled the answer was vague: "Headed east." As with the Henderson flight, the timing of this one is uncertain, but based on Rickett's testimony, if there was such a flight, it seems most likely to have gone out the morning of July 9.[3]

The principal source concerning other possible flights is the late Robert E. Smith, who came forward in response to the *Unsolved Mysteries* reenactment of the Roswell events (September 20, 1989, rebroadcast in January 1990). Smith, who was a sergeant assigned to the First Air Transport Unit at Roswell AAF in July 1947, claimed to have been involved in loading mysterious sealed crates aboard "three or four" 1st ATU C-54s. Smith says one of the other sergeants working with him showed Smith and other soldiers a small piece of the foil-like debris, which he had taken as a souvenir.[4]

There is ample reason to question Smith's account. It includes a wide range of information about aspects of the crash/retrieval/cover-up operation to which it is unlikely he, a junior noncommissioned officer, would have been privy or even in a position to hear rumors about. Still more damning, it also incorporates a conveniently deceased "distant cousin" of Smith's who was in the Secret Service in 1947 and "was at Roswell at this time, more or less as a representative of President Truman." This "presidential representative" recognized Smith at the base but did not speak. Presumably, the distant cousin was one of "a lot of people in plainclothes [sic] all over the place . . . strangers on the base."

Let us also not forget what Smith said he and others with him saw "several nights before this." As Smith related, "[W]hen we were coming back to Roswell, a convoy of trucks covered with canvas passed us. The truck convoy had red lights and sirens [!]," and Smith and his buddies saw it enter the base and head for the hangar where he claimed he later helped load crates aboard transport aircraft.

Further, Smith said "one crate took up the entire plane," and the flights went to Los Alamos. However, a crate that size would have been impossible to maneuver through a C-54's cargo door. Even if that small problem were somehow solved, the airstrip at Los Alamos was still under construction in July 1947, and when completed two months later was far too short to accommodate a C-54.[5]

Of course, it is possible Smith did have something to do with loading debris from the Foster Ranch aboard at least one 1st ATU transport. He was in the right place at the right time. However, like so many other Roswell witnesses and "witnesses," his melodramatic embellishments and factual errors call his entire story into question.

In addition, Smith came forward after the *Unsolved Mysteries* broadcast. When his account is studied alongside the impressive "reenactment" featured on that program, the parallels between the two are striking to say the least—not the least being a convoy of vehicles with dramatically flashing red lights.

Taken together, the factors discussed above reduce Smith's claims to an interesting tale of no probative value. Yet Smith's story still is cited by the advocates of the Roswell saucer crash scenarios.

As should now be quite clear, it is highly unlikely there were more than four flights which carried Foster Ranch debris out of Roswell, and only two of these—the Marcel and Henderson flights—with any substantial quantity of material aboard. Apart from the limited amount of reliable testimony about the veritable airlift itself, we are faced with the question of where a quantity of debris requiring the use of several very large aircraft to transport it could have come from.

Although the area of the debris field was described by some as being very large, others, including its discoverer, Mack Brazel, said otherwise. Also, accounts of the character and condition of the debris itself, as well as what Brazel did with it, indicate it would be rather compact and not at all heavy when gathered up. Moreover, every description of the alleged crashed craft suggests it was relatively small—if a disk, thirty feet in diameter; if lifting-body-like, twenty-two to thirty feet long with a span of twelve to fifteen feet. Is it credible that, while remaining essentially intact, such a small, crewed vehicle could possibly shed enough of its structure to create wreckage requiring four or five C-54s, a B-29, and at least two other aircraft to transport it?

THE BODIES

Here, too, the evidence is sketchy, to say the least, although the principal witness, former 393rd Bomb Squadron member Robert Slusher, at first blush seemed to me to be quite sincere and credible. "Tim," another former 393rd member, has recollections similar to Slusher's and, reportedly, a diary containing notations that seem to support his and Slusher's memories.[6]

In a twist that immediately sends up a red flag of doubt, Tim has insisted on anonymity, citing a series of alleged mysterious, sometimes threatening telephone calls. Given that it was Tim who provided the leads that directed researchers to Slusher, and that Slusher always has been quite willing to talk publicly and has never had even a hint of a threat, Tim's fears appear contrived and call into question his credibility. So, too, does the fact that he was completely unknown to the UFO research community until, on his own initiative, he made himself known in early 1989, by writing a letter to prominent ufologist and ufological historian Barry Greenwood. Adding to this is Tim's recent resurfacing and "enhanced" recollections, which I discuss below.

It will be recalled that Slusher told me he was a crewman on a B-29 (according to Tim, tail number 44-7301) which allegedly carried a mysterious crate under armed guard to Fort Worth AAF on the afternoon of Wednesday, July 9. Apart from the cargo and its escort housed in the airplane's forward bomb bay, according to Slusher and Tim, the flight was unusual in a number of ways. It was hastily ordered. The outbound leg was flown at much lower than normal altitude, with the crew-space pressurization off. As soon as the cargo and passengers were unloaded, the flight returned to Roswell at normal altitude and pressurized. Supposedly Major Marcel was a passenger on the return trip. In Texas, Slusher told me, the plane was met by a group of military personnel, which included three military policemen and a mortician who had been a schoolmate of the B-29's bombardier, 1st Lt. Felix A. Martucci, identified by Leonard Stringfield as "Capt. FM."[7]

Tim gave Stringfield testimony that is consistent with Slusher's in virtually all important respects, the principal difference being the makeup of the guard detachment. He has also shown Stringfield his diary, in which he logged his flight activity. According to Stringfield, one of these entries reads: "July 9, 1947, DEH [the Civil (now Federal) Aeronautics Administration station designation for Roswell AAF], Ship 7301. B-29. Cross country. Ft. Worth and return. Flight time 1 hr., 55 mins."[8]

What was in the crate? The reported presence of a mortician in the greeting party at Fort Worth is suggestive, to say the least, although the coincidence that made it possible to identify the man's profession, Martucci's old school tie with him, seems all too convenient.

Stringfield, Randle, and Schmitt attempted to follow up with Martucci. They report that, after an initial fruitless contact, someone who had served with the former bombardier was asked to telephone him, on the theory he might be more forthcoming with an old comrade in arms. Allegedly, after several attempts, this fellow got through to a young woman, who rather hysterically refused to discuss anything or put Martucci on the line. This, of course, has been interpreted to mean that Martucci and his family had been threatened with dire consequences if they did not keep what they knew to themselves. The person who pursued the matter at Stringfield's request and the source of the "shush-up" story? It was none other than Tim.[9]

The only source identified to date who has claimed certain knowledge that strange bodies were sealed in a crate that was flown out of Roswell is, once again, Frank Kaufmann. Since providing this testimony, Kaufmann has changed his story, claiming the bodies were flown out on two separate flights, on one of which he flew as copilot with Pappy Henderson in command, and that the "crate flight" was a diversion.[10]

The simple truth is, assuming there was such a crate and such a flight as described by Slusher and Tim, we do not know what was in the large wooden box. Perhaps it was a transferring general officer's furniture, as Slusher and Tim report was speculated by members of the B-29 crew. More likely, there was no such crate and no such flight—about which no supporting testimony and of which no documentation has been found. All we have is that offered by Slusher and Tim, with a bit of dubious, indirect backup from Kaufmann.

After years of silence, the ufological community heard from Tim again in early 2000. He contacted George A. Filer, eastern regional director of the Mutual UFO Network (MUFON) and publisher of *Filer's Files*, an online compendium of UFO sighting reports and the like, including a great deal of Roswell-related material. In his April 2000 issue, Filer posted a long message from "Another New [sic] Roswell Witness." Filer does not name his correspondent, but the content of the man's missive leaves no doubt whatsoever that it is Tim (bored and writing from a safe house?). Tim now "recalls" never-before-revealed memories of how, "three to six months later, the wives [of the men involved in the alleged saucer and bodies retrieval] began talking among themselves about the cleanup detail," and how, when he asked one of the cleanup crew "what he had seen out there," the man "was upset and told [Tim], 'You don't want to know.' "

This fellow, Tim wrote, "was a neighbor of ours. I think he was a baker because he would leave for work in the early morning, like 0130 hours. . . . Based on the wives [*sic*] gossip we heard he had seen a body." It would appear Tim has been reading about the late Sergeant Brown, who, it will be recalled, was a cook at Roswell AAF and, according to a daughter, was pressed into service as a guard at the saucer crash site and later at the hangar where the crated bodies were stashed for a time.

Making things more interesting, Tim mentions but does not describe "two weird experiences" he and fellow KC-97 aerial tanker crew members had at March Air Force Base, California, "with something that officially was not there."[11] Perhaps he will soon elaborate on this cryptic tease. In fact, I think we can count on it.

Apart from the obvious difficulties about the crate flight tale arising principally from Tim's emulation of Frank Kaufmann, there are a few other niggling questions. These are prompted by the claim that the mission was carried out with a B-29 bomber.

Why would a bomber have been used for such a mission? Just down the ramp were the First Air Transport Unit's C-54s, designed and built specifically to transport large, bulky cargo. Allegedly, the 1st ATU's planes and crews did all the other "heavy lifting" of the Roswell debris. Moreover, while personnel/cargo pallets that could be inserted in the bomb bays of B-29s and other bomber types were available, they were problematic, difficult to install and remove, and so on, and consequently were used only when no other reasonable alternative was possible. If the crate required guarding in transit, once again, a C-54 would have been ideal. There were fold-down passengers seats in the cargo space, which was voluminous.

Supposedly, one objective was to minimize attention drawn to the shipment of the crate and its attendants. Once again, using an aircraft and an aircrew whose routine, day in, day out jobs were to haul cargo and passengers would have been far less conspicuous than the B-movie thriller approach described by Slusher and Tim.

Finally, there is the matter of Major Marcel being aboard during the return trip, the day after he had flown to Fort Worth. Marcel himself has told us Eighth Air Force commander Roger Ramey had sent him back to Roswell within at most a few hours of his arrival in Texas on July 8.[12]

I once thought it was likely there had been a crate flight. Given the above considerations, however, this exciting element of the Roswell story no longer flies with me. Once again, a facet of the conventional wisdom has lost its luster, and with this dimming, the whole saga no longer shines quite so brightly.

NOTES

1. See app. A and C.

2. Sappho Henderson, Robert Shirkey, affidavits, app. H.

3. Rickett as attributed in William L. Moore, "Crashed Saucers: Evidence in Search of Proof," in *MUFON Symposium Proceedings* (Seguin, Tex.: Mutual UFO Network, 1985), p. 167.

4. Robert E. Smith, affidavit, app. H; *Recollections of Roswell—Part II*, available from the Fund for UFO Research.

5. Smith affidavit, app. H. When the Los Alamos airfield began operations on September 1, 1947, it was nothing more than an unlighted 4,950-foot dirt airstrip with a tar paper shack for a terminal; at its elevation of 7,150 feet, the strip was far too short for a C-54 (James Rickman, Office of Public Affairs, Los Alamos National Laboratory; Philip J. Klass, "Roswell UFO: Cover-ups and Credulity," *Skeptical Inquirer* [fall 1991]: 73).

6. Leonard H. Stringfield, *UFO Crash/Retrievals: The Inner Sanctum, Status Report VI* (Cincinnati, Ohio: self-published, 1991), pp. 13–18.

7. Personal interview with Robert A. Slusher, May 23, 1993; Slusher affidavit, app. H.

8. Stringfield, *Status Report VI*, p.15.

9. Kevin D. Randle and Donald R. Schmitt, *UFO Crash at Roswell* (New York: Avon, 1991), pp. 267–68; Stringfield, *Status Report VI*, p.17.

10. See chap. 5.

11. George Filer, *Filer's Files*, no. 14, April 10, 2000.

12. See, e.g., app. A.

TEN

RICKETT, LaPAZ, AND THE CIC

The testimony of the late Lewis S. "Bill" Rickett, the senior Army Counter Intelligence Corps noncommissioned officer at Roswell AAF in July 1947, once seemed to me to have added to our knowledge of both what was found by Mack Brazel and what the army did about it, while at the same time introducing some significant misinformation and confusion. Thanks to the diligent archival research and analysis of Robert Todd, it is now clear the misinformation and confusion far outweigh any illumination Rickett's testimony may have provided.

Rickett was first located and interviewed by William L. Moore in 1983. In subsequent years before his death in November 1992, he was interviewed many times by a number of researchers. Although I did not have an opportunity to interview him myself, I have carefully reviewed the transcripts and audio- and videotapes of several of the interviews conducted by my colleagues, testimony attributed to Rickett by various authors, and related information, as well as the results of Todd's work.

It is important to note that in his later years, when most of the interviews took place, Rickett was in poor and failing health. It is evident when listening to and watching him on audio- and videotape that his memory was faulty and many people and events were confused in his mind, chronologically and otherwise. During a single interview, he frequently contradicted himself on various mostly but not always substantively minor points.

When all is said and done, it seems fairly likely Rickett did visit the debris field with Cavitt during recovery operations there, as he claimed. It also seems probable he was involved in at least a minor way in arranging shipment of some of the debris. Rickett remembered seeing only the foil-like material at the debris field. He said it was unusually strong, but interestingly and significantly, he also said several times there were not many pieces—"forty or fifty, small"—and they covered but a tiny area—"not any bigger than this apartment." As I noted above, he also confirmed the security measures that the army at some point put in place on the Foster Ranch.[1]

ORDERS, INTERVIEWING THE VAQUEROS, Y MAS

Under a bit of scrutiny, Rickett's most intriguing recollections have evaporated. He told of working with famed meteoriticist Lincoln LaPaz on the case sometime in the fall of 1947, an account summarized in chapter 2.

To begin with, Rickett was quite emphatic that he received his orders to work with Dr. LaPaz directly from Col. Doyle Rees at Kirtland AAF, near Albuquerque.[2] However, as Rees told me himself, the colonel was not assigned to Kirtland until September 1948, a year later and after establishment of the independent air force and its Office of Special Investigations (OSI), which took over army air forces CIC functions.

Rees told me he was in no way involved in the Roswell matter, which took place well before he "came on watch" in New Mexico. He does remember both Rickett and his boss, Capt. Sheridan Cavitt, quite well and fondly. Both men transferred to the air force and continued serving at Roswell under OSI District 17 (New Mexico, Arizona, and part of western Texas), which Rees commanded. Rees also told me he and LaPaz were good friends and that they worked closely together on a number of OSI projects, mostly UFO investigations. Further, he remembers LaPaz doing UFO-related field work with some of his agents, and although he has no memory of it, he said it is quite possible Rickett was on one or more of these assignments.[3] It is important to note that Rickett remembered such an assignment, one having nothing to do with Roswell but closely resembling Rickett's description and interwoven with his account of the Roswell work he says he did with LaPaz.[4]

Rickett made a particular point that LaPaz's fluency in Spanish was very helpful in the Roswell investigation as they traveled about the New Mexico countryside interviewing Spanish and Mexican ranchers and cowboys.[5] However, despite his surname, LaPaz, a native of Ohio, did not speak a word of Spanish. I was told this by several of LaPaz's colleagues and former students and Spanish-speaking former OSI agent Edgar J. Bethart, who worked with LaPaz. In a letter dated July 4, 1993, this was confirmed in no uncertain terms by LaPaz's daughter Jean, who not only was his daughter but worked very closely with him: "[M]y father was *not* fluent in spoken Spanish. He neither spoke nor read that language, requiring the assistance of either an interpreter during interviews with Spanish-speaking individuals or a translator for scientific articles published in Spanish."[6]

There are other difficulties with Rickett's memories of his association with LaPaz. For example, in one interview he discusses at length a conversation between LaPaz and Mack Brazel, at which he says he was present. In another interview, he says he never met Brazel. Another example is Rickett's insistence in one instance that he got his orders directly from a superior officer at Kirtland, Col. Doyle Rees, while in another he said Cavitt got the order to support LaPaz and assigned him to the job. In still another interview, he said Cavitt was directly involved in the LaPaz "visit," escorting the scientist to his room at the Roswell AAF visiting officers' quarters.

In a 1995 interview, Cavitt told me he remembered a visit from LaPaz at Roswell, but that this was some time after the July 1947 incident and in connection with an investigation of a sighting of one of the mysterious, not-quite-meteor-like green fireballs that began plaguing New Mexico skies in December 1948. Cavitt remembered nothing about Rickett's involvement in that investigation, but he said it was entirely possible, even quite likely.[7]

Hours spent studying Rickett's accounts convinced me he worked with LaPaz on at least one and probably more UFO field investigations in New Mexico, but that it was unlikely any of them had anything to do with the alleged crashed-saucer event. However, it seemed to me that, if LaPaz had been involved with Roswell in some way, it was certainly possible he may have discussed the case and his thoughts about it with Rickett during their days on the road together. Blurred by the effects of time, failing health, and "recollections" inadvertently introduced by interviewing researchers, memories of these activities and conversations with LaPaz could easily have merged in Rickett's mind with those of his very real if relatively minor July 1947 involvement in the Roswell "captured disc" incident.

BUT . . . WAS LAPAZ INVOLVED?

As with so much about this remarkable case, the answer to the above question once seemed to be, "Possibly, but . . ."

In April 1993 I received a most interesting telephone call from Earl L. Zimmerman, a retired OSI agent. He was responding to an article which I had written for the magazine of the Association of Former OSI Special Agents, in which I solicited Roswell-related information from the association's membership.[8] In addition to other intriguing information, Zimmerman said LaPaz had told him of his involvement in the Roswell investigation.[9]

Zimmerman had been stationed at Roswell AAF in July 1947 and, in addition to his official duties as a classified-communications ground radio operator, he moonlighted as a bartender at the base officers' club. That summer, he told me, he heard "many rumors about flying saucers in the club and around the base, including something about *investigating the discovery of one under the guise of a plane crash investigation*" (emphasis added).[10]

Some time later, Zimmerman was selected for service with OSI and transferred to OSI District 17 headquarters at Kirtland Air Force Base, where he served while waiting to be sent to OSI agent school.[11] "In early 1949," Zimmerman told me,

> I worked with Dr. Lincoln LaPaz of the University of New Mexico on an extended [air force] research project at the university's research station on top of Sandia Peak [immediately northeast of Albuquerque]. . . . We worked in three-man, one-week shifts, and Dr. LaPaz was in charge.
>
> During this project, which lasted for several months, I got to know Dr. LaPaz very well. When I mentioned to him I had been stationed in Roswell during 1947, he told me he had been involved in the investigation of the thing found in the Roswell area that summer. He did not discuss the case in any detail, but he did say he went out with two agents and interviewed sheepherders, ranchers, and others. *They told these witnesses they were investigating an aircraft accident.* I seem to recall LaPaz also saying they found an area where the surface of the earth had been turned a light blue and wondering if lightning could cause such an effect. [Emphasis added][12]

Another retired OSI agent, Edgar J. Bethart, was the CIC officer assigned to Alamogordo Army Air Field in July 1947. Alamogordo is located about ninety air miles southwest of Roswell, and Bethart frequently "liaised" with Cavitt, Rickett, and others at Roswell. He told me he remembers them and the July 1947 excitement well, but that he heard only the weather balloon story at the time. Bethart, the Spanish-speaking former agent mentioned above, also remembers LaPaz quite well, having "chased flying saucers all over southern New Mexico with him." Bethart says he cannot recall discussing Roswell with LaPaz. However, he does remember hearing that the scientist and another CIC or OSI agent found "a large, circular burned spot somewhere on the prairie" while investigating a flying saucer report "sometime in the nineteen forties or early fifties."[13]

In 1994, Robert Todd published the results of his acquisition and study of formerly classified reports written by LaPaz and others concerning LaPaz's work on the green fireball phenomenon, carried out for the Air Force in close cooperation with OSI District 17. In one of these documents, a report to District 17 dated February 21, 1949, LaPaz discusses in some detail his investigation of a green fireball sighted near Roswell on January 30, 1949, and his fieldwork on the case with OSI agent Lewis Rickett, who was still stationed at the former Roswell AAF, then called Walker Air Force Base. In his report, LaPaz commends Rickett by name for his valuable support.

Another report turned up by Todd, dated February 11, 1949, was written by the Walker AFB OSI detachment commander, Lt. Paul Ryan. Ryan reports on "an almost house-to-house search" conducted east of Roswell by LaPaz and OSI agents Rickett and Jack Williams. Ryan goes on to discuss an aerial and ground search for physical evidence, conducted in the vicinity of Lamesa, Texas, and then writes, "Special Agent RICKETT continued this search throughout Southeast New Mexico and West Texas from 1400 hours, 2 February 1949, to 2400 hours, 5 February 1949, in the company of Dr. LINCOLN LA PAZ of the University of New Mexico."

In the same article, Todd discusses his follow-up on my contact with Earl Zimmerman and his correlation of what Zimmerman had told both of us with records concerning the establishment of the Sandia Peak observation post. He confirmed what I had learned from OSI District 17 commander Doyle Rees, that the post was set up in an attempt to photograph green fireballs. In addition, Todd's correspondence with Zimmerman, together with what he learned about LaPaz's green fireball hunt at and around Roswell, leaves little doubt that this was the incident Zimmerman was told about by LaPaz.[14]

Finally, I was told by James Winchell, a former student and assistant of LaPaz's, that when seeking to locate meteorities, he and LaPaz often told those they interviewed that they were investigating an aircraft accident. They did this to give their questions a "routine feel" and thus minimize competition from amateur meteorite hunters.

Clearly, LaPaz's green fireball work has been confused with the alleged flying saucer crash. Without a reasonable doubt, both Zimmerman and Rickett were recalling the Roswell-area green fireball sighting and the subsequent investigation. Both blended those memories with others, direct and indirect, of the 1947 incident and what they had heard and read about it. So another exciting element of the case bites the dust, and with it any significant evidentiary value that may once have attached to Rickett's testimony.

JACK WILLIAMS, CLAIR MILLER, AND FRIENDS

The third CIC agent assigned to Roswell AAF in July 1947 was Sgt. Jack B. Williams. Unfortunately, based on information provided by several former CIC/OSI agents who served with or knew Williams, he is almost certainly dead, although, to my knowledge, this has yet to be confirmed.[15]

However, one of these former agents, retired Air Force Maj. William M. O'Brien, provided some interesting recollections about Williams. O'Brien told me he and Williams served together in 1960–61 at OSI District 12, St. Louis, Missouri.[16] O'Brien recalled that District 12 was commanded by a Maj. John (actually, Russell) Womack, whom O'Brien thinks may have served with Williams at Roswell. O'Brien told me, "Jack spoke to me several times of the 1947 incident. He mentioned there was considerable CIC activity, and that he and other agents had been posted to watch the skies with binoculars at night for an extended period." On one occasion, O'Brien remembers, Major Womack overheard Williams talking about Roswell, called him into his office, "and chewed him out." Williams never again discussed the matter with his District 12 colleagues.

The New Mexico skies produced many UFO reports in the late 1940s and early 1950s. The green fireball sightings were prominent among them and, because of their proximity to nuclear weapons research facilities and other highly sensitive installations, they generated considerable high-level interest and concern. Both what O'Brien recalls being told by Williams and the incident in which Womack braced Williams certainly are quite consistent with this, and thanks to Robert Todd's research, it is now known that Williams participated in the investigation of the January 1949 green fireball sighting near Roswell. In addition, it turns out Womack was also involved in the green fireball investigations when assigned to OSI District 17 at Kirtland Air Force Base in early 1950s.[17]

As we have seen, it takes very little for decades-old memories, especially those of similar matters to become intertwined, which is what I am convinced is the case here. Green fireballs and not a crashed flying saucer were behind the excitement and extra duty Williams was talking about around the District 12 water cooler.

Another possible CIC/OSI link to Roswell is Clair Miller, a retired OSI warrant officer, mentioned by Rickett as someone stationed at CIC headquarters (700th CIC Detachment), Washington, D.C., in July 1947. Rickett claimed to have talked with Miller at a meeting of former CIC/OSI agents sometime in 1980. In retirement, Rickett and Miller lived near each other in Florida, but this was their first meeting in about twenty-five years. In a 1989 interview with Schmitt, Rickett claimed he asked Miller about what happened to the material recovered at Roswell, and Miller responded, "Let's just say you didn't ask me. . . . I'll forget you asked me about that." Yet in a videotaped interview done the following year, with Schmitt doing the interviewing, Rickett mentioned Miller and specifically and unequivocally stated he never talked with him about Roswell.[18]

I wrote to Miller in March 1993, referring him to my Association of Former OSI Special Agents magazine article (Miller was the founding president of AFOSISA). He responded immediately with this curiously phrased note: "Regrets! I was stationed with the 700th CIC Det. in Washington, DC at the time. Not being directly involved in the activities in New Mexico, my knowledge would be very minimal. Anyhow, that is almost 46 years ago."[19]

I followed up with a telephone call. Miller was quite friendly and remembered Rickett very well, even volunteering the information that he had died recently. While repeating his denial of any knowledge of Roswell, Miller offered to help me track down others who might know something, which he did, leading to some helpful information. However, when it came to the cryptic conversation reported by Rickett, he merely chuckled and changed the subject. Questions about what he knew of the Roswell case produced responses similar to his "Regrets!" note.[20] Further attempts on both counts during a follow-up conversation elicited similar responses, and in a letter of April 4, 1993, Miller offered a slightly different version of his "I know nothing" answer: "I have no recollection relating to the 1947 Roswell/Corona case. I was stationed in Washington, DC at the time. I may have approved investigative expenditures relating to that case; but, that is 46 years of water under the bridge and my mind is blank. Sorry!!!!!!!"[21]

At the time, I was inclined to interpret Miller's words and unwillingness to discuss his alleged conversation with Rickett as polite attempts to avoid spilling the beans. In retrospect, it seems much more reasonable that the latter actually was a matter of avoiding speaking ill of a recently deceased former colleague, and that the former mean what they say and nothing more.

LESS THAN MEETS THE EYE

At every turn, the conventional wisdom Roswell diminishes under scrutiny. What seemed so promising when tarted up by hopeful expectation and a will to believe, the moral equivalents of colored spotlights at night on a carnival midway, begins more and more to look like not much more than clever manipulation of ordinary things and the words of a fast-talking barker enticing the rubes to step right up and marvel at strange creatures and other wonders from far-off lands.

Speaking of which, it is now time to dispose of the bodies.

NOTES

1. Audiotaped interview conducted by Mark Rodeghier, January 1990.

2. Ibid.; transcript of audiotaped interview conducted by Donald R. Schmitt, October 29, 1989.

3. Telephone interview with Doyle Rees, October 1992; letters from Rees to me, December 8, 1992, and August 20, 1993; various telephone conversations with Rees, 1992–93.

4. Rodeghier interview with Rickett, January 1990.

5. Ibid.; Kevin D. Randle and Donald R. Schmitt, *UFO Crash at Roswell* (New York: Avon, 1991), p. 119.

6. Letter to me, July 4, 1993; audiotaped telephone interview with Edgar J. Bethart, January 26, 1993.

7. Rodeghier interview with Rickett, January 1990; Schmitt interview with Rickett, October 1989; Randle and Schmitt, *UFO Crash*, p. 119; my personal interview with Sheridan W. and Mary Cavitt, July 7, 1995.

8. Karl T. Pflock, "Update: Roswell Army Air Field, July 1947," *AFOSISA Global Alliance* (April 1993): 28–29.

9. Audiotaped telephone interview with Earl L. Zimmerman, April 25, 1993; Zimmerman affidavit, app. H.

10. Zimmerman affidavit, app. H.

11. In an August 20, 1993, letter to the author, Doyle Rees confirmed Zimmerman's assignment to his District 17 headquarters at the time in question. Rees wrote that he thought very highly of Zimmerman.

12. Zimmerman affidavit, app. H.

13. Bethart interview, January 26, 1993.

14. Robert Todd, "LaPaz, Roswell, and Green Fireballs," *MUFON UFO Journal* (July 1994): 3–5.

15. These include Charles R. Shaw, William M. O'Brien, Edgar J. Bethart, Clair Miller, and Doyle Rees.

16. Doyle Rees provided me with the correct name and sought unsuccessfully to make contact with Womack for me.

17. Letter to the author from William M. O'Brien, February 5, 1993; audiotaped telephone interview with O'Brien, February 24, 1993; Loren E. Gross, *UFOs: A History—January–March 1950* (Port St. Lucie, Fla.: Arcturus Books, 1990), pp. 3, 91 (nn. 5 and 6).

18. Schmitt interview with Rickett, October 29, 1989; *Recollections of Roswell—Part II*, available from the Fund for UFO Research.

19. Letter to me from Clair Miller, March 22, 1993.

20. Telephone interview with Miller, April 14, 1993.

21. Letter to me from Miller, April 4, 1993.

ELEVEN

DISPOSING OF THE BODIES

D id the army recover cadavers of hapless extraterrestrials somewhere in Lincoln or Chaves or, even farther away, in Catron County; take them to the Roswell AAF hospital for preliminary examination; and then ship them out to Fort Worth AAF and, ultimately, on to another facility? In March 1994, as I was finishing *Roswell in Perspective*, the interim report on my investigation, I thought the answer could well be yes, at least with respect to a site in the general vicinity of Roswell.

Now I know I was a victim of my own wishful thinking and what seemed to me a very convincing story told by Glenn Dennis, a down-to-earth guy whom I liked very much—as it turns out, too much. This was reinforced by the seemingly plausible and supportive accounts of the crate flight (see chapter 9) and the alleged admissions of Pappy Henderson.

There also were other stories, stories I found wanting even then. In this chapter I will deal with those and the Henderson tale.

DOUBTFUL TALES

Of the alleged hundreds of Roswell witnesses (more about this particular issue anon), only four persons claiming firsthand knowledge of alien bodies have been interviewed by Roswell authors and identified publicly. These are Frank Kaufmann, who also claimed to have seen a crash survivor; the late Jim Ragsdale; a Lt. Col. Albert Lovejoy Duran; and one Gerald Anderson, who, like Kaufmann, told not only of seeing bodies but also a survivor, this at a third alleged crash site on the Plains of San Agustin in Catron County, about two hundred miles west-northwest of Roswell.[1]

New Mexico Jones, the anonymous person who telephoned Kevin Randle claiming to be an archaeologist, is the only other purported firsthand witness to the bodies with whom a researcher has talked and made public the details of his account. I exclude unquestionably real archaeologist W. Curry Holden from the list of firsthand witnesses to alien cadavers. Nothing in what little he told Randle just before his death at ninety-six gives any reason to believe he saw bodies, or for that matter, anything at all extraordinary, unless one is desperate to wring *something* out of the words, "I was there and I saw it all."

Other tales of alien bodies in direct or at least close connection with Roswell are second- and thirdhand or even more removed. Except for Dennis's, all are inconsistent in important ways with the more solidly established or, at least, generally accepted elements of the Roswell story.

Of the so-called firsthand witnesses, Kaufmann has claimed extensive knowledge of the bodies in the context of both the conventional wisdom and revisionist scenarios. In fact, along with Dennis's account, it is his that breathed life back into the Roswell bodies after researchers had hit a dead end with the Barney Barnett story, made public by Berlitz and Moore in their 1980 book *The Roswell Incident.* For a time, Ragsdale's tale was part of the revisionist scenario but then morphed into a more commercially viable form. Jones's anonymous account has been advanced uncritically in support of both versions of the Roswell legend, and although it has been asserted that Jones has been identified, this information has never been made public and no independent confirmation of Jones's claims has been developed.

For reasons set forth at length earlier, neither Kaufmann nor Ragsdale can be considered credible. Because of his anonymity and other concerns, also covered earlier, Jones's alleged recollections cannot be given any evidentiary weight. As for Duran, he surfaced in 1994 as a throwaway footnote in Randle and Schmitt's second book, then promptly sank from sight, never to be heard of or from again.[2]

As for Gerald Anderson, his story seemed too good to be true. It was.

Anderson was one of a number of self-described witnesses who came forward after the *Unsolved Mysteries* broadcasts in which the Barney Barnett story figured prominently. When he was a child of five, Anderson related, he and several family members stumbled upon a crashed saucer and its crew, all but one dead. While the Anderson clan was examining the wrecked saucer and attempting to communicate with the survivor, a group of archaeology students and their professor, a Dr. Buskirk, showed up, soon followed by a man in a pickup truck who "looked like Harry Truman" (Barnett somewhat resembled Truman, and a photo of him was shown on *Unsolved Mysteries*).

Next in the parade vividly recalled by Anderson was a U.S. Army contingent. The officer in command took charge of things, and he and his men prepared the way for a large, well-equipped detachment that in short order began arriving by both ground and air. According to Anderson, this officer, a redhead like the one who threatened Glenn Dennis (an alleged fact mentioned on *Unsolved Mysteries*), was quite nasty, and after swearing all the civilians to secrecy with attendant dire consequences if they broke their oaths, ran them off the site.

Apart from his phenomenally detailed memory of these events, especially for someone who was a child of five at the time they transpired, Anderson's story was soon found to include more than a few questionable elements. For example, he said his family was on the Plains searching for moss agate. Kevin Randle soon determined that agate, moss or otherwise, did not occur in the area where the events were alleged to have unfolded. By strange coincidence, Dr. Buskirk turned out to have the same name as one of Anderson's high school instructors, a teacher of anthropology, no less.

Randle also caught Anderson falsifying the bill for a long-distance telephone conversation he had with Randle. The altered bill was offered in an attempt to refute Randle's revelation that he had interviewed Anderson for more than an hour, during which time he had become suspicious of the man's story.

The final straw was what purported to be a diary kept by Ted Anderson, an uncle of Gerald's whom he said had been one of the family party when the crashed saucer had been discovered. The handwritten document, dated July 1947, included a brief account of the incident on the Plains of San Agustin. It was sent to ufologist Stanton Friedman under a typewritten letter from Uncle Ted's daughter Vallejean, a Catholic nun.

Forensic analysis revealed that the ink used to write the "1947" diary did not exist before 1970. Confronted with this difficulty, Anderson explained that his uncle wanted to give copies to various family members and so made multiple handwritten duplicates in the early 1970s. However, it seems Uncle Ted was killed in an auto accident in 1965, five years before the ink he supposedly used in this transcribing was manufactured. Meanwhile, Kevin Randle determined that the typewriter used to write the cover letter under which the diary was forwarded to Friedman seemed certain to have been also employed in altering the problematic telephone bill mentioned above.

There is more, but it is just icing on the cake. Clearly, Anderson's creative imagination was more remarkable than his memory.[3] However, it appears very likely that much of his story was based upon real events that he experienced firsthand or had read or been told about in some detail. I will explore this below.

It seems there can be no reasonable doubt that not one of the purported firsthand witnesses to alien bodies and a lonesome survivor is credible. Not one. This leaves only accounts attributed to others who supposedly had such firsthand knowledge.

Beverly Bean has testified her father, the late Sgt. Melvin Brown, told her he saw strange bodies on a truck at a crash site and later guarded the hangar in which they were temporarily stored. However, no other testimony or other evidence has emerged to corroborate Bean's claims. In addition, the description of the bodies she attributes to her father is significantly inconsistent with that provided by all other alleged witnesses. So, although this testimony is interesting, it offers scant comfort to those who want to believe bodies were found.

Barbara Dugger, granddaughter of Sheriff George Wilcox and his wife, Inez, has testified her grandmother told her the sheriff "went out to the site; it was in the evening. There was a big burned area, and he saw debris. He also saw four 'space beings.' One of the little men was alive. Their heads were large. They wore suits like silk." Dugger's aunt, George and Inez Wilcox's daughter Phyllis McGuire, says, "My mother talked to different members of the family about the event and said that there was a crash and there were bodies, but they could not talk about it."[4]

This dramatic testimony is thirdhand, from the sheriff to his wife to his daughter and granddaughter. Moreover, Dugger's account, which has been cited in support of both Roswell scenarios, includes a live alien and a large burned spot on the crash site, making it significantly inconsistent with other reports except, significantly, those of Frankie Rowe and Frank Kaufmann. Enough said.

Then there is the story attributed to John G. Tiffany, who told Stan Friedman and Don Schmitt his father claimed to have seen or to have had knowledge of unusual bodies. According to this account, during the summer of 1947, the elder Tiffany had been on a flight crew sent from Wright Field, Ohio, to an unnamed destination in Texas. "Once on the ground there, they picked up some of the debris and a large container that looked like a giant Thermos jug." Ostensibly, the debris was very light and very tough, with a "glasslike surface" and resistant to all attempts by Tiffany and his compatriots to "mark it, bend it, or break it." (One wonders what would have prompted such foolishness by military personnel charged with the custody of the material and why those in charge would have permitted it.) As for the bodies, while Tiffany said he was uncertain if his father was speaking from direct experience or only repeating what he had been told by others, he claimed his father described to him three dead beings, of which "two were intact and one had been dismembered. They had smooth features and skin, and all wore some sort of flying suit." Like Sergeant Brown, Tiffany's father seems not to have left any record of his alleged experience, and citing concerns about his U.S. government job, the younger Tiffany has refused to discuss the matter further.[5]

Thus, like so many of the tales of otherworldly bodies snatched up and stashed in various government facilities, Tiffany's gives us nothing useful to go on, at least as far as alien remains are concerned. However, the item described as a giant Thermos jug does suggest that the witness's father indeed was involved in transporting items recovered from a site near Roswell, probably the Foster Ranch debris field or somewhere nearby. I will explore this in due course, but now I must return to the body-tale count, beginning with the ever-more-significant role of Frank Joyce in the scheme of things Roswellian.

Joyce, the Radio KGFL announcer and United Press stringer who might have had a scoop had he taken Mack Brazel seriously the first time he spoke with him, has made a number of claims about his role in the Roswell story. The first, of course, is that he was the first newsman to speak with Brazel about his find, talking with the rancher on the telephone as he sat in Sheriff Wilcox's office. Although there is no corroborative evidence available, it seems reasonable to give Joyce the benefit of the doubt on this.

Joyce's second claim to fame is that it was he who broke the saucer crash story on July 8. It is true Joyce transmitted the news to UP that day. However, as I have shown, the real credit for breaking the story goes to George Walsh of rival radio station KSWS. Still, this is an understandable exaggeration or misrecollection, and the UP broadcast wire carried exchanges on July 8 that confirm Joyce's subsequent involvement in getting the story out.[6]

Frank Joyce's third significant claim is that he tried to persuade Walter Haut it was not a good idea to put out his sensational press release. He told me he ran after Haut as he left the KGFL station, urging him to hold off, but Haut dismissed his concerns by saying something like, "It's okay—the Old Man authorized it." Joyce also said he telephoned Haut at the base a short time later to try again, only to be brushed off once more. Later the same afternoon, Joyce told me, Haut called him to say he should have listened to him and not issued the release, and that he was being transferred out of Roswell forthwith.[7] I had discussed this with Haut the previous day, and he denied emphatically anything like this happened. He also pointed out he remained at Roswell AAF until being released from active duty in August 1948, more than a year later.[8]

The most important of Joyce's claims is that, late on July 8, Mack Brazel came to KGFL and told him the alleged cover story, indicating he was under considerable pressure from the army. Joyce has told researchers, including myself, that he pointed out to Brazel how different his new story was, "especially the part about the little green men." To which Brazel responded, "Only they weren't green."[9]

When I first considered this claim in *Roswell in Perspective*, I noted it raised two questions. First, and most obvious, nothing in what Joyce had said about his first contact with Brazel even implies "men"— dead, alive, little, green, or otherwise—were discussed, although Joyce did hint darkly that there was more to what Brazel told him than he had revealed circa 1992–94. No one else had suggested Brazel ever mentioned entities of any sort, alive or dead, and this remains the case.

The second question arises from a May 1982 interview with William L. Moore. In the transcript prepared by Moore, Joyce is quoted as claiming Walter E. Whitmore Sr., owner of KGFL, made the "LGM" remarks to him in 1952:

> . . . I later said to Mr. Whitmore on his deathbed—I had gone to see him while he was dying of cancer some years later—I went to see him at his home and I said, "Mr. Whitmore, you remember that time we went out to that ranch and all that stuff about the flying saucer and the weather balloon and so on?" And he said, "Yes." And I said to him, "Mr. Whitmore, what do you really think that was?" And he said, "I just think it was something that the military wanted to cover up." And that's all he would say. Later, as I was leaving, he called me back into the room and said, "Frank, I know you've heard some of those crazy stories about little green men." Now when he said that, it caught me by surprise, and I just said "Yes." And he said, "Well, they weren't green." And that's all he would say; just, "they weren't green." I couldn't get him to say any more about it and I never saw him again before he died.[10]

Joyce told me Moore misquoted him, so I contacted Moore. In November 1994, Moore sent me a copy of the letter in which Joyce provided corrections to and approved the transcript of their interview. One of the corrections was that it was Brazel with whom he had the exchange about LGMs. It seems Joyce had told Moore about his conversation with Brazel after the formal interview was concluded and they were walking to Joyce's car. Moore told me he made the error in notes he wrote later. In subsequent versions of the paper from which the above quote was taken, Moore presented the corrected version of Joyce's deathbed exchange with Whitmore—sans LGMs—although without acknowledging the previously published error. Still, earlier in the audio-taped portion of the interview, Joyce is quoted at length with respect to Brazel's alleged visit to KGFL, and nothing there even hints at a mention of LGMs by either the rancher or Joyce.[11]

Recently, ufologists Thomas Carey and Donald Schmitt reported on a May 1998 interview they conducted with Joyce. Carey and Schmitt write that Joyce told them, "I'm going to tell you fellows something I've never told anyone. Don't stop me once I get started, or I might realize what I'm doing and shut up." They then offer their "reconstruction" of the telephone conversation Joyce had with Brazel as the rancher sat in the Chaves County sherrif's office, "based on Joyce's comments to us in this interview":

Brazel: [angrily] Who's gonna clean all that stuff up? That's what I wanna know. I need someone out there to clean it up.

Joyce:	What stuff? What are you talking about?
Brazel:	[somberly] Don't know. Don't know what it is. Maybe it's from one of them flying saucer things.
Joyce:	Oh, really? Then you should call the Army air base. They are responsible for everything that flies in the air. They should be able to help you or tell you what it is.
Brazel:	[At this point, according to Joyce, Brazel really started "losing it."] Oh, God. Oh, my God. What am I gonna do? It's horrible, horrible, just horrible.
Joyce:	What is? What's horrible? What are you talking about?
Brazel:	The stench! Just awful.
Joyce:	Stench? From what? What are you talking about?
Brazel:	They're dead.
Joyce:	What? Who's dead?
Brazel:	Little people.
	[At this point, Joyce thought to himself, "This is crazy!" He decided to play the role of devil's advocate to a story he did not believe.]
Joyce:	What the . . . ? Where are they? Where did you find them?
Brazel:	Somewhere else.
Joyce:	Well, you know, the military is always firing rockets and experimenting with monkeys and things. So, maybe . . .
Brazel:	[Shouting] God dammit! They're not monkeys, and they're not human!

According to Carey and Schmitt, Joyce then told them he had a telephone call from Brazel

a day or so later . . . to tell me that he didn't have the story quite right the first time. So, I invited him over to the station. When he arrived, I could see the military waiting for him outside in the lobby, and he appeared to be under a great deal of stress. He then told me the new story, and that's when I challenged him about it and made the little green men comment, referring back to our original telephone conversation. That's when he replied that they weren't green, and out he went.[12]

Clearly, this new account is a significant departure from what Joyce previously had testified concerning his contacts with Brazel and raises obvious credibility questions. But there is more.

As I first pointed out in 1994, when assessing Joyce's recollections of July 1947 events, it is important to consider them in the context of other, highly unusual claims he has made. Despite being on the table for twelve years when I attempted to highlight them six years ago, these have received next to no notice from Roswell authors and believers. They involve a ride Joyce says he took to the Foster Ranch in 1947, sitting next to Walter Whitmore Sr. at the wheel of his "big Hudson" (according to his son, Whitmore drove a Cadillac), with a tall, mysterious man wearing a golden-yellow flight suit—"the Traveler"—in the back seat (Joyce has also told the story with the Traveler in the front passenger seat and himself in back). Among other things, Joyce alleges the Traveler never spoke, but used mind control to guide Joyce to a strange, dreamlike rendezvous with Mack Brazel in a tack room and corral on the ranch. This bizarre tale is detailed in Joyce's published interview with Moore, first made public in

1982, and Joyce has related the story to me and presented it publicly at least once himself.[15] Moreover, it is disturbingly similar in tone, mood, and content to other alleged experiences unrelated to Roswell with which Joyce regaled me off the record during our first interview in 1992.

It seems to me nothing more needs to be said about Frank Joyce's credibility with respect to the bodies or much else of consequence to the Roswell story. However, what of the recollections attributed by Kevin Randle and Don Schmitt to retired Air Force Brig. Gen. Arthur E. Exon?

When first made public in 1991, it seemed Exon's memories of the possibility that bodies had been flown from Roswell to Wright Field in 1947 might be based upon firsthand information. If so, this would be highly significant, especially since Exon also seemed to have firsthand knowledge of the debris field and crash site, as well as a shadowy high-level group established to keep the truth about Roswell under wraps. However, in a lengthy September 1992 telephone conversation, Exon told me his comments about bodies and debris at Wright Field were based solely upon rumors he heard from colleagues at Wright Field and nothing more. As for the "control group," he said he merely was making educated guesses as to who likely would have been selected for such a group. Finally, with respect to his alleged knowledge of the debris and crash sites, he told me he remembered flying over several sites in New Mexico quite some time after July 1947, on missions having nothing to do with the Roswell incident. One such location might have fit what he had been told about the crash site by ufologists because it had vehicle tracks running to it.[14]

PAPPY'S LITTLE JOKE

Consider now the accounts of Sappho Henderson and Mary Kathryn Groode, respectively widow and daughter of First Air Transport Unit command pilot Pappy Henderson, and Dr. John Kromschroeder, a dentist, retired naval officer, and friend of Pappy Henderson. All three have testified Pappy told them he flew Roswell debris to Wright Field and at some point saw some strange bodies. Groode and her mother said Henderson had never said a word about his experience until 1980 or 1981, when he saw a newspaper article about Roswell, which he took to mean the matter was no longer classified. Pappy's widow said he described "strange," small "beings . . . with large heads for their size. He said the material that their suits were made of was different than anything he had ever seen." She added she seemed to recall his mentioning "the bodies had been packed in dry ice to preserve them."

Groode, the Hendersons' daughter, said her father described the "alien beings as small and pale, with slanted eyes and large heads. He said they were humanoid looking, but different from us." She also thought her father said he had seen three bodies. Kromschroeder claimed Henderson told him he had flown both "wreckage and alien bodies to Wright Field" and "described the beings as small." Kromschroeder also said Pappy showed him a piece of unusual metal, which he told his friend was a piece of the crashed flying saucer that had carried the aliens to their deaths.[15]

Kromschroeder's credibility is shaky at best. Among other things, he is a devotee of devastatingly discredited Pleiadean contactee-photographer Eduard "Billy" Meier. In addition, he claims to have applied metallurgical knowledge acquired in his dental profession to an analysis of Henderson's metal fragment, finding it to be somehow out of the ordinary, and to have applied an electrical current to the fragment, causing the material to emit a soft blue glow while remaining cold to the touch.[16]

This is all very interesting. However, it hardly gives us reason to have any confidence in the dentist's story beyond the possibility that Henderson did indeed show him a bit of metal, saying it was from a flying saucer, the dead crew and wreckage of which he had secretly airlifted from New Mexico to Ohio.

What of the testimony of Henderson's widow and daughter? At first blush, it seems entirely sincere and credible. The former likely is true. However, when we get to know Pappy better, the latter becomes most unlikely.

When Henderson left the air force not long after the 1947 incident, he and his wife decided to settle in Roswell. The family lived in Roswell for an additional thirteen years, and Pappy became a successful roofing contractor. The Hendersons were a very popular couple. They numbered among their friends such key Roswell affair personalities as Glenn Dennis and his second wife, Walter Haut and his wife, and Mr. and Mrs. Robert Shirkey. Besides being an avid partygoer and bridge enthusiast, Henderson was renowned for his sense of humor and as an active and accomplished practical joker well known for his clever gags.[17]

So it would seem tales of transporting alien bodies and flying saucer wreckage would be right up Henderson's alley. This becomes more than mere speculation when the testimony of Jonathan Smith, one of Henderson's former comrades in arms, is considered. It seems that among Henderson's souvenirs were fragments of a German V-2 rocket, which he acquired while stationed overseas. Smith told author Kal Korff that Henderson delighted in showing friends and others these bits of World War II vintage wreckage and claiming they were from a "crashed UFO."[18]

It is not a great leap from this information to the possibility that, inspired by a tabloid article about Berlitz and Moore's *Roswell Incident*, which was published in 1980, Henderson made John Kromschroeder one of the victims of his little joke. Given Kromschroeder's strong interest in UFOs and, especially, his naive acceptance of Meier's claims, he would have been an all but irresistible target. An elaboration about seeing the strange bodies thrown in for good measure, bolstered by probably unwitting family members, would make the gag even more delicious. Of course, this cannot be proven, but the circumstantial evidence is strong enough to discount the Henderson story unless and until something solidly supportive of it comes along.

This leaves Glenn Dennis, to whom the next chapter is devoted.

NOTES

1. The best representation of the Anderson story is found in Stanton T. Friedman and Don Berliner, *Crash at Corona* (New York: Paragon, 1992).

2. Kevin D. Randle and Donald R. Schmitt, *The Truth About the UFO Crash at Roswell* (New York: Evans, 1994), p. 8.

3. For detailed discussion of the Anderson saga see George M. Eberhart, *The Plains of San Agustin Controversy* (Chicago and Washington, D.C.: Center for UFO Studies and Fund for UFO Research, 1992); Randle and Schmitt, *Truth*; Kal K. Korff, *The Roswell UFO Crash: What They Don't Want You to Know* (Amherst, N.Y.: Prometheus Books, 1997); Kevin D. Randle, *The Randle Report: UFOs in the '90s* (New York: Evans, 1997); Philip J. Klass, *The Real Roswell Crashed-Saucer Coverup* (Amherst, N.Y.: Prometheus Books, 1997).

4. Dugger affidavit, app. H; McGuire affidavit on file with the Fund for UFO Research. See also videotaped interviews in *Recollections of Roswell—Part II*, available from the Fund for UFO Research.

5. Tiffany as attributed in Kevin D. Randle and Donald R. Schmitt, *UFO Crash at Roswell* (New York: Avon, 1991), pp. 103–104.

6. Audiotaped personal interview with Frank Joyce, November 3, 1992.

7. Ibid.

8. Haut interview, November 2, 1992.

9. Joyce interview, November 3, 1992.

10. As attributed in William L. Moore, "The Roswell Investigation: New Evidence in the Search for a Crashed UFO," *MUFON Symposium Proceedings, 1982* (Seguin, Texas: Mutual UFO Network, 1982), p. 94.

11. Ibid., p. 92; Karl. T. Pflock, "Little Green Men," letter to the editor, *MUFON UFO Journal* (December 1994): 19.

12. Thomas J. Carey and Donald R. Schmitt, "Mack Brazel Reconsidered," *International UFO Reporter* (winter 1999): 18.

13. Moore, "Roswell Investigation," pp. 89–94; Joyce interview, November 3, 1992; Joyce presentation before New Mexico MUFON, spring 1993.

14. Randle and Schmitt *UFO Crash*, pp. 108–12, 231–34; telephone interview with Arthur E. Exon, September 30, 1992.

15. Henderson, Groode, and Kromschroeder affidavits, app. H. See also videotaped interviews with all three in *Recollections*.

16. Kromschroeder affidavit, app. H; videotaped interview in *Recollections*; and Randle and Schmitt, *UFO Crash*, p. 95.

17. A number of persons who were friends of the Hendersons in their Roswell days have told me about Pappy's talent as a practical joker. Among these are Glenn Dennis, Walter Haut, and Robert Shirkey, none of whom have any reason to undermine the credibility of the Pappy Henderson story, in fact, quite the opposite.

18. Korff, *Roswell UFO Crash*, pp. 94–95.

TWELVE

GLENN DENNIS

Now we come to the heart of the body of evidence on which rests the case for dead aliens having been recovered somewhere in the vicinity of Roswell in July 1947. Glenn Dennis's account is bizarre. Dennis himself says, "If someone else was telling this story, I wouldn't believe him." I should have listened to him.

Consider, the story sounds like a B-grade thriller conceived by Oliver Stone on a good day: strange inquiries about body preservation methods and small, child-size caskets; threats and manhandling ordered by a ruthless army officer; strangely marked debris unlike that described by others, seen in the back of a military ambulance; Dennis's being escorted out of Roswell AAF hospital and off the base by military policemen; further threats from the military conveyed through Sheriff Wilcox and Dennis's father; a bizarre tale of an autopsy of three weird bodies told and illustrated with drawings of the corpses by a nearly hysterical nurse; and the disappearance of that nurse without a trace.

When I began my investigation, I was more skeptical of this testimony than anything else about the case. A couple of attentive viewings of unedited videotape of an interview with Dennis conducted by representatives of the Fund for UFO Research had me saying to myself, "Would you buy a used car from that guy? No way!"

Then, in late 1992, I met and interviewed Dennis for the first time. Despite myself, I was favorably impressed and decided I might have jumped to conclusions about the man. During the ensuing two years, I got to know Dennis very well and found that I liked and trusted him. I also learned that he was well respected in both Roswell and Lincoln, where his principal residence was located and where he served in various civic capacities. Although many I spoke with found his story hard to swallow, everyone qualified this by saying something like, "If Glenn said it happened, then you can bet it did."

In addition, two witnesses were found who provided testimony that seemed to lend important support to Dennis's story. The first of these was L. M. Hall, a former Roswell chief of police and in 1993 a member of the Roswell City Council. In a personal interview, Hall told me he had sketchy recollections of Dennis telling him of a call from the base about small caskets, "probably a couple of days after the stories about a crashed flying saucer appeared in the Roswell papers." Hall said he thought Dennis was trying to catch him with "one of those 'gotcha' jokes" because he said the army wanted the caskets for " 'those aliens,' something to that effect," implicitly referring to the crashed-saucer story.[1]

Clearly, Hall's recollections were fragmentary and uncertain. His memory of Dennis referring to the army needing coffins for "those aliens" is unlikely at best, since in 1947 the term *alien* had not yet become virtually synonymous with *extraterrestrial being*. Moreover, if Hall was correct in recalling that the conversation took place a day or two after the crashed-disk story was bannered in the *Roswell Daily Record*, it would seem the army's dire threats had not had much impact on Dennis. Still, the possibility the newly minted embalmer had said something to someone at the time of the incident was at least a hopeful sign.

A critical difficulty with Dennis's story is the alleged disappearance of his friend, the army nurse who he said claimed to have been involved in the examination of several strange bodies. Dennis testified that she was transferred overseas, to London, a matter of days after she told him of her bizarre experience. Sometime later, he said, he was told by other nurses at the Roswell AAF hospital that they had heard rumors she had been killed in a plane crash somewhere in Europe or Great Britain, and he claimed a letter he wrote to her was returned, marked "DECEASED."

Research by myself, aviation writer and ufologist Don Berliner, Kevin Randle, and others failed to uncover evidence of an aircraft accident in which the nurse was or could have been a victim. No official records of the existence of a nurse with the name Dennis gave me and other investigators—birth and school documents, military service files, and so on—or her presence at Roswell AAF in July 1947 were found. Similarly, no record of her family could be located.

Some suggested the nurse never existed. This was my primary problem with Dennis's story. The person he claimed was a firsthand witness to alien bodies was too conveniently missing. Then Stan Friedman, who had been doggedly tracking down members of Squadron M, the base medical unit, got a lead. He found someone who claimed to remember the nurse.

In July 1947, David Wagnon was nineteen and a private first class in the Army Air Forces, serving as a technician in the Roswell AAF hospital. In a September 1993 interview, he told me, as set down in an affidavit he signed in November 1993,

> I do not recall anything about a crashed flying saucer incident during the time I was stationed at RAAF, but I do remember an Army nurse named Naomi Self, who was assigned to the base hospital. She was small, attractive, in her twenties, and, I believe, a brunette. I seem to recall Miss Self was transferred from RAAF while I was still stationed there, but I am not at all certain about this.

Wagnon also told me another reason he remembered "Self" so well was that she was very attractive and, unfortunately for PFC Wagnon, an officer.

In independent interviews with Wagnon, both Friedman and I got the same story. Dennis had identified the nurse as Naomi Self in an interview with Friedman on August

5, 1989, according to the transcript even spelling out the last name. Dennis had referred to the nurse as Naomi, then Friedman asked, "Do you remember her last name?" Dennis replied, "Yeah, Self, S-E-L-F." The alleged correct spelling of her name (see below) was known to me at the time I drafted the affidavit based upon my interview with Wagnon, but I deliberately misspelled it in the document in order to facilitate assessment of information received from others claiming knowledge of the nurse.

I was very careful not to lead Wagnon, simply including Naomi Self in lists of names I asked him one by one if he remembered and, if so, what he remembered about each person. I did not spell out any of the names for him. Friedman told me he used the same approach. Wagnon seemed quite truthful. Moreover, he did not come forward, he had to be found by Friedman. It appeared that, thanks to his testimony, the most troublesome cloud of doubt over Dennis's story might have a silver lining.

These developments, coupled with my personal experience with Dennis and those who knew him, caused me to revise my assessment of the man and his story. When the time came to write *Roswell in Perspective* in late 1993, I was convinced Dennis was telling the truth as best he could remember it. While there were some inconsistencies and overly dramatic elements in his story, I chalked them up to honest failings of memory and understandable exaggeration, not as indications of attempts to deceive and calculated hype. I was certain the Roswell affair involved strange bodies. The only significant uncertainties seemed to be whether these bodies were of earthly or extraterrestrial origin and what became of them and why.

REEMERGING DOUBTS

My Roswell investigation did not end with the publication of *RiP* in June 1994. I continued to pursue leads, with a particular emphasis on Dennis's story. In January 1995, an Associated Press story based on an interview with Dennis appeared in newspapers across the country. The article, by AP reporter Tim Korte, included something I had never heard before. Dennis had told Korte the nurse had told him the two doctors, pathologists, whom she had assisted in their examination of the bodies were from the army's Walter Reed Hospital, near Washington, D.C. As skeptical ufologist Philip Klass has pointed out, this called into question Dennis's claim to have been consulted about the effects of embalming fluid.[4] If army pathologists were on the scene, Dennis's advice would not have been needed.

This new revelation introduced other difficulties as well. In March 1994, Dennis had told me he recently had a flash recall that, shortly after returning to his office from the meeting at which the nurse had told him of the bodies, the *Roswell Daily Record* had been delivered (he later changed this, saying he saw the paper on his desk that evening when he went into his office to write an obituary). This was the July 8 edition with its lead story of the army's "capture" of a crashed flying saucer. This "established" that the autopsy and Dennis's confrontation with the redheaded captain (or colonel) had taken place the day before, July 7. But for that to be the case, the doctors would have had to leave Washington that morning—before Mack Brazel arrived in Roswell, alerting the army to his discovery.

If Dennis's claims about the newspaper and the pathologists both were true, the bodies had to have been discovered sometime before July 7. In which case, it is hardly likely that base intelligence officer Jesse Marcel would have been available to take Sheriff Wilcox's call about Brazel. He and quite probably CIC detachment commander Capt. Sheridan Cavitt all but certainly would have been out of pocket, on the site where the bodies had been found. So which of Dennis's recollections could be trusted?

I contacted Tim Korte and asked him if his story as published had the matter of the Walter Reed pathologists correct. The journalist checked his notes and told me there was no discrepancy. That's what Dennis had told him. I followed up with Dennis, who told me he had been misquoted. What he claimed to have said was that he had suggested to the Roswell base hospital mortuary officer that he should contact Walter Reed about body preservation, the effects of embalming fluid, and so on.[5]

The March 1995 issue of Philip Klass's *Skeptics UFO Newsletter*, or *SUN*, reported on the AP story and raised the same issues that had occurred to me. I called Klass and told him what Dennis had related to me. Phil told me an article that had appeared sometime earlier also quoted Dennis as saying the two pathologists had come in from Walter Reed. He read me the relevant portions of the piece, "Embalming E.T.," by mortician John Sime.

I contacted Sime by telephone on April 12, 1994. He said he was "90 percent certain" that this is what Dennis had told him, although there was nothing in his interview notes about it. Sime also sent me a copy of his article, which had appeared in the November 1994 issue of the *American Funeral Director*, a national magazine. Sime wrote, "The nurse also stated [to Dennis] that the two men following her out of the storage room [where the autopsies allegedly took place] were pathologists from Walter Reed hospital in Washington, D.C."

As if it were needed, the May 1995 issue of *SUN* carried further confirmation. The story reported that in a March 20, 1994, on-camera interview with Dayton, Ohio, television investigative reporter Carl Day, Dennis had said, "The guys . . . they were flown in from Walter Reed Hospital in Washington and they were doing a partial autopsy."

Once again I raised the issue in a telephone conversation with Glenn Dennis. This time he did not deny having told AP reporter Korte that the army doctors were from Walter Reed. He claimed he did not recall having done so and grudgingly admitted he "probably" had said it in his interview with Day.[6] There was no "probably" about it.

Once again I was forced reluctantly to reconsider my assessment of Dennis just as I had begun working on a long article about him for the now-defunct *Omni* magazine. I had been commissioned to interview Dennis and write a piece that would present his story unfiltered by my and others' opinions and interpretations. Shortly after speaking with Sime, I journeyed to historic Lincoln, New Mexico, where Dennis and his wife Kay reside for most of the year. For two days, I was their guest and spent hours interviewing Glenn, with Kay chiming in now and then. I got everything on audiotape, and there were several follow-up telephone conversations, one of them in connection with the Carl Day interview. Approved in writing by Dennis, the article appeared in the fall 1995 *Omni*, along with two other features about Roswell.

During our interview, I asked Dennis again about his on-camera conversation with Carl Day, asking, "Did the nurse know who the doctors were or where they came from?" Dennis replied, "I asked her, and she said she'd never seen them before. She told me she heard one say to the other that they'd have to do something when they got back to Walter Reed Army Hospital." This exchange appears in my *Omni* article, and this particular version of Dennis's recollections about where the doctors had come from and why he thought it was Walter Reed is what he now tells everyone who asks about the matter. Like other discredited features of Roswell witness accounts, the flash "recollection" about the newspaper and its "confirming" headline has quietly gone by the board.[7]

THE NAME GAME

Stan Friedman located Glenn Dennis in late summer 1989 when he was in New Mexico working on the *Unsolved Mysteries* segment that would catapult the Roswell affair into the minds of the general public to stay. Friedman conducted an audio-taped interview with Dennis on August 5, 1989, during which, according to the transcript of the conversation, Dennis identified the "missing" nurse as Naomi Self, "S-E-L-F."

In an attempt to facilitate a thorough search for information about the nurse, Friedman confidentially provided the name to Kevin Randle and Don Schmitt. It appears likely that, unbeknownst to Friedman, Dennis had independently provided the name to Randle and Schmitt and to Mark Wolf, a video-documentary producer with whom they were working. Thus began the search for the missing nurse or, at least, evidence and testimony that might independently back up Dennis's story about her.

In a 1994 interview with journalist and ufologist Paul McCarthy, Schmitt claimed that not only had his and Randle's efforts failed to turn up any trace of the nurse, but also that they could find no official records of the five nurses whose photographs were published in the 1947 Roswell Army Air Field yearbook. Schmitt claimed the search covered every possible base and said, "Once again it appears as if they really covered their tracks," implying the U.S. government had purged official records in order to keep the crashed-saucer, alien-bodies tale under wraps.[8]

The following year, researching an article about the missing nurse that appeared in the same issue of *Omni* as my piece, and having no reason not to believe what Schmitt had told him, McCarthy was stunned when, in the space of three days, he came up with the records of the five yearbook nurses. Naomi Self remained among the missing, but contrary to Schmitt's dramatic claim, here was everyone else.

At the time, four of the five women from the yearbook were deceased. The fifth, retired Air Force Lt. Col. Rosemary J. Brown (in 1947, Rosemary A. McManus), was still living and residing in a Wisconsin nursing home not far from where Schmitt lives. McCarthy interviewed her and learned,

> . . . Yes, she had been stationed in Roswell in July 1947. She remembered the other four yearbook nurses, but not Nurse X [Self], and not Glenn Dennis himself.
> What's more, she told me, she had witnessed nothing to suggest a crash at

Roswell or any other unusual goings-on at the base hospital. "I had no sense of any-thing weird happening at all. . . ."[9]

Brown has since passed away, but not before being interviewed by U.S. Air Force Capt. James McAndrew, the principal investigator in the air force's reluctant Roswell research effort, and Victor Golubic, a ufologist who pursued a diligent and thorough search for any trace of the missing nurse. Brown told them the same story she had told McCarthy.

I conducted my first interview with Glenn Dennis on November 2, 1992. During that meeting, I told Dennis that the Fund for UFO Research was working with staff of the U.S. Congress to arrange for a formal congressional request for the nurse's records. He responded by telling me other Roswell researchers did not have the spelling of her name quite right. It was not Self, as he had so careful spelled out for Stan Friedman in 1989, but Selff, double *f*. He then volunteered her middle name, Maria, which he said he had not given to any other ufologist. He asked me not to share the middle name with my colleagues and to conduct any investigation I pursued quietly.

Since this was the first time we had ever met and Dennis knew next to nothing about me, I was surprised by this turn of events. I asked him why he would trust me with this information. He said he really did not think the other researchers knew what they were doing, "don't really trust 'em," but that with my "background and connec-tions" I might actually be able to learn something. He really wanted to know what had happened to the nurse, he said.

In a later telephone conversation (May 26, 1994), Dennis told me Naomi's grand-father had immigrated the United States because he had "had a real hard time" in the "old country," and he had changed the family name "to make it American" by short-ening it to Selff. Dennis said he did not recall Grandfather Selff's native land and was not even certain he ever knew it, though less than a year later, during our April 1995 interview for *Omni*, he told me he thought her mother was Italian and her father Greek.

Other than a possible confirmation of Selff's existence from David Wagnon, my efforts came up dry. Among these was an attempt to contact her through a service pro-vided by the U.S. Social Security Administration (SSA). In mid-1993, Dennis had told me that he was beginning to think she actually had not been killed in an airplane crash, but rather that this was a cover story, disinformation to discourage any further inquiries by him and others. As he later repeated during our interview for *Omni*, "This is just my surmise, but I think when she was transferred, they discharged her and arranged for her to join an order, enter a convent. Everything was done with the [Catholic] church's help." After all, he pointed out, she had planned to become a nun when she left the service anyway.

By mid-1993, "Sister Naomi" would have been in her seventies and probably retired. I had learned that, while the SSA would not reveal the whereabouts of persons on the Social Security rolls, it would forward what it considered important postage-paid letters to them, leaving to the recipients' discretion whether or not to make con-tact with their correspondents.

I drafted a letter to Selff and a cover letter to the SSA, and sent them to Dennis to sign. Months went by. They either had not gotten to him or had gotten lost. He told me he did not remember for sure. Finally, almost a year later, he signed new copies I prepared, and I mailed them to the SSA in June 1994. In late July, the cover letter and envelope addressed to Naomi Selff was returned by the SSA. A form letter advised that Dennis's communication did not meet the agency's requirements: "We will forward letters only when the letter has important information that we feel [the addressee] does not know, and he/she would want to be informed."

Meanwhile, Golubic and McAndrew had come on the scene, and both were in touch with me. They not only had found the records for the nurses in the Roswell AAF yearbook, they had found them for *every* army nurse who had served in 1947. There was not one Naomi Maria Selff. Nor was there anyone whose name even slightly resembled Naomi Selff, with or without the middle name Maria.

Moreover, Golubic informed me he had conducted a photographic lineup with David Wagnon. It included all the nurses assigned to Roswell AAF/Walker Air Force Base during 1947 and 1948. From this he had determined with little room for doubt that Wagnon's memories were of one of the five women whose photos were in the base yearbook. Wagnon was quite sincere in his efforts to help, but he was mistaken in his recollections.

Golubic's efforts were far-reaching and exhaustive. Dennis claimed Selff was a native of St. Paul, Minnesota, and had done all her schooling there. Golubic conducted a fruitless genealogical search of Minnesota families with surnames similar to Selff (there were no Selffs). He searched massive files of Cadet Nurse Corps identification cards from the mid-1940s with no hits. He located and interviewed a nurse who had been assigned to Roswell just before July 1947 and another who reported in soon after. Both remembered the five women in the yearbook. Neither recalled Naomi Selff. He located and interviewed Col. J. Comstock, the Roswell AAF hospital commander in July 1947. Comstock remembered nothing of either Selff or anything to do with an alleged saucer crash or examination of strange bodies in his facility.

Still Golubic did not give up. Learning that Kevin Randle had made multiple unsuccessful Freedom of Information Act requests for copies of the hospital morning reports, which record the names and serial numbers of personnel going on or returning from leave, reporting for duty or being transferred out, and so on, Golubic decided to give it a try himself. He knew that errors were frequently made in searching and reviewing records in response to FOIA requests. After several attempts, his efforts were rewarded with Roswell AAF Squadron M (medical staff) morning reports covering the period October 1, 1946, through December 31, 1947. Naomi Selff was nowhere to be found in those documents, nor was any name that came even somewhat close.[10]

In late 1995, Golubic told Dennis he had a problem. Naomi Selff seemed not to have ever existed. This did not faze Dennis, who told the surprised researcher that the name he had given Randle, Schmitt, Friedman, Wolf, and me was not his friend's real name at all. It seems he did not like or trust any of us, and so had provided versions of a name that were only close to the real one. He refused to give Golubic the real name, but did condescend to share with him what he claimed was the first letter of the nurse's real surname.

About the same time, word got around the Roswell research fraternity that Dennis had told one of our number that the nurse's name actually was Naomi Sipes. This struck me and others as highly unlikely, since it was so close to Naomi Selff that it certainly would have been spotted and considered by the bevy of investigators on the nurse's trail. No Naomi Sipes had been turned up.

According to Kevin Randle, "When it was pointed out that no documentation, no corroboration, that nothing verified the existence of the nurse, Dennis changed the tale again. He had not supplied anyone with the right name. In fact, the last name didn't even begin with an 'S.' "[11]

In April 1995, during the interview for my *Omni* article, Dennis and I had the following exchange about the nurse's name:

KTP: You have provided some researchers with what you say is the nurse's real name. Why?

GD: I would like to know what happened to her and have someone verify my story.

KTP: It has been alleged you made up the name you gave researchers.

GD: No, no way. I have never done that.

KTP: Others have suggested that you provided the wrong name or, possibly, a misspelled name, due to imperfect memory. Is that possible?

GD: Yes, I guess it's possible I don't have her name quite right.

KTP: Several researchers are attempting to locate the nurse under the name Naomi Maria Selff, which has been published by UFO skeptic Philip J. Klass. Is this her true name?

GD: I promised her I would never reveal her real name, so I can't confirm or deny. If she's still alive, I don't want her to get in any more trouble. I don't want her or her family to be bothered, either.

KTP: Anyone who could conceivably confirm your story seems to be dead. Obviously, as long as you refuse to provide the nurse's name so it can be fully and openly checked out, people will continue to consider your story suspect. Doesn't this concern you?

GD: It doesn't make a damn bit of difference to me. They can believe it or not.

KTP: Would you be willing to give *Omni* the nurse's true name so the magazine can attempt to locate her?

GD: To answer the first question: definitely not, and I've already said why. If I ever got proof she was dead, I probably would make her name known or confirm it.[12]

Baloney by any other name—Naomi Maria Selff, if you like—is still baloney.

THE "NURSE"'S DRAWINGS AND WHAT PROBABLY INSPIRED THEM

One of the features of Dennis's account that seemed to lend it substance were the drawings of alien bodies he claimed had been sketched for him by Naomi Self/Selff/Sipes/X. Dennis told me and other ufologists that, when he and the nurse met at the Roswell AAF officers' club the day after the incident at the base hospital, she had given them to him. During our interview for *Omni*, I asked about this:

KTP: Why do you think she came to you instead of someone else?

GD: Because she'd seen me at the hospital and thought I knew something, I suppose. . . .

KTP: She took notes during the examination [of the alien bodies]. Did she also make drawings?

GD: No. She did that, that night. . . .

KTP: Why did she decide to make the drawings?

GD: She made the drawings for me—but only after I'd made a solemn oath I'd never reveal her connection to them. [But she had done the sketches the previous night, before Dennis had been able to contact her and arrange their meeting or make a solemn oath about anything.] She wanted to know if I saw the same things she saw. She asked me if they brought the—I think she called them "creatures"—to the funeral home. I told her I hadn't seen the bodies, that they hadn't been taken to Ballard's [the funeral home where Dennis worked].

KTP: What did she make the drawings on and with what? Were there any notations?

GD: They were in pencil, and she did them on the back of a prescription pad. . . .

KTP: What did she do with the drawings after she showed them to you?

GD: She gave them to me. She said she wanted me to have them. I think maybe it was for her protection. She said, "Guard them with your life."[13]

Dennis told me he kept the drawings hidden for a long while, then put them in a personal file at the Ballard Funeral Home, occasionally taking them out and looking at them. Yet, as he told me more than once, when he finally ended his on-again, off-again employment at Ballard's in 1962, he inexplicably left all his files and the vitally important drawings behind.

Not long after their initial interview in early August 1989, Dennis gave Stan Friedman sketches he claimed to have made from his memory of what the nurse had drawn. This seems to have been a short while after he and Friedman had gone to the funeral home, in search of the original drawings. The filing cabinets were still there in the basement, but they were empty. The mortuary manager told the duo that he and another man, Joe Lucas (who at one time had been a business partner of Dennis's), had hauled all the old files to the city dump some years before.[14]

The Dennis drawings were first made public in Kevin Randle and Don Schmitt's 1991 book *UFO Crash at Roswell*, credited as "drawings by Glenn Dennis . . . based on the actual drawings done . . . by the nurse who participated in the preliminary autopsies. . . ."[15] I subsequently learned from Dennis that "his" drawings had actually been done by well-known New Mexico artist Walter Henn, a neighbor of Dennis's in Lincoln. Henn had worked from rough sketches and verbal descriptions given by Dennis as the artist drew.

In early 1995, I spoke with Henn by telephone, a partially audio-taped conversation. The artist was rather indignant about not being given credit for his work. He told me he understood that the credit line in Randle and Schmitt's first book could have been an honest mistake, but when "the second edition"—actually *Crash at Corona* by Stan Friedman and Don Berliner, published in 1992—still gave the credit to Dennis, he became very angry. He had contacted Dennis after seeing his work miscredited in the Randle and Schmitt book and had been assured by his neighbor that the "error" would not be repeated. Ironically, *Crash at Corona* got it doubly wrong, giving the credit to Glenn "Davis."

I asked Henn how it had come to pass that he had done the drawings for Dennis. He told me Dennis had approached him "a few years ago," saying he had been interviewed by a "UFO researcher," undoubtedly Friedman, who wanted to see the drawings the nurse had done. These were missing, so Dennis had decided to reproduce them as best he could, but needed professional help to do the job right. According to Henn, Dennis said, "We could make a lot of money out of this," and suggested Henn sign the drawings. The artist demurred, saying, "No, I don't care about signing these, but give me a byline."

Henn told me, "If I wanted to be vindictive about the thing, he [Dennis] could be sued for that, because that's not a right thing to do. But I'm not going to do anything like that. But I also don't want to be part [of] or party to anything that's going to make him more of a hero."

At the time, I attributed Henn's concerns to sour grapes, but as the case against Dennis's credibility began to build, I reassessed this and other factors bearing on the origin and inspiration of the drawings, some of which I had been aware of before my chat with Henn. In 1994, I learned that the *Roswell Daily Record* had run two front-page stories about the alleged crashed-saucer incident in June 1987. The first of these, appearing in the Sunday, June 7 edition of the paper, reported that Stan Friedman had claimed "he has seen documentation that indicates as many as four aliens, small in stature, and not resembling any biological species known on earth, were also found by RAAF [Roswell Army Air Field] crews about two miles from the Corona crash site."

The following day, the newspaper ran a follow-up story featuring frontal and profile drawings of artist Vincent DePaula's conception of what the faces and heads of "the aliens who crashed near Corona might have looked like." These drawings are remarkably similar to the Dennis-Henn "reconstructions" of the facial and profile sketches allegedly done by Naomi Selff.

According to Robert Shirkey, the former Roswell AAF assistant operations officer, the day after the drawings appeared in the *Daily Record*, Glenn Dennis casually mentioned them to him. In 1994, Shirkey told me that, as he and Dennis and their wives were leaving after dinner at the home of Walter Haut, Dennis said something to this effect: "Bob, you know those pictures of the aliens in the paper yesterday? Well, that's really what they looked like." When Shirkey sought more information, Dennis refused to elaborate. He also denied such a conversation had taken place when I asked him about it.

A little more than two years later, on August 5, 1989, Shirkey drove Stan Friedman from Roswell to Lincoln so the ufologist could interview Dennis for the first time. This is what was said about alien likenesses, presented here as set down in the verbatim interview transcript:

GD: . . . then later on 2 or three days or so after this was over [!], then where she drew me the diagram of what she had saw [*sic*] and what it was all about another thing she was telling me on the anatomy this is what I was wondering. *The other day on the TV I saw where they had pictures of little guys*[.]

STF: It was probably from my interview?

GD: Was that from your deal?

STF: Yeah, I'll show you the slide[.] I've got it with me.

GD: Ok this [Friedman's slide] is what it was, and I was wondering where they got that information on the other day because you were talking about the eyes and the heads and all that ok and I have a diagram somewhere that she drew me[.]

STF: I'd love to see that.

[Emphasis added.]

It is very likely the drawings Friedman had exhibited on local television a day or two before he interviewed Dennis and then showed Dennis in Lincoln were those done by Vincent DePaula. According to the *Roswell Daily Record* story of June 8, 1987, in which DePaula's drawings were featured, they had been created at the request of an unnamed "UFO researcher."

It is also more than a little noteworthy that later in the Friedman-Dennis interview this exchange took place:

GD: . . . See[,] I understand these bodies weren't in the same location as where they found [the crashed saucer]. . . .

STF: Where did you get that?

GD: I understand the bodies were found several miles away[,] a few miles away from the crash site itself.

STF: *Was that from the stuff I sent you* or stuff you heard before?

GD: The impression I got or I heard out there was there was reason I think, this is my reasoning, the way I reason it out, they said that the bodies weren't in the vehicle itself, *the bodies were separated a couple or 2–3 miles from it.* [Emphasis added.]

Clearly, enough motivation and conveniently available raw material existed to have inspired and facilitated Dennis's creative imagination and spawned his alien autopsy drawings, with the innocent assistance of artist Walter Henn. Whatever may be the exact genesis of these controversial renderings, it is a safe-as-houses bet they are not representations of Dennis's memories of nonexistent sketches drawn by the nonexistent Naomi Maria Selff.[16]

It is also a very safe bet that the notion of bodies being found at a second, relatively nearby site—mentioned by Dennis to Friedman in August 1989 and by Frank Kaufmann to Kevin Randle and Donald Schmitt in early 1991 (see chapters 2 and 5)—originated with Friedman's remarks as quoted in the prominently featured, page-one *Roswell Daily Record* article of June 7, 1987. As I have noted, there is good reason to believe at least Dennis had read the piece when it first appeared, and he may well have seen it again in the material Friedman sent him just before their interview.

Dennis was vague when he told Friedman where and how he had come to hear that the alien bodies had been found at a second site. However, when I interviewed him for *Omni* in April 1995, he said *Nurse Selff had told him* she had overheard the doctors she assisted "saying the bodies were found with or in some wreckage two or three miles from where everything else was located."

It would appear two key Roswell witnesses fed bogus information back to ufologists, one of whom indirectly put the idea in their heads in the first place. In turn, these ufologists—including myself—have repeated it in their writings and speeches. If this is not being used by intelligence agency training staffs as a textbook example of how to take advantage of "useful idiots" to give currency to disinformation, it should be.

THERE WAS A NURSE

Most of those who had examined Dennis's tale and concluded it was, to be polite about it, an example of good old fashioned New Mexico tall-tale telling, decided there was no real-life person who inspired the fantasy of Naomi Selff. I never counted myself among them, and on reading the U.S. Air Force's *Roswell Report: Case Closed* (1997), I am even more certain there was a real nurse Dennis had in mind as he "remembered" Naomi Selff. *Case Closed* includes this intriguing sidebar article, entitled "The 'Missing Nurse'?":

> 1st Lt. Eileen M. Fanton was assigned to the Roswell Army Air Field Station Hospital from December 26, 1946 until September 4, 1947. Fanton, who is deceased, was retired from the U.S. Air Force at the rank of Captain on April 30, 1955, for a physical disability.
> In this [Dennis's] account, the missing nurse is described as single, "real cute, like a small Audry [*sic*] Hepburn, with short black hair, dark eyes and olive skin." Lieutenant Fanton was single in 1947, 5'1" tall, weighed 100 pounds, had black hair, dark eyes, and was of Italian descent.
> Dennis also stated that the nurse was of the Catholic faith, and had been "strictly raised" according to Catholic beliefs. Fanton's personnel record listed her as Roman Catholic, a graduate of St. Catherine's Academy in Springfield, Ky. and as having received her nursing certification from St. Mary Elizabeth's Hospital in Louisville, Ky.
> The witness [Dennis] also recalled that the "missing nurse" was a lieutenant, was a general nurse at the hospital, and had sent him correspondence at a later date which stated she was in London, England with a New York, N.Y. APO number (military overseas mailing address) as the return address. Records revealed that Fanton was a First Lieutenant (promoted from Second Lieutenant to First Lieutenant in June 1947), and she was classified as a "nurse, general duty." Records also indicated that of the five nurses assigned to the Roswell AAF Station Hospital in July 1947, she was the only one that later served a tour of duty in England. Furthermore, she was assigned to the 7510th USAF Hospital, APO 240, New York, N.Y., where she served from June 1952 until April 1955. The 7510th USAF Hospital was located approximately 45 miles north of London at Wimpole Park, Cambridge, England.
> An additional similarity between Fanton and the "missing nurse" is that her personnel record indicated that she quickly departed Roswell AAF and it is probable that the hospital staff would not have provided information concerning her departure. Fanton's unannounced departure from Roswell AAF, on September 4, 1947 was to be admitted to Brooke General Hospital, Ft. Sam Houston, Texas, for a medical condition. This condition was first diagnosed in January 1946 and ultimately led to her medical retirement in 1955. Therefore, if someone other than a family member con-

tacted the Station Hospital at Roswell AAF and inquired about Fanton, as Dennis stated he did [concerning the allegedly missing nurse], the staff was simply protecting her privacy as a patient. . . .[17]

That Fanton probably was Dennis's Nurse Selff is further suggested by the fact that, according to Victor Golubic, she is the woman David Wagnon was recalling as the nurse who possibly was Dennis's friend. In addition, before this had been established, Wagnon told me he seemed to "recall Miss Self was transferred from RAAF while I was still stationed there" and remembered whispered "rumors about Miss Self having a D&C (dilatation and curettage) in the base hospital, the tissue being sent off (probably to Brooke Army Medical Center in San Antonio, Texas), and the biopsy report coming back with some indication of fetal tissue."[18]

TRANSFORMING REALITY INTO PSEUDOREALITY

It appears very likely that a genuine army nurse of Dennis's acquaintance was not the only element from real personal experience that contributed to his story. Diligent research by Capt. James McAndrew turned up several other people and events that very likely played important roles in shaping what Dennis told ufologists and many others he remembered or thought he remembered about events in July 1947.

After years of ignoring citizen inquiries, the air force was compelled finally to take the Roswell matter seriously when in 1993 New Mexico Congressman Steve Schiff requested the U.S. General Accounting Office, the investigative and audit agency of the U.S. Congress, to look into the case (see chapter 17). When the air force released *The Roswell Report: Fact vs. Fiction in the New Mexico Desert*, the first report arising from its congressionally inspired investigation, it was roundly and rightly criticized for not addressing the alien bodies issue. McAndrew, a principal investigator for the first report, was assigned to rectify this failing. He presented the results of his efforts in *The Roswell Report: Case Closed*, published in 1997, just before the fiftieth anniversary of the alleged saucer crash and from which I have already quoted. (Ironically, *Case Closed* was released on June 24, the fiftieth anniversary of Kenneth Arnold's sighting over Mount Rainier, the event that launched the modern UFO era.)

In essence, McAndrew found that witnesses and "witnesses" such as Gerald Anderson, Jim Ragsdale, Frank Kaufmann, Frankie Rowe, Barney Barnett, and Glenn Dennis had wittingly or unwittingly drawn upon actual personal experiences and/or events about which they had heard, read, or seen depicted in motion pictures and on television to construct their accounts of crashed saucers and dead extraterrestrials. The events identified by McAndrew included high-altitude manned and unmanned research balloon launches and mishaps, anthropomorphic dummy drops and recoveries, and a fiery, fatal military aircraft accident. They took place over a thirteen-year period, from 1947 to 1959. Constrained by superiors worried about negative legal, public relations, and political consequences, McAndrew was compelled to leave it to his readers to decide for themselves which witnesses were innocently misremembering and which were being more creative.

Unfortunately, McAndrew's solidly documented and sourced report was the subject of misinformed ridicule and neglect from the day of its release—some of the former from me, on national television (NBC-TV *Nightly News*, June 24, 1997) and in newswire-service interviews (e.g., see the *Albuquerque Tribune*, June 25, 1997). The anthropomorphic dummies were ready-made for laughs and cheap shots. So, too, was the notion of flawed memories blending events widely separated in time, even though it is well-known that the vagaries of human memory frequently result in such misassociations. The naysayers' job was made even easier by the incredibly inept Pentagon press conference at which *Case Closed* was unveiled. All this made it difficult for anyone who had actually read the report to suggest openly that McAndrew was on to something.

I am quoted in the *Albuquerque Tribune* as saying, "People on all sides are going to laugh." Unfortunately, I was right. McAndrew's study has either been ignored or quietly if sneeringly criticized by such skeptical ufologists as Phil Klass, for such sins as "restoring respectability" to the likes of Gerald Anderson by suggesting his tall tale probably incorporated large elements of fact—if not truth.[19] This appears to be because anti-UFOlogists seem to prefer Anderson, Dennis, and others as unvarnished bald-faced liars who made up their stories out of whole cloth, rather than as lying or possibly mistaken transformers of truth into pseudotruth.

Since opening my mouth and inserting my left cowboy boot, I have carefully read *Case Closed* and independently looked into many of the claims its author makes. There is no question that McAndrew's findings are flawed, largely because all too often he tries to stretch his data to make it explain more than it can. However, on key issue after key issue, his evidence and analysis are compellingly persuasive, in no respect more so than with Glenn Dennis's account.

I have already cited the example of Captain Fanton as a model for Naomi Selff. The aftermath of a horrific June 26, 1956, aircraft accident supplies the essential elements of Dennis's bodies-at-the-base-hospital story. On that early summer day, a U.S. Air Force KC-97G aerial refueling tanker lifted off the runway at Walker Air Force Base (formerly Roswell Army Air Field). Four and a half minutes later, the fully loaded "flying gas tank" suffered a propeller failure. A propeller blade apparently punctured the plane's huge deck fuel tank, igniting an intense cabin fire and turning the plane into a blazing inferno. The aircraft immediately spun out of control and crashed, its eleven crew members all instantly killed by the fire and impact explosion.

The charred and dreadfully mangled remains of the eleven airmen were recovered, enclosed in body bags, and taken to the Walker AFB hospital, which was little changed from July 1947. The following day, air force identification specialist George Schwaderer arrived from Wright-Patterson AFB and set to work, wearing a standard hospital staff gown and mask. When interviewed, Schwaderer recalled that because of his working garb and the nature of what he had to do on the job, he often was mistaken for a pathologist.

Partway through the identification process, the work was removed to a refrigerated compartment at the base commissary. This was compelled by the overpowering odor from the burned and fuel-drenched bodies and the small hospital's lack of proper storage space. On the same day, three of the victims were autopsied by Dr. Alfred S. Blauw, a local civilian physician. The autopsies were performed at the Ballard Funeral Home, where Glenn Dennis was employed. All three victims had "extreme, multiple" injuries, and two of them had suffered extensive third-degree burns and loss of their lower extremities. One of the bodies was described in the autopsy report as having "multiple fractures of all bones of the skull" and "partially cooked strands of bowel . . . over the abdomen and chest." The report also included descriptions of a detached hand and the fingers and arms of the victims, as well as one with a "face completely missing."

Dennis claims Nurse Selff told him of three bodies three-and-a-half to four feet tall with black skin. She also described skulls that were flexible and body tissue in "strings," possibly because it had been pulled and shredded by predators after the saucer crash. According to Dennis's account, the nurse went into some detail about a severed hand and the fingers, arms, "deeply set" eyes, and "concave" noses of the "creatures." Then there was the odor, which the nurse said became so overpowering that the bodies had to be removed from the hospital, and the two "pathologists," both strangers at the hospital.[20]

As I read McAndrew's account of the aftermath of the KC-97 crash, I found myself in amazed agreement that this had to be the source of Dennis's recollections. I also had forcefully brought to mind the first words out of the mouth of an experienced aircraft-accident investigator whom I had shown the Dennis-Henn sketches a few years before, without mentioning Roswell: "What airplane crash is this from?" When I asked what prompted his question, he said the facial and profile drawings strongly reminded him of what he'd seen in more than one fatal air crash in which the victims had been badly burned.

There are other real-life events and people McAndrew relates to various elements of Dennis's story, most of which are very convincing. However, my focus here is the credibility of Dennis's claims concerning the nurse and the alien bodies she allegedly told him about. My conclusion on this score can be summed up by harking back to L. M. Hall's gotcha-joke comment quoted at the beginning of this chapter: Gotcha, Glenn.

As I reviewed my files and writings and listened to audiotapes of my interviews with Glenn Dennis in preparation for writing this chapter, considering the evidence from what I am confident now is as objective a perspective as possible, I was quite frankly more than a little embarrassed. How could I have overlooked or dismissed as unimportant or almost willfully turned a bind eye to so many clues that what Dennis was telling me and others simply did not hang together? How is it I had set aside my initial negative evaluation and been so deeply drawn into believing what the former mortician said were memories of a series of dramatic events that had occurred in 1947? This was completely contrary to my professional training as an intelligence officer and my experience in the political trenches of Washington.

I have a carefully cultivated and tried and true personal First Rule of Ufology and Politics: Trust no one and delight in the occasional pleasant surprise. Why did I not apply it with Dennis? Was it because so much of what Dennis claimed was rooted in reality, giving it the ring of truth, possibly even convincing him for a time that it really had happened as he was telling it, or at least close to it? In truth, I think it was this compounded by what was an unrecognized, deep-seated, and innocently stubborn bias on my part, perfectly summed up by the words emblazoned on the poster adorning *X-Files* FBI agent Fox Mulder's office wall: I Want to Believe. In this respect, I am not alone, nor is this a failing confined to the "believer" side of the ufological divide. It is mirrored in the "True Unbelieverism" of many who think of themselves as skeptics.

NOTES

1. Hall affidavit, app. H. Hall told me he does not remember the exact term Dennis used in reference to the bodies. *Aliens* almost certainly was not it, and other details of Hall's recollections are probably less than reliable, since the conversation was clearly of little consequence to him until many years later.

2. Audiotaped telephone interview with David N. Wagnon, September 17, 1993; Wagnon affidavit, app. H.

3. Wagnon interview, September 17, 1993.

4. Philip J. Klass, *The Real Roswell Crashed-Saucer Coverup* (Amherst, N.Y.: Prometheus Books, 1997), p. 188.

5. Telephone conversations with Tim Korte and Glenn Dennis, late January 1995.

6. Telephone conversation with Glenn Dennis, April 14, 1995.

7. Karl T. Pflock, "Star Witness," interview with Glenn Dennis, *Omni*, fall 1995, p. 104.

8. Paul McCarthy, "The Case of the Missing Nurses," *Omni*, fall 1995, pp. 108–109.

9. Ibid., pp. 109, 111.

10. Kevin D. Randle, *The Randle Report: UFOs in the '90s* (New York: Evans, 1997), pp. 190–91.

11. Ibid., pp. 191–92.

12. Pflock, "Star Witness," p. 132.

13. Ibid., pp. 104–105.

14. Ibid., p. 105.

15. Kevin D. Randle and Donald R. Schmitt, *UFO Crash at Roswell* (New York: Avon, 1991), illustration immediately preceding p. 145.

16. From time to time, Dennis hinted to me and to an associate of mine that the nurse's sketches still existed, that he had them carefully hidden away. Independently, my associate and I attempted to persuade Dennis to come forward with this proof of his story. He dismissed my importunings with a laugh or a "We'll see." He told my associate he was afraid something might happen to him or his family if he did so, saying, "They'll come out after I'm gone."

17. James McAndrew, *The Roswell Report: Case Closed* (Washington, D.C.: U.S. Government Printing Office, 1997), pp. 82–83.

18. Wagnon affidavit, app. H.

19. Philip J. Klass, e-mail message to me, August 6, 1997.

20. McAndrew, *Roswell Report*, pp. 96–99.

THIRTEEN

NOT SO MUNDANE

By late 1993, as I was sitting down to write *Roswell in Perspective*, I had established to my satisfaction that there no longer was any reasonable basis for believing the mere weather balloon explanation for the Roswell events. Whatever happened, whatever fell to earth on the Foster Ranch, whatever was retrieved, I was certain there was nothing routine or mundane about it, or at least there was something behind it that was not. On the other hand, of course, I knew this did not necessarily mean a crashed flying saucer or anything else exotic in an unearthly sense was involved.

Recognizing this, I and several other investigators had expended considerable effort looking into possible down-to-earth but other-than-ordinary explanations. Crashed secret experimental aircraft, captured German V-2s or other rockets gone astray, nuclear weapons accidents or training activities gone wrong, Japanese balloon bombs, wayward Soviet spy craft, and a variety of classified and unclassified scientific and technical research projects were considered and all found wanting. However, I discovered—or, rather, rediscovered—one project that had been considered by others and dismissed as not having anything to do with Roswell.

ROBERT TODD GETS CURIOUS

As it happens, I was not the only UFO researcher who had zeroed in on this undertaking, a constant-level, high-altitude balloon research-and-development program conducted for the U.S. Army Air Forces by New York University. Robert G. Todd, an archival investigator to whom ufology owes a great but largely unacknowledged debt of gratitude, had "gotten there first." As I was to learn sometime later, my independent research benefited in no small degree from Todd's diligent and painstaking efforts.

In the fall of 1990, Todd was sleuthing through a collection of Federal Bureau of Investigation documents having to do with UFOs, which had been released as the result of Freedom of Information Act requests filed by well-known ufologist Bruce Maccabee. Reading an FBI document concerning alleged "UFO crash debris" found by a Danforth, Illinois, farmer in August 1947, Todd noted something interesting. According to the report, when FBI agents had asked a senior U.S. Army civilian employee to examine the material, they were told it might be something from an army project with the code name Mogul. The FBI men were given no further details. Project Mogul was classified Top Secret, and they had no "need to know."

Todd's Sherlockian curiosity was aroused. He filed a FOIA request with the U.S. Air Force Historical Agency, resulting in the release of a document from the papers of Gen. Curtis LeMay in which there was a reference to Mogul that linked the project to the Army Air Forces' Watson Laboratories in Red Bank, New Jersey. Following this lead, Todd found that Mogul—which had been declassified almost two decades earlier—was somehow connected with the NYU constant-level balloon effort.

Pursuing matters further, Todd found that in May 1947 a Project Mogul field team from Watson Labs under Dr. Albert P. Crary had set up shop at Alamogordo Army Air Base, about ninety air miles southwest of Roswell. He also discovered that an NYU balloon-project group had arrived at Alamogordo AAB soon after, linking up with the Watson Labs team and relocating the project's balloon-launch operations from the East Coast, where they had been secretively conducted since the fall of 1946. He further learned that New Mexico Institute of Mining and Technology atmospheric physics professor Charles B. Moore had served as the balloon project engineer and was part of the group at Alamogordo. In spring 1992, Todd located and contacted Moore in Socorro, New Mexico, home of New Mexico Tech, and they began exchanging information about Mogul, the associated NYU project, and the Roswell incident.[1]

I contacted Professor Moore the following year, after having been told by ufologists Stan Friedman and Don Berliner that he had approached them in Socorro in response to an announcement run in the local paper on November 4, 1992, a couple of months after their *Crash at Corona* had hit the bookstores. Friedman and Berliner were to be in town seeking more information about the Roswell affair, and they invited anyone who had anything to offer to meet with them at their motel on November 16. Moore, who with the help and encouragement of Todd had been digging into his files and memories for several months, was one of those who responded. He brought with him some of the NYU project reports, which included flight-train schematics and flight data. When he suggested parts of one of the balloon and instrumentation arrays he and his team had launched from Alamogordo might be what Mack Brazel had stumbled upon, the two ufologists appear to have dismissed the idea out of hand. Berliner even told me they thought Moore and B. D. "Duke" Glidenberg, another former Alamogordo research balloonist who had come to see them with a similar suggestion, might even be part of the continuing Roswell cover-up.[2]

I had a somewhat different reaction. I quickly realized Moore was C. B. Moore, the scientist who had made one of the most impressive—and still unexplained—early UFO sightings, near Arrey, New Mexico, on April 24, 1949. I also recalled his contact with Friedman and Berliner was not the first with ufologists concerning the Roswell affair. William L. Moore (no relation to C. B.), coauthor of *The Roswell Incident*, had interviewed the New Mexico Tech professor a number of times in 1979. Moreover, the two had even discussed the possibility that something from the NYU project might have precipitated the short-lived furor in July 1947:

. . . In the summer of 1947, Moore . . . was directly involved in a New York University–sponsored high-altitude-research-balloon project based out of the North Field of White Sands, near Alamorgordo, New Mexico, a project which, he said, he believed was responsible for "at least *some* of the flying-saucer reports in the area." . . .

When asked whether the Roswell device might have been a weather balloon or other scientific balloon, Moore replied: "*Based on the description you just gave me,* I definitely rule this out [emphasis added]. There wasn't a balloon in use back in '47, or even today for that matter, that could have produced debris over such a large area or torn up the ground in any way. I have no idea what such an object may have been, but I can't believe a balloon would fit such a description."[3]

It seems ufologist Moore had told Professor Moore that whatever had crashed had plowed a huge gouge or gouges in the ground and that the debris field was very densely covered with shattered wreckage. As he carefully stated, the scientist's response was based upon the information given him by the ufologist-author. In the summer of 1992, Charlie Moore was to learn from Robert Todd that he had be grossly misinformed.

In his efforts to assist Bill Moore in his investigation, the scientist provided him with copies of drawings and documents from the NYU project. One item was an annotated schematic drawing of an NYU flight train launched in New Mexico on July 7, 1947. The drawing of Flight 11A was published in Moore and Berlitz's *Roswell Incident*. This is where I first saw the schematic of Flight 11A, and I immediately was struck by the multiballoon device's unusual appearance and great size, about three hundred feet from top to bottom in flight.[4] It was easy to see how it and its sisters could have generated flying saucer reports. Other than that consideration and a fleeting, wondering thought about the ultimate purpose of the rig, I did not think anything more of it at the time. After all, it was part of a university research effort, and the former project engineer had said with some certainty that, if what he had been told was accurate, it was not one of his flight trains that had launched the Roswell incident.

In May 1993, Professor Moore and I met for the first time, in my motel room in Socorro (there are definite patterns in the Roswell saga!). One of the first things I raised with him was his "No way!" response to ufologist Bill Moore. It was then I learned that, when "a friend" (Robert Todd) had sent him a copy of the July 9, 1947, *Roswell Daily Record* article giving Mack Brazel's description of what he had found, Professor Moore quickly had changed his mind. He told me that what Brazel described very closely matched various types of equipment flown by the NYU project and in condition, quantity, and distribution was what might be expected to be found where one of the project's flights had touched down and been dragged along by the wind.

Moore then explained that the university program was connected with a highly classified military project called Mogul, a code name he learned for the first time only a year before, from a person he declined to name at that time but whom he later told me was Robert Todd. Over the next several months, I was to collect a good deal more information about the NYU program and the very sensitive project it supported, and in June 1994, I was the first to go public with the connection between Roswell and Project Mogul, in *Roswell in Perspective*. Soon after, in September 1994, the air force would make publicly available a vast amount information about Mogul and the related NYU activities and their role in the crashed flying saucer story.

PROJECT MOGUL AND FLYING SAUCERS

Project Mogul, classified Top Secret and so sensitive that even its code name was classified, was of such importance that it had a "1A" priority, a status shared in 1947 only by the Manhattan Project. Mogul was inspired in the fall of 1945 by a memorandum from Columbia University geophysicist William Maurice Ewing to U.S. Army Air Forces Com. Gen. Carl A. "Tooey" Spaatz.[5]

Ewing had been instrumental in developing "sofar" (sound fixing and ranging), a technique for position fixing at sea by exploding a charge under water, measuring the time for the shock waves to travel to three widely separated receivers, and calculating the position of the source by triangulation. Ewing believed that, by taking advantage of a postulated "acoustical duct" in the tropopause, the interface between the troposphere and the stratosphere (at an altitude ranging between thirty thousand and fifty thousand feet depending upon atmospheric conditions), a conceptually similar technique could be used for global long-range detection of rockets passing through the duct zone and, most important, nuclear weapons bursts. He was convinced this had the potential of making possible both an early warning system against rocket attack and, of more immediate concern, detecting Soviet atomic bomb tests, which were expected in the near future (the first Soviet detonation of a nuclear device took place on September 22, 1949).[6]

Spaatz enthusiastically embraced Ewing's idea, and Project Mogul was established under the auspices of the Air Materiel Command's new Watson Laboratories. Its objectives were to prove Ewing's concept and, to take advantage of it, develop the necessary detection instrumentation and a quiet, reliable, and long-duration flight platform to lift that instrumentation into the "sound channel" and keep it suspended there for extended periods.[7]

The first few months of the project were inauspicious, and in November 1946, the late Col. Marcellus Duffy, a highly respected, experienced, "can-do" research-and-development officer who had been a key participant in the development of most U.S. military weather equipment during World War II, was put in charge as the Mogul project officer, operating from a high-security New Jersey field site. Duffy selected Capt. Albert C. Trakowski as his deputy, and Dr. James Peoples served as the Mogul project scientist. Duffy turned to New York University's Athelstan F. Spilhaus, a World War II colleague, to guide development of the flight platform under an AMC/Watson Laboratories contract, with the work to be done by the Research Division of NYU's College of Engineering as "Project 93."[8]

Spilhaus, a brilliant idea man, almost immediately seized upon the notion of using large, constant-level balloons as Mogul platforms. In 1946, this was cutting-edge technology. No one had ever done anything like it. Spilhaus called on C. B. Moore to translate this bold idea into reality. A chemical engineering graduate of Georgia Tech who had served with Spilhaus in the army air forces weather service during World War II, Moore was then pursuing graduate studies in physics at NYU. He was appointed Project 93 engineer and worked directly under project director Charles S. Schneider.[9]

Duffy had barely gotten the key Project Mogul and supporting NYU players in place when Col. Carl Maier, founding chief of the Electronic Subdivision of AMC's Engineering Division, at Wright Field, Ohio, had him reassigned to his staff, leaving Captain Trakowski in charge as the Watson Labs Mogul project officer.[10] Trakowski was up to the challenge, and the project went forward rapidly. Watson Labs scientists and technicians quickly scrounged off-the-shelf sound-detection and data-gathering instrumentation for early test activities and, working with Columbia University acoustical experts, began developing and fabricating new listening devices designed especially for Mogul applications.

Moore and his NYU associates had no or, in a few cases, carefully limited knowledge of the Watson Labs activities and the ultimate military-scientific purpose of their own work. They worked independently and conducted several test flights from the grounds of NYU and nearby locations in New Jersey and Pennsylvania, using neoprene meteorological sounding balloons to lift their flight trains.[11] Moore quickly concluded that constant-volume balloons were needed to accomplish his mission. Neoprene stretches as a balloon rises, changing the balloon's volume and lift, significantly complicating the task of reaching and, especially, sustaining the desired operational altitude. Moore hit on the idea of using polyethylene, which up until then had never been used in balloon construction. He arranged for the H. A. Smith company and General Mills to supply the project with these advanced devices on a top-priority basis.[12]

The Watson Labs Project Mogul group and the associated NYU balloon-project team "went on the road" for the first time in the late spring of 1947. The Watson Labs people, led by Albert Crary, arrived in New Mexico in mid-May, and later Moore and others from NYU and their equipment, joined by Mogul project officer Trakowski and project scientist Peoples, flew west from New Jersey aboard a C-47 transport, one of several aircraft dedicated to Project Mogul. Arriving at Alamogordo AAB on June 1, they set up shop in a hangar in the field's North Area. Their neighbors were a group of army air forces radar men under the command of Captain L. H. Dyvad and also assigned to Watson Labs. They were in New Mexico to track V-2 rocket launches out of the adjacent White Sands Proving Ground.

Taking advantage of his project's high-priority status and the mutual Watson Labs association, Moore persuaded Dyvad to give him a hand in tracking his balloon and instrumentation trains. Mogul project scientist Peoples had decided not to have the NYU group bring its ground-side radiosonde (meteorological data collection and radio transmission and tracking) equipment to New Mexico, so Moore turned to using radar instead, inadvertently contributing a key and contentious element to the Roswell mystery.[13]

Aircraft also were used to track the flight trains and monitor their data transmissions. Moore told me of one instance in which the project B-17G bomber even provided "air cover" for a grounded flight train. The pilot took the big four-engine plane "right down on the deck," buzzing a group of oil-rig workers who had seen the strange contraption coming down and were chasing after it. He then circled low over the downed array to keep the curious civilians away until a ground team could arrive and retrieve everything.

The NYU group launched both Mogul constant-level-flight/detection-instrumentation experimental arrays, called service flights, and simple meteorological ones, the latter to chart local "wind fields" and check current conditions before releasing the former. The meteorological flights were clusters of three to seven neoprene sounding balloons lifting a string of three to five ML-307B radar-reflecting targets linked together one above the other, like a very large kite tail. Each corner-reflector target measured about three feet on a side, and Moore used multiple targets, because he found the radar-signal return from a single target was too faint to be useful.[14] Moore and his team were the first to group corner-reflector targets in this fashion, and no one else was doing it at the time. Similar multiple-target hookups were used on many of the service flights, and one set of these other-than-ordinary radar targets was to play a central role in the Roswell mystery.

Three numbered service launches, Flights 4, 5, and 6, were made during this first New Mexico field activity at Alamogordo, on June 4, 5, and 7 respectively. All three of the arrays were huge and complex, looming almost 700 feet from top to bottom in flight. Each employed twenty to thirty neoprene meteorological sounding balloons (the special polyethylene balloons were not yet available) and several payload, data-transmitter, altitude-control, parachute, and disposable-ballast packages. All this was linked together with a complex rigging of heavy-duty monofilament nylon line and an even stronger central flying line, the keel of the flight train, made of hand-braided nylon "lobster twine," plus various fittings, many of which were cobbled together or fabricated on site as experience suggested a need.[15]

Flight 5 was airborne for almost six hours, rose as high as fifty-eight thousand feet, successfully maintained a period of constant-level flight at fifty-one thousand feet, and grounded east of Roswell, where it was recovered by members of the NYU team under the watchful eyes of the Project Mogul B-17 crew as mentioned above. Flight 6, less successful, flew for about three hours, and about half of the array was recovered approximately eighteen miles east-southeast of Alamogordo. Flight 4 was another matter entirely, as we shall see.

According to Moore, in addition to the "for the record" numbered service flights and the numerous meteorological launches, several unnumbered test launches were made by his NYU team. How many of these there were is uncertain, but some apparently were "all-up" arrays and others, scaled-down versions. All were used to test various equipment, launch and flight-control techniques, and so on before attempting for-the-record, numbered launches.[16] Other balloons lofted test-support instrumentation and still others, explosives, which were set off at altitude to test the detection microphones being experimented with.[17] Members of the Watson Labs Mogul team also made explosive shots on the ground for the same purpose, and attempts were made to detect the low-frequency rumbling roar of V-2 rockets launched from White Sands, with both balloon-borne and ground-based microphones.

No effort was made to recover any of the meteorological or explosives flights, and it is uncertain how many of the unnumbered constant-level and instrumentation test flights were recovered.[18] None of the June flights carried identification tags, nor did any of those flown the following month. One of the numbered service flights, Flight 4, also was among the missing and is not included in any of the Project 93 reports covering June 1947 activities. Soon after recovering the remains of Flight 6, the NYU group returned to the East Coast to prepare for the next series of launches with the new nonextensible polyethylene balloons.

Moore's team returned to New Mexico in late June 1947, again enlisting the aid of Captain Dyvad's radar men in tracking its aerial behemoths and their lesser cousins. As before, the team conducted numerous unlogged flights—several constant-level/instrumentation experiment arrays, many meteorological clusters, and substantial numbers of test-support (explosives and instrument) launches, all using the same sort of rigging, instruments, and tracking gear and radar targets employed during the earlier New Mexico series. The first numbered service launch of the second round was Flight 7, lifting off at 5:21 A.M. on Wednesday, July 2. This was one of the last two Mogul-service arrays employing neoprene balloons, and it included twenty of them. Flight 7 measured about 450 feet from top to bottom in the air, and after nearly seven hours aloft, it grounded in the Sacramento Mountains about thirty-one miles east of Alamogordo AAB. All that was recovered by the NYU team was a single balloon neck.

At just after 3 A.M. the next day, Thursday, July 3, the world's first polyethylene balloon flight was launched by Charlie Moore's group. This was Flight 8, a service-flight array over 200 feet tall, employing ten conical General Mills balloons, carrying a Mogul microphone, and launched in anticipation of a V-2 rocket firing, which was postponed after the NYU team had released their ungainly bird. Flight 8 was aloft about three hours before touching down approximately twenty miles west-northwest of the base, and project personnel last saw it from the air, dragging north across the desert. Nothing from this flight was recovered.

In early 1994, when I was writing *RiP*, I strongly suspected the next numbered flight was the Roswell culprit. At that time, no information was available for Flight 9. It was missing from all the NYU/Project Mogul documentation I had gathered. Professor Moore and former Mogul project officer Trakowski told me they could recall nothing about it. However, Moore said he remembered several flights were "classified out" of the NYU Project 93 reports and reports on subsequent balloon programs in which he was involved. He thought Flight 9 might have been one of those. It was the only flight in the NYU project's Alamogordo numbered launch sequence of July 1947 that was missing from the project reports, and it seemed likely to have been launched on Friday, July 4, or possibly the day before, making it a good Roswell "saucer" candidate. Moore and Trakowski were firm in their recollections that Friday, July 4, was *not* a holiday for the NYU and Watson Labs Mogul teams at Alamogordo. Theirs was a crash project, and they worked very long hours, seven days a week.[19] The mystery of Flight 9 is now resolved, as I will explain below.

Just after 5 A.M. on Saturday, July 5, Flight 10 was launched, employing a single fifteen-foot polyethylene balloon. Never recovered, it was last seen twenty-six hours later over Pueblo, Colorado, still drifting north. Two days later, Monday, July 7, the last numbered Mogul service launch of the July series, Flight 11A, the flight depicted in *The Roswell Incident*, was sent aloft. With seven polyethylene and two neoprene meteorological sounding balloons, this three-hundred-foot array flew for nearly seven hours before grounding about fifteen miles due west of Roswell Army Air Field. None of the Flight 11A material was recovered.

About 10:30 on the morning of Tuesday, July 8, the NYU team, having exhausted their entire stock of polyethylene balloons, boarded a C-54 transport along with most of the members of the Watson Labs Mogul group and flew back to New Jersey.[20] Unbeknownst to them, about the same time their plane began its takeoff roll, Colonel Blanchard was probably dictating the "flying disc" press release to Walter Haut at 509th Bomb Group headquarters in Roswell.

When the news broke about a flying saucer being found on the Foster Ranch, it must have caused great consternation at Alamogordo AAB.[21] Project Mogul's hosts and Watson Labs personnel still at the base undoubtedly quickly became concerned the project might be in danger of being compromised as a result of the news coverage of Mack Brazel's discovery, which was likely to be something from one of the numerous unrecovered NYU arrays. Several of the flights had already been responsible for reports of flying saucers over the Tularosa Valley, in which Alamogordo is located. Moreover, there had been some press inquiries to the base about "unusual activities" in the North Area. Added to this growing public and media attention, the possibility that someone without a need to know had physical evidence of the NYU team's Project Mogul–related balloon operations meant something had to be done to divert press and public attention.[22]

On the afternoon of July 9, the local press was invited to the base for a demonstration of the alleged "study and training" activities of the "Watson Laboratories AMC experimental group for long range radar detection." This cleverly capitalized on the current flying saucer excitement, and there is little room for doubt that it was done to preclude compromise of Mogul security.

Captain Dyvad's men conducted the "demonstration," with Watson Labs project officer Maj. W. D. Pritchard fronting for them. Pritchard was not assigned to Mogul but coordinated with Mogul's Alamogordo field chief Albert Crary and through Crary was privy to Mogul information. He told the press the purpose of the work "was study and training of officers and enlisted men of the army in observing and tracking of objects slower than airplanes by eye and radar device."[23]

As reporters watched and took photographs, the "experimental group" used a stepladder (a Charlie Moore technique) to launch a cluster of meteorological balloons trailing two radar targets (something they had never done before Moore had shown them how) and demonstrated how they radar-tracked them in flight.[24] Major Pritchard explained to the newsmen that his group "had not realized that our balloon and corner reflector radar experimental device was in any way related to the widely-discussed 'flying disc' observed over the nation until reading news dispatches on Thursday [sic]. . . . [A]fter reading the detailed description on [sic] the recovery of one of our reflectors or a similar one from another base, we suddenly became aware of the possibility." Whether by design or not is uncertain, but the demonstration and Pritchard's explanation dovetailed well with General Ramey's weather balloon announcement of the day before, and the secret of Project Mogul was safe.[25]

Although early on the evening of July 8 Ramey had told the press in Fort Worth the special flight carrying the Roswell debris to Dayton had been canceled, apparently it had not. At 6:17 P.M. that evening, the FBI's Dallas office sent a Teletype message to

FBI headquarters in Washington, D.C., and the FBI office in Cincinnati, Ohio, advising that the Roswell "object" was being flown to Wright Field by "special plane." The telex said the "disc is hexagonal in shape and was suspended from a ballo[o]n by cable, which ballo[o]n was approximately twenty feet in diameter." The message went on to state "the object found resembles a high altitude weather balloon with a radar reflector, but . . . telephonic conversation between . . . [Eighth Air Force headquarters in Fort Worth] and Wright Field had not borne out this belief."[26] It requires very little thought to recognize the distinct possibility that the "disc" and associated equipment described in this message may well have been from one of the NYU project's flight trains.

Albert Trakowski told me that "a few days" after the Roswell excitement had come and gone, he received a telephone call from his predecessor as Mogul project officer, Col. Marcellus Duffy, now stationed at Wright Field and serving in the Air Materiel Command subdivision with oversight responsibility for Mogul, where one of his duties was to monitor upper air programs. According to Trakowski, Colonel Duffy told him "some guy awakened him the night the plane came in and showed him some debris," telling him it had been found in New Mexico and had stirred up considerable press interest as possibly being from a flying saucer. Trakowski said Duffy told him he strongly suspected the material was from something that had been flown in connection with Mogul, but of course, he could not reveal this. So he said he offered the literally if narrowly true opinion that "no doubt it is from a meteorological device," further and probably inadvertently reinforcing the cover story for Mogul.[27]

In correspondence and telephone conversations not long before his death in 1992, Colonel Duffy gave Robert Todd a similar account. Todd told me that Duffy at no time told him that what he had been asked to identify was associated with Project Mogul, which he was unwilling to discuss without official assurances that he could do so.[28] However, in a November 6, 1991, letter to Todd, Duffy wrote,

While stationed at Wright A.F.B. [sic] in 1947, I received a call at home [on the adjacent Patterson Army Air Field] one evening saying that what was currently being described by the press as a "flying saucer" was being flown in to Wright Field and would be brought to my home that evening for identification. You can imagine how excited my wife and children were. I identified the "flying saucer" as a weather observation balloon. I'm reasonably sure that this was the one found by the rancher near Roswell, but can't swear to it.

In a follow-up letter dated November 13, Duffy added,

In my previous letter I stated that I identified the "flying saucer" as a "weather observation balloon." I should have said I identified it as "weather observation equipment." It could have been a drop-sonde, corner [radar] reflector, [or some other type of weather observation equipment]. . . . I'm not sure that a balloon was part of what I identified. . . . I didn't attach any great importance to this particular incident at the time.

So, despite what General Ramey told the press, it appears certain that at least some of the debris discovered and collected on the Foster Ranch was taken to Wright Field not long after it had been found. By interesting coincidence, the C-54 carrying the NYU and Watson Labs personnel back to the East Coast made an overnight stop at Wright Field. Professor Moore told me he clearly remembers the group had heard about the "flying saucer" recovery on their trip east, and that they decided the report had been made by people who had found the remains of Flight 11A, undoubtedly thinking the gadget was not of this earth because they had never before seen polyethylene balloons.

However, Moore had all but forgotten the stopover and the role it played in his recollections until, in December 1994, he located Eileen Ulrich Farnochi, one of the data analysts on the Watson Labs Mogul team. She had vivid memories of the trip to New Jersey and the stopover in particular, this especially because, as there were no quarters available for women on the base, she and Vivian Bushnell, the other data analyst, were put up in the YWCA in downtown Dayton, where they had to share their quarters with hoards of bedbugs.

I spoke with Farnochi in February 1995, supplementing what Moore had told me with her recollections. As she put it in a letter to Moore, she had "the impression that somebody (who? [Moore remembers it was Mogul project scientist Dr. James Peoples]) told us that our plane had been followed by reporters from New Mexico. Their story was that a space ship (?) had landed in the desert in the area where we were conducting tests and that the ship (?) and/or the contents thereof had been put on our plane" and taken to Wright Field. Both Farnochi and Moore recall that reporters attempted to interview members of their party, but according to Moore, Peoples arranged for the NYU-Watson Labs group to evade them and board the plane without so much as a "no comment" being required. Farnochi recalls, "When we got back to the labs, the incident was mentioned, but I don't recall any big commotion about it. I think it was quickly dismissed and forgotten."[29]

Thus it was that until 1992, when he first learned of Mack Brazel's description of what he had found, Moore remained under the impression that the Roswell furor had been caused by the discovery of one of the NYU group's polyethylene balloons. Moreover, until being approached by ufologist Bill Moore in the late 1970s, it was a matter that he had not thought about for years. When reminded of it, he still was of the opinion that it was one of the polyethylene-balloon flights that had sparked the excitement, though it did not then seem to him that this was what created the spectacular debris field the author described.

WHAT GOES UP...

Those who saw and handled the debris discovered by Mack Brazel and have come forward publicly have provided generally consistent descriptions of a variety of materials. Others who have reported what they remember being told by firsthand witnesses offer similar memories. These include: dull-silver, foil-like material, something like aluminum or tinfoil, although some of these persons have claimed it would not tear and could not be permanently creased or wrinkled; small, brownish balsa-wood-like struts or beams, which, allegedly, a match or cigarette-lighter flame would not burn, were flexible but too strong to break, and which resisted being cut or grooved by pocket knives and fingernails; tough, brownish, parchmentlike paper; silklike threads or fibers; strands of material resembling heavy gauge monofilament fishing line; and peculiar designs done in pink and purple pastels and embossed on the beams or struts and/or imprinted on whitish tape.

Certain individuals have described items or characteristics not mentioned by others. Dr. Jesse Marcel remembers "a brittle, brownish-black plastic-like material, like Bakelite," and—*alone among all who claim to have examined any of the debris*—he recalls at least one of the struts he saw on his family's kitchen floor as having a cross section like an I-beam. Lewis Rickett is reported to have talked of handling a piece of very thin, very light sheet material which "looked like metal," was about two feet square and slightly curved, and which he could not bend, even with great effort. Sallye Tadolini described a piece of "fabric" Bill Brazel showed her, which was "about the thickness of very fine kidskin leather and a dull metallic grayish silver" in color. Jesse Marcel Sr. is reported to have said he thought CIC Captain Cavitt found "a black, metallic-looking box several inches square" on the debris field, and in his December 1979 interview with Bob Pratt, he cryptically mentioned "some material that's hard to describe. I'd never seen anything like that and I still don't know what it was." In the same interview and another audio-taped in 1981, Marcel referred to some "porous material you could blow through," which he and Cavitt found on the site. In other interviews, Marcel talked of one of his men doing something very unlikely. According to Marcel, this unnamed fellow—a military intelligence man—struck a large piece of the recovered material with a sledgehammer but could inflict no permanent damage.[30]

There was another witness to the debris. This is the late Walter E. Whitmore Jr., son of the majority owner of Roswell's radio station KGFL. I first met and interviewed Whitmore in October 1992. In *Roswell in Perspective*, I called him "Reluctant," because he wished to remain anonymous "for the time being." He told me he wanted to come forward with the truth and the physical evidence he had, and would do so one day. At the time, however, he was concerned this might adversely affect the positive economic results Roswell was just beginning to experience from the growing public interest in the crashed-saucer story. Whitmore definitely did not relish the idea of being the guy who rained on the city's UFO-dollars parade. Small-town life can be tough.

I attempted to get Whitmore to permit Professor Moore to examine the material or at least to let me take photographs of it that Moore and others could examine. He blew hot and cold on this and never gave me a definitive answer, one way or the other. After almost two years of trying, I finally got him to agree that he would work something out with Max Littell of Roswell's International UFO Museum for the material to be turned over to the museum after Whitmore's death, provided the museum committed to exhibiting it with the full true story behind it, a condition to which Littell verbally agreed.

After Whitmore died in April 1995, I discussed the matter several times with Littell. Each time he told me he and Whitmore's widow were trying to find the debris, but so far without any luck. This, of course, was before I became aware of the Littell-Ragsdale deal. In light of that and similar developments, if the Whitmore "stash" has been located, I would be surprised if it also was not immediately "lost" again, this time permanently.

Thus, all that is now available to us with respect to Whitmore's claims is his testimony, which he provided to me in two audiotaped, in-person interviews, supplemented by telephone conversations and correspondence. In July 1947, Whitmore was a law student at Denver University and had returned home for the Fourth of July holiday, only to find Mack Brazel, a stranger to him, ensconced in his room. This is what Whitmore told me about the debris field and how he managed to get to it:

> . . . Brazel sketched a map for me, showing which roads to take and how to find the site. I drove there [from Roswell] alone in my 1946 Chevrolet, a distance of 65 or 70 miles. No one was there when I arrived, I do not remember seeing any sign that anyone had been on the site, and I saw no one else while I was there. Although I now believe the army was already aware of Brazel's find at the time, I am certain I was on the site before any military personnel got there.
>
> The site was a short distance from a ranch road. The debris covered a fan- or roughly triangle-shaped area, which was about 10 or 12 feet wide at what I thought was the top end. From there it extended about 100 to 150 feet, widening out to about 150 feet at the base. This area was covered with many, many bits of material. The material was very light. I could see it blowing in the wind. Many pieces had been blown out of the main area, and I could see them stuck to bushes as far as a city block away.
>
> Most of what I found was white, linen-like cloth with reflective tinfoil attached to one side. Some pieces were glued to balsa-wood sticks, and some of them had glue on the cloth side, with bits of balsa still stuck to it. Most of the pieces were no larger than four or five inches on a side, although I found one or two about the size of a sheet of typing paper. None of the sticks was more than a foot or so long.
>
> One of the larger pieces of foiled cloth, measuring about 8 by 12 inches, had writing on the cloth side. Someone had used a pencil to do some figuring, arithmetic. There were no words, only numbers. I did not see any writing or markings on any of the other debris.
>
> I collected some of the foiled-cloth material, including the piece with the writing on it, and a few of the sticks, filling a large, 9 by 12, envelope with it. . . .
>
> . . . I still have the material I collected on the ranch site in July 1947. It is . . . stored in a safe and secure place [for years his bank safe-deposit box, later at home, in what he called his junk room]. . . .[31]

Clearly, Whitmore was describing materials of an earthly origin that very well could have been part of an NYU-Mogul flight array. With the exception of the large, strong piece or pieces of "metal" described by Rickett and Marcel Sr., and perhaps the "fabric" remembered by Tadolini, the same is true of the materials described by others.

Admittedly, this requires discounting some of what the witnesses say they recall about certain properties of the debris, something I was loath to do a few years ago. Back then, while I had no doubt one of the NYU group's flights was responsible for the great majority of what had been found on the Foster Ranch, I kept the door open to another possibility. Speculating that there might have been a midair collision or near miss of earthly and unearthly craft, I thought it possible, if unlikely, that the debris with remarkable properties could have been from a downed or damaged flying saucer.[32]

Now, however, armed with much additional countervailing information and my will to believe in check, I am certain it is entirely reasonable to disregard testimony about anomalous properties. We now know volumes about the activities of the NYU balloon project team in New Mexico and the types of equipment and materials they used in their flight arrays, key elements of it absolutely unique. We also know that time, unconscious adoption of things heard from or suggested by others, and the subtle and not so subtle influences of celebrity can introduce sometimes startling distortions into even relatively recent memories, especially on the part of those prone to exaggerate, innocently and otherwise.

The simple truth is that, as we shall see, the overwhelming majority of the evidence and testimony—even that of those witnesses who attribute "unearthly" qualities to the debris—points unequivocally to "all that junk all over out there" on the Foster Ranch as being something from an NYU Mogul service flight train.[33] The tantalizing claims about super strength and other unusual properties seem significant only when lifted out of the context of much more mundane memories, dazzling us with amazing possibilities.

... MUST COME DOWN—SOMEWHERE

It is obvious that, with the help of New Mexico's seemingly inexhaustible winds, the NYU balloon, instrument, and radar-target Mogul service arrays were large enough to create a debris field of the size(s) described. These huge flight trains included hundreds of square feet of polyethylene and/or neoprene balloon envelopes, many square feet of radar-reflective material, several parchment parachutes, much hardened balsa strutting, and so on.

Six years ago, I thought NYU Flight 9 was the Roswell culprit. This Mogul service flight is missing from the Project 93 reports on the NYU team's July 1947 operations, and it seemed likely to have been one of the flights lofted with the new polyethylene balloons, which I thought could account for Major Marcel's mystery material. Information recorded in the field diary of Alamogordo Mogul group chief Albert Crary deflated this idea.

In the spring of 1994, Professor Moore was able to obtain from Dr. Crary's widow a copy of the portion of the diary for the period May 24 through July 15, 1947. He kindly furnished me with a copy and a transcription he prepared from the handwritten text, offering the following in his cover letter,

> ... [T]he diary provides an explanation for NYU Flight #9 and a reason for its absence from the flight summary. When the need for the instrumented flight vanished with the further postponement of the V-2 firing [due to an accident] at WSPG [White Sands Proving Ground] on the evening of July 3, 1947, . . . the balloon cluster (probably of meteorological balloons) was released without instruments.
>
> After the cancellation of the V-2 firing, the balloons inflated for the hastily cobbled-together second flight on July 3rd would surely have been stored inside North Hangar for later use if they had been made of polyethylene, since they were in short supply. The fact that Crary recorded they were released with a dummy load suggests to me that those balloons were of the meteorological sounding variety, of which we had a large supply.
>
> Crary's diary and the NYU report both indicate that Flight #8 launched that morning was tracked somewhat by radar. From these, I would conclude that radar tar-

gets were probably also included initially in the devices to be carried by Flight #9. . . . [However,] I think that we would have removed the radar targets from the flight train if there was to be no tracking. . . .

Moore told me that this also explained why Flight 9 was not written up in the NYU project reports. Only those flights from which useful performance data were obtained were summarized in those documents. Since no data were gathered on Flight 9, it was ignored. However, a photographic record remains, preserved by Eileen Farnochi. Some of these photos appear in this book.[34] They confirm Moore's thoughts about the flight. It was a small cluster of neoprene sounding balloons with no instrumentation and carrying no radar targets. It included nothing unusual or mysterious, used no then-exotic polyethylene. My Flight 9 notion had been shot down.

If something from one of the flights launched by Moore and his NYU colleagues was found by Mack Brazel, and I was all but certain of that, which flight was responsible? The only other candidate among the numbered service flights was the unrecovered Flight 4, launched on June 4, during the NYU team's first sojourn at Alamogordo. Like Flight 9, it was missing from the project's reports, indicating it had either been "classified out" or had not been a productive launch.

It appears that Dr. Crary's diary provides the only remaining contemporaneous record of this flight: "June 4 Wed. Out to Tularosa Range and fired charges between 00 and 06 this am. No balloon flight again on account of clouds. Flew regular sonobuoy mike up in cluster of balloons and had good luck on receiver on ground but poor on plane." When coupled with the recollections of project engineer Moore, a plausible and likely picture comes into focus. In a March 27, 1995, white paper, "The New York University Balloon Flights During Early June, 1947," Moore provides the following account:

> Crary's diary entries for June 4 are puzzling because they are contradictory. My examination of his original handwritten entries suggests that he copied them later from other notes; the entries from June 2 through the first half of June 5 appear to have been written at one sitting with the same pencil and without any corrections or false starts. During the hectic operations in June, he apparently used field notes to record events as they occurred and then transcribed them later into his diary. This is evident in some later entries, where the events of an entire week were lumped together. . . .
> One interpretation of the June 4 entry is that the launch scheduled for making airborne measurements on Crary's surface explosions after midnight was canceled because of clouds but, after the sky cleared around dawn, the cluster of already-inflated balloons was released, later than planned. The initial cancellation and the later launch were recorded sequentially, as they occurred, in his field notes which he later transcribed into his permanent diary, without elaboration.
> According to C. S. Schneider's progress report for May, 1947, NYU Flight #3 from Bethlehem, PA on May 8 was the last attempt to carry instruments aloft before June 4, whereas the ascent on June 5 was identified as NYU Flight #5. On this basis, I think that the June 4th balloons carried NYU Flight #4, although there is no mention of this flight in the NYU flight summary because no altitude data were obtained.
> . . . Since we had spent the time after our arrival at Alamogordo in preparing for a full-scale flight, I think that we would not have improvised on the morning of June

4, after the gear was ready and the balloons were inflated; we would have launched the full-scale cluster [measuring 657 feet from top to bottom], complete with the targets for tracking by the Watson Labs radar. Tracking was essential whenever an acoustic instrument was flown so that the microphone's location could be determined, relative to the surface and airborne explosions that Crary created. . . .

I have a memory of J. R. Smith watching the June 4th cluster through a theodolite on a clear, sunny morning and that Capt. Dyvad reported that the Watson Labs radar had lost the targets while Smith had them in view. It is also my recollection that the cluster of balloons was tracked to about 75 miles from Alamogordo by the crew of the B-17. As I remember this flight, the B-17 crew terminated their chase while the balloons were still airborne (and J. R. was still watching them), in the vicinity of Capitan Peak, Arabela and Bluewater, NM. I, as an Easterner, had never heard of these exotically-named places, but their names have forever afterward been stuck in my memory. This flight provided the only connection that I have ever had with these places. From the note in Crary's diary, the reason for termination of the chase was due to the poor reception of the telemetered acoustic information by the receiver aboard the plane. We never recovered this flight and, because the sonobouy [microphone], the flight gear and the balloons were all expendable equipment, we had no further concern about them but began preparations for the next flight.

As I noted above, neither this flight nor any of the other NYU arrays launched during June and July carried any sort of identification or "if found, please contact" tags. The equipment was expendable. The general expectation of the scientists involved seems to have been that anybody finding anything would dismiss it as meteorological equipment and not suspect anything more sensitive was involved.

The "scientific johnnies," unsurprisingly more concerned with the substance of their work than security, seem not to have considered that anyone familiar with sonobouys would have found one lying out in the New Mexico desert or mountains to be somewhat out of place. The normal operational venue for such devices was at sea. Naval antisubmarine aircraft dropped them into the water, where the buoy-suspended microphone listened for screw and other noises emitted by enemy submarines and transmitted what it picked up to circling planes and warships waiting to pounce. Neither did it seem to occur to the NYU group that, if found, their radar targets might have been considered to be out of the ordinary. If they had, there might never have been any Roswell mystery, let alone the larger-than-reality legend the mystery spawned.

So Flight 4 was last seen near Capitan Peak, about seventy-five air miles northwest of Alamogordo AAB, approximately twenty-three miles south of the Foster Ranch debris field site. Were weather conditions such that Flight 4 could have continued flying those twenty-three miles and in the right direction to make a fateful, self-destructive touchdown, creating the "crashed-saucer" debris?

Ufologist Kevin Randle was able to obtain microfilm copies of U.S. Weather Bureau Analysis Center 1947 maps of the winds aloft over the continental United States, which he provided to Moore. Utilizing the data from these maps for the period June 3 through 7, ground-track data from NYU Flights 5 and 6, launched on June 5 and 7, respectively, and additional detailed winds data obtained by Dr. John Lewis of the National Severe Storms Laboratory, Moore established with great confidence that conditions indeed were such that Flight 4 could easily have gotten from the vicinity of Arabela to the Foster Ranch. Or, as he put it more cautiously in a letter to Randle, "[O]n the basis of the information now available to us [as of October 21, 1995], . . . NYU Flight #4 can not be ruled out as the possible source of the Foster Ranch debris." This conclusion, concurred in by expert colleagues of Moore, was reinforced a short while later by Moore's acquisition and study of detailed surface winds data for the critical period.[35]

While there was no absolute proof that Flight 4 dropped out of the New Mexico sky onto the Foster Ranch on June 4, dying there and leaving its scattered bones to be found by Mack Brazel ten days later, it seemed to me the circumstantial case for such a scenario was very strong. Accused murderers have been condemned to death on far more shaky presentments. When I combined Moore's analysis with a consideration of what all but certainly was aboard Flight 4 and what would have happened to the array when it descended to earth, the case became nearly airtight.

Flight 4 was a near twin to NYU Flight 2, lacking only a radiosonde. The schematic diagram for NYU Flight 2 shows what truly remarkable and ingenious contraptions it and Flight 4 were. When airborne, Flight 4 towered 657 feet from the lower ends of its ballast tubes to the top of its uppermost balloon, soaring 102 feet taller than the Washington Monument. Twenty-one standard-size (three feet in diameter before inflation) neoprene meteorological sounding balloons were attached at twenty-foot intervals along the flying line, and two, each about three times larger than the others, topped off the array. Spaced along the length of the flight train were the payload, a sonobuoy microphone; explosive cut-off squibs used to regulate the flight's altitude; pressure switches; batteries; aluminum launching and assembly rings fabricated from tube stock by Moore's team; four red or orange reinforced-parchment (on later flights, silk) parachutes; and, grouped together one above the other roughly one-third of the way up the array, three oddly shaped corner-reflector radar targets not in general use in the continental United States.

What might have happened when Flight 4 touched down on the New Mexico high desert? Professor Moore and I have discussed this many times. Drawing upon his experience with other NYU flights and subsequent decades of research ballooning, here is how he described the likely fate of Flight 4 in a letter to skeptical ufologist Phil Klass:

> The standard weather balloons used in this flight did not "crash." Instead they probably descended slowly to Earth after some of the neoprene balloons lifting the train burst as a result of prolonged exposure to sunlight. When the bottom part of the balloon train touched the ground, the upper portion of the train was held aloft by the remaining balloons which were probably blown downwind by the breezes at the surface. A landing like this usually caused the equipment at the bottom of the train to be dragged through the underbrush and to be ripped off when any of it snagged in the shrubbery.

Often, after the equipment was ripped off as a result of wind forces, the upper part of the train had enough lift that it would rise again and float downwind until another balloon burst from degradation in the sunlight, whereupon the descent, dragging and equipment-shedding would be repeated. . . .36

Clearly, this could have created a debris field as described by Major Marcel—"three-quarters [of a] mile long and two hundred to three hundred feet wide." It also is consistent with the much smaller area of debris described by Walt Whitmore Jr. (who did not necessarily visit exactly the same spot as that examined by Marcel and Cavitt), and the somewhat larger one recalled by Mack Brazel's daughter Bessie and Brazel himself.37

It is equally clear that the northeast-southwest orientation of the debris field as remembered by Marcel is consistent with Flight 4, which would have approached the Foster Ranch from the south-southwest. Marcel interpreted what he saw to mean the device responsible for the debris was flying from northeast to southwest, but it is just as likely to have been moving in the opposite direction.

"ONE HELL OF A HULLABALOO OUT OF NOTHING"

So the case for Flight 4 and against a crashed flying saucer continued to build. There was no doubt the huge array could have gotten to the Foster Ranch and, as it drifted to its end, created a long trail of debris while leaving behind smaller deposits of its disintegrating self. This, plus comparing what I knew about the construction, size, and components of Flight 4 with descriptions of the debris recovered from the Foster Ranch and the recollections of those involved in the NYU and Mogul projects and the acquisition of the equipment used by them, established for me beyond any reasonable doubt that Flight 4 all but certainly was the Roswell crashed saucer.

The debris Mack Brazel brought into Roswell included "smoky gray . . . rubber strips." Brazel's daughter Bessie remembers "grayish" and "rubber-like" material scattered about the landscape. Fort Worth newspaper photographer J. Bond Johnson vividly recalls the pile of "smelly garbage" he encountered in General Ramey's office, which appears in several of the photographs he took in that office the evening of July 8.38

When launched, the neoprene meteorological sounding balloons employed on Flight 4 were ivory in color. The significantly smaller and visually tracked latex pilot balloons used by the army air forces' Air Weather Service and army artillery weather units were pigmented in several colors to permit them to be seen against the sky under various weather conditions. Sounding balloons, whose purpose was to lift equipment to very high altitudes, were left unpigmented to preserve maximum elasticity, yielding longer flight life and maximum lift and altitude.

When exposed to sunlight, the ivory, unpigmented neoprene quickly becomes tawny and, after a few days exposure, a dirty gray. Mack Brazel made his discovery on June 14, ten days after Flight 4 took to the air, plenty of time for the remnants of its balloons to become "smoky gray."

The large pile of dark gray strips of material clearly shown in J. Bond Johnson's photographs appears to Professor Moore to have been the tattered, sun-exposed remains of at least three burst neoprene sounding balloons. That it is likely this is what it was is reinforced by Johnson's recollection of the unpleasant odor it emitted. Neoprene balloons, especially those that have burst after inflation, give off an acrid odor. (I can attest to this from personal experience launching—and all too often breaking while inflating—such balloons as a research assistant on a San José State University Meteorology Department project in the early 1960s.) During World War II, Moore discovered that dipping neoprene balloons in very hot water before inflating them reduced breakage and enhanced balloon life in flight. He used this technique with the NYU balloons. This heating also enhances dramatically the very unpleasant "eau de neoprene."

Moore and his team used very strong (150- and 300-pound test) monofilament nylon line in rigging their flight trains. This is consistent with the material reported to resemble heavy-gauge monofilament fishing line. Also used was hand-braided lobster twine, composed of many fine nylon threads. Moore told me the twine's individual strands strongly resembled silk threads when the twine unraveled, which it did easily when snapped or cut. The silklike threads recalled by some debris witnesses could well have been strands of damaged lobster twine.

The brittle, brownish-black Bakelite-like material remembered by Dr. Marcel from his boyhood likely was just that, Bakelite, pieces of the sand-ballast tubes that dangled at the bottom of Flight 4. The black metal box vaguely recalled by his father? A number of such boxes were aboard the flight, housing instruments and batteries. The porous material "you could blow through"? Moore told me he seemed to recall a strong, open-weave mesh fabric was used to reinforce some attachment-point eyelets on the flight arrays.

What about the tough, brownish, parchment-like material? Flight 4 included four parachutes made of parchment, three of them attached just below the radar targets. The parachutes used by the NYU group were dyed red or orange, but according to Moore, the colors faded very rapidly in sunlight. A few days on the prairie, and the Flight 4 parachutes would have been sun bleached to "brownishness."

In a 1979 interview, Mack Brazel's daughter Bessie told ufologist Bill Moore the odd material she helped her father collect included "something made out of the same metal-like foil that looked like a pipe sleeve. About four inches across and equally long, with a flange at one end. . . ." She said she recalled several of these, which she also described as "aluminum collars about four inches around." Professor Moore told me the NYU team had considerable difficulty with its "amateurish first flight from Bethlehem, PA in early April, 1947." He explained, "[We had] problems connecting all of the lines to each other and, after the launch, with the remaining lines (used to hold the balloons during launching) fouling and restraining the balloons that we wished to cut free aloft when the balloon train exceeded the desired altitude." So for the second and later flights, they redesigned the flight trains and used aluminum rings cut from three-and-a-half- or four-inch tubing "as attachment aids through which we could slip our double-ended handling lines, . . . removing them by holding [only] one end at launch." These rings are shown and labeled in the schematic diagram of Flight 2, Flight 4's virtual twin.[39]

The small Foster Ranch house in which Mack Brazel and, during summer months, his family lived. It is here where he, U.S. Army Air Forces intelligence officer Maj. Jesse Marcel, and U.S. Army Counter Intelligence Corps officer Capt. Sheridan Cavitt allegedly spent the night of July 7, 1947, before going to the debris field. *(Karl Pflock)*

Main Street, Roswell, New Mexico, ca. 1947. On the right, the Wilmot Hardware sign. Owner Dan Wilmot reported seeing a flying saucer pass over town the night of July 2, 1947. For years Roswell researchers thought this might have been the Roswell saucer en route to its doom. *(Tony Redmon and Robert Shirkey)*

Roswell jail, ca. 1947. The sheriff's office was located in the jail. It was here that Mack Brazel brought some of the debris he found and where Chaves County Sheriff George Wilcox telephoned Major Marcel at Roswell AAF to tell him of the find. *(John Price)*

Members of U.S. Air Force Office of Special Investigations District 17, photo taken at Kirtland Air Force Base, New Mexico, September 1948. This was a meeting of all members of Dist. 17, who were stationed at several locations in New Mexico and western Texas. The group includes several important and secondary Roswell incident witnesses and sources. Front row, kneeling, from left to right: Capt. Sheridan Cavitt, WO Edgar Bethart, and, fifth from left, Col. Doyle Rees. Second row, standing: second from right, M.Sgt. Lewis "Bill" Rickett, and third from the right, Sgt. Jack Williams. Third row, standing: fifth from left, Lt. Russell Womack. *(Edgar Bethart)*

Radio Station KGFL, ca. 1949. Station majority owner Walter E. Whitmore Sr., hoping to recoup being scooped by rival KSWS on the crashed-saucer story, hid rancher Mack Brazel overnight and recorded a never-broadcast interview with him. *(Walter E. Whitmore Jr.)*

Frank Kaufmann/Joseph Osborne/ Mr. X/Steve MacKenzie (left), whose testimony has formed the cornerstone of the two principal Roswell crashed-saucer scenarios, receiving a medal from Lt. Col. Payne Jennings, 509th Bomb Group and Roswell AAF deputy commander, ca. 1945–1946. *(Roswell AAF Yearbook, Walter Haut)*

Walter E. Whitmore Sr. It was his seques-tering of Mack Brazel that likely led to claims Brazel had been kept "in jail" by the army. *(Walter E. Whitmore Jr.)*

George "Jud" Roberts, partner in KGFL with Walter E. Whitmore Sr., poses with then nameless Roswell International UFO Museum alien, later named R.A.L.F. (Roswell Alien Life Form). Roberts confirmed Whitmore kept Mack Brazel at his home overnight and claimed to have received threatening calls from Washington, D.C., that caused him to scrub broadcast of the Brazel interview. *(Karl Pflock)*

Left to right: former mortician Glenn Dennis, Karl Pflock, Walter Haut. Dennis claims to have learned of alien bodies at Roswell AAF from an army nurse who later mysteriously disappeared. Haut was the Roswell AAF public relations officer who released the announcement of the recovery of a crashed flying saucer near Roswell. *(Karl Pflock)*

Arthur McQuiddy, in 1947 editor of the *Roswell Morning Dispatch*. McQuiddy was scooped on the crashed-saucer story by *Dispatch* affiliate radio station KSWS and the *Roswell Daily Record*. He claims to have had an interesting discussion of the incident with 509th Bomb Group commander Col. William H. Blanchard. *(Karl Pflock)*

Col. William H. "Butch" Blanchard, in July 1947 commander of the 509th Bomb Group and Roswell AAF. Blanchard dictated the crashed-saucer announcement to his public relations officer 1st Lt. Walter Haut. *(U.S. Air Force)*

Main entrance to the Roswell AAF/Walker Air Force Base hospital, ca. 1956. It was at this facility where, according to Glenn Dennis, preliminary autopsies were performed on alien bodies. *(U.S. Air Force)*

Rear of Roswell AAF/Walker AFB hospital dispensary, ca. 1954. This is the ramp at which Glenn Dennis alleges he saw army ambulances loaded with odd-looking debris. *(U.S. Air Force)*

Air force Capt. Eileen M. Fanton, likely model for Glenn Dennis's missing nurse, "Naomi Maria Selff." *(U.S. Air Force)*

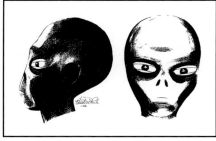

Artist conception of Roswell aliens drawn for an unnamed Roswell researcher (possibly Stanton Friedman) by Vincent DiPaula. These drawings appeared on the front page of the June 8, 1987, *Roswell Daily Record,* illustrating the second of a two-part story detailing the Roswell theories of ufologists William L. Moore and Stanton Friedman and the contents of alleged government documents confirming the reality of Roswell. Note strong similarity to Dennis-Henn sketches Dennis provided to Friedman two years later. *(Clifford Stone)*

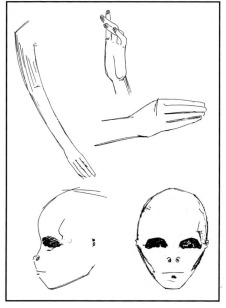

Sketches by artist Walter Henn under the direction of Glenn Dennis, allegedly based upon drawings of the alien cadavers at the Roswell AAF hospital made for Dennis by the mythical Nurse Selff. *(Glenn Dennis)*

U.S. Air Force KC-97 aerial-refueling tanker. An aircraft of this type crashed on takeoff from Roswell AAF/Walker AFB on June 26, 1956. Charred bodies of crew members were brought to the base hospital, likely providing the factual inspiration for Glenn Dennis's alien bodies tale. *(U.S. Air Force)*

U.S. Army Air Forces B-29 heavy bomber, the type operated by the 509th Bomb Group, Roswell AAF. A B-29 flew Major Marcel and a quantity of Foster Ranch debris to Eighth Air Force Headquarters, Fort Worth AAF, Texas. *(U.S. Air Force)*

A 1st ATU C-54 transport in flight, ca. 1946. Planes of this type allegedly transported saucer wreckage and alien bodies out of Roswell AAF. *(Roswell AAF Yearbook, Walter Haut)*

Capt. Oliver Wendell "Pappy" Henderson (left) and his 1st Air Transportation Unit C-54 crew, with their transport plane in background. Henderson claimed to have seen alien bodies and saucer debris and to have flown one or the other or both to Wright Field, Ohio. Frank Kaufmann says he copiloted a B-25 bomber with Henderson, transporting some of the bodies to Wright Field via Andrews AAF, near Washington, D.C. *(Roswell AAF Yearbook, Walter Haut)*

U.S. Army Air Forces B-25 bomber. The day before Major Marcel was dispatched to Fort Worth, an airplane of this type, converted for use as a command executive transport, probably flew to Fort Worth AAF with some or all of the debris brought to Roswell by Mack Brazel. *(U.S. Air Force)*

U.S. Army Air Forces B-26 bomber. According to Eighth Air Force executive officer Col. Thomas DuBose, the debris brought from Roswell aboard the 509th Bomb Group B-25 was transferred to the Eighth Air Force command transport, a B-26, and flown to Strategic Air Command headquarters near Washington, D.C. DuBose said the flights were ordered by Maj. Gen. Clements McMullen, SAC deputy chief of staff. *(U.S. Air Force)*

Maj. Gen. Clements McMullen, in July 1947, deputy chief of staff, Strategic Air Command. *(U.S. Air Force)*

Maj. Gen. Curtis LeMay and Brig. Gen. Roger Ramey during World War II. LeMay, in July 1947 deputy chief of air staff for research and development and later chief of staff of the air force, was very close to Col. William Blanchard and General Ramey and had oversight over Project Mogul. Ramey, in 1947, commander of the Eighth Air Force, of which the 509th Bomb Group was a part, issued the weather balloon "explanation" for the Roswell crashed-saucer story. *(U.S. Air Force)*

Brig. Gen. Roger Ramey in his Fort Worth AAF office posing with the remnants of New York University balloon project Mogul service Flight 4, evening of July 8, 1947. Note the pile of sun-degraded neoprene sounding-balloon fragments near Ramey's right foot. The other material is shattered remnants of at least two radar-reflecting targets. (*J. Bond Johnson/Fort Worth Star-Telegram*)

General Ramey and his executive officer Col. Thomas DuBose with the Flight 4 debris. The document Ramey holds in his left hand (see also above photo) is believed by many Roswell enthusiasts to be a classified message containing the "real truth" about the incident. (*J. Bond Johnson/ Fort Worth Star-Telegram*)

WO Irving Newton posing with NYU Flight 4 debris in General Ramey's office. Newton, a Fort Worth AAF meteorologist, was called in to identify the alleged flying saucer debris—which he did, as battered radar target parts and sounding-balloon fragments. (*Charles A. Cashon, U.S. Air Force/Pierre Lagrange*)

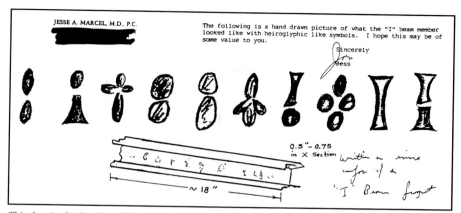

JESSE A. MARCEL, M.D., P.C.

The following is a hand drawn picture of what the "I" beam member looked like with heiroglyphic like symbols. I hope this may be of some value to you.

Sincerely
Jess

0.5"- 0.75
in X Section

~ 18"

This drawing by Dr. Marcel shows in greater detail his recollections of the shapes of the markings on the "I-beam." *(Roswell International UFO Museum)*

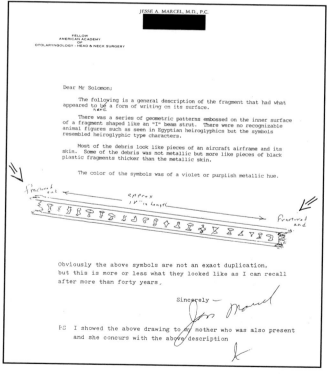

JESSE A. MARCEL, M.D., P.C.

FELLOW
AMERICAN ACADEMY
OF
OTOLARYNGOLOGY - HEAD & NECK SURGERY

Dear Mr Solomon;

The following is a general description of the fragment that had what appeared to be a form of writing on its surface.

There was a series of geometric patterns embossed on the inner surface of a fragment shaped like an "I" beam strut. There were no recognizable animal figures such as seen in Egyptian heiroglyphics but the symbols resembled heiroglyphic type characters.

Most of the debris look like pieces of an aircraft airframe and its skin. Some of the debris was not metallic but more like pieces of black plastic fragments thicker than the metallic skin.

The color of the symbols was of a violet or purplish metallic hue.

Fractured end

approx
18" in length

Fractured end

Obviously the above symbols are not an exact duplication, but this is more or less what they looked like as I can recall after more than forty years.

Sincerely — Marcel

PS I showed the above drawing to my mother who was also present and she concurs with the above description

Dr. Jesse Marcel Jr., a boy of eleven in July 1947, was shown some of the Foster Ranch debris by his father, Maj. Jesse Marcel Sr. He recalled at least one small, thin member that looked like an I-beam. On its edges were odd pinkish-purple markings. Dr. Marcel provided this description and sketch to a correspondent. Note Dr. Marcel's "fractured end" annotations. *(Roswell International UFO Museum)*

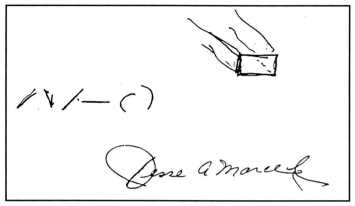

In 1981, Doctor Marcel's father told interviewer Linda Corley his son was mistaken about seeing an I-beam. He drew and signed this sketch of the "little member"s' rectangular cross section and his recollection of the markings on them for Corley. *(Miller Johnson)*

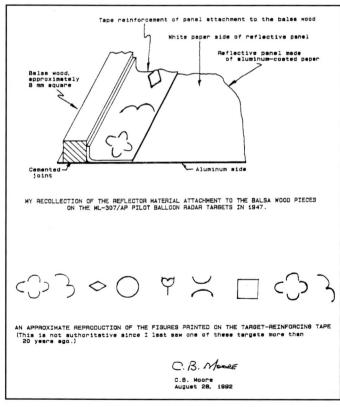

Tape reinforcement of panel attachment to the balsa wood

White paper side of reflective panel

Reflective panel made of aluminum-coated paper

Balsa wood, approximately 8 mm square

Cemented joint

Aluminum side

MY RECOLLECTION OF THE REFLECTOR MATERIAL ATTACHMENT TO THE BALSA WOOD PIECES ON THE ML-307/AP PILOT BALLOON RADAR TARGETS IN 1947.

AN APPROXIMATE REPRODUCTION OF THE FIGURES PRINTED ON THE TARGET-REINFORCING TAPE (This is not authoritative since I last saw one of these targets more than 20 years ago.)

C. B. Moore

C.B. Moore
August 28, 1992

NYU constant-level balloon project engineer C. B. Moore also remembered odd pinkish-purple markings, these on tape reinforcing the radar targets he was launching on his balloon and instrumentation flight trains. Note that the senior Marcel's and Moore's recollections of the markings bear a crude similarity, with Marcel's easily seen as segments of Moore's, and that both recall structural members of rectangular cross section, not I-beams. *(C. B. Moore)*

Scientists Albert P. Crary (left) and W. Maurice Ewing. The latter developed the concept that led to Project Mogul and the NYU constant-level balloon project. Crary directed Mogul field operations at Alamogordo Army Air Base. His field diary has provided information invaluable to the solution of the Roswell mystery. *(U.S. Air Force)*

Col. Marcellus Duffy (left) and Maj. Athelstan Spilhaus (third from left), ca. 1945. In late 1946, Duffy was brought in by Maj. Gen. Curtis LeMay to reorganize and reinvigorate Project Mogul. He asked Spilhaus, then director of research, NYU College of Engineering, to take on the job of developing flight platforms for Mogul. *(C. B. Moore)*

Capt. Albert Trakowski, who succeeded Colonel Duffy as Mogul project officer and was serving in that capacity at the time of the Roswell incident. *(U.S. Air Force and Albert Trakowski)*

Mogul project scientist James Peoples. His decision not to have the NYU team bring radiosonde tracking equipment to Alamogordo AAB in June 1947 led project engineer C. B. Moore to use multiple radar targets on his flight trains, a unique arrangement of an uncommon device. *(U.S. Air Force)*

Mogul field operations director Albert Crary tracking Flight 9 with a theodolite. *(Eileen Ulrich Farnochi and C. B. Moore)*

NYU project engineer C. B. Moore at work, ca. 1947. *(U.S. Air Force and C. B. Moore)*

Preparation for and launch of NYU Flight 9, evening of July 3, 1947. Flight 9 was once thought by the author and other Roswell researchers to be the Roswell "culprit." *(Eileen Ulrich Farnochi and C. B. Moore)*

Schematic diagram of NYU Mogul-service Flight 2, except for the radiosonde identical to Roswell "culprit" NYU Flight 4, launched from Alamogordo on June 4, 1947. Note especially the multiple radar targets, parachutes, launching rings, and the plastic ballast tubes. *(New York University, C. B. Moore)*

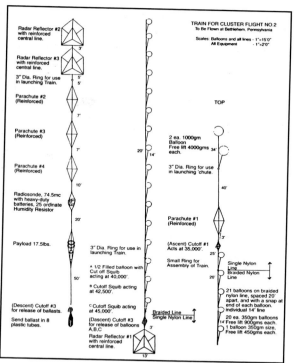

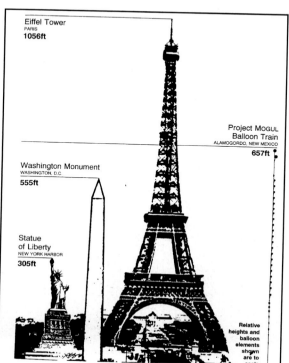

NYU "Mogul" Flight 4 was huge. *(U.S. Air Force)*

Professor C. B. Moore, in 1947 the NYU constant-level balloon project engineer, displays a later (ca. 1953) model of the type of radar target he used on NYU Flight 4. *(David Thomas)*

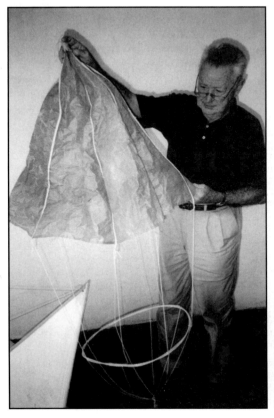

Professor Moore with a parchment parachute similar to those used on NYU Flight 4. Some debris field witnesses recalled the debris included tough, parchmentlike paper. *(David Thomas)*

Sonobuoy microphone package of the type used on some Mogul service flights by the NYU team. John Tiffany recalled his father seeing a large Thermos-like item in a collection of odd material on a special flight he crewed on from "somewhere in Texas" to Wright Field, Ohio. A sonobuoy microphone like this was the payload on Flight 4. *(U.S. Air Force)*

Roswell International UFO Museum founders (from left) Glenn Dennis, Max Littell, and Walter Haut, with the museum's alien, R.A.L.F. Haut was the Roswell AAF public relations officer who issued the crashed-saucer announcement. Dennis, who in 1947 worked at a Roswell funeral home that had a contract with the base, claims a key role in the case. *(Karl Pflock)*

The late U.S. Congressman Steven H. Schiff (R–N.M.). After his repeated requests to the Department of Defense for information about Roswell were ineptly handled, Schiff asked the U.S. Government Accounting Office to look into the matter. Schiff's initiative led to the U.S. Air Force's admission and public release of extensive information about what actually was behind the Roswell incident. *(U.S. House of Representatives, Mary Martinek)*

Ufologists Stanton Friedman and Karl Pflock in a "show of support" for each other's books about Roswell at the 1995 Mutual UFO Network symposium in Seattle. *(Philip J. Klass)*

Karl Pflock (far left) and Kevin Randle debate the Roswell case during the fiftieth anniversary celebration of the event, Roswell, July 1997. *(Bill Eatwell)*

The late Roswell case exploiter Philip Corso prepares to participate in a broadcast of *CNN Talk-Back Live* from near one of the alleged Roswell crash sites. Corso's science-fiction cum spy-thriller book *The Day After Roswell* was one of the most audacious and sleazy capitalizations on the incident. *(Bill Eatwell)*

Most important, what of the struts or beams, the strange markings, and the foil-like debris that were the central focus of attention, the items and features most vividly remembered by those who actually saw and handled the debris from the Foster Ranch and gave rise to notions of a crashed flying saucer from another planet? The ML-307B/AP, "gable type" radar corner-reflectors used by the NYU research and development team were designed late in World War II for the U.S. Army Signal Corps.[40] The radar-reflective material most generally used was aluminum foil laminated onto a sturdy white or brown paper, but on some batches of targets, a tough, aluminum coated paper was employed. Formed into right-angle triangles about three feet high, this material was glued onto balsa struts heavily coated with "something like Elmer's Glue" to strengthen them. These assemblies were arranged in a pattern which gave the appearance of abutting roof gables and was designed to present a radar-reflecting geometry from any angle.[41]

The targets were folded for shipment and storage, and it was soon discovered this and, on occasion, rigorous flying conditions stressed and weakened the paper-backed foil where it was attached to the struts. When this problem was identified, the manufacturer began using adhesive tape to reinforce the structure of the targets, lapping it over the struts and securing it to both sides of the reflector sheeting. The vendor was a New York City toy or novelty company, a "we'll make anything outfit" with numerous wartime contracts.[42] To solve the ML-307 problem, the company used tape it had on hand for manufacture of its civilian product lines. This was clear or milky and semi-opaque, about two inches wide. *It had pink and purple flowerlike figures imprinted on it.*

Professor Moore remembers these figures as being "embossed on the back of the tape" and not very bright in color but having "very sharp edges, sharply incised." Moore told me, "What sticks in my mind, Karl, is that every time I'd prepare a target for flight, I would always look at that tape and I would wonder, 'Why in the hell did anybody [use it]? What's the significance of this?' " Moore's confidence in these recollections is based not only on his 1947 activities but also many balloon flights during the succeeding two years on which the curiously "decorated" targets were employed.

Several others associated with Mogul, the NYU project, and the design and acquisition of these targets during World War II remember the oddly patterned tape. These include former NYU project technician Herbert Crowe, who was a member of the flight-train assembly and launch team; former Mogul project officer Trakowski; retired air force general Joseph Fletcher; and former signal corps and army air forces procurement officers George Trad, John Peterson, and Edwin Istvan. It was Istvan who placed the original order. Trakowski told me he well remembered the first time he and others in his air forces weather service group saw the tape-reinforced targets. They all had a good laugh, shaking their heads and thinking, "What next?"[43]

Keeping the rather unmilitary ML-307B's in mind, consider the testimony of several key first- and secondhand witnesses to the Roswell debris. Loretta Proctor remembers Mack Brazel talking about *"tape* which had printing on it [emphasis added]. The color of the printing was a kind of purple. He said it wasn't Japanese writing; from the way he described it, it sounded like it resembled hieroglyphics [*sic*]." Brazel's sister, the late Lorraine Ferguson, is reported as remembering him saying some of what he found "had some kind of unusual writing on it—Mac[k] said it was like the kind of stuff you find all over Japanese or Chinese firecrackers; not really writing, just wiggles and such." Brazel's son, Bill, says his father mentioned some of the debris had "figures" on it. He said this was the same term his father used when he talked about Indian petroglyphs.[44]

Mack Brazel's daughter, Bessie, who helped her father gather up some of the debris, remembers "grayish silver" foil attached to "sticks, like kite sticks" with "a whitish *tape* [emphasis added]. The tape was about two or three inches wide and had flower-like designs on it. The 'flowers' were faint, a variety of pastel colors, and reminded me of Japanese paintings in which the flowers are not all connected."[45]

In an April 1979 letter to *Roswell Incident* coauthor Bill Moore, Dr. Jesse Marcel wrote, "In reference to the UFO incident of 1947 or 1948 I omitted one startling description of the wreckage for fear it might have been the fanciful imagination of a twelve-year-old. Imprinted along the edge of some of the beam remnants, there were hieroglyphic-type characters. I recently questioned my father about this, and he recalled seeing these characters also, and even described them as being a pink or purplish-pink color." In his interview with Bob Pratt, the senior Marcel talked of thin "members" along the length of which were "little markings, two-color markings as I can recall. Like Chinese writing to me, nothing you could make sense out of." A year and a half later, during an interview with college student Linda Corley, he made a rough sketch of what he recalled of these markings. In a 1993 telephone conversation, Dr. Marcel told me, "Some of the geometric forms could resemble the petals of a flower . . . maybe flowerlike . . . a solid form, purple color, violet hue."[46]

Former Fort Worth Army Air Field weatherman Irving Newton also remembers the strange markings. As a young army air forces warrant officer, Newton was called to General Roger Ramey's office on the evening of July 8 to examine and identify the "flying saucer" brought from Roswell by Major Marcel. In a July 1994 interview, Newton recalled,

> I told them that this was a balloon and a RAWIN [radar-wind] target. I believed this because I had seen many of these before. . . .
>
> While I was examining the debris, Major Marcel was picking up pieces of the target sticks and trying to convince me that some notations on the sticks were alien writings. There were figures on the sticks[,] lavender or pink in color, appearing to be weather faded markings, with no rhyme or reason. . . .

The markings were not something Newton recalled having seen before. He found them peculiar but, unlike Major Marcel, not by any means out of this world, since he had no doubt about the nature and planetary origin of the device on which they appeared.[47]

The parallels between the descriptions of the markings/tape with markings on the debris found by Mack Brazel and collected by Marcel and those on the novelty/toy-company tape used to reinforce the radar targets flown by the NYU balloon-project team are impossible to dismiss. To my mind, they are virtually conclusive.

Only Dr. Marcel recalls the small struts on which he, his father, and others saw the odd markings, as having an I-beam-like cross section. His father spoke repeatedly of solid "rectangular members," measuring "perhaps three-eighths of an inch by one-quarter of an inch thick and just about all sizes. None of them were [sic] very long. I'd say about three feet." He said this material was "weightless. You couldn't even tell you had it in your hands . . . just like balsa wood." Quite a good match with the balsa members used in constructing ML-307 radar targets.

In the May 1981 tape-recorded interview with Linda Corley mentioned above, the elder Marcel called into question his son's recollections of an I-beam or beams: "Jesse didn't have that right to begin with. . . . He said they looked like I-beams. But it wasn't. . . . Let me give you a cross section of what it looked like." He drew a solid rectangular cross section. He also sketched his recollections of the "alien writing," showing figures quite unlike those drawn by his son and appearing much more like segments of those recalled by Professor Moore.[48]

The senior Marcel's description of the "beams" is the most detailed we have. Bessie Brazel Schreiber remembers "sticks, like kite sticks." Former Associated Press reporter Jason Kellahin remembered "sticks" attached to "silver colored fabric, perhaps aluminized cloth." Walter Whitmore told me of seeing and collecting "balsa wood sticks." Loretta Proctor and Bill Brazel remember only small fragments. Proctor remembers "a little sliver of wood looking stuff. . . . [It was] about the size of a pencil and about three or four inches long. . . . It was a kind of a brownish tan . . . [and it] looked like plastic, . . . that was kind of what it looked like." Brazel recalls material "like balsa wood in weight, but a bit darker and much harder. . . . [Y]ou couldn't scratch it with your fingernail like ordinary balsa, and you couldn't break it either. It was pliable, but wouldn't break. Of course, all I had was a few splinters."

With the exception of the struts' alleged strength, again we have very good match-ups with NYU-project targets. As for the reported super strength, consider that Proctor and Brazel said all they saw and handled were "slivers" and "splinters." In addition, Dr. Marcel told me he recalled at least one of the beams with the strange markings as "being broken off. It looked like it had been severed or broken. It was not a finished edge." A drawing he has made shows a beam with jagged ends, which Marcel labeled "fractured."[49] Clearly, the beams were not indestructible.

As for the foil-like material, we have various descriptions, but the great majority quite directly match the radar-reflective sheets used in the NYU team's radar targets. For example, Whitmore spoke of "white, linen-like cloth with reflective tinfoil attached to one side. Some pieces were glued to balsa wood sticks." Jason Kellahin told me he saw "pieces of silver colored fabric, perhaps aluminized cloth. Some of the pieces had sticks attached to them." Bessie Schreiber said she picked up "double-sided material, foil-like on one side. . . . Sticks, like kite sticks, were attached to some of the pieces with a whitish tape." She also said the "material could not be torn like ordinary aluminum foil," which, of course, foil backed by tough paper could not.[50]

It has been suggested that the radar targets flown from Alamogordo AAB by the NYU group would have been recognized easily for what they were because they were in wide use by military weather units. It also has been claimed that what Warrant Officer Newton identified and the press viewed and photographed in General Ramey's office was not the real saucer wreckage flown in from Roswell. Some Roswell authors and Major Marcel himself claimed a battered radar target and a shredded weather balloon from the Fort Worth AAF weather office were substituted for the real goods.[51]

These assertions do not stand up to scrutiny. Model 307B/AP radar targets were not in general use in the continental United States at the time. Irving Newton noted this in his July 1994 interview: "They were normally launched by a special crew and followed by a ground radar unit. . . . *We did not use them at Fort Worth*. However, I was familiar with them because we used them and their products on various projects in which I was involved. *These were used mostly on special projects and overseas*" (emphasis added). Neither were such targets issued to the weather and flight service unit at Roswell AAF. In fact, few if any air forces weather squadrons had access to tracking radars and so would not have been issued the targets. It is also worth noting that almost four years later people were still mistaking ML-307 radar targets in flight and on the ground as flying saucers.[52]

Other than the NYU team, the only known activity in New Mexico that was using balloon-borne radar targets in 1947 was a group making upper-air observations in support of the V-2 rocket firings at White Sands Proving Ground. Prior to that, very limited use was made of them to provide wind data for the Trinity atomic bomb test on July 16, 1945. Neither of these operations employed balloon clusters and multiple radar target arrays like those used by the NYU group. Unlike the Watson Labs radar at Alamogordo, their radars operated on the frequency for which the targets were designed. Only one target per flight was required, and one sounding or pilot balloon provided sufficient lift for this.[53]

So, while Mack Brazel and Maj. Jesse Marcel (and others at Roswell AAF and in the region) would have had no trouble identifying routinely used balloon-lofted weather equipment such as radiosondes, it is highly unlikely either of them had ever seen an ML-307B/AP radar target until they came upon the remains of three of them on the Foster Ranch. Mack Brazel's statement to reporters on July 8 about previously having found "weather observation balloons on the ranch" and that "I am sure what I found was not any weather observation balloon" is consistent with this. So, too, is Major Marcel's reaction to what he found, apparently particularly inspired by the odd pinkish-purple markings.

Ironically, it is these markings, so often pointed to as evidence that the Foster Ranch debris was from another planet, that tie the "saucer wreckage" directly to the NYU balloon group and Project Mogul. The radar targets used by Moore and his colleagues were taken from U.S. Army Signal Corps stock in New Jersey. There is every indication that the complete lot was put into storage when World War II ended, with not one target ever having been distributed to any operational unit. These were the targets with the telltale tape, the "alien writing."[54]

Finally, the photographs of the debris taken in General Ramey's office unquestionably show the remains of more than one ML-307B radar target and several sun-degraded neoprene sounding balloons.[55] The press conference at which these tattered exhibits were displayed was held shortly after Marcel had arrived in Fort Worth and less than forty-eight hours after Mack Brazel arrived at the Chaves County sheriff's office. Even in the well-nigh impossible event that the army had enough detailed information about the nature and appearance of the alleged saucer wreckage to decide some shredded weather balloons and battered radar targets would be enough to fool the press, assembling the props for the conference would have been no simple trick.

Quietly rounding up the targets from distant units would have required some deft scrambling. Even if that were successful, there would not have been enough time to properly "age" torn neoprene, and military weather stations did not keep sun-discolored balloon bits handy just in case a general officer needed it for a cover-up show-and-tell routine. Even if all of this had been possible, why would the cover-up artists have whipped up a display of the remains of several targets and balloons when one of each would have done nicely?

Mack Brazel had it right when he told his family the excitement over his find was "one hell of a hullabaloo out of nothing."[56] Prophetic words from an old cowboy. To which I would add, what are the odds that a vehicle from another planet would be constructed of materials so closely similar to those used by the NYU project and, on top of that, that such a "camouflaged" craft would crash so conveniently close to the NYU project's base of operations? Astronomical? At least. One hell of a hullabaloo out of nothing indeed.

NOTES

1. Robert Todd's continuing efforts to fill in the blanks about the Roswell-NYU-Mogul collection were the essential element in cracking the Roswell mystery.

2. Telephone conversations with Stanton T. Friedman and Don Berliner, December 1992.

3. Charles Berlitz and William L. Moore, *The Roswell Incident* (New York: Berkley, 1988), pp. 40–41.

4. Ibid., p. 42.

5. Personal interview with Charles B. Moore, May 23, 1993; audiotaped telephone interview with Moore, October 6, 1993; audiotaped telephone interview with Albert C. Trakowski, March 21, 1994. See also United States Air Force, *The Roswell Report: Fact versus Fiction in the New Mexico Desert* (Washington, D.C.: U.S. Government Printing Office, 1994).

6. Re Ewing and "sofar," see, Daniel N. Lapedes, ed., *McGraw-Hill Dictionary of Scientific and Technical Terms*, (New York: McGraw-Hill, 1978); Isaac Asimov, *Asimov's Biographical Encyclopedia of Science and Technology* (New York: Avon/Equinox, 1972).

7. See n. 5 above.

8. Ibid; Charles B. Moore, James R. Smith, and Seymour Goldstein, Technical Report Number 1, Balloon Group, Constant Level Balloon Project (Project 93) of the Research Division, College of Engineering, New York University, April 1, 1948. See app. B.

9. See n. 5 above, Moore. Moore is now emeritus professor of atmospheric physics, New Mexico Institute of Mining and Technology.

10. See n. 5 above, Trakowski.

11. These were flights 2 and 3 in the numbered NYU flight series.

12. See n. 5 above, Moore.

13. Ibid.

14. Ibid.

15. Ibid. See flight-configuration schematic in app. B.

16. See n. 5 above.

17. Moore told me that at one point, Charles Schneider had to justify the use of the "aerial mines" to the Civil Aeronautics Administration, citing national security.

18. See n. 5 above, Moore.

19. See n. 5 above, Moore, Trakowski.

20. See n. 5 above, Moore.

21. See n. 5 above, Trakowski.

22. Ibid. Trakowski remembers hearing a local radio report of a flying saucer in the Alamogordo area, which he told me definitely was an NYU flight.

23. "Fantasy of 'Flying Disc' Is Explained Here," *Alamogordo News*, July 10, 1947 (Pritchard was incorrectly identified in a United Press story of the same date as "James R. Pritchard, public relations officer at the Alamogorodo [*sic*] air field"); United States Air Force, *Fact versus Fiction*, "Report of Air Force Research Regarding the 'Roswell Incident,'" attachment 32, "Synopsis of Balloon Research Findings."

24. Ibid.

25. As Moore pointed out to me in a letter of January 29, 1995, Pritchard and company picked just enough true bits and pieces from Mogul's activities to make a plausible cover story.

26. See app. C.

27. See n. 5 above, Trakowski.

28. Robert G. Todd, e-mail message to me, July 2, 2000. I am grateful to Todd and Professor Moore for providing me with copies of Colonel Duffy's letters.

29. Audiotaped telephone interview with Eileen Ulrich Farnochi, February 1995; letter, Farnochi to Charles B. Moore, January 9, 1995, copy in my files; letter, Moore to me, January 29, 1995.

30. See, e.g., Berlitz and Moore, *Roswell Incident*, p. 73.

31. Audiotaped personal interviews with Walter E. Whitmore Jr., October 31, 1992, and May 16, 1993. A significantly contradictory version of this story is attributed to Whitmore in Berlitz and Moore, *Roswell Incident* (pp. 97–99). I asked Whitmore about this during our October 31 interview, and he emphatically stated that Berlitz and Moore had misquoted him. He told me he pointed this out to Moore in detail after the book was published in 1980, but no corrections were made in subsequent printings or for the 1988 paperback edition.

32. Karl T. Pflock, *Roswell in Perspective* (Washington, D.C.: Fund for UFO Research, 1994), p. 116.

33. "All that junk all over out there," is a statement attributed to Mack Brazel by his 1947 neighbor Sallye Strickland Tadolini. See Tadolini affidavit in app. H.

34. Letter from Charles B. Moore to me, August 22, 1994, and numerous telephone and in-person conversations.

35. C. B. Moore, *The New York University Balloon Flights During Early June, 1947* (Socorro, N.M.: self-published, 1995); letter from Moore to Kevin D. Randle, October 21, 1995, copy in my files; telephone conversations with Moore, October 31 and November 1, 1995; United States Weather Bureau Analysis Center winds-aloft maps, June 1947, copies in my files courtesy of Professor Moore.

36. Letter from Charles B. Moore to Philip J. Klass, September 25, 1995, as quoted in Philip J. Klass, *The Real Roswell Crashed-Saucer Coverup* (Amherst, N.Y.: Prometheus Books, 1997), pp. 120–21.

37. Marcel interview with Bob Pratt, app. A; Schreiber affidavit, app. H; "Harassed Rancher Who Located 'Saucer' Sorry He Told About It," *Roswell Daily Record*, July 9, 1947; Whitmore interviews, October 31, 1992, and May 16, 1993.

38. Johnson made this reference in an audiotaped telephone interview with Kevin Randle (February 27, 1989; copy in my files) and went on to say, "Anybody in his right mind, with the stench that that had, would want to get it out of his office pretty quick."

39. Audiotaped telephone interview with Bessie Brazel Schreiber, August 26, 1993; William L. Moore, "Crashed Saucers: Evidence in Search of Proof," *MUFON 1985 UFO Sym-*

posium Proceedings (Seguin, Tex.: Mutual UFO Network, 1985), p. 158; letter from Charles B. Moore to me, January 29, 1995.

40. See n. 5 above.

41. Ibid.

42. Among these was a contract for aluminum chaff, used to foil enemy radars, which is why the company was thought to be a good candidate to build the targets. Besides Moore and Trakowski, others have recalled that this was the case, among them: Maj. Gen. Joseph Fletcher, USAF (ret.), who during World War II was instrumental in pioneering the use of radar to gather weather data, including the development of corner-reflector targets; former U.S. Army Signal Corps and Army Air Forces procurement officers George Trad, John Peterson, and Edwin Istvan; the late Athelstan Spilhaus, director of the NYU project who as an army air forces officer was involved with the development of the targets; and the late Col. Marcellus Duffy. In 1993, Trad told Professor Moore that he remembered a "father-and-son company called Merrick Manufacturing on Canal Street" in New York City as the target contractor. See n. 5 above. Letter from Charles B. Moore to me, January 29, 1995; transcript of interview with Marcellus Duffy conducted by Patrick Huyghe, November 30, 1991, copy in my files courtesy of Professor Moore and Robert Todd; letter from Marcellus Duffy to Robert Todd, November 13, 1991, copy in my files.

43. See n. 5 above; telephone conversation with Professor Moore, February 1995.

44. Proctor affidavit, app. H; transcript of telephone interview with Loretta Proctor conducted by Kevin Randle, April 20, 1989, in Kevin D. Randle, *Roswell UFO Crash Update: Exposing the Military Cover-Up of the Century* (New Brunswick, N.J.: Global Communications, 1995), p. 164; Berlitz and Moore, *Roswell Incident*, pp. 89 and 95.

45. Schreiber affidavit, app. H.

46. Stanton T. Friedman and Don Berliner, *Crash at Corona* (New York: Paragon House, 1992), p. 16; app. A, Marcel Sr. interview; audiotaped telephone interview with Dr. Jesse A. Marcel Jr., September 23, 1993.

47. Newton July 21, 1994, statement in United States Air Force, *Fact versus Fiction*, attachment 30 to "Report of Air Force Research Regarding the 'Roswell Incident.' "

48. App. A; audiotaped personal interview with Jesse A. and Viaud Marcel, May 5, 1981, conducted by Linda Corley, tapes provided to me by Stanton T. Friedman.

49. Marcel Jr., September 23, 1993. The sketch is included in the photo insert. It is worth noting that while, in many interviews, including one with me, Loretta Proctor has claimed that when Mack Brazel showed a "sliver of a wood looking stuff" to her and her husband, Floyd, Brazel and Floyd Proctor tried and failed to cut and burn the material. Yet in the April 20, 1989, interview with Kevin Randle cited above she explicitly denied this.

50. Kellahin and Schreiber affidavits, app. H.

51. See for example, Berlitz and Moore, *Roswell Incident*, pp. 75–76.

52. Karl T. Pflock, "Roswell, Radar Targets, and All That," *MUFON UFO Journal* (September 1995): 12–13.

53. See n. 5 above; telephone conversation with Charles B. Moore, August 20, 1994; letter from Moore to me, February 9, 1996.

54. See n. 5 above; letter from Charles B. Moore to me, January 29, 1995; telephone conversation with Moore, August 20, 1994.

55. See n. 5 above; letter from Charles B. Moore to Robert Todd, August 21, 1992, copy in my files courtesy of James W. Moseley and Robert Todd; letter from Moore to Col. Richard Weaver, May 6, 1994, copy in my files courtesy of Professor Moore.

56. Schreiber affidavit, app. H.

FOURTEEN

THE TERROR AND OTHER EXAGGERATIONS

On close and careful examination, the seemingly impressive case for a crashed flying saucer at Roswell dissolves, and a quite different picture comes into focus. No saucer wreckage. No bodies. No missing nurses. Instead, there is revealed the story of a highly classified, very sensitive U.S. Army Air Forces research-and-development project, how it almost was compromised by a combination of complacency, chance, and hubris, and what military authorities did to forestall such a security breach.

Yet doubts still linger, doubts I shared not all that long ago. In this chapter I examine some of the "whys" behind this. Be prepared for some surprises.

JAIL TIME AND THREATS MOST DIRE?

Often cited by doubters as a basis for skepticism are the sometimes tearfully related accounts of dire threats against witnesses and their families and other acts of intimidation and repression. A reader's letter published in the spring 2000 *International UFO Reporter* under the headline "Going Neanderthal Over Mogul Debris" concisely sums up the doubters' views, offering in the bargain a prime example of what my friend and ufological gadfly James W. Moseley calls Saucer Logic:

> Although I've made an effort to follow the evolving debate over the Roswell incident, I do not recall any of the Project Mogul proponents addressing the question of why witnesses to a balloon crash would need to receive rough treatment at the hands of the U.S. military to shut them up. . . .
>
> The significance of balloon debris, no matter how secret, would have been lost on all but the most technically skilled scientists involved. Consequently, there would have been no need for the various methods of intimidation and pressure reportedly used against civilians, especially Mack Brazel. They didn't know enough to be dangerous!
>
> This "behavioral mismatch" remains one of the strongest arguments that the Mogul story is disinformation.
>
> *Terry Hansen*
> *Bainbridge Island, Washington*

Hansen does not seem to have considered the possibility that the tales of "rough treatment" may be dramatic exaggerations or even utterly untrue, that there really was no "behavioral mismatch." Moreover, as I have shown, there were things aboard NYU Flight 4 that could and did raise questions in the minds and inspire the imaginations of even technically knowledgeable people.

Still, Hansen and other doubters have a point. The *reported* actions of military authorities *are* greatly out of proportion to any reasonable concerns about Project Mogul security, not to mention violations of law and the constitutional rights of American citizens.

I, too, once found some of the tales of intimidation credible. Even after I was certain Project Mogul and the supporting activities of the New York University team at Alamogordo played a central role in the incident, this caused me to think something far more sensitive might well be involved. It would have been quite consistent with concerns about Mogul security for the army quietly to contact the Roswell newspapers and radio stations and ask them to spike or downplay the story. Anything more dramatic would have been overkill and contrary to the low-key, no-big-deal weather balloon and radar-tracking and training cover stories that clearly were intended to protect Mogul. Taking the sort of heavy-handed actions testified to by some could have backfired, reigniting press interest and exposing the project to hostile foreign powers.

These considerations do make one wonder. However, an examination of the claims of Gestapo-like tactics and established, "inconvenient" facts leaves little room for any reasonable doubt about what did and did not happen.

It has been alleged that the army held Mack Brazel against his will for as long as eight days. According to one of his neighbors, the late Marion Strickland, Brazel complained of being "held in jail" at Roswell Army Air Field and was not allowed to leave the base. Kevin Randle and Donald Schmitt have written that Edwin Easley, in July 1947 the Roswell AAF provost marshall, told Randle that Brazel "was kept under guard in the [base] guest house for a number of days."[1]

Also cited as evidence that the rancher was in some sort of military custody are reports that Brazel was being escorted and kept (mostly) incommunicado by military personnel in Roswell. Friends told of seeing him in downtown Roswell, "surrounded by the military." Army men reportedly also waited outside the *Roswell Daily Record* office while Brazel gave an interview to the *Record* and Associated Press reporter Jason Kellahin. It has been implied that the military brought him there to tell a cover story authorities had dictated to him.

Seeming to lend further support to the Mack-in-jail story is the testimony of Brazel's son Bill and former radio station KGFL announcer Frank Joyce. Bill has told several ufologists that, when he arrived on the Foster Ranch from Albuquerque on July 10, his father was not there and did not return until two or three days later. He also has claimed "they had shut him up for about a week." Joyce told me and others that when Brazel visited him at the radio station, probably on the evening of July 8, army personnel waited for him outside as he told Joyce his allegedly revised story. Joyce said he could tell "the Army had gotten to him," and quoted Brazel as saying, "It'll go hard on me," which Joyce took to mean Brazel had to stick to the new story or risk government retribution.[2]

All this seems quite impressive until we learn that Randle did not record his interview with Easley and has no independent verification of what he recalls the now-deceased officer told him. Similarly, there is nothing to back up Frank Joyce's dramatic claims, and I have already shown that Joyce has a rather fertile imagination and a tendency to "enrich" his recollections as time goes by.

While Bill Brazel seems to think his father was away from the ranch for several days, we have the countervailing testimony of his sister Bessie Schreiber, who was there with her father and helped him pick up the "bunch of garbage." She does not remember her father "taking any overnight or longer trips away from the ranch around that time."[3]

Over against this is the testimony of several witnesses that Mack spent at least one night in Roswell, not in the custody of the army but as the guest of Walter Whitmore Sr., majority owner of KGFL. Whitmore's station had been scooped by the rival KSWS on the breaking captured flying disk story, and he was determined to recoup with an exclusive interview of Brazel. According to the late Jud Roberts, minority partner in KGFL, Whitmore went looking for Brazel, found him somewhere in Roswell, and took him to his home. There he conducted and wire-recorded an interview, which he intended to release to the Mutual Network. Roberts told me and others that Brazel spent that night at the Whitmore home. The recollections of Whitmore's son, the late Walter Jr. (see chapter 13), lend credence to this.[4]

The possibility that Whitmore had established some control over and working relationship with Brazel is given considerable weight by this unequivocal statement in the July 9, 1947, *Roswell Daily Record* report on the interview given in the newspaper office the evening before: "Brazel was brought here late yesterday by W. E. Whitmore, of radio station KGFL." Lending further support is what Jason Kellahin told me: "Walter E. Whitmore, owner of KGFL, . . . was also present during the interview. Whitmore did his best to maneuver Brazel away from the rest of the press." It would seem Whitmore, not the army, was "managing" Brazel, this much to the army's chagrin, according to the younger Whitmore, who told ufologist Bill Moore that evening the army was "having a fit" because they could not locate Brazel.

Directly related to Brazel's situation is the alleged threat to revoke KGFL's broadcast license if Whitmore aired the recorded interview with the rancher. To have been effective and consistent with the timing of other events, the threat would necessarily have been delivered late on July 8 or early the morning of July 9.

The two sources for this claim, Jud Roberts and Walter Whitmore Jr., are both deceased. So, too, are the persons who allegedly delivered the threats, T. J. Slowie, secretary of the Federal Communications Commission, the commercial-radio licensing authority; Dennis Chavez, then one of New Mexico's U.S. senators; or, perhaps, then U.S. Secretary of Agriculture Clinton Anderson, another New Mexico Democrat politician.

The younger Whitmore told me it was his father who received the call (from Slowie) or calls (from Slowie and either Chavez or Anderson). Whitmore Sr. was a significant player in the state's Democratic Party and a friend of both Chavez and Anderson, so it is not out of the question that he might have received a friendly warning call from one of these men. Roberts claimed it was he who received the call—"it may have been someone in the office of Clinton Anderson or Dennis Chavez"—

suggesting "we might lose our license in as quickly as three days," and that it was he who, on his own, decided to kill the story.

What are we to make of all this? To my mind, the threat story seems likely to be at most an exaggeration of what may have actually happened, perhaps a joking chat between Whitmore or Roberts and Slowie, Chavez, or Anderson. By the morning of July 9, not only was the original flying disk story already worldwide news, so too was the weather balloon "explanation." Radio station KSWS, which broke the story the day before, did not have its broadcast license threatened. It is unlikely that such an effort against either station could have been coordinated so quickly among the military, the FCC, and the office of Senator Chavez or Secretary Anderson. Such a thing would be difficult with today's high-speed communications. It would have been all but impossible in 1947. Quite simply, such a threat would have been counterproductive and prohibitively difficult to execute as quickly as it was said to have been carried out.

It is known from a contemporaneous source that Whitmore was squiring Brazel around on the evening of July 8. We have testimony that backs this up and that the rancher spent at least one night at Whitmore's home, a likely possibility considering the lateness of the hour at which the interview in the newspaper office took place and the lengthy drive Brazel would have to make home.

As with so much about Roswell, memories and testimony are confused and conflicting. We simply do not know what actually took place and never will. However, all things considered, it seems very likely to me that Brazel's "detainment" was a product of the senior Whitmore's considerable and well-known persuasiveness, not army compulsion. Brazel's complaint had nothing to do with being physically locked up, but rather was the chafing of a private, quiet man used to running his own life in the wide-open spaces who suddenly found himself swept into the bewildering and embarrassing situation of being a media celebrity and the subject of some scrutiny from military authorities. As the *Roswell Daily Record* reported on July 9, "Brazel . . . told his story of finding what the army at first described as a flying disk, but the publicity which attended his find caused him to add that if he ever found anything else short of a bomb he sure wasn't going to say anything about it."

Whitmore probably brought Brazel to the *Record* office with the thought that a nationally distributed Associated Press wire story could give his recorded interview with Brazel a boost, whetting the public appetite for more, but he likely quickly realized it was too late. The flying disk balloon had burst. It was rapidly becoming a nonstory and was yesterday's news by the next morning when KGFL went on the air. End of story.

What of the other claims of threats and intimidation? There are five—count 'em, five—persons who have made such assertions. Who are they? Glenn Dennis, Frankie Rowe, Ruben Anaya, Jim Ragsdale, and Barbara Dugger, granddaughter of Chaves County Sheriff George Wilcox and his wife, Inez.

Dennis alleges he was personally threatened in the Roswell AAF hospital. Later, he claims, Sheriff Wilcox visited his father with the warning that the military had asked for the names and addresses of the entire Dennis family and that Glenn should forget about what he had seen and heard. Rowe, usually with tears welling in her eyes, tells of the visit from the army man with the "loud, booming voice," who told her that, "if he found out that any of us had talked, they might just take us out into the middle of the desert and shoot all of us." Anaya spoke of he, his brother, and two friends being told by Senator Chavez to keep their mouths shut about what had happened with New Mexico Lt. Gov. Joseph Montoya, who in any case was a "damn liar." Ragsdale told of mysterious break-ins and what he said he thought was an attempt on his life, all of which he attributed to his possession of pieces of the downed flying saucer.

Finally, we have the story of Barbara Dugger, whose mother Elizabeth Tulk, is the daughter of Sheriff George Wilcox and his wife, Inez. In a March 1991 interview, Dugger alleged that decades after the fact, her grandmother told her the military visited her grandparents at the sheriff's office and threatened that "if we [George and Inez Wilcox] ever told anything about the incident, not only would we be killed, but our entire family would be killed."[5]

This is a stand-alone claim, which makes it suspect in light of what both Dugger's mother and the Wilcox's other daughter, Dugger's aunt Phyllis McGuire, have said to Roswell researchers about their memories of the events of July 1947. McGuire was in the sheriff's office when the military arrived, and Tulk's husband Jay dropped in soon after. The Tulks and McGuire have never said anything about death threats. The closest any of them has come is McGuire's recollection that, after she had "pestered" her parents about what had happened, her mother told her the army had asked the sheriff not to say anything further about the incident—rather like what former reporter Jason Kellahin recalled from his attempt to interview the sheriff the evening of July 8: "Wilcox said the military indicated to him it would be best if he did not say anything."[6]

As we have seen, Dennis, Rowe, Anaya, and Ragsdale simply are not credible. Each of their stories is, in a word, incredible. Similarly lacking in credibility is Dugger's unsupported secondhand account, given just weeks after the Roswell case and tales of the harsh cover-up measures had been given currency by the *Unsolved Mysteries* broadcasts. Without the claims of these witnesses, without the jailing of Mack Brazel, without the silencing of radio station KGFL, all that is left of the Roswell Terror is the great paper sweep.

DISAPPEARING PRESS RELEASES AND SUCH

Because no copy of the Roswell AAF crashed-disk press release has ever been found, it has been assumed and asserted by saucer crash proponents that the army conducted a sweep of the Roswell newspaper offices and radio stations, rounding up and destroying all copies. As I have shown, the real reason no copy of the release exists is because a written one almost certainly never was distributed, that the only written copy likely was the one Walter Haut read from when he contacted the local media by telephone. This is borne out by the July 8 United Press Association wire exchange in which the UP Santa Fe bureau advises the UP Denver office that the "army gave verbal announcement. No text."

Two of those who certainly would have remembered a roundup of press release copies have no memory of anything of the sort. George Walsh, the former KSWS station manager who broke the captured flying disk story, told me the only notice of the army's about-face he remembered his station getting was an Associated Press wire item reporting Ramey's weather balloon announcement. Similarly, Art McQuiddy, the former editor of the *Roswell Morning Dispatch,* told me the only thing he recalled with any certainty was a telephone call from Roswell AAF advising him the earlier announcement was in error. When I asked Walter Haut about it, the former airbase public relations officer who put out the release said he remembered nothing dramatic happening and assumed his copy had simply been thrown out just as had all the other releases he had cranked out.

So where did this tale originate? With Frank Joyce. He told me and others that KGFL, where he worked, was swept clean of "every scrap of paper that had anything about the event on it." He added the claim that the files of the United Press Association Santa Fe bureau office, to which he reported the story as a UP stringer, had been cleaned out. Yet as I have explained, Joyce gave Roswell researchers, including myself, copies of July 8 UP wire stories and communications about the alleged saucer crash, which he received on the radio station's Teletype and filed away, and Jud Dixon, the UP–Santa Fe man at the time, told me no one raided his office.

Once again, we find a facet of the Roswell saga to which there is "less than meets the eye." Like a number of others, this one turns out to be a mutation born of exaggeration of a less-than-accurate account by one of the witnesses, someone who played a part in real events less dramatic than he now recalls.

As Terry Hansen observes, if all that were involved was debris from a New York University Mogul-service flight, "there would have been no need for the various methods of intimidation and pressure reportedly used against civilians." Precisely.

ANOTHER LOOK AT LYDIA SLEPPY'S STORY

There is another dramatic story closely related to claims that U.S. government authorities sought to intimidate the Roswell press and broadcast-news outlets. This comes to us from Lydia Sleppy, who in July 1947 worked at Albuquerque radio station KOAT, an affiliate of Roswell's KSWS. Sleppy has claimed that the FBI cut her off in mid-sentence as she was attempting to transmit by Teletype a story about the Roswell crashed saucer dictated to her over the telephone by KSWS general manager John McBoyle. Sleppy said that, as she began to type, the warning bell on her machine rang and an incoming message something like this automatically began printing, pre-empting her: "THIS IS THE FBI. YOU WILL IMMEDIATELY CEASE ALL COMMUNICATION." If true, this is rather startling evidence of a coordinated attempt to suppress news about whatever was found in the vicinity of Roswell.

Sleppy was located by ufologist Stanton Friedman in October 1990, who had been directed to her by her son, a forest ranger whom a Friedman associate had contacted in connection with another UFO case. I interviewed Sleppy three years later. As for McBoyle, when contacted by a number of ufologists before his death in 1992, he reportedly either refused to talk about the incident at all or dismissed his callers with, "Forget about it. It never happened."

When I spoke with Sleppy, I found her to be pleasant, open, and quite straight-forward. She related her account in a fashion that suggested she was telling the truth as she genuinely remembered it, neither too detailed and certain nor too vague and hesitant. One thing did give me pause. This was her claim to have seen formations of flying saucers several times in the late 1940s. Unlike some investigators, I do not con-sider multiple sightings by a witness the basis for automatic dismissal of all the person's claims about UFO-related experiences. However, when a witness tells me, as Sleppy did, of lying on her Albuquerque front lawn with neighbors to watch saucers go over time and again, a warning flag definitely goes up.

Sleppy told me, as she had told Friedman, that she asked KOAT assistant man-ager Karl Lambertz to sit in as she took down McBoyle's story, holding out the possi-bility of a corroborating witness. My efforts to locate Lambertz led me to his widow, who told me her husband had never said anything about such an incident and that, in fact, until I contacted her, she had never heard anything about the Roswell affair at all.[7] With both McBoyle and Lambertz gone, everyone directly involved other than Sleppy was out of the picture.

About three weeks after I spoke with Sleppy, I interviewed Merle Tucker in his Albu-querque office. In 1947, Tucker owned KOAT and, in whole or part, other New Mexico radio stations, including KSWS, which comprised the "Rio Grande Network." He told me he remembered both the incident and Lydia Sleppy. When the Roswell story broke, Tucker had been in Washington, D.C., pursuing applications for additional broadcast licenses, and it was not until he returned to New Mexico a week or so later that he learned of McBoyle's call. He told me he did not remember any details of what supposedly hap-pened, including anything about the forestalled Teletype transmission. All he knew about that, he said, he had been told by other writers who had interviewed him. He did remember having been concerned about anything his staff had done having an adverse effect on his pending license applications, but to his relief, no problems surfaced. He did say Lydia Sleppy was a fine, upstanding woman, and if she told me the FBI had stopped her from sending the message, then he was quite sure it had happened as she said it did.[8]

All well and good, but not evidentiary. In 1994, I reported Sleppy's story in *Roswell in Perspective*, not entirely sure about its validity. It seemed to me at the time that it was possible, even if it had nothing to do with a crashed flying saucer. It might well have been intended to protect Project Mogul security. After all, New Mexico was the center of U.S. nuclear weapons research, as well as other highly sensitive activi-ties. It was not out of the question that the FBI was keeping close tabs on potential sources of security leaks and on occasion took swift action to plug them.

Subsequently, I did some further investigating. Merle Tucker told me the Teletype in KOAT's office had both a send and receive capability, but did not know if it was possible for an incoming message to be automatically printed on it without some enabling action being taken first. I was told by several journalistic old-timers that in the 1940s send-and-receive Teletypes definitely had to be manually set in one mode or the other. If a machine was set to send, it could not receive an incoming message. A bell would ring to alert someone to switch over to receive.

In his 1997 book, *The Roswell UFO Crash,* author Kal Korff reported that he, too, had learned that a machine of the type KOAT probably had in its office required the operator to switch manually from one mode to the other. In other words, it would have been impossible for an incoming message to interrupt Sleepy's transmission without her taking action to permit it.

Korff also looked into FBI communications security monitoring in New Mexico in 1947. According to him, his inquiries to FBI headquarters and the bureau's Dallas, Texas, field office revealed

the agency had no "wire" in place at the time the alleged events occurred and they were in no position to monitor any news transmissions! Furthermore, the inquiry also revealed that the agency had *never* opened a file on Lydia Sleppy nor had they ever bothered "eavesdropping" on any of the Teletype communications of radio station KOAT in Albuquerque. As one agent bluntly put it, "You better believe . . . that with the way J. Edgar Hoover ran things back then someone would have made a report on this. Hell, we've got stuff here on file that goes back to the bureau's very first day of existence. We definitely keep our paperwork around here and there's plenty of it."[9]

This conforms with what I learned about what was and was not possible with respect to monitoring of and interference with electronic communications in the mid-1940s. While what Sleppy alleged to have happened could quite easily be done today, it would have been impossible in July 1947.

Setting aside the technical roadblocks for a moment, once again, why would the government take such heavy-handed action against a news organization, regardless of the security issue involved? A polite appeal to a sense of patriotic duty would have sufficed.

HUNDREDS OF WITNESSES?

One of the questions frequently put to me by those who doubt the earthly answer to the Roswell mystery goes something like this: "If there was no saucer crash, how do you explain the hundreds of witnesses who have testified that there was such an event?" To which I reply, "Nothing to it. There aren't hundreds of witnesses."

The dozens upon dozens of witnesses element of Roswell mythology began with this statement in Randle and Schmitt's *UFO Crash at Roswell:* "In the course of completing this work, more than two hundred people were contacted and interviewed. . . . Some witnesses . . . asked that their names be withheld." There follows a list of 182 persons who had been interviewed and granted permission for their names to be used, with the authors admonishing their readers, "Remember, this is not the entire list." This is followed by another list of 89 persons (90 names were listed, but one, Harold Arner, also appeared on the interviewee list). These were persons "contacted in an attempt to learn more about the events of July, 1947." Curiously, one of these is Walter Whitmore Jr.[10]

Together, these lists total 271 persons, and with those who wished to remain anonymous, deceased persons who are known or thought to have had some role in the Roswell affair, and others who have surfaced since, the grand total of "witnesses" exceeds 300, a figure I have heard Kevin Randle and Don Schmitt use numerous times, implying that all these people had something material to contribute to the Roswell story.

Using and consistent with the Randle-Schmitt distinction between persons interviewed and "persons contacted in an attempt to learn more about the events of July 1947" and, with the exception of Whitmore, dropping the latter group entirely, the list of so-called witnesses is cut by almost a third. Continuing the culling, a scan of the list of 182 persons interviewed by Randle and Schmitt reveals some odd witness candidates, for example: ufologist Don Berliner, who told me he was included because he remembered having heard a national radio broadcast of the crashed-disk story in 1947; Bill and Don Bogel, the current owners of the old Foster Ranch; Fortean writer John Keel; Donald Keyhoe, pioneering UFO author (in an interview conducted in 1976, more than a decade before Randle and Schmitt began their Roswell investigations); Coral Lorenzen, cofounder of the Aerial Phenomena Research Organization (interviews conducted in 1972 and 1983); UFO-abduction psychiatrist John Mack; the late Ed Reece, modern military affairs archivist at the National Archives; and ufologist Leonard Stringfield. Clearly, some of these people had or claimed to have information relevant to an investigation of Roswell. Others seem most unlikely to have had such information. *None* legitimately can be called a witness to the events of 1947 in more than a hearsay sense.

Also included is Jay West, purportedly in 1961 a United Press International stringer working in Alamogordo. According to Randle and Schmitt, West "became friendly with the base [presumably, Holloman Air Force Base, formerly Alamogordo Army Air Base] public information officer. The PIO had found a file that mentioned the Roswell crash that included a map. The PIO got a topographical map of the crash site. According to West, they made trips out to try to locate the crash. West described the map as showing the debris field and then, two and a half miles to the east, a second crash site."[11]

Curiously, other than the above, which appears in the timeline section of *UFO Crash at Roswell,* and the entry in the list of interviewees ("conducted in person, Nov 1989"), West and his story appear nowhere else in the book, including the index, and he is given similarly short shrift in Randle and Schmitt's second book, *The Truth About the UFO Crash at Roswell.* Yet, clearly, West could be the key to the Roswell mystery, the lever needed to pry the lid off the crashed-saucer cover-up.

Early on, Fred Whiting of the Fund for UFO Research and I sought to learn more about West from Randle and Schmitt. The answers we got were vague and rather evasive. Meanwhile, with the help of a friend with extensive experience in New Mexico and national journalism, I attempted to track down Jay West. We came up completely dry, rather like the quest for Glenn Dennis's nurse.

A few years later, on August 3, 1999, I received an e-mail message from Kevin Randle asking, "Did you talk to Frank Lovejoy Duran [previously mentioned alleged witness to alien bodies]? This was a source that Schmitt developed and seemed to be quite impressed with."

Replying in the negative, I took the opportunity to once again bring up Jay West. The next day, Randle replied, "Jay West was a guy that Schmitt supposedly met in Florida (if I remember the story correctly) while he was down there interviewing either DuBose or Rickett. West provided him with the information but no documentation. We did search files at White Sands and I took a FOIA request into Holloman . . . ," presumably with negative results, although Randle did not tell me this explicitly.

Randle then added, "[I]t was Schmitt who came up with the Catholic nuns [who allegedly made and logged a sighting of the Roswell object in flight on July 4, 1947]. He was the one who worked through the church and was supposedly able to corroborate the story through the convent. He told me about searching through boxes of dusty old church records to find the names of the nuns."

I will return to the issue of Don Schmitt and his exaggerations and what this means for the Roswell story, but first let us finish our consideration of the "hundreds of witnesses" question. Clearly, Jay West is problematic at best. He is not alone in this regard.

When all is said and done, those who can unequivocally be considered genuine first- or secondhand witnesses to events in and around Roswell or at Fort Worth Army Air Field number just 41. Of these, 23 are known, claim, or can reasonably be thought to have seen physical evidence, debris recovered from the Foster Ranch. Of this group, only 7 have asserted that what they saw had unusual properties or exhibited something else suggestive of otherworldly origins.[12]

When all is said and done, the testimony of the latter group—seven people—constitutes the entire remaining case for Roswell as the crash of a flying saucer. And the great majority of what even these witnesses have said points away from that conclusion and, instead, to one of the New York University project's flight trains.

Funny what a little careful arithmetic can reveal.

THE CURIOUS CASES OF JESSE A. MARCEL SR. AND DONALD R. SCHMITT

As is by now more than a little obvious, the tendencies of a number of key players in the Roswell story to exaggerate, embellish, and just plain lie have had a significant impact on what has come to be widely accepted as the truth about the case. There is more.

The late Jesse Marcel Sr. was the man on the spot when the news broke that army elements stationed at Roswell Army Air Field had "captured" one of the elusive flying saucers. It was Major Marcel who, along with Capt. Sheridan Cavitt, had conducted the initial investigation on the Foster Ranch and collected a substantial quantity of the debris they found there. Soon after, he was sent to Eighth Air Force headquarters in Fort Worth with at least some of the debris, where he was photographed and very likely interviewed by the press. These are objectively established facts.

A number of Marcel's claims about the properties of some of the debris, such as remarkable strength and resiliency and lack of flammability, have become staples of the pro-crashed-saucer argument and have shown up in the accounts of other witnesses—and "witnesses." Since the other credible persons who are known to have been on the debris field have never offered any testimony to back up Marcel's claims and, in fact, have actually contradicted them, it is necessary to scrutinize Marcel himself to assess how much confidence can be placed in his more startling assertions.

In his December 1979 interview with reporter Bob Pratt and in numerous other interviews later, Marcel provided a good deal of rather impressive background information on himself. For example: He claimed to hold a bachelor's degree in physics from George Washington University, obtained after attending five other universities. He said he was a private pilot before World War II, having begun flying in 1928, with a total of eight thousand hours of flight time, three thousand of them as a pilot. He told Pratt and others that when assigned to the 1009th Special Weapons Squadron in Washington, D.C., it was he who wrote the report on the first Soviet atomic bomb test on which the speech President Truman gave announcing the test was based. During the war, he said, he saw duty as a bomber pilot, bombardier, and waist gunner, receiving five air medals for downing five enemy aircraft.[13]

This is an impressive record and suggests Marcel's Roswell recollections could be trusted. However, a look behind the claimed record suggests extreme caution is in order. Researcher Robert Todd obtained Marcel's complete military personnel file (excluding only medical records) and checked it and other sources to see if he could confirm what Marcel had said about himself. Among other things, Todd found that not only did George Washington University not have a record of granting Marcel a degree, it had nothing in its files showing he had even attended GWU. Todd also discovered that on the "Classification Questionnaire for Reserve Officers" Marcel filed out in February 1942 as part of his application for appointment as an army air corps reserve officer, he claimed to have attended Louisiana State University for a year as a special student taking non-credit courses. A check with LSU turned up no record of Marcel's attendance.

On the same classification form, Marcel listed numerous hobby activities, including amateur radio and photography, but did not indicate he was a pilot or even that he had any flying experience at all. (How likely is it a pilot applying for appointment as an *air corps* officer would omit the fact that he had been flying for fourteen years?) Later documents in Marcel's file explicitly state that he had no flying experience and that he was not a rated pilot.

When the White House was informed of "Joe One," the first Soviet nuclear weapon test, it issued a written press release about it. President Truman did not go on the air with an announcement. Research by Todd turned up files on the first Soviet test and the work of the 1009th Special Weapons Squadron in connection with it. Todd also located a copy of the White House statement, including corrections. In none of this material is Marcel mentioned, nor is there anything else backing up his claim.

Concerning Marcel's war record, his personnel file confirms he flew on combat missions—as a combat intelligence officer, not as a pilot or in any other rated-aircrew capacity such as bombardier. It also shows he was awarded two air medals—not five— these not for having shot down enemy planes, but because he had accumlated enough time on combat missions to qualify for them.[14]

Obviously, Marcel had a tendency to embellish his personal history. In addition, according to his efficiency report (performance review) for the period July 1, 1947, to April 30, 1948—during which time the Roswell affair unfolded—his "only known weakness" was noted as "an inclination to magnify problems he is confronted with."[15]

Something rarely if ever noted is Marcel's claim to have had a UFO sighting shortly before being called upon to investigate Mack Brazel's find. In his 1979 interview with Bob Pratt (Appendix A), he related that one night while driving south to the base from his home in town, he saw a formation of lights moving from north to south. . . . We had no aircraft that traveled at that speed. . . . [They] were visible only maybe three or four seconds from overhead to the horizon. They were bright lights flying in a perfect vee formation. And I hesitated to open my mouth about that because I knew nobody would believe me [but he was the base intelligence officer. Was it not his duty to report what he had seen flying over his highly sensitive base?], but two or three days later some GI said, "I saw something in the skies the other night." And he described exactly what I saw. [But, once again, Marcel seems not to have taken any official action on the matter.]

This experience, coupled with the prevailing atmosphere of public and official excitement and concern about flying saucers, would certainly have "primed" Marcel to interpret anything unusual that seemed to have fallen from the sky as at least possibly being connected with saucers.

Taken together, this information about Marcel suggests his more exciting statements about the debris he retrieved from the Foster Ranch, as well as his later assertions about a debris switch and cover-up in Fort Worth, cannot be taken at face value without credible backup from other sources, backup which has yet to be uncovered.

Finally, a recent as yet independently unconfirmed claim posted on a UFO online discussion site by author Kal Korff suggests there may be other good reasons to discount what Marcel said about such matters. In his July 5, 2000, posting, Korff alleged that in the mid-1970s he had a close, confidential ufological working relationship with the late Leonard Stringfield, an important figure in crashed-saucer research and lore. In April 1978, Stringfield and Chicago radio personality Steve Tom conducted a telephone interview with Marcel, this less than two months after Stanton Friedman had discovered and first spoken with Marcel. According to Korff, "Marcel had indicated he never even considered the 'alien' part of things as a possible explanation until UFO 'researchers' started SUGGESTING that idea to him."

The February 1995 issue of *Milwaukee* magazine carried a feature article that would deal a blow to the credibility of the leading pro-saucer-crash-at-Roswell team, Kevin Randle and Don Schmitt. The piece, "Out of This World," by freelance journalist Gillian Sender, was a profile of Schmitt, who lives in the Milwaukee metropolitan area. The first page carried this tease line: "Can a man who stretches the truth about himself be trusted to report accurately about UFOs and extraterrestrial life?"

Sender, who about two years before had written a very positive, even flattering article about Schmitt, had subsequently done some digging. What she uncovered surprised her. In her *Milwaukee* profile, she revealed that Schmitt's claims that he possessed bachelor of arts and master's degrees and earned his living as a medical illustrator while pursuing a doctorate at Concordia College were false. She also pointed out that Schmitt was given to embellishing in other respects, citing as an example his continual references to his books with Randle as bestsellers, when neither of them had ever appeared on a bestseller list. This led her to wonder if much of what the team of

Schmitt and Randle had written about Roswell, which in substantial measure depends not upon objective evidence but rather the authors' credibility, might also be embellished and even outright false.

The March issue of the magazine carried an anonymous letter to the editor claiming that rather than earning his keep as a medical illustrator, Schmitt delivered mail from the Hartford, Wisconsin, post office. Printed below the letter was a note by Sender reporting that she had confirmed with Hartford Postmaster Ken Eppler that Schmitt was a full-time letter carrier and had been employed at the Hartford post office since 1974. I followed up on this and other of Sender's discoveries, with her, Eppler, and other sources. Everything proved to be as reported.

When the storm over Schmitt's "exaggerations" broke, it recalled to mind stories I had heard about and from Schmitt of his alleged ongoing adventures as a U.S. Drug Enforcement Agency undercover operative, involved hairbreadth escapes and improbable life-threatening knife and other wounds. Schmitt enjoyed cultivating a secret-agent aura about himself, spinning tantalizing tidbit-tales about which he said he could not elaborate for security and other reasons.

As a former CIA intelligence officer, I found his subtle bragging completely inconsistent with what would be expected from someone who actually was engaged in such dangerous, shadowy work. I dismissed it as Walter Mitty–ish "wannabe" talk, but did not consider it a sign that something might be critically wrong with Randle and Schmitt's Roswell work. Like Lydia Sleppy's front-lawn saucer watches, I treated it as nothing more than a caution flag. I should have know better, as should Kevin Randle, a former intelligence officer himself.

Randle had known and worked closely with Schmitt since 1988 and never had any reason to question his honesty in any way. He had braced his friend about the charges and claims in Sender's article and the anonymous letter. Schmitt told him they were a pack of lies. Unsurprisingly and to his credit, Randle believed his friend and colleague and vigorously fought to defend him against what he saw as a smear campaign.

Schmitt also struck back, obtaining this misleading letter from Postmaster Eppler, which Eppler told me Schmitt had drafted:

> In the letter section of the March 1995 issue of *Milwaukee* magazine, it is implied that Donald Schmitt has worked full-time for the U.S. Postal Service since 1974. Not only is this untrue, but I have never made such a statement to *Milwaukee* magazine or anyone else.

Randle distributed copies of the letter throughout the world of UFO research, asking, "What does this say about the credibility of the rest of the article about Don?" In short order, Randle would discover what I and others had already established: Schmitt did work at the Hartford post office and had been there since 1974, starting in a part-time capacity, as all Postal Service mail-carrier and mail-handler employees do.[16]

Soon after receiving this blow, Randle wrote to me and others that he had been wrong, saying, "My only excuse is that I believed my friend and he let me down." However, he also made it clear that, while he was disappointed by Schmitt's lies about his personal life, he had no reason to believe his colleague's unfortunate proclivity extended to his investigation of Roswell. It was not long before he was proven wrong on this score, too.[17]

In Randle and Schmitt's *UFO Crash at Roswell* it is claimed that the team submitted the names of eleven men who had served at Roswell Army Air Field in July 1947 to the Departments of Defense and Veterans Affairs, only to be told records did not exist for these men. In its 1994 *Roswell Report*, the air force revealed that a quick, names-only check (Randle and Schmitt had provided no serial numbers) with the National Military Personnel Records Center turned up the records of eight of the "missing" eleven. The other three names were so common, there were multiple "hits."[18]

As I discussed in chapter 12, in his article "The Case of the Vanishing Nurses" in the September 1995 *Omni* magazine, ufologist Paul McCarthy told of his surprise on finding the records of the five Roswell AAF hospital nurses whose photographs appeared in the base yearbook. In their second book, *The Truth About the UFO Crash at Roswell*, Randle and Schmitt claimed that an exhaustive search had been made and the records of those nurses and the disappeared Naomi Maria Selff did not exist. McCarthy made a telephone call to the NMPRC, and three days later he had the records of all five real nurses and later interviewed the sole surviving one.

Then, as mentioned above, we have Albert Lovejoy Duran, allegedly a former military man who was part of the special team that recovered alien bodies, and Jay West, reportedly a former news service stringer who had seen an official file with a map pinpointing the debris field and saucer crash sites. As Randle told me in 1999, both of these men and anything even hinting at confirmation of their alleged accounts remain more than a little elusive.

What do all these curious matters have in common? Don Schmitt. It was he and an associate—not Randle—who supposedly made the exhaustive and fruitless searches for the records of the nurses and men who had served at Roswell AAF. It was he who supposedly located and interviewed Duran and West.

Clearly, Schmitt's storytelling prowess was not limited to personal matters. These revelations were the last straw for Randle, whose own reputation and credibility had been undermined by his association with Schmitt's exaggerations and bald-faced lies. On September 10, 1995, he sent me and numerous others a long "To Whom It May Concern" letter in which he wrote,

The "day-job" of Don Schmitt has never been the issue. . . . It was the lies he told about it. When I asked him, repeatedly, about it, he told me he didn't work at the Post Office. . . . To compound the lie he had Postmaster Ken Eppler write a letter that he and Schmitt knew was misleading. . . .

I had believed that his lying related only to his personal life. Now I learn that it doesn't. . . .

. . . I do not believe anything that Schmitt says and neither should you. . . . I'm not sure he understands the truth. And this has slipped into his research. HIS research. . . . When there is corroboration for what he said, when others had backstopped the work and reported the same things, I have great confidence. If it is work he claims to have done himself, I have no confidence. The search for the nurses proves that he will lie about anything. . . . He has destroyed his work and badly damaged mine. I believed him to be honest, I believed him to be honorable, and I trusted him to tell me the truth. I was taken in by him.

Having been so thoroughly bamboozled by another Roswell player, Glenn Dennis, I empathize with Randle, who I am sure has done his level best to get at the truth about the affair according to his own lights. Especially when reinforced by friendship and the unqualified trust it entails, the will to believe can be a harsh mistress indeed.

As this controversy boiled around him, the heat finally began to get to Schmitt. He quietly resigned as director of special investigations of the J. Allen Hynek Center for UFO Studies and, later and even more quietly, his seat on the CUFOS board.

In most other fields, such a scandal would be career ending, but not in ufology, which is far more forgiving than it should be. Schmitt is now back on the Roswell trail, with Tom Carey as his sidekick. He speaks frequently at the International UFO Museum in Roswell. He and Carey are with some regularity digging up new "witnesses" and attempting to reinvent old ones, as, for example, they have done with Mack Brazel and Frank Joyce in a recent article, previously cited, in the *International UFO Reporter*, the CUFOS quarterly magazine. In ufology, there is life after lies for those with chutzpah and a gift for saying what those with a will to believe want to hear.

Clearly, there is not much left to Roswell as a flying saucer/UFO incident. Fragments of testimony by seven witnesses still might offer a glimmer of hope to some whose will to believe and capacity to accommodate contradiction are very sturdy and substantial. But what I turn to next should give even those hearty souls pause.

NOTES

1. Kevin D. Randle and Donald R. Schmitt, *The Truth About the UFO Crash at Roswell* (New York: Evans, 1997), p. 30.

2. Charles Berlitz and William L. Moore, *The Roswell Incident* (New York: Berkley, 1988), p. 94; Kevin D. Randle and Donald R. Schmitt, *UFO Crash at Roswell* (New York: Avon, 1991), pp. 42–43, 128; Kellahin affidavit, app. H.

3. Schreiber affidavit, app. H.

4. Roberts affidavit, app. H; transcript of January 19, 1990, interview of Roberts conducted by Kevin Randle, in Kevin Randle, *Roswell UFO Crash Update: Exposing the Military Cover-Up of the Century* (New Brunswick, N.J.: Global Communications, 1995), pp. 170–71; Randle and Schmitt, *UFO Crash*, p. 71.

5. Dugger affidavit, app. H.

6. Randle and Schmitt, *UFO Crash*, pp. 46–47.

7. Telephone interview with Mrs. Karl Lambertz, June 4, 1993.

8. Audiotaped personal interview with Merle Tucker, May 27, 1993.

9. Kal K. Korff, *The Roswell UFO Crash: What They Don't Want You to Know* (Amherst, N.Y.: Prometheus Books, 1997), p. 43.

10. Randle and Schmitt, *UFO Crash*, pp. 272–81.

11. Ibid., p. 218.

12. The forty-one are (* indicates saw or likely saw debris): Robert I. Barrowclough,* William H. Blanchard,* Bill Brazel,* Mack Brazel,* Charles Cashon,* Sheridan W. Cavitt,* Jud Dixon, Thomas J. DuBose,* Walter Haut, J. Bond Johnson,* Frank Joyce, Jason Kellahin,* Jesse A. Marcel Jr.,* Jesse A. Marcel Sr.,* Viaud Marcel,* Phyllis McGuire, Arthur McQuiddy, Irving Newton,* Bud Payne, Robert Porter,* Floyd Proctor,* Loretta Proctor,* Roger Ramey,* Lewis Rickett,* Jud Roberts, Bessie Schreiber,* Robert Shirkey,* Lydia Sleppy, Robert Slusher, Sallye Tadolini,* Merle Tucker, Jay and Elizabeth Tulk, George Walsh, Walter E. Whitmore Jr.,* George* and Inez Wilcox, Dan and Mrs. Wilmot, and William Woody and his father.

The seven who asserted what they saw had unusual properties or aspects suggestive of other than earthly origins are: Blanchard (via the "flying disc" press release), Bill Brazel, Marcel Sr., Marcel Jr., Loretta Proctor, Rickett, Tadolini.

13. Robert G. Todd, "Major Jesse Marcel: Folk Hero or Mythomaniac?" *KowPflop Quarterly* (December 8, 1995).

14. Ibid.

15. Korff, *Roswell UFO Crash*, figure 13.

16. Philip J. Klass, *The Real Roswell Crashed-Saucer Coverup* (Amherst, N.Y.: Prometheus Books, 1997), p. 153.

17. Ibid.

18. United States Air Force, *The Roswell Report: Fact versus Fiction in the New Mexico Desert* (Washington, D.C.: U.S. Government Printing Office, 1995), "Report of Air Force Research Regarding the 'Roswell Incident,' " p. 16.

FIFTEEN

THE FORMERLY CLASSIFIED RECORD AND OTHER "MINOR" MATTERS

What we now know about matters directly bearing on the Roswell incident and what was behind it leaves no room for any reasonable doubt that what happened had nothing whatever to do with the crash and hush-hush retrieval of a flying saucer. Beyond the specifics of the Roswell events themselves, actual and alleged, there is another body of evidence that secures the Roswell coffin even tighter than one of Glenn Dennis's hermetically sealed numbers. This is the formerly classified UFO record from the period 1947 through 1955. For good measure, there also is the history of national defense policy, planning, and execution by the United States and other major powers during the past fifty-three years.

In 1992, I plunged into the Roswell crashed-saucer maelstrom with an enthusiasm and an unrecognized will to believe that, together, gave me a severe case of tunnel vision. Intent upon digging up the truth about the Roswell affair I focused too tightly on that alleged event and directly related matters. My archival burrowings were aimed at finding documents and references specific to *Roswell*.

Had I cast my net wider, my ufological endeavors during the past eight years would have taken a decidedly different turn. It is quite likely that after a thorough review of the formerly classified UFO files available at the time, I would have concluded the consensus in ufology before publication of *The Roswell Incident* was on the money: Roswell was a case of justifiably short-lived mistaken identity precipitated by the flying saucer flap of 1947. Whether that would have been for better or worse is a question I leave to others to answer.

THE TALE TOLD BY THE ONCE-CLASSIFIED FILES

Stated plainly, the relevant, extensive, authentic formerly classified official United States government record establishes beyond any reasonable doubt that no physical evidence unequivocally establishing the nature and origin of UFOs was in the possession of or known to American authorities at any time before mid-1955, positively excluding Roswell as a crashed-saucer retrieval.[1]

It is important to understand the records in question were written decades before passage of the Freedom of Information Act in 1975 made it possible to peer behind the wall of official secrecy. They were created by those whose job it was to crack the flying saucer mystery, who wrote and spoke with the certainty that no unauthorized person would ever be privy to their words. They were the products of and addressed to men who had fought World War II and were fighting the Cold War, men used to doing their duty with little fear of being second-guessed, top-notch professionals who sat in the highest ranks of American intelligence and official science. They had no qualms about being forthright with each other inside the comfortable precincts of Pentagon conference rooms and protectively enfolded by security classifications and compartmentation. In fact, their responsibilities demanded it.

They were candid with each other, utterly so. This is shown in the formerly classified record, much of which—including many of the most telling documents—was publicly available before the crashed-saucer revival began in the late 1970s, and most of which had been released by the mid-1980s, well before Roswell was resuscitated by Kevin Randle and Don Schmitt in 1991.

This record entails no fewer than forty-one documents. Seven were originally classified Top Secret, thirty-one were Secret, and the remaining three were Confidential or Restricted. Of these, seventeen were declassified before publication of *The Roswell Incident* in 1980 and twenty-eight of them before release of *UFO Crash at Roswell* in 1991, *Crash at Corona* in 1992, and *The Truth About the UFO Crash at Roswell* and my own *Roswell in Perspective* in 1994. Here is what this historic file reveals.

During the summer of 1947, U.S. Army Air Forces intelligence quickly concluded the " 'flying saucer' situation is not at all imaginary or seeing too much in some natural phenomenon. Something is really flying around."[2] Thus the report "Flying Discs," classified Secret and dated July 30, 1947 (declassified, mid-1980s), the first Air Force study of flying saucers. Conducted by the Collection Branch of Brig. Gen. George F. Schulgen's Air Intelligence Requirements Division, a headquarters component of army air forces intelligence, the report referenced eighteen "reported sightings of 'Flying Discs,' " but noted one "has not yet been received" and four others (including Kenneth Arnold's attention-getting sighting of June 24, 1947) "have not been analyzed." Witness statements were attached. Completed three and a half weeks after Mack Brazel drove into Roswell with pieces of what he had found, the study made no mention of physical evidence, one way or the other, and contained no reference to Roswell.

In August or early September 1947, this report was forwarded by Schulgen to Lt. Gen. Nathan F. Twining, commander of Air Materiel Command, Wright Field, Ohio. Schulgen requested an AMC opinion on flying saucers and a recommendation on how to address them. Twining's command was responsible for the army air forces' cutting-edge aeronautical and propulsion research and technical and scientific intelligence analysis.

In a Secret letter dated September 23, 1947 (declassified, 1969), Twining responded, "[T]he considered opinion of this Command concerning the so-called 'Flying Discs' " is that "the phenomenon reported is something real and not visionary or fictitious," and that it was possible "at least some of the objects are controlled either manually, automatically or remotely." Twining recommended "a detailed study" be carried out, noting "due consideration must be given" to the possibility flying saucers were "the product of some high security" domestic project, the chance "some foreign nation has a form of propulsion[,] possibly nuclear, which is outside of our domestic knowledge," and *"the lack of physical evidence in the shape of crash recovered exhibits which would undeniably prove the existence of these objects"* (emphasis added). The general made no mention of Roswell.

This is the first known official denial of the existence of physical evidence of flying saucers, made by the man in charge of his service's technical intelligence and engineering analysis and development. The Air Materiel Command's intelligence and engineering divisions would have been responsible for cooperatively evaluating and reporting on any saucer artifacts recovered by elements of what, as of September 18, 1947, was the independent U.S. Air Force, as is alleged to have happened near Roswell. If such had occurred, there is no question Twining would have known about it—and he would not have lied about it to his superiors. If security required a classification higher than Secret to discuss such an obviously relevant matter, his letter would have been so classified.[3]

On October 30, 1947, General Schulgen sent forward a draft intelligence collection memorandum, spelling out detailed information to be gathered on "Flying Saucer Type Aircraft." This Secret document (declassified, 1976), contains no reference to physical evidence, no reference to Roswell. Its emphasis is on the possibility the saucers might be highly advanced Soviet aircraft based upon German designs. (A bogus version of this draft collection memorandum circulated in ufology for a decade, accepted as genuine by most researchers, pro- and anti-UFO alike. In early 1997, the fraud was discovered. More on this below.)

On December 22, 1947, Maj. Gen. George C. McDonald, director of air force intelligence, sent a Secret letter (declassified, 1986) to Maj. Gen. L. C. Craigie, head of air force research and development. McDonald concurred in Twining's recommendation for a flying saucer study. He based his decision upon "conclusions reached as a result of the study of the problem made in this office" and forwarded with his letter the results of that study.

The undated report, a "reanalyzed and rewritten" version of an October 6, 1947, memorandum, was classified Secret (declassified, 1986). In addition to analysis of sighting reports, it included investigations to determine possible stimuli for such reports: highly classified U.S. projects, natural phenomena, advanced foreign aircraft projects, and "the possibility that the 'flying saucer' episodes might be the result of a deliberately planned subversive effort to create mass hysteria, possibly Communist-inspired." The first of four conclusions read in part, "Flying discs, as reported by widely scattered observers, probably represent something real and tangible, *even though physical evidence, such as crash-recovered exhibits, is not available"* (emphasis added). Once again, there was nary a word about Roswell.

On December 30, 1947, General Craigie issued a Secret directive (declassified, 1969) to AMC establishing Project Sign. The project was tasked to determine whether the flying saucers were a national security threat and, if so, what they were and where they came from. Craigie made no mention of physical evidence or Roswell.

On March 17–18, 1948, the new Air Force Scientific Advisory Board, chaired by rocket expert Theodore von Karman, held its first substantive meeting. Comprised of leading scientists and other significant figures, the AFSAB advises the chief of staff of the air force on scientific and technical matters critical to his service's mission—including the nature of potential threats and how to counter them. The proceedings of the March meeting were Secret (transcript declassified, 1996).

Briefing the distinguished board on March 17 was Col. Howard M. McCoy, chief of T-2, Air Materiel Command's intelligence division, the home of Project Sign. After telling the board with some enthusiasm about the *"only . . . recent item of captured equipment* [emphasis added]," an advanced propeller-driven Soviet fighter, McCoy turned to flying saucers:

> We have a new project—Project SIGN—which may surprise you as a development from the so-called mass hysteria of the past Summer when we had all the unidentified flying objects or discs. *This can't be laughed off. . . .* We are running down every report. *I can't even tell you how much we would give to have one of those crash in an area so that we could recover whatever they are* [emphasis added].

McCoy said not a word about Roswell, and it did not come up during discussion by and questions from the board.

A few months later, McCoy asked the Central Intelligence Agency for help in learning "whatever they are." In a Secret October 7, 1948, letter (declassified, mid-1990s), McCoy noted, "To date, *no concrete evidence as to the exact identity of any of the reported objects has been received. Similarly, the origin of the so-called 'flying discs' remains obscure"* (emphasis added). He continued, "The possibility exists that some of the sighted objects are of domestic [U.S.] origin," and asked for "any available evidence which might serve to indicate that these objects have a domestic origin." Roswell was not even hinted at in this missive.

About the same time, an air force study of the "so-called 'flying discs' " was completed. According to a Top Secret October 11, 1948, memorandum, on July 27, 1948, Maj. Gen. Charles P. Cabell, McDonald's successor as director of air force intelligence, asked his staff to conduct a study to "determine the tactics of flying objects and the probability of their existence." The memorandum, signed by Col. Brooke E. Allen, chief of the Air Estimates Branch, and addressed to his boss, General Cabell, transmitted a Top Secret report, "Analysis of Flying Object Incidents in the U.S.," and summarized the study effort and its "tentative conclusions." A Top Secret memorandum for the record forwarding this document for Allen's signature noted suggestions had been made to Project Sign "for pursuing flying object phenomena *to the end that positive identification might be achieved"* (emphasis added). All of these documents were declassified in the mid-1980s. None of them included any mention of Roswell, even implicitly.

Allen wrote, "[A]n exhaustive study was made of *all information pertinent to the subject in this Division [Air Force intelligence] and the Intelligence Division of Air Materiel Command"* (emphasis added). Further, "Because *the subject matter is of such an elusive nature,* this study is presented as a preliminary report to be reconsidered *when information on hand warrants it"* (emphasis added). Nonetheless, Allen continued, "it must be accepted that some type of flying objects have been observed, *although their identification and origin are not discernible,"* and "it would be unwise to overlook the possibility that some of these objects may be of foreign origin." He also suggested "several possible explanations" for the objects' appearance over the United States, *"assuming the objects might eventually be identified as foreign or foreign-spon-sored devices"* (emphasis added). Allen mentioned nothing of physical evidence, nothing of Roswell.

Neither, apparently, did the Top Secret study he forwarded to Cabell. This document no longer exists. However, another, also Top Secret and all but certainly little more than an updated version of the earlier one, was declassified in 1985. Prepared by air force intelligence with the concurrence of the Office of Naval Intelligence, it is dated December 10, 1948. It contains the same problem statement and language regarding conclusions about the reality and possible purposes of the saucers referenced and used by Allen. It also states "their identification and origin are not discernible," but strongly suggests the possibility that, if they are of foreign origin, they could be Soviet developments of German designs. One of the report's principal conclusions is that *"if it is firmly indicated that there is no domestic explanation,* the objects are a threat and warrant more active efforts of identification and interception" (emphasis added). This Top Secret document makes no reference to physical evidence, none to Roswell.

General Cabell seems to have taken his staff's warnings seriously. In a Secret letter dated November 3, 1948 (declassified, 1986), Cabell wrote to Air Materiel Command, "The conclusion appears inescapable that some type of flying object has been observed. Identification and the origin of these objects is not discernible to this Headquarters. It is imperative, therefore, that efforts to determine *whether these objects are of domestic or foreign origin* must be increased *until conclusive evidence is obtained* [emphasis added]. The needs of national defense require such evidence in order that appropriate countermeasures may be taken. . . . Request immediate information as to your conclusions to date. . . ." Cabell made no reference to Roswell, and his insistence that "conclusive evidence" be secured more than hints that physical evidence was not in hand.

Just five days later, November 8, AMC intelligence chief McCoy responded to Cabell in a Secret letter (declassified, 1986) drafted by Project Sign staff. After outlining Sign's work sorting the saucer-sighting wheat from the chaff and plans for additional winnowing, McCoy wrote:

> Although explanation of many of the incidents can be obtained from the investigations described above, there remains a certain number of reports for which no reasonable everyday explanation is available. *So far, no physical evidence of the existence of the unidentified sightings has been obtained. . . .*
>
> *The possibility that the reported objects are vehicles from another planet has not been ignored.* However, *tangible evidence to support conclusions about such a possibility are [sic] completely lacking. . . .*
>
> . . . In view of the above, the following conclusions are drawn:
>
> a. In the majority of cases reported, observers have actually sighted some type of flying object. . . .
>
> b. *There is as yet no conclusive proof that unidentified flying objects . . . are real aircraft.*

c. Although it is obvious that some types of flying objects have been sighted, *the exact nature of those objects cannot be established until physical evidence, such as that which would result from a crash, has been obtained.*" [emphasis added]

Yet again, Roswell was nowhere mentioned in any way, shape, or form, not even to suggest that, for a fleeting moment in 1947 it was thought physical evidence had been recovered, but alas . . .

As the study directed by Cabell was going forward, Project Sign prepared its famous Top Secret "Estimate of the Situation," concluding the saucers were intelligently controlled vehicles from another planet. This went up through channels all the way to Air Force Chief of Staff Hoyt S. Vandenberg, apparently arriving on his desk early in October 1948. Vandenberg sent it back to AMC without his approval, and it was ordered destroyed.[4]

However, a copy or two survived for a while, and the late Maj. Dewey J. Fournet had the opportunity to read one in 1952 when he was serving as headquarters monitor and liaison in the Pentagon for the air force UFO investigation, by then known as Project Blue Book. In a May 23, 1992, letter to ufologist Jim Melesciuc, Fournet wrote, "The UFO 'Estimate of the Situation' . . . did indeed exist. It (or a copy of it) was in the UFO files that I inherited when I became program monitor. . . . It recapped all seemingly unexplainable UFO reports received by the AF to that time. *It very explicitly mentioned that absolutely no artifacts had been recovered*" (emphasis added).[5] Fournet said nothing about Roswell in his letter, which he surely would have if he recalled any mention of the incident in the estimate, since by then Roswell was a hot topic again.

After hearing from AMC's McCoy, Air Force intelligence director Cabell made a recommendation to Secretary of Defense James Forrestal concerning publicity on flying saucer incidents. In a Secret November 30, 1948, memorandum (declassified, mid-1990s), Cabell informed Forrestal that "we must accept that some type of flying objects have been observed, *although their identification and origin are not discernible,*" and advised him attempts were continuing "to determine the nature and origin of these objects." Cabell, suggested inquiring reporters be told "the Air Force is investigating carefully all valid reports." Roswell was not mentioned in Cabell's memorandum.

A few months later, in February 1949, Project Sign issued its final report, classified Secret (declassified, 1961). It included these observations: *"No definite and conclusive evidence is yet available that would prove or disprove the existence of these unidentified objects as real aircraft of unknown and unconventional configuration. It is unlikely that positive proof of their existence will be obtained without examination of the remains of crashed objects"* (emphasis added). Yet again, no mention of Roswell.

Things had not changed almost four years later when H. C. Cross of the Battelle Memorial Institute wrote to Capt. Edward J. Ruppelt, head of Project Blue Book (née Sign and Grudge). Battelle, a private research group headquartered in Columbus, Ohio, was under contract to the air force to provide technical and scientific support, a contract on which Blue Book piggybacked work it needed done. In a Secret January 9, 1953, letter (declassified, mid-1980s), Cross presented a "preliminary recommendation . . . on future methods of handling the problem of unidentified flying objects." A key factor shaping Cross's recommendations was the "distinct lack of reliable data with which to work." Since one of Battelle's fortes was metalurgical and other materials analysis, and since it was a trusted air force partner in highly sensitive, highly classified work, it hardly seems likely Cross would have been kept in the dark about any physical evidence of the existence and nature of flying saucers, wherever it might have been collected. Needless to say, Roswell did not receive a mention in Cross's letter.

Not long after receiving the letter from Battelle, Blue Book's Ruppelt presented a Secret-level briefing to U.S. Air Defense Command officials. He said it was possible other planets harbored beings capable of visiting earth. "However," he said, "there is no, and I want to emphasize and repeat the word, *no* evidence of this in any report the Air Force has received . . . we have never picked up any hardware," no "pieces, parts, whole articles, or anything that would indicate an unknown material or object."[6] It is hardly necessary to note that Ruppelt spoke not a word about Roswell.

At the time Cross and Ruppelt wrote and spoke, Battelle was working on a statistical analysis of UFO reports for the Air Force, published as a Confidential report on May 5, 1955 (declassified, 1956). This is the controversial "Project Blue Book Special Report No. 14." While, in my opinion, the results of the study strongly suggest UFOs are real, anomalous phenomena, its authors chose in many respects to ignore their own data. One thing they did not ignore, however, was the lack of physical evidence. In their summary they wrote, "It is emphasized that there has been a complete lack of any valid evidence of physical matter in any case of a reported unidentified aerial object." Roswell missed the cut once again.

The air force was not the only U.S. agency worrying the UFO problem in the 1940s and 1950s. The Central Intelligence Agency took note of the situation at least as early as 1949, and, inspired by the spectacular and, in my view, still unexplained radar-visual sightings over and around Washington, D.C., in July 1952, the agency became actively involved.

Senior CIA officials were briefed several times on the subject, and the lack of physical evidence was addressed at least twice, in Secret briefings given on August 14 and 15, 1952 (declassified, 1978). The first paper presented four theories offered to explain UFOs, one being "the man from Mars—space ships—interplanetary travelers" explanation, for which the briefer said "there is no shred of evidence." The next day's briefing paper declared, "Finally, no debris or material evidence has ever been recovered following an unexplained sighting."[7] Roswell did not come up.

The CIA *did* take UFO reports seriously, but with a focus on worries about exploitation of the excitement about flying saucers for psychological warfare and breaching U.S. air defenses. With these concerns uppermost, the agency convened a panel of scientists to consider the evidence. Known to ufology as the Robertson Panel after their chairman, Dr. H. P. Robertson, the five scientists met for four days in January 1953, receiving presentations on seventy-five of what the air force said were the best cases in its files.

The Secret report of the meeting and the conclusions of the group, dated February 16, 1953 (declassified, 1958 and 1969), makes clear the panel was not disposed to take seriously the possibility of alien spaceships or even highly advanced Soviet technology. It also reveals that among the seventy-five cases presented by the air force, not one included any artifacts. Roswell was not mentioned, even in passing.

This brief survey of formerly classified U.S. documents covers only a small fraction of the thousands of pages of official UFO material now available to ufologists, that fraction which most forcefully limns the reality that those like myself find so disappointing: While saucers may have crashed back in the good old days, alas, none was scooped up and stashed away by the U.S. government or any of its allies. A consideration of national security policy and programs underscores this.

"WATCH THE SKIES!"

If a flying saucer of extraterrestrial origin or even just bits and pieces of such a craft had been recovered by U.S. authorities near Roswell in 1947, this would have set off loud, clanging alarm bells within the nation's defense, intelligence, and top political realms. The reality of alien visitation would necessarily and appropriately have been regarded as a potential threat of the greatest possible magnitude. The best scientific and technical talent would have been put to work analyzing and exploiting the captured materials, equipment, and bodies. Crash programs would have been launched to develop and deploy saucer-detection systems and antisaucer weapons as quickly as possible. All this would have involved literally thousands of people and entailed expenditures of billions of dollars.

That flying saucer reports were taken very seriously early on as indicators of a potential national security threat is demonstrated quite clearly in the formerly classified record discussed above. This statement from General Cabell's November 3, 1948, letter to AMC sums up these concerns, what was required to address them, and, if the threat was confirmed, the need to defend against it: "It is imperative . . . that efforts to determine whether these objects are of domestic or foreign origin must be increased until conclusive evidence [of the origin and nature of the flying saucers] is obtained. The needs of national defense require such evidence in order that appropriate countermeasures may be taken."

As I have shown, Cabell's urgent request for action and information was inspired by reports of strange and wonderfully capable things seen in the sky, not by knowledge of a captured flying saucer. The responses to his request and other subsequent investigation and analysis of flying saucer reports did not lead to "appropriate countermeasures being taken"—as surely they would have, had Roswell yielded up physical evidence of visitors from outer space.

In the years following Roswell, American national defense programs, planning, and expenditures, as well as those of our allies and adversaries, showed no signs of a response to an actual or perceived security threat linked to that event. Roswell did not even figure into the concerns and actions of those working the flying saucer problem, let alone the development of defense and intelligence programs.

In point of fact, while various forward-looking programs such as the Hermes ballistic missile and Boeing jet bomber projects were pursued, the general state of U.S. defenses—including homeland early warning and air defense—was poor and generally declining during the five years from the end of World War II to the Communist invasion of South Korea in June 1950. Notably, in July 1947, there were at least three programs underway that might have figured in any planned antisaucer defense, two intended to develop supersonic air-to-air missiles and one to develop a ground-to-air hypersonic ballistic-missile interceptor. All were canceled within a year after the Roswell incident.

During the 1950s and 1960s, the Soviet strategic bomber threat led to the creation of a massive North American continental air defense system, involving the expenditure of billions of dollars and the development of myriad new weapon and associated systems. The advent of Soviet intercontinental ballistic missiles in the late 1950s spawned massive U.S. strategic ballistic missile and anti-ballistic-missile efforts. The Soviet leap into space led to the spare-no-expense creation of a space surveillance program and significant research-and-development expenditures on anti-satellite weapons. The quick-and-dirty emergency version of the former, the Navy Space Surveillance System, cobbled together with off-the-shelf technology, was up and running less than three years after Sputnik I was put on orbit in October 1957. The technology and know-how to do this were available in 1947, and it would have been a quite reasonable and appropriate response to an alien threat discovered near Roswell. Yet it did not happen.

Nowhere on the long list of threats and counterthreats from 1947 to date is there anything extraterrestrial or counter-extraterrestrial. For about a year and a half, from mid-1947 through early 1949, and again for about two years from late 1951 through early 1953, the American defense and intelligence community, in particular the air force, took seriously the idea that flying saucer reports might involve sightings of machines posing a threat to national security, wherever they might hail from. During the earlier period, it was generally accepted that "something real is flying around," and during the latter that idea was strongly held by a number of influential senior officers, some of whom were convinced the "something" was from outer space. Not once, however, did these concerns result in actions other than efforts to gather more data in the hope of finding out what UFOs were, where they came from, and if they were dangerous.

By early 1953, after some worried consideration of the burden the previous year's flood of UFO reports had placed on the country's defense and intelligence communications and following the Robertson Panel's recommendations to deal with that concern and related psychological warfare concerns, the saucer threat, rightly or wrongly, ceased to be thought of in official circles as one posed by "something" flying around but rather by the reports themselves. The ensuing policies of ridicule, explain 'em away, and the like, together with the earlier intelligence-gathering and analysis efforts keying on the conclusion that people were seeing solid, machinelike objects, possibly even spaceships, were the sum and substance of the national security response to flying saucers. This most definitely would not have been the case if a saucer and the bodies of its unfortunate crew had been recovered in New Mexico in 1947.

FORGERIES FOR FUN, FAME, AND FORTUNE

As I have outlined, the record revealed by numerous authentic formerly classified official documents as well as in the history of national defense policy and action leaves no reasonable doubt that a flying saucer did not crash near Roswell in 1947. Over against this there now is a virtual flood of forged allegedly official and allegedly still highly classified documents which purport to confirm just the opposite. Prior to Roswell, ufology was relatively free of fake documents. Most of those that did show up were obvious hoaxes or were quickly exposed as or reasonably concluded to be fraudulent. Rarely were any intended or taken as much more than practical jokes.[8] The new wave of Roswell-inspired and decidedly more serious fakery has dramatically confused and created dissension within the ranks of ufology. The seemingly endless wrangling and debating over the authenticity and content of this material have damaged the field's already shaky credibility, severely strained its limited resources, and diverted energies that would have been better put to use addressing the UFO phenomena themselves.

Beginning with the so-called Operation Majestic-12/Majic-12/MJ-12 Eisenhower briefing paper, which was made public in 1987 almost simultaneously by Roswell author William L. Moore and British ufologist Timothy Good, documents of all sorts and sizes have surfaced. Majestic-12 allegedly is a super-secret group established by President Truman in 1947 to keep under wraps and to carry out study and exploitation of what was found at Roswell and recovered from later saucer crashes, manage human contact with extraterrestrial visitors, and so on.

The Eisenhower briefing paper makes specific reference to Roswell. Tellingly, it "confirms" the original scenario set down by Moore and his coauthor Charles Berlitz in *The Roswell Incident* as further elaborated by Moore and associates such as Stanton Friedman during the early 1980s. Other documents refer to or purport to be products of MJ-12 and such subprojects as Snowbird, Redlight, Aquarius, Sigma, and Pounce. Some of these forgeries are quite subtle, others are embarrassingly clumsy.

Most of the fake papers that came on the scene during the mid-1980s seem to be products of a relatively clever orchestrated campaign designed specifically to create the illusion of genuine documentary backup for the Roswell crashed saucer tale. The Eisenhower briefing document, conveniently lacking all of the technical attachments it references, provides the foundation for this. Others, like the so-called Aquarius Document, build upon this foundation with their references to various interlocking projects, MJ-12 classification authority notations, and the information-compartmentation codeword *MAJIC*, first appearing on the Eisenhower briefing paper, which carries the impressive if bogus classification label "TOP SECRET/MAJIC—EYES ONLY."

A common element in all cases is William L. Moore. Either the documents were anonymously delivered to one of his associates (e.g., the MJ-12 Eisenhower briefing paper, in the form of an undeveloped roll of 35-mm film, allegedly arrived in television producer Jaime Shandera's mailbox in December 1984) or were handed over or shown to Moore by someone "inside," or were discovered by him in U.S. government archives. Whatever the alleged original source, it was Moore who got the documents into circulation in ufology by one means or another.[9]

In later years, additional material showed up. For example, in March 1994, Don Berliner, UFO and aviation writer, board member and now chairman of the board of the Fund for UFO Research, received an undeveloped roll of 35-mm film (!) in his home mailbox. When developed, the film was found to contain images of sections of the "TOP SECRET/MAJIC—EYES ONLY" and, oh, yes, also "RESTRICTED" Majestic-12 Group Special Operations Manual, SOM1-01, "Extraterrestrial Entities and Technology, Recovery and Disposal," dated April 1954.

Despite such immediately obvious anachronisms as its internally contradictory classification markings (Top Secret is the highest level of U.S. classification; Restricted was the lowest and was no longer even being used in April 1954) and a reference to "downed satellites" more than three years before Sputnik I, the SOM1-01 created a considerable stir. Stanton Friedman featured it, albeit without endorsement, in his *TOP SECRET/MAJIC*, published in 1996, and even though expert analysis by researchers on both sides of the UFO-belief divide has definitively shown the manual to be a fraud, it continues to be touted by some as authentic.

Which brings me to Tim Cooper, a Big Bear Lake, California, resident. Cooper, who purports to be a private investigator, has produced literally thousands of pages of copies (and, recently, some purported originals of) allegedly official classified documents. Cooper claims he began receiving this material in 1992, and he says it has come to him from various sources, including someone who delivers them to his post office box and the daughter of a deceased former senior CIA official he calls "Cantwheel."

Of course, MJ-12, Roswell, and all or most of its assorted activities, subprojects, and so on are referenced in the Cooper documents, which sport the usual classification markings and such. But there is more. Such old ufoological (*not* a typo) chestnuts as the U.S. Army Interplanetary Phenomena Unit show up. There is a barely literate "philosophical" paper attributed to J. Robert Oppenheimer and Albert Einstein. And so, on and on.

Cooper has been hanging around the fringes of ufology for at least ten years. He has contacted leading researchers such as Len Stringfield, Stan Friedman, and Timothy Good, spinning tales for them and feeding them documents he claimed had been leaked to him. In 1993, he even wrote a lengthy paper for the Fund for UFO Research, "The White Sands Proving Grounds UFO Incidents of 1947: A Preliminary Report," which to its credit the fund did not publish. In a presentation he gave at the 1999 National UFO Conference in San Antonio, Texas, fund board member and Mutual UFO Network Corporate Secretary Thomas Deuley stated, "Documents from Timothy Cooper came to the Fund for UFO Research with proposals to do this and do that with them. The Fund Board was not particularly impressed with the documents but did give him a small grant. The preliminary report was so poorly written and full of wild speculation that the fund killed the project."

Cooper got to me in 1994. I received a telephone call from him a couple of months after my *Roswell in Perspective* was published. Stan Friedman had suggested he get in touch. He had, he said, information I might find interesting and useful to my continuing Roswell work.

After a few niceties, Cooper launched into one of his staple stories, which first was published in 1991 in one of Stringfield's saucer crash/retrieval reports. It concerned his father (described in Stringfield's report as "Bob"), a retired U.S. Air Force noncommissioned officer who worked as a print shop manager in the service and had in July 1947 been stationed at Alamogordo Army Air Base. While at Alamogordo, Cooper told me, his father was directed personally by base commander Col. Paul Helmlek to print a highly classified report on the recovery of a flying saucer, complete with forty or fifty photographs of several grounded egg-shaped craft and surgical tents and men in protective suits. Also in the photographs were Oppenheimer and Theodore von Karman.[10]

Helmlek had arrived at the print shop escorted by a detail of military policemen toting Tommy guns. As the armed men proceeded to surround the building, the colonel ordered everyone out of the shop except Cooper's father, whom he handed a portfolio, ordering him to print it but not to read the contents and to forget what he saw in the photographs. After the print job was done, Helmlek took the portfolio and all copies of the report and departed.

I immediately recognized the story, which, for reasons that should be obvious, I had never taken seriously. However, I was interested in what else Cooper might have to offer, so I stayed in touch with him. Among other things, he provided a large extract from his never-published Fund for UFO Research paper and, of direct interest here, a copy of a file copy of a memorandum allegedly written by then-Central Intelligence Group (forerunner of the CIA) Director Roscoe Hillenkoetter. The subject of the memo, dated "19 Sep 1947," was "Examination of Unidentified Disc-like Aircraft near Military Installations in the State of New Mexico: A Preliminary Report" (see the style used by Cooper in the title of his would-be Fund for UFO Research paper). It carried the odd heading "Memorandum for the Military Assessment of the Joint Intelligence Committee," and briefly outlined the discovery of a debris field seventy-five miles northwest of Roswell Army Air Field, the recovery of "unidentified planform [sic] aircraft in the state of New Mexico on 6 July 1947," and a "subsequent capture of another similar craft . . . on 5 July 1947" (emphasis added). It went on to discuss the course of action that would be taken "until a clear directive from the President is issued."[11]

The misuse of the term planform (which means a view of an aircraft or other object from directly above or below, not a type of aircraft design), the "subsequent" saucer capture that took place the day before the first one, and other oddities made me doubt the authenticity of the document. However, it did include features of language and subject matter that suggested whoever created it had borrowed or copied portions of text from a real document.

Imagine my delight when I learned from Stan Friedman that he had received from Cooper what purported to be a copy of a letter allegedly written by Secretary of State George C. Marshall. Dated September 27, 1947, the letter referred to "MAJIC military communications" being sent to the addressee. Friedman had asked the Marshall Foundation to examine the letter, and it immediately was recognized as "a retyped and slightly reworded version of a well-known letter from Marshall to Republican presidential candidate Thomas Dewey during the 1944 campaign."[12]

Quite a while before this, however, I had decided Cooper was a ufological "wannabe," seeking to become a ufological somebody by latching onto the coattails of someone already established in the field. I also suspected he was himself responsible for the bogus documents he had passed on to me, Friedman, Good, and others. I questioned Cooper quite closely and in no uncertain terms expressed my doubts about much of what he told me and the Hillenkoetter memo. Soon he stopped calling me, having no doubt concluded I would not be of any willing help to him.

Apparently, Cooper's next targets were Robert and Ryan Wood. Robert, a retired aerospace engineer with a decades-long interest in UFOs who is the Mutual UFO Network director of research, and his son Ryan, a computer industry professional, gave Cooper a sympathetic ear. Soon they were rewarded with reams of documents and, allegedly, alien-autopsy photographs, all of which they vigorous support as either 100 percent authentic or as "authentic forgeries," that is, government disinformation, or as some combination of both. Despite devastating analyses of the documents that give every indication that all or most of them were created by Cooper himself, despite Cooper's unequivocally deceptive responses to key questions during a polygraph examination (which the Woods curiously interpret as evidence of Cooper's honesty, perhaps because of the positive results they got from remote viewers), and despite a host of obvious absurdities, the Woods continue to defend their man. The will to believe marches on.[13]

Others, from the ranks of both pro- and anti-UFOlogists—notably Kevin Randle, Phil Klass, Tom Deuley, Tim Good, Robert Todd, Stan Friedman, and ufological historian Barry Greenwood—have thoroughly discredited this shameful bogus material. A very long book could be written about the Roswell-inspired and related documents, the clues to their origins, and the remarkable work done to expose them for what they are. I hope someone will write it.

As for me, I am going to end my consideration of this terrible problem with a brief discussion of the bogus document that fooled everyone for more than a decade: the cleverly modified version of the Schulgen intelligence collection memorandum of October 30, 1947. For years many ufologists thought this document a possible Roswell smoking gun.

The seemingly authentic copy was provided to then Fund for UFO Research Chairman Bruce Maccabee by *Roswell Incident* coauthor William L. Moore sometime in 1986. Moore told Maccabee he had located and copied it at the National Archives in late 1985 or early 1986. The document consists of a cover letter signed by General Schulgen forwarding an attached draft intelligence collection memorandum on "current intelligence requirements on Flying Saucer type aircraft" for final review, editing, and distribution. The draft document contains the statement that "it is the considered opinion of some elements that the object may represent an interplanetary craft of some kind," as well as references implying knowledge of saucer construction, propulsion, and the like. Some have taken these features as indicating the collection memo was drafted based upon what had been discovered at Roswell.

Copies of the final version of the memorandum have been located. They do not include the reference to the interplanetary craft opinion and other curious language. This was long quite reasonably assumed to have reflected more conservative opinion prevailing as the memo went through the approval process, routine adjustments in the statement of technical requirements, and so on. Having contributed to, prepared, and responded to such intelligence collection requirements myself, I knew this sort of jiggering was the rule.

In June 1987, the Fund for UFO Research published a Maccabee compilation of "Documents and Supporting Information Related to Crashed Flying Saucers and Operation Majestic Twelve." It included the Schulgen cover letter and draft collection memo. While some researchers had mild reservations about the Schulgen document, it was generally accepted as genuine and considered noncontroversial. In fact, it was used as supporting documentation in various publications about the Roswell case and was even included in a 1993 Fund for UFO Research briefing document for members and staff of the United States Congress which I helped prepare. The Schulgen document became a "given" in the case for a crashed saucer at Roswell.

Then in January 1997, having been bothered for years by niggling doubts about certain features of the document, Robert Todd requested a copy of the document from the National Archives. When he received it, he discovered it had been declassified in 1976, well before Moore said he had located it, and did not include the tantalizing prose. Todd then set about comparing the real thing he had just received and the version of it that ufologists had accepted as genuine since 1987. He quickly discovered that the latter was a retyped and edited "copy" of the actual item.

Here are some of the "adjustments" Todd noted. First, paragraph four of the genuine draft collection memorandum, with words (in one case, a critical part of a word) *deleted* by the forger, whom I shall call "Will," shown in italics:

> The strange object, or phenomenon, may be considered, in view of certain observations, as long-range aircraft capable of a high rate of climb, high cruising speed *possibly subsonic at all times* and highly maneuverable and capable of being flown in very tight formation. For the purpose of analysis and evaluation of *the* so-called "flying saucer" *phenomenon*, the object sighted is being assumed to be a manned *aircraft, of Russian origin, and based on the perspective thinking and actual accomplishments of the Germans.*

Having made his critical deletions, Will then placed a period after *craft* and added the following sentence:

> While there remains the possibility of Russian manufacture, based on the perspective thinking and actual accomplishments of the Germans, it is the considered opinion of some elements that the object may in fact represent an interplanetary craft of some kind.

Next, consider paragraph three of the draft enclosure to the collection memo, "Items of Construction," with Will's *additions* in italics:

> Composite or sandwich construction utilizing various combinations of metals, *metallic foils*, plastics, and perhaps balsa wood *or similar material.*

Clearly, Will's intention here was to incorporate references that could be interpreted as being based upon statements of Roswell witnesses about unusual foil and balsa-wood-like structural members.

More changes along similar lines were made, and the interested reader can compare the genuine and forged documents, which are reproduced in their entirety in this book. As Todd put it, Will clearly meant "to make the UFO field believe the primary motivation behind the memo was the crashed alien spaceship supposedly recovered during the Roswell incident."[14] He succeeded remarkably well, and even when it became abundantly obvious that the version of the Schulgen memo that had been accepted for so long was a fake, there was great resistance in the ranks of ufology. The truth finally prevailed, but instead of making a special effort to inform the field of this forgery, it was quietly dropped from discussion and new publications, and the Fund for UFO Research simply stopped distributing its 1987 documents collection.

The will to believe dies hard.

NOTES

1. Mid-1955 is the latest date for which directly relevant documentary evidence exists. However, developments in public policy and defense programs since then make it highly unlikely that such physical evidence subsequently has come into the hands of or has been accepted as authentic by the American or any other government.

2. U.S. Army Air Forces, Air Intelligence Requirements Division, Assistant Chief of Air Staff for Intelligence, "Flying Discs," July 30, 1947. Except as noted, copies of this and other documents cited herein are in my files. I am grateful to Robert Todd, William LaParl, Stanton Friedman, Philip Klass, Don Berliner, Simone Mendez, and Clifford Stone for providing me with many of them.

3. A great deal of tortured reasoning has been applied to this letter in an effort to demonstrate Twining knew about Roswell and was seeking to keep it under wraps while at the same time encouraging an intelligence-gathering effort on flying saucers. See for example Kevin D. Randle and Donald R. Schmitt, *The Truth About the UFO Crash at Roswell* (New York: Evans, 1994), chap. 13. A far more plausible interpretation along these lines is found in Michael D. Swords, "The Summer of 1947: UFOs and the U.S. Government at the Beginning," in *The Roswell Report: A Historical Perspective*, ed. George M. Eberhart (Chicago: Center for UFO Studies, 1991), pp. 9–38.

4. Edward J. Ruppelt, *The Report on Unidentified Flying Objects* (New York: Doubleday, 1956), pp. 41–45, passim. A dramatic interpretation of the Estimate of the Situation episode, in which Vandenberg (allegedly a member of the alleged original Roswell "control group") saddled the Project Sign staff with an impossible "catch-22" in order to keep the lid on Roswell, is championed by Kevin D. Randle in his *UFO Casebook* (New York: Warner, 1989), pp. 28–31.

5. After leaving the Air Force, Fournet was actively involved in the effort to get at and make public the truth about the nature of flying saucers and what the government knew about them. Among other things, he served as a member of the National Investigations Committee on Aerial Phenomena (NICAP) board of governors and as a consultant for the 1956 docudrama feature film *Unidentified Flying Objects* (which as a boy of thirteen I sat through three times one Saturday afternoon).

6. Philip J. Klass, *The Real Roswell Crashed-Saucer Coverup* (Amherst, N.Y.: Prometheus Books, 1997), pp. 209–10.

7. Philip J. Klass, *UFOs: The Public Deceived* (Amherst, N.Y.: Prometheus Books, 1983), pp. 17–18.

8. One of these, the infamous 1957 "Straith letter" to Space Brother contactee George Adamski, was perhaps the premier UFO-related hoax document before the so-called MJ-12

papers began surfacing thirty years later. See James W. Moseley, "In Which We Offer a Possible Solution to the Long-time Mystery of the Infamous 'R. E. Straith' Letter Written to George Adamski Many Years Ago (Circa 1957)," *Saucer Smear*, January 10, 1985.

9. In a November 16, 1993, telephone conversation, journalist and ufologist Bob Pratt told me that in the mid-1980s—before MJ-12 surfaced as "fact"—he, Moore, and former Air Force Office of Special Investigations agent Richard Doty collaborated on a novel, which he referred to as the "MJ-12 novel." The book, which never found a publisher, was based upon research by Moore and Pratt, working independently, with "technical advice" from Doty. According to Pratt, Moore wanted to do a nonfiction book, but Pratt persuaded him that they did not have enough documentation, so they agreed to do a "fact"-based work of fiction.

For some years rumors have circulated that when Moore and Stanton Friedman had failed to find any significant documentation backing their Roswell claims, Moore suggested he might create and release some fake Roswell documents in the hope of "smoking out" the real thing. In a July 5, 2000, message he posted on an online UFO discussion list, writer Kal Korff claims that not long before Moore released the MJ-12 papers, he was told by Friedman that "he did not object if fake government memos were created concerning UFOs as long as it resulted in the release of the real thing."

10. Leonard H. Stringfield, *UFO Crash/Retrievals: The Inner Sanctum* (Cincinati: The author, 1991), pp. 21–22. Stringfield also includes three additional accounts provided by Cooper. Cooper's account to me of his father's alleged memories was a bit embellished from that which he told Stringfield, including Oppenheimer, Von Karman, surgical tents and suited men, and several silvery egg-shaped craft instead of just one "saucer-like" craft.

11. The entire document is reproduced in facsimile in Timothy Good, *Beyond Top Secret* (London: Sidgewick and Jackson, 1996), p. 466.

12. The story of this document and others provided to Friedman by Cooper appears in Stanton T. Friedman, *TOP SECRET/MAJIC* (New York: Marlowe, 1996), pp. 144–60 (see especially, pp. 158–60).

13. "New Documents Said to Support MJ-12 Claims," *CNI News*, November 16, 1998; "Dr. Robert Wood Emerges as New Promoter of MJ-12 Authenticity, Endorses Recent Batch of Flawed Documents from Secretive Source" and associated articles, *Skeptics UFO Newsletter* (January 1999): 1–6; "Timothy Good Discovers More 'Anomalies' in Cooper Documents," *Skeptics UFO Newsletter* (July 1999): 2; "Failed Polygraph Yields Unexpected Benefit," press release, September 1999, Wood and Wood LLC (see the Majestic Documents Web site at www. majestic-documents.com/press/9-99.html); "Woods' Press Release Claims Cooper's Failure to Pass Polygraph Test on His 'New MJ-12 Papers' Does Not Challenge Their Authenticity," *Skeptics UFO Newsletter* (September 1999): 1; "Tim Cooper Offers His Diverse Views on His Majestic-12 Documents" and "Woods' Credulity Revealed by Their Explanations for Why Cooper Failed His 'Lie Detector' Test," *Skeptics UFO Newsletter* (March 2000): 3–5; "Cooper (Unwittingly) Shows His Disinformation Skills on Internet," *Skeptics UFO Newsletter* (May 2000): 3.

14. Robert G. Todd, "Bill Moore and the Roswell Incident: The True Believers Deceived," *Spot Report*, March 7, 1997. Composite and sandwich-construction materials were of considerable interest in the immediate post–World War II years, to provide lightweight but strong aircraft components. During the war the Chance-Vought Aircraft Division of United Aircraft Corporation had developed "Metalite" sandwich construction, consisting of thin sheets of aluminum alloy bonded to and separated by a low-density balsa core. At the same time Schulgen's staff was drafting the intelligence requirements document on flying saucers, Chance-Vought was developing "Fabrilite," consisting of thin laminates of plastic-reinforced Fiberglas bonded to a balsa core. Leonard Bridgman, *Jane's All the World's Aircraft, 1949–1950* (New York: McGraw-Hill, 1949), pp. 204c–205c.

SIXTEEN

BANDWAGON, GRAVY TRAIN, AND THE WILL TO BELIEVE

Vallée's Law holds, in effect, that high-profile cases tend to make bad ufology—rather like the old legal adage, "Hard cases make bad law." One of the reasons for this is that publicity tends to draw publicity seekers and others who want to be part of the excitement, not to mention those who smell an opportunity to make a buck. All too often, the problem is further compounded by those who refuse to let go when confronted with the inconvenient facts.

As we have seen, Roswell is no exception, is in fact the eight-hundred-pound gorilla of all such cases. Roswell has become a household word and a virtual mini-industry.

Inspired by the efforts of Roswell-affair luminaries Glenn Dennis and Walter Haut, who in association with Max Littell founded the International UFO Museum and Research Center in 1992, the town finally realized there was money in crashed saucers. In 1995 it staged its first crash-celebration festival. This and the one the following year were warm-ups for the fiftieth anniversary event in 1997, which drew about 45,000 people and poured an estimated $5 million into the New Mexico economy. It has been downhill since, however, with the 2000 event barely making a ripple and leaving vendors who paid high fees for stalls in which to peddle their alien this and thats grumbling. Perhaps the bloom is off the Roswell rose, at least as far as trapping tourists with an annual festival goes.

All is not lost, however. The museum is still Roswell's main attraction, drawing about 180,000 visitors a year and significantly enhancing the town's retail and lodging economy. Recently, the museum announced it would pay "up to $1 million for the first scientifically verified piece of debris from the legendary 1947 crash of an alien spacecraft near Roswell," up quite a bit from the $3,000 offered for physical proof of flying saucers in 1947.[1] Perhaps museum elders are hoping to recover from the embarrassment they suffered a few years ago when their much-touted fragment of Roswell debris turned out to be a piece of jeweler's scrap.

In any event, such a prize should motivate a good many people to go traipsing all over the alleged crash and debris field sites in search of a bit or piece the army may have missed, which ought to both annoy and delight the ranchers who own the property or hold U.S. Bureau of Land Management lease rights to it. If they are smart, they will follow the example of fellow rancher Hub Corn, who owns the land where the revisionist-scenario, or Frank Kaufmann, "crash" site is located. Corn charges visitors fifteen dollars a head to come on his place for a look-see.

I want to make clear that I do not disapprove of all this. Those who have been writing books, doing television documentaries, making motion pictures, and lecturing about Roswell—including myself—have been raking it in to one degree or another for years. It is about time the local folks got their share. My only objection to such booster- and hucksterism is when, as for example with the Jim Ragsdale scam, it is based on out-and-out lies without benefit of the sly carny's wink that says, "Hey, it's all in fun. And wouldn't it *really* be fun if it were all *true?* Step right up . . ."

THE ALIEN AUTOPSY FILM

A world-class version of the sort of utterly dishonest thing I am referring to is the infamous alien autopsy film foisted upon the world in 1995 by British music promoter and video producer Ray Santilli, U.S. television producer Robert Kiviat, and the Fox Television Network. On a January 13, 1995, British Broadcasting Corporation television program, rock star Reg Presley announced that he recently had been shown a film of the autopsy of one of the Roswell aliens. Not long after this startling revelation, Santilli claimed he had acquired the footage from the man who had shot it, an elderly retired cameraman who had been in the U.S. Army at the time of the incident.

This ignited a firestorm of interest and controversy, which Santilli expertly manipulated. When he judged the frenzy level was right, he staged a preview at the London Museum. This took place on May 5, 1995, with more than one hundred journalists, ufologists, and television and motion picture producers in attendance. There followed a great scramble to strike a deal with Santilli for the right to exhibit the film publicly.

Robert Kiviat, an independent television producer who formerly had been on the staff of NBC's *Unsolved Mysteries* and Fox's *Encounters*, emerged as the lucky winner. He landed exclusive first broadcast rights for the film, and Santilli reeled in a licensing fee of $125,000.

In did not take Kiviat long to strike a lucrative deal of his own with the Fox network, which bought a one-hour, prime-time special project for its *Encounters* series. Santilli recognized the upcoming broadcast as a superb advertising opportunity, and he began production on a videotape entitled *Roswell: The Footage*, for which he charged a mere $59.

Santilli's marketing campaign was a masterful extension of his earlier run-up to the preview. All sorts of hints were dropped in interviews and online postings and discussions. President Truman could be seen in some of the footage. There were scenes inside tents at the crash site, showing the preliminary examination of one (perhaps more) alien cadavers. There were others in which pieces of the saucer were displayed, including a control panel with (alien) hand-shaped impressions molded into its surface. Santilli and those working with him never quite said for certain that Truman and the rest would appear on the Fox special or in his video, but that quickly became the word in the ufological rumor mills, and Santilli did nothing to discourage it. Excitement over the upcoming television show continued to build, as did the advance orders for the videotape.

According to writer Kal Korff, the Kiviat-Fox special originally was intended to be broadcast live from studios in the United States and Great Britain. The film was to be shown, and experts of all sorts were to present their analyses of it on camera, with a verdict rendered at the wrap. Korff had known Kiviat for some time, and he offered to put together a team to attempt to authenticate the film. Kiviat readily agreed.

Soon, however, things began to change. The focus of the program shifted from a genuine attempt to assess the truth about the film to all-too-typical tabloid television sensationalism. Seeing the handwriting on the wall, Korff and his associates bowed out.[2]

When the show, "Alien Autopsy: Fact or Fiction?" aired on August 28, 1995, it was little more than an infomercial for Santilli's video. While there were those on the program who raised doubts, the general drift was that this was the real McCoy. Even famed forensic pathologist Cyrl Wecht declared that the body looked very real to him.

What the presentation lacked in objectivity and thoughtfulness, it made up for in the ratings. It was a smash success, and Fox rushed to air it again, this time with additional material.

While Truman and the scenes at the crash site were not shown—and did not appear in the videotape—this seemed not to bother anyone but the few ufologists, skeptics and "believers" alike who were interested only in the truth about the whole affair. These were the same doubters who raised such telling points as the utter uselessness of the obviously unsealed protective suits worn by the "doctors" in the film, the fact that the cord on the wall telephone in the autopsy room was not marketed until some years after 1947, the absurd "scoop out the guts" handling of the cadaver's internal organs, the blood oozing from the scalpel incisions when the decedent had been dead for days, and, of course, the bizarre aspect of the alleged alien itself, which had all the realism of a dummy made for a 1950s "B" science-fiction thriller. In fact, the entire black-and-white film looked like a clip from one of these drive-in specials.

As the controversy raged and more and more problems surfaced, Fox continued to rebroadcast the show, and Santilli continued to peddle thousands of copies of his tape. While some in ufology, notably British ufologist Philip Mantle and his German associate Michael Hesseman, continued to defend the autopsy film, the overwhelming view was that it was a fraud.[3] In fact, the case for the prosecution was brilliantly presented in the March 1996 *MUFON UFO Journal*, the magazine of the world's leading UFO-enthusiast organization. This cover story, "Santilli's Controversial Autopsy Movie" by Kent Jeffrey, utterly devastated the credibility of both the film and Santilli. Thereafter, the alien autopsy flick faded from the ufological screen—but not before making Santilli, Kiviat, and Fox a lot of money.

Then it came back to make Kiviat and Fox a little more. This time, in a breathtaking show of what we in New Mexico call *cojones*, the producer and network took a slightly different tack. On the December 28, 1999, Kiviat-produced Fox special "The World's Greatest Hoaxes: Secrets Finally Revealed," Kiviat and the network told the world that the alien autopsy film was a hoax—but forgot to mention the inconvenient fact of their central, if at least technically innocent, role in promoting the fraud in the first place.

Viewers did get to see one of the segments supposedly filmed in a tent at the crash site, where two alleged physicians struggled to save the life of a barely surviving alien. Image enhancement resulted in the identification of one of the doctors as Elliot Willis, a British film-industry technician. "Doctor" Willis was interviewed on the Fox special, and he revealed that his former employer, AK Music, had produced the tent sequence for Santilli. His partner in the scene, he said, was, appropriately enough, a local butcher.

LIEUTENANT COLONEL CORSO

I met the late Philip J. Corso on January 29, 1994. He was, he said, in New Mexico to refresh his memories before sitting down to write his memoirs. He had with him Dennis Hackin, whom he identified as his coauthor. My wife, Mary Martinek, and I had driven down to Roswell that morning from our home in Placitas to meet Corso at the International UFO Museum and join him and others on a trek to the debris field, the ranch house where Brazel, Marcel, and Cavitt allegedly spent the night forty-seven years before, and two of the alleged crash sites.

Before Mary and I arrived at the museum, Corso had met privately with Glenn Dennis and, if memory serves, Walter Haut and Max Littell. He told them he had been involved in the project that was set up to learn the secrets of the Roswell saucer and put them to use in national defense, against both our earthly enemies and the aliens. He showed Dennis and the others sketches of the Roswell aliens, complete with strange helmets and other interesting features.

We spent a very long day driving over the cold, windy prairie. It was almost as windy inside the vehicle as it was outside. Corso spent a good deal of the time regaling us with tales of his more than twenty years' service as a U.S. Army officer, as well as cryptically discussing his interest in the Roswell incident. He said he had played "a small part" in the aftermath of the affair, "nothing much," and would be including it as one minor story in his memoirs. It struck me that he really knew very little about the case and was actually in the process of picking as many brains about it as he could.

As we bounced about the countryside, Corso also made the mistake of telling a tale about how, when he was serving in some army intelligence capacity in Rome during the 1950s, the local CIA contingent had interfered with his activities, jeopardizing a very sensitive operation. He paid a visit to the CIA station chief, read him the riot act, and even physically braced the man, shoving him up against his office wall to underscore that he meant business. Unfortunately for Corso, I had known this fellow when I was in the agency. I knew he would never have put up with anything like that for a moment—especially given that he was a big, strapping man and Corso was slightly built and, if he made a valiant effort, barely scraped the five-six mark.

I dismissed Corso as just another blowhard and effectively forgot about him. In late spring of 1997, the news broke about a new Roswell blockbuster book called *The Day After Roswell*, due out just in time for the fiftieth anniversary of the incident. The author was none other than Philip Corso, who somewhere along the line had shed Dennis Hackin and now was writing with William J. Birnes, today the publisher of *UFO* magazine.

Dennis Stacy, then editor of the *MUFON UFO Journal,* asked me to review *The Day After Roswell,* and I requested a set of galley proofs from the publisher, Pocket Books. When the galleys arrived, I discovered Corso had not only shed his original co-author but also 99.9 percent of his memoirs. My guess was that he had soon discovered that no one was interested in the memoirs of just another undistinguished retired lieutenant colonel and had, on his own or with a little help, decided his now-amazing role in the Roswell story would sell much better. Apparently so did Pocket Books, which had scheduled an eighty-thousand-copy first printing of the hardcover book, which to my great surprise included a foreword by U.S. Senator Strom Thurmond, a venerable South Carolina Republican.

As I read *The Day After Roswell,* I did not know whether to laugh or cry. Other than referring to some of the real and bogus documents long known to ufologists, Corso provided absolutely nothing to back up his claims about crashed saucers and alien technologies. Nothing. He relied entirely on the credibility implied by his army career and testified to in the foreword to his book written by a distinguished U.S. senator, saying in effect, "Trust me. How could a fine fellow like me be lying?"

A check of Corso's records confirmed he had retired from the U.S. Army in 1963 as a lieutenant colonel after twenty-one years' service, principally as an intelligence and artillery (antiaircraft missiles) officer. He seemed to have served about four years in some capacity on the National Security Council staff during the Eisenhower administration and was on General MacArthur's staff in Japan during the Korean War. He had testified before congressional committees concerning Korean and Vietnam war POWs and other Americans believed still to be held in Russia, Korea, China, and Vietnam. From 1961 until his retirement, he served in and was at least for a few months chief of the Foreign Technology Division of army research and development in the Pentagon, reporting directly to the legendary Lt. Gen. Arthur Trudeau, chief of R&D and former head of army intelligence. It is Corso's alleged adventures during this latter assignment that were the focus of his book.

In his book, Corso played upon contemporary paranoia about government cover-ups. He exploited not only all of the various versions of the Roswell non-crash-retrieval (a laughably garbled conglomeration of which began the book), but also virtually every UFO-related theme and notion, old and new. His was a veritable unified field theory of practically everything ufological and ufoological.

While on army R&D's foreign technology desk, Corso claimed, he was responsible for the army's "Roswell Files" and seeding into American industry the alien technologies they contained. However, it was many years earlier—to be exact, on the night July 6, 1947—that Corso said he got his first inkling of Roswell. As he made his rounds as the post duty officer at Fort Riley, Kansas, an enlisted bowling buddy called him over and into the fort's old veterinary building to look at the cargo of a truck convoy headed from Roswell to Wright Field, Ohio. Corso forced open a crate and saw an alien being floating in a large glass container. Somehow he knew it was from outer space. His mind reeling, he claimed, the young Corso continued his rounds, desperately forcing from his mind this chance "close encounter," which foreshadowed his FTD assignment decades later.

In 1961, as Corso was taking up his FTD duties of analyzing and evaluating foreign military technologies, General Trudeau handed him a far more important job. He was entrusted with a locked file cabinet containing not only reports on the crashed Roswell saucer and medical evaluations of the ship's dead genetically engineered crew, but also actual bits and pieces of fabulous technologies from another world. It seems these wonders had not been exploited for various bureaucratic and security reasons, and Trudeau was determined to push things forward. Corso's job was to insinuate these technologies into government and industrial R&D through existing defense contracts and programs, allowing them to be absorbed and developed while knowledge of their true origins evaporated like the morning dew.

Corso claimed he set about his mission eagerly. He worked long into many Pentagon nights writing reports for Trudeau, setting out his evaluations of the alien technologies and his brilliant insights into their workings and potential applications, something for which his two years of college-level industrial arts studies well qualified him, of course. He donned mufti and showed up at such places as IBM, Bell Labs, Dow Corning, and army research labs at Fort Belvoir, Virginia. Like a stealth nuts-and-bolts Johnny Appleseed, he presented his gifts to awestruck and eternally grateful scientists and engineers, then faded back into the Pentagonal woodwork.

My mind boggled. If Corso's egoistic fever dreams were taken as fact, he was responsible for nothing short of making possible the cornerstones of the technological revolution of the second half of the twentieth century—the integrated-circuit chip, lasers (a handheld cow-mutilator was found at Roswell), fiber optics—plus many other militarily and scientifically important capabilities—night-vision systems (a "two-piece set of dark elliptical eyepieces as thin as skin" was in Corso's file cabinet, rather like those peeled off the alien's eyes in the Santilli film); Kevlar armor; stealth; the Strategic Defense Initiative (SDI, or Star Wars); high-speed, nap-of-the-earth night flying; and on and on and on. Corso's work made it possible for the West to win the Cold War while keeping our kids entertained with video games.

But wait, that's not all. Corso also personally and privately briefed Attorney General Robert Kennedy on the strategic significance of space. He did not tell Kennedy about the alien threat, but he knew the president's brother understood there was more to the story than merely forestalling Soviet dominance of space. Corso asserted he was certain this led to President John F. Kennedy's commitment to put a man on the moon before the sixties were out. Oh, yes, and Corso's musings on the need for mankind to train and adapt for spaceflight, inspired by his knowledge of the Roswell aliens, led to the establishment of NASA's Space Camp for kids.

But there was still more. Not only did the technological revolution, notably SDI, spawned by Corso's secret labors win the Cold War, it won the far more sinister war with the aliens, turning their own technologies against them. For some reason the shadowy aliens, who lurked menacingly around the fringes of Corso's narrative to be invoked when he needed them to pump up the drama, did not press their advantage for fourteen years. Then, with Corso on the job, it was too late.

And still more. It seems the naughty CIA was in cahoots with its putative adversary, the Soviet KGB, and worked diligently to thwart Corso's efforts and learn the secrets of Roswell. But Corso stood up to them, even more dramatically than he had in Rome:

[T]he CIA had a tail on me all throughout my four-year tenure at the White House. . . . Then, when I came back to Washington in 1961 to work for General Trudeau, they put the tail back on and I led him down every back alley and rough neighborhood in D.C. that I could. He wouldn't shake. So the next day, . . . I led my faceless pursuer right to Langley, Virginia [CIA headquarters], past a sputtering secretary, and straight into the office of my old adversary, the director of covert operations Frank Wiesner, one of the best friends the KGB ever had. I told Wiesner to his face that yesterday was the last day I would walk around Washington without a handgun. And I put my .45 automatic on his desk. I said if I saw his tail tomorrow, they'd find him in the Potomac the next day, with two bloody holes for eyes; that is, if they bothered to look for him.[4]

What a guy! Of course, what else could we expect from someone who claimed he numbered J. Edgar Hoover among his best friends and, in a career-ending move, tipped off U.S. Senator Kenneth Keating ("one of my friends") to Soviet intermediate-range ballistic missiles in Cuba. There *were* two small problems, though. Frank Wiesner was not the CIA's deputy director for plans (clandestine operations) in 1961, and CIA Headquarters had not yet relocated from miscellaneous buildings in Washington, D.C., to Langley.

The litany of Corso's earth- and mankind-saving works went on and on, but more telling were the many other things he got wrong. Here are but a few examples:

- He claimed he and General Trudeau played a major role in developing and launching Corona, the world's first spy-satellite program, because they wanted a means to detect UFO landings in the Soviet Union. He wrote they "slipped the Corona photo-surveillance payload directly into the ongoing Discoverer program, reverse-engineering Discoverer to make the payload fit," and identified Discoverer as a NASA project. He also told of the "jubilation at the Pentagon" when the photos from the *first* Corona mission were developed.

  Corona was a CIA-Air Force project; NASA and the army had nothing to do with it. It began in 1958, three years before Corso was assigned to the Pentagon. It was a "black" program hidden inside the Air Force's Discoverer space-medicine research project, which had been established expressly as a cover for Corona. The first mission, launched on February 28, 1959, more than two years before Corso went to work for Trudeau, failed and did not even have a camera aboard. The first photography was provided by the *fourteenth* mission, Discoverer 14, code named "Limber Leg" and launched on August 18, 1960, almost a year before Corso joined army R&D.

- He claimed such advanced, Corso-seeded Star Wars technologies as missile-launched high-energy lasers and directed-particle-beam weapons have been deployed, thwarting the evil aliens' designs on Earth, which Corso said was the secret real purpose of SDI. No such deployments have taken place, and the secret real purpose of Star Wars was to convince the Soviets they could no longer afford to stay in the arms race, a purpose it served with stunning success.

- A retired army officer, Corso at least twice misidentified the Wac-Corporal, an old army research rocket, as a *navy* system, saying it was the rocket that blew up on the pad in an attempt to put the first U.S. space satellite on orbit in December 1957. Actually, of course, this was Vanguard, a navy-developed system.

- He claimed the B-2 stealth bomber was spawned by Lockheed. It was a Northrop creation. This is a notably odd slip-up, as elsewhere in the book Corso hinted broadly that an earlier U.S. flying-wing bomber, the *Northrop* YB-49, was a product of Air Force exploitation of Roswell technology. He wrote that the YB-49's quadruple vertical stabilizers were so uncannily reminiscent of the head-on Roswell craft sketches in his files that it was hard not to make a connection between the spacecraft and the bomber.

- He alleged the F-117 stealth fighter is almost crescent shaped, like the space vehicle that crashed into the arroyo outside of Roswell. Of course, the F-117 is arrowhead shaped and employs rather mundane and obsolescent technologies to work its stealthy wonders.

- He wrote that Willy Ley, the late science writer and spaceflight enthusiast, was a German rocket scientist and part of Wernher von Braun's team at Alamogordo/White Sands in 1947. Ley was neither, and had fled Nazi Germany in the 1930s.

- Corso also stated the "Backfire," a supersonic Soviet swing-wing jet bomber was operational in the 1950s, and his Nike missile battalion in Germany (1957–58) and others like it were there to defend against this threat. The Backfire, the Russian equivalent of our B-1, was not deployed until the 1980s.

One would think a military technology and intelligence whiz like Corso, who remembered precisely and at length the text of memos and the details and nuances of conversations thirty-five and more years after the fact, could get such simple things straight. But these lapses paled beside his greatest failing, one of honor.

I was flabbergasted when I discovered Senator Strom Thurmond, president pro tempore of the United States Senate, chairman of the Senate Armed Services Committee, the longest-serving U.S. senator, retired army reserve major general, D-Day paratrooper, American political legend and icon, had written a brief foreword to Corso's book, praising Corso as a patriot and commending him for his service to his country—but including not a word about the book's content. My surprise grew when I read Corso's account of an alleged 1960s-vintage conversation in which, according to Corso's telling, Senator Thurmond winkingly signaled his knowledge of the intrepid colonel's work with alien technology.[5]

I called the senator's press secretary—who turned out to be Chris Cimko, whom I had worked with in the Pentagon—and learned Corso, who had put in two short stints on Thurmond's staff in the 1960s and 1970s, had asked the senator to write a foreword to his memoirs, *I Walked with Giants: My Career in Military Intelligence*, not a book about his Roswell-related exploits and U.S. government cover-up of a UFO crash. Cimko was horrified and acted quickly. Quoting Senator Thurmond from his June 5, 1997, press release on the matter:

> I did not, and would not, pen the foreword to a book about, or containing, a suggestion that the success of the United States in the Cold War is attributable to the tech-

nology found on a crashed UFO. I do not believe in UFOs, do not believe that the United States is in possession of such a vehicle, and do not believe that there has been any government cover-up of a UFO crash.

The outline of "I Walk[ed] with Giants" provided to me by Mr. Corso indicated he was writing a book of his recollections and observations on topics such as World War II, the Korean War, the Vietnamese Conflict, intelligence, espionage, and counter-espionage operations. There was **absolutely no mention**, suggestion, or indication that any of the chapters and subjects listed dealt with Unidentified Flying Objects and government conspiracies to cover-up the existence of such a space vehicle. [Emphasis in original]

Clearly, Corso had pulled a bait and switch. Senator Thurmond demanded that Pocket Books remove his name and foreword from the second and subsequent printings of *The Day After Roswell*. He got what he asked for, but the book continued to sell like hotcakes and eventually was released in a mass-market paperback edition. Many within ufological circles, possessed of a hearty will to believe, still suspect there might be something to Corso's story, that all the melodrama and error can be chalked up to the colonel's coauthor, William J. Birnes. Before his death, Corso reinforced this wishful thinking by claiming he had not seen the final manuscript before it went to the publisher.

Recently, longtime ufologist Larry Bryant obtained Corso's FBI files through a Freedom of Information Act request. This reveals a man continually trying to advance his personal agenda and extreme right-wing politics through lies and exploitation of members of Congress and the FBI. One of the documents in Corso's file includes this comment from his dear friend J. Edgar Hoover: "Corso is a rat."[6] That says it all, but those who have a need to will go on believing.

GIGO & READING THE RAMEY MESSAGE

Two recent examples of the will to believe in action are civil engineer Robert Galganski's attempts to prove an NYU-Mogul flight train could not have created the Foster Ranch debris field, and various attempts to read the words on a piece of paper seen in photographs taken in Brig. Gen. Roger Ramey's office.

Galganski assumes the anecdotes in which it is claimed a vast area of the high desert was densely covered with debris are accurate and true, ignoring the inconvenient facts on the other side of the question. He applies his considerable technical skills to demonstrate that the total surface area of the radar targets and balloons of an NYU array did not come even close to the extent of that reportedly thickly covered with debris. From this, Galganski concludes such an array was not responsible for what was found.[7]

Of course, what he conveniently forgets is that there is no good reason to believe the testimony he relies upon is true and accurate and very good reason to consider it is not, or at the very least, to suspend judgment about it. Oddly, especially for an engineer, Galganski refuses to accept that the GIGO—garbage in, garbage out—principle applies to his work. As the late science-fiction author Robert Heinlein once observed with respect to the fallacy inherent in the Marxist labor theory of value, no matter how much effort, skill, talent, knowledge, and love are applied to making mud pies, the end product is still mud. Similarly, manipulating unreliable, unverified data, no matter how skillfully done, does not make it any more reliable or useful, no matter how much one might wish it were so.

Somewhat more rooted in reality are the attempts of the Roswell Photo Interpretation Team (RPIT) and others to ferret out the meaning of words on a piece of paper Brig. Gen. Roger Ramey is seen holding in two of the photographs taken of him on July 8, 1947, as he poses beside the NYU-Mogul debris brought to Fort Worth by Maj. Jesse Marcel. J. Bond Johnson, the man who took the photographs in Ramey's office, founded and heads RPIT, which is dedicated to analyzing the images he and Fort Worth Army Air Field public information officer Maj. Charles Cashon captured in Ramey's office.

When first contacted by Roswell researchers in 1989, Johnson had very hazy memories of the events forty-two years before, but seemed to accept the weather balloon and radar target explanation. It was not long before he found the opinions of crashed-saucer proponents persuasive, and he seems sincerely to believe he was duped by the army in 1947.[8] He now devotes much of his time to proving this through interpretation of what is shown in his and Cashon's photos. Among other things, Johnson and RPIT claim they have "proved conclusively" that the debris photographed in Ramey's office could not possibly have been part of a New York University balloon project flight train, this despite all the evidence to the contrary.[9]

More important, however, are the group's and others' attempts to read the Ramey "message," which they have decided is a highly classified communication containing information that would establish once and for all that a flying saucer crashed somewhere near Roswell. However unlikely as it might seem that an army air forces general officer, commander of the Eighth Air Force, would be so foolish as to have something like that in his hand at a press conference, such things have happened. For example, Presidential National Security Advisor McGeorge Bundy was photographed with President Lyndon Johnson during the Gulf of Tonkin crisis in 1964. A few months later, the front page of the *New York Times Sunday Magazine* carried the photo, in which millions could and did read a highly classified code word on a document Bundy was holding. Such mistakes do happen, so while the RPIT notion that Ramey was holding a classified message is not likely to be true, it is possible.

It is certainly more than a little likely that what Ramey was holding was something about the incident concerning which he had called the press conference. It could have been talking points for him to refer to, or a script for him to read from during a later radio statement he made about the incident. However, virtually everyone who has examined enhanced images of the document concurs that it is some sort of message form, probably a TWX, or military radio-telegraph message. Perhaps it was from Wright Field or Air Weather Service headquarters outside Washington, D.C., providing a tentative identification of what had been recovered.

That this is the case is suggested by what aerospace engineer and ufologist Brad Sparks discovered as long ago as the early 1980s. In 1980, Sparks was the first person to be able to read a word in the Ramey message: "BALLOONS." In 1985, working from a good blowup copy of one of the photographs, he was able to pick out: "WEATHER BALLOONS," "'DISC,'" "LAND," and "FORT WORTH."[10]

More exotic interpretations have been offered by RPIT and others. For example, "VICTIMS OF THE WRECK WERE TAKEN BY CONVOY," and "MAGDALENA" (a town near the alleged Barney Barnett/Gerald Anderson crash site), and so on. Recently, Donald Burleson, a New Mexico MUFON and International UFO Museum official, claims he, Don Schmitt, and Tom Carey have dug out a variety of exotic tidbits, among them "FOR ATOMIC," "SITE TWO AT CARLSBAD," and what Burleson thinks might be the meaning of "TEMPLE," which some say is the one-word signature line of the message. According to an informant of Burleson's, "Temple" was the code name for none other than FBI Director J. Edgar Hoover. The FBI has refused to confirm or deny this, but in my experience, both official and as a private researcher, I've never seen a message from the FBI director's office during Hoover's tenure that was not signed "Hoover." Given his ego, I think it unlikely he ever would have hidden his light under a codeword bushel.[11]

My intention here is not to ridicule the idea that something useful might be gleaned from the Ramey message, filling in a few blanks and adding to the sum of our knowledge of the incident.[12] Rather, it is to point out how easy it is to read into it things one wants to find, and to suggest the power of the will to believe in a more general sense. Despite the tremendous weight of evidence supporting the earthly answer to Roswell, those who do not like that answer keep plugging away, trying with some desperation to do an end run around that evidence with their own "facts" born of innocently wishful thinking.

NOTES

1. "Greenbacks for Proof of Little Green Men," *Saucer Smear,* July 15, 2000, p. 5; *IUFOMRC Newsletter* (July 2000): 5.

2. Kal K. Korff, *The Roswell UFO Crash: What They Don't Want You to Know* (Amherst, N.Y.: Prometheus Books, 1997), pp. 204–207.

3. Michael Hesseman and Philip Mantle, *Beyond Roswell: The Alien Autopsy Film, Area 51, and the U.S. Government Coverup of UFOs* (New York: Marlowe, 1997).

4. Philip J. Corso, with William J. Birnes, *The Day After Roswell* (New York: Pocket Books, 1997), p. 87.

5. Ibid., pp. 252–53.

6. Federal Bureau of Investigation, File Number 62-HQ-110017, "Philip James Corso."

7. Robert A. Galganski, "The Roswell Debris: A Quantitative Evaluation of the Project Mogul Hypothesis," *International UFO Reporter* (March/April 1995); Galganski, "An Engineer Looks at the Project Mogul Hypothesis," *IUR* (summer 1998).

8. Audiotaped telephone interview with J. Bond Johnson conducted by Kevin Randle, February 27, 1989, copy in my files; Don Schmitt and Kevin Randle, "Fort Worth, July 8, 1947: The Cover-Up Begins," *International UFO Reporter* (March/April 1990); Don Schmitt and Kevin D. Randle, "The Fort Worth Press Conference: The J. Bond Johnson Connection," *International UFO Reporter* (November/December 1990). Both *IUR* articles are reprinted in *The Roswell Report: A Historical Perspective*, ed. George M. Eberhart (Chicago: Center for UFO Studies, 1991), pp. 56–69.

9. "RPIT Claims Roswell Debris Not from Balloon-Borne Radar Target," *Skeptics UFO Newsletter* (November 1999): 3–4.

10. Brad Sparks, e-mail message to me, June 20, 2000.

11. Donald R. Burelson, "A New Discovery in the Ramey Letter," letter to the editor, *MUFON UFO Journal* (July 2000): 13.

12. For example, quiet work independent of RPIT is underway, with very preliminary results demonstrating that RPIT's "interpretations" definitely are off the mark, but that something interesting and perhaps surprising eventually may be teased out of the Ramey message.

SEVENTEEN

THE CONGRESSIONAL INQUIRY
Insights from an "Insider"

A great deal has been written about the congressional inquiry into the Roswell incident. Much of it has been speculation, much has been inaccurate, and some has wronged a good and honest man, the late U.S. Congressman Steven H. Schiff. Steve Schiff, a Republican, represented the First Congressional District of New Mexico for almost a decade (January 1989 to March 1998) before his untimely death from cancer a week to the day after his fifty-first birthday.

My wife, Mary Martinek, was on Steve's staff during his entire tenure in the House of Representatives, in Washington as his legislative director, then in New Mexico, first as his district director and then as chief of staff. Steve was more than Mary's boss. He was our friend.

I played a leading role in the effort that ultimately led Steve Schiff to launch a congressional inquiry into the Roswell affair. Some have suggested I and those with whom I worked took improper advantage of my connections with Steve and his staff. This is absolutely not true. We did what is done quite properly every day in a democratic republic by people with causes or interests they want their elected representatives to pursue for them.

PRIMING THE PUMP

In early June 1992, I had taken the plunge back into full-time writing after eleven years as a congressional staffer, deputy assistant secretary of defense, and Washington "inside the Beltway" consultant. I had a list of subjects I wanted to pursue and write about. Well down that list was Roswell. The year before I had read Randle and Schmitt's *UFO Crash at Roswell,* and it seemed to me that they might be onto something. In short order, Roswell moved to the top of my list.

One evening, my wife brought home a slim brochure about the Roswell events. Mike Cook, the press secretary in her office, had received it from Bruce Donisthorpe, a member of the staff of Republican Congressman Joe Skeen, who represented and still represents Roswell. Skeen had been approached by constituents who wanted his help in getting the government to open up about the incident. Donisthorpe knew Cook was interested in UFOs, and he was trying to get a better understanding of the matter before recommending a course of action to Skeen. Was there anything to this? If so, what would be the best way to deal with it? Cook knew of my long-standing involvement in ufology, so he wanted me to look over the material.

The brochure, a compilation of press clippings and brief summary information, had been prepared by the Fund for UFO Research. The contact person listed was Fred Whiting, fund secretary-treasurer. This was a delightful surprise to me, as I had known and worked with Fred in the early 1980s when both he and I were congressional staffers. It had been nearly ten years since we had been in touch.

I gave Fred, who had left Capitol Hill to become a Washington public relations executive, a "voice from the past" call, and after catching up and explaining how I had learned of his involvement, we discussed Roswell. It seemed that, on behalf of the fund, Fred single-handedly had been pursuing an effort to spark some Capitol Hill interest in the case. He had talked with several key staff members of both the House and Senate. Most would not touch the issue with a ten-foot pole. A couple seemed genuinely interested, but were reluctant to take the lead.

Fred's latest initiative was aimed at Congressman Skeen, whose sprawling district included not only Roswell but the debris field and the alleged crash site. He had persuaded Glenn Dennis (who had attended high school with Skeen and was actively involved in local and state Republican politics) and Walter Haut, both Skeen constituents, to meet with the congressman. They had left the fund brochure with Skeen, who in turn passed it to Donisthorpe, who handled defense and national security issues for the congressman, and who then turned it over to Cook, who brought me into the picture. This is how things work—or do not—in Washington!

Fred and I agreed to join forces on the congressional initiative and began planning how to take advantage of an upcoming opportunity. Stanton Friedman and Don Berliner's book on Roswell, *Crash at Corona,* was slated for publication in August. Berliner was a Fund for UFO Research board member, and Friedman was a fund research grantee. Fred had arranged for a book-launch press conference at the National Press Club on August 31, at which Friedman, Berliner, and Dr. Jesse Marcel would appear. Fred and I decided to capitalize on this by arranging a meeting or meetings with congressional staff so they could hear the story from Roswell researchers and one of the witnesses.

The afternoon of August 31, Fred, Dr. Marcel, Freidman, and I met in Congressman Schiff's office with my wife; Cook; Monty Tripp, minority council for the House Government Operations Subcommittee on Information, on which Steve Schiff served; and, by speaker phone, Donisthorpe, who was in New Mexico. Following the briefing, Tripp presented the information to the subcommittee's senior Republican member and her majority counterpart. Both agreed the subcommittee would be willing to take action if a subcommittee member, Schiff, requested it.

Steve was advised of this, and he discussed the entire situation with his colleague Joe Skeen. The two congressmen concluded that the government operations committee, with its broad charter for oversight of executive-branch agencies, would be a good venue for any investigation, if one were needed, so Steve agreed to take the lead.

However, other more pressing matters took precedence, so any further pursuit of sub-committee action was put on hold.

Meanwhile, Fred and I decided a constituent letter campaign might help things along. Together, we drafted a letter for Fred's signature, which was sent to the long list of persons the Fund for UFO Research knew to have been involved in one way or another in the Roswell affair. Most were New Mexico residents, many of them Steve Schiff's constituents. All were urged to write to the congressman asking him to look into the case.

Throughout the fall of 1992 and the early months of 1993, letters poured into Steve's office. During this time, Steve and I occasionally discussed Roswell, and he made it clear he considered the issue was not, to quote him, "chasing flying saucers" but instead government accountability. He wanted to do something responsive for his and Skeen's constituents, but was leery of doing anything dramatic or high profile. Quite frankly, he did not think the matter warranted it, and he was concerned not to appear "some kind of nut."

Fred Whiting and I continued our "consciousness-raising" efforts on Capitol Hill. We expanded the letters campaign to encourage interested persons to write to their representatives and senators, not just Steve Schiff. We expanded the Roswell information booklet into a substantial briefing package and distributed copies to congressional staff and members who had expressed interest in the case.

We also sought to obtain the cooperation of all active Roswell investigators in making information available to Congress. This effort met with some success, but in general was disappointing, as in many cases our colleagues all too often seemed more interested in protecting their commercial competitive advantage than in advancing a congressional investigation that might get at the truth.

THE PENTAGON RUN-AROUND

In early March 1993, Steve decided it would be best to handle the situation as a routine constituent information inquiry. Members of Congress continually receive requests for help in obtaining information or action from federal agencies. All congressional offices have a standard "fill in the blanks" form letter for the purpose. Nine times out of ten, such a request is forwarded to the appropriate agency, the agency responds to the congressman with what has been requested or reasonable answers as to why the request cannot be accommodated, the member of Congress passes this along to the constituent, and that is that.

Steve decided to direct such an inquiry to the new secretary of defense, former House of Representative Armed Services Committee Chairman Les Aspin. However, this was an instance in which the usual form letter would not suffice. Steve asked me to draft something on which he could base his letter to Secretary Aspin, a common practice when an issue is complex and unfamiliar to a congressman and his staff. Needless to say, I was glad to be of assistance.

On March 11, 1993, Steve wrote to Aspin outlining the basic elements of the Roswell story as they were then thought to be, pointing out that the inconsistency between repeated official denials and the public record and testimony of those involved has led to a great deal of sensational speculation and called into question the credibility of the Departments of Defense, Army, and the Air Force [Schiff was a colonel in the air force reserve]. . . . I believe a full and honest review and reporting of the facts of the case would serve the interests of both the United States Government and affected citizens, and help put the matter to rest once and for all.

He went on to request "such a review be undertaken on a priority basis" and that he be briefed by "representatives of the Department of Defense and the responsible Military Departments" and be given a written report "providing a current, complete, and detailed description and explanation of both the nature of what was recovered and all official actions taken on the matter."

A month later, the congressman received a brief reply from the office of the assistant secretary of defense for legislative affairs. Signed by air force colonel Larry Shockley, it advised that Steve's March 11 request had been bucked to the National Archives for action. Obviously, bureaucratic routine had triumphed over institutional common sense. Although Congressman Schiff understood the realities of Washington were such that not all congressman are treated equally, that those who sit on committees directly responsible for an agency's budget and programs are considered "more equal" and receive more attentive consideration, this was an outrageous brush-off.

Ironically, I know from my conversations with Steve that, if he had received a response that gave good reason to believe his request had been taken seriously and followed up on with a genuine effort to "answer the mail," he would have passed the result along to his constituents and Congressman Skeen, and as far as he was concerned, there the matter would have ended. Instead, he was blown off, and he got his back up. He directed my wife, whom he had made the "stuckee" on the issue, to contact Rudy deLeon, Secretary Aspin's special assistant, and let him know in no uncertain terms that he expected his request for oral and written briefings to be honored.

On April 20, deLeon, who had worked for Aspin as a senior House Armed Services Committee staff member before joining him at the department of defense, responded with a letter advising he also found "these unexplained occurrences of great interest; however, these records are too old to be available here at the Pentagon." He recommended that the congressman "contact the National Archives for additional information as I believe Colonel Shockley has already done on your behalf."

On May 10, the congressman wrote once again to Secretary Aspin. He made clear that, while he understood that whatever records may exist on the forty-six-year-old incident probably had long since been archived, he also knew there was nothing in the holdings of the National Archives pertinent to his request. He insisted that Aspin see to it that his request for information be honored:

Wherever the documents may be, what is at issue is my request for a personal briefing and a written report on a matter involving actions taken by officials of the U.S. Army and U.S. Air Force, agencies under your purview.

I realize the research required to uncover the relevant documents and related materials will take time and considerable effort, and I am prepared to wait a reasonable amount of time for this to be accomplished. However, I expect the job to be done and my request to be addressed as set forth in the penultimate paragraph of my March 11th letter.

What had begun as a routine constituent request had escalated into a matter of government accountability and appropriate courtesy to an elected representative of the people.

About two weeks later, Steve received a letter dated May 20, from R. Michael McReynolds, director of the textual reference division of the National Archives, confirming that archives held no documents relevant to the Roswell matter. McReynolds noted that he was responding to the congressman's letter of March 11, which he had received from the "Department of the Air Force" (actually, the Office of the Secretary of Defense, where Colonel Shockley, an air force officer, was assigned). McReynolds wrote that he had received the congressman's letter on *May 6, 1993*, more than two months after Shockley claimed to have forwarded it and a month after the congressman's office had contacted deLeon. Clearly, the Pentagon could not even pass the buck competently.

Three months passed without any further word from the secretary of defense or any of his minions. On August 13, a very exasperated Steve Schiff tried again. He forwarded copies of his May 10 letter and previous correspondence and insisted

> on the courtesy of a reply to my letter [of May 10], **which is now three months old.**
>
> *To reiterate, while I am prepared to wait a reasonable amount of time for the briefing I requested, I do insist that the Department do the research on my inquiry and report the findings to me.*
>
> I also must insist on having my letters to the Department of Defense acknowledged and acted upon. I look forward to your response to my letters, and to the scheduled briefing. I will expect a reply to this inquiry by September 7th. [emphasis in the original]

September 7 came and went without any response from the Pentagon.

ENTER THE GAO

In October 1993, Comptroller General Charles Bowsher, the head of the General Accounting Office, paid a visit to Steve Schiff. The GAO, the investigative and fiscal accountability arm of Congress, fell under the oversight of the House Committee on Government Operations, on which, as I have explained, Steve served. Bowsher's budget was coming up for consideration in the committee and he and some of his senior staff were under considerable scrutiny, facing allegations of misuse of travel funds and other not insubstantial irregularities. Moreover, Bowsher had managed to get on the wrong side of a number of powerful congressmen and senators, among them New Mexico's Senator Pete Domenici, and he was anxious to gain Steve's support or at least a sympathetic ear in the upcoming budget review hearing.

As the courtesy call was coming to a close, Bowsher said something he no doubt almost instantly regretted. He asked the congressman, "Is there anything we can do for you?"

Steve and I had discussed possible ways to get the defense department to take his request for Roswell information seriously. Based on my experience with GAO's oversight work when I was in the Pentagon, I had suggested he might want to consider asking it to look into things for him. Besides having the effect of lighting a fire under the Pentagon, such an investigation might turn up something substantive that could be the basis for a government operations committee inquiry. Steve thought the idea interesting, but told me all he really wanted to do was get the department of defense to act on his months' old request. "A GAO inquiry might be overdoing it," he said.

"Is there anything we can do for you?" Bowsher asked. Steve explained his Pentagon-Roswell problem and wondered if, maybe, the GAO might be of any assistance. Later, Steve told me that Bowsher was somewhat taken aback, but responded, "Well, that's a bit unusual, but we're willing to take a stab at it. Let me discuss it with my people and get back to you."

Having been in similar situations during my Washington days, I can imagine the consternation of Bowsher's senior staff when he told them what had transpired between him and the congressman. After considerable agonizing, early in 1994 the GAO suggested an investigation seek to determine defense department "requirements for reporting air accidents similar to the crash near Roswell and identify any records concerning the Roswell crash." Congressman Schiff agreed to this, and the GAO began preparations for its work.

A few days later, Steve was in the offices of the *Albuquerque Journal* for one of his regular meetings with the editorial board. As he usually did, he also stopped by the newsroom, where he chatted with reporter Steve Brewer. Brewer asked if the congressman had anything new on his plate, and Schiff laughingly mentioned the GAO Roswell-records investigation. The next morning, January 13, 1994, the story ("Schiff Reopens UFO Case") was on the front page of the *Journal* and on the national news wires. The story immediately was picked up and played heavily by the *Washington Post* and other major newspapers and media.

I am sure that this was the first time that Steve Schiff realized what he had gotten into. He knew from me that the case was of intense interest in the ufological community. Of course, he also knew of its importance to many New Mexicans. However, until he and his inquiry became the subject of intense media interest, he really had no idea the chord the Roswell affair struck with the general public.

I am equally certain that, while the GAO was nervous about the assignment from the beginning, the media attention caused a reconsideration of the situation at the highest levels. I have been told by knowledgeable confidential sources that, while in response to media inquiries the agency's press officers attempted to downplay everything, senior GAO officials pondered what to do. It was decided to make a bare-minimum effort, just enough to give the congressman something to show his constituents, and get the whole thing out of the way as quickly and quietly as possible.

Two investigators were assigned to the job, Gary Weeter and Jack Kriethe. They went to work unaware of the decision of their superiors, and on February 8, 1994, the GAO Director for National Security Analysis, whom I had gotten to know when I was in the Pentagon, wrote to the secretary of defense formally advising him of the GAO investigation.

Anticipating the need to respond to and support the GAO effort, the air force had already begun its own investigation on the strength of the news reports. The job was assigned to the air force director of security and special program oversight, an official whose office was cleared for access to the most sensitive information.

Finally, someone in the Pentagon had gotten the message.

ROSWELL CENTRAL

The ensuing year and a half were hectic and often surreal. In March, I completed work on *Roswell in Perspective,* which was published by the Fund for UFO Research three months later. Soon after I delivered the manuscript to the fund, I met with the GAO's Jack Kriethe and gave him a copy. About the same time, Randle and Schmitt's second Roswell book was published. The release of both books added fuel to the fire.

Steve Schiff's office, the GAO, and the air force were inundated with mail, offers of help, and requests and often demands for information. At every opportunity the congressman emphasized the views that he began with and held to throughout his inquiry. First, "Generally I'm a skeptic on UFOs and alien beings, but there are indications from the run-around that I got that whatever it was, it wasn't a balloon. Apparently, it's another government cover-up." Second, "The issue to me is not flying saucers. The issue is government accountability. The public has a right to know what their government is doing."[1]

Hopes in the ufological community ran high, and one of the most difficult things for Fred Whiting and me and the GAO public affairs and congressional offices to do was "managing expectations." Fred and I tried to make clear the limited scope of the GAO's investigation, but had little success. The broad UFO-interest community was convinced this was going to blow the lid off the Roswell cover-up, and that was that.

We counseling patience and keeping a low profile, but it did little good. For example, Operation Right to Know, a group that had been demanding release of all government UFO files and underscoring its campaign with an annual demonstration in front of the White House, decided a demonstration in front of the GAO offices would be a welcome show of support for Steve Schiff's initiative. They even invited the congressman to take part. No amount of argument that this would be counterproductive helped. The demonstration took place, under the bewildered and bemused gaze of GAO staff on lunch and smoke breaks.

It also seems to have caught the attention of those in top-floor corner offices. Weeter and Kriethe began getting pressure to wrap up their work, and frequently were told how close they were to going over budget.

On September 8, 1994, the air force released its report on the results of its investigation, a twenty-three-page document summarizing its findings and the contents of some thirty-three attachments, which were not immediately distributed but were made available for viewing in the Pentagon library (everything was published in a single huge volume the following year, under the title, *The Roswell Report: Fact versus Fiction in the New Mexico Desert*).[2] Until one was demanded, a copy was not sent to Steve Schiff. Neither was he given any notice that the report was to be released. Once again, the air force had forgotten basic courtesy and its own long-range self interest. Ironically, at about the same time, in a Pentagon promotion ceremony, the chief of staff of the air force awarded the congressman the silver eagles of an air force reserve colonel.

The air force report arrived at the same basic conclusion I had about Project Mogul, without of course any of my reservations and speculations about other possible and more exotic factors. Amusingly, this led to speculation that the air force and I were in cahoots and that I had put them onto the Mogul idea. The credit for the latter goes to Robert Todd, who was not in any sort of unholy league with the Pentagon, but merely providing leads and the results of his research as so many others, including myself, had done to Steve Schiff and the GAO.

THE TRUTH ABOUT THE GAO REPORT

In the late spring of 1995, the GAO investigation came to a screeching halt. Highly reliable confidential sources have advised me that one day investigators Weeter and Kriethe were told they were out of funding for the investigative phase of their work, and it was time to write their report. Neither man was happy with this, Kreithe in particular believed a good deal more needed to be done, but the bureaucratic-political handwriting was on the wall: Give the congressman his damn' report, make it good enough to cover his and our butts, and move on.

In early June 1995, Weeter informally reviewed with Mary Martinek, the congressman's chief of staff and my wife, the points they were covering and their findings. *No* draft document was provided to the congressional office, as has been alleged by those who have sought to suggest Steve Schiff brought undue influence to bear in an attempt to have the report provide answers he wanted to hear. As I understand it, the one concern of any consequence conveyed to Weeter was that the proposed report lacked "beef," that it needed to be fleshed out.

On June 14, Weeter and Kriethe, accompanied by their division chief Richard Davis and the GAO's director of congressional relations Tom Hagenstad, met with Congressman Schiff, my wife, and other members of the congressman's staff. At this meeting, the GAO provided a copy of its draft report and briefed the congressman and his staff on its contents. It is standard GAO procedure to obtain comments from their requester before preparing their "final," for-comment draft, which is circulated to the agencies under review to give them an opportunity to correct factual errors and, if they wish, provide formal comments, which are then included in the published report.

Some time before, Steve had told me he thought message traffic to and from Roswell Army Air Field was likely to contain references to the alleged crashed-saucer incident, a reasonable presumption. At the June 14 meeting, he noted that there was no reference in the draft report to outgoing messages from Roswell AAF and asked if the GAO had looked for these. He was told that during their records searches, the investigators had reviewed Roswell AAF, Fort Worth AAF, and U.S. Army Air Forces Headquarters message traffic at the National Personnel Records Center in St. Louis. However, none of the GAO representatives could recall having seen any outgoing traffic from Roswell AAF.

Steve asked the GAO to look into this, and the investigators followed through by contacting the chief archivist at the NPRC. He advised that Roswell AAF outgoing messages for the period October 1946 through December 1949 had been destroyed, likely sometime in the 1950s. On June 20, the GAO informed the congressional office of this, *advising the destroyed records were listed on the Roswell AAF document disposition register as permanent records and therefore they should not have been disposed of.* Staff provided the information to Steve.

The GAO incorporated this new development in their for-comment draft dated and distributed for comment, with an *information* copy to the congressman's office, July 5, 1995. In the "Results in Brief" section, the for-comment draft included this statement:

> . . . [O]ur investigation indicates that . . . RAAF outgoing messages (October 1946 through December 1949) have been destroyed. These records were listed as "permanent" records. Senior government records management officials told us that *because these were permanent records, they should not have been destroyed.* [emphasis added]

In the "Search for Records" section, this was elaborated upon:

> The Chief Archivist for the Center [NPRC] provided us with documentation indicating that . . . RAAF outgoing messages from October 1946 through December 1949 have been destroyed. According to Center officials, the document disposition form did not indicate what organization or person destroyed these records or exactly when the records were destroyed. . . .
> . . . Both the Chief Archivist and a senior Air Force records management official told us that *because the RAAF outgoing messages . . . were listed as "permanent" records on the document disposition form, they should not have been destroyed.* [emphasis added]

On July 7, the GAO received a fax message from the NPRC chief archivist advising that it had misrepresented what he had told them. Accordingly, the GAO revised the text of its report, and as published it contained no reference to the outgoing messages as permanent records which should not have been destroyed. Instead, it stated, "the document disposition form did not properly indicate the authority under which the disposal action was taken," an error that was common during the period in question. In other words, what seemed a serious breach of government records management rules turned out to be a bureaucratic oversight.

While the GAO had taken care to inform the congressman of the erroneous information about the allegedly permanent records, *it did not bother to inform either him or his staff of this new development or the changes made to reflect it,* nor of other textual changes that were made before the report when to press. (Another bureaucratic oversight?) Thus, when the congressional office received its copies of the final report, no one there had any reason to know it was in any way substantively different from the July 5 for-comment draft.

As a result, when Steve Schiff released the GAO report, his press announcement made a point of the destroyed records which the congressman had been given to believe should not have been disposed of.[3] This was entirely reasonable based upon what he and his staff had been told by the GAO on June 20 and given in writing in the for-comment draft of its report on July 5. Perhaps someone should have gone through the final report with a fine-tooth comb, comparing it with the July 5 draft. It might have prevented this additional bit of confusion from being added to the already confused state of Roswell affairs. Unfortunately, Steve and his staff relied upon the GAO, a professional organization whose duty it is to give its bosses, the members of the United States Congress, accurate information—which includes keeping them informed of important changes in previously provided material.

Skeptical ufologist Phil Klass has made much of the "false charge" about destroyed records and Steve's statement to him in a July 29, 1995, interview that the GAO had provided him with two drafts of its report, implying this was an indication that the congressman had been exercising undue influence on the outcome of the GAO's work.[4] Taking the latter first, it should now be obvious that the two drafts in question are the "first cut" provided and briefed on June 14 and the information copy of the for-comment draft provided on July 5. Nothing out of line was involved.

As for the "false charge" issue, perhaps Klass should ask the "confidential source" who provided him with a copy of the for-comment draft why the GAO did not inform the congressman immediately when it found out it had made a serious error.

NOTES

1. "N.M. Congressman Spurs Probe of UFO Reports," *Washington Post* article as published in the *Santa Fe New Mexican,* January 14, 1994; "Goofy Issues Aside, Schiff Still Tackles the Day-to-Day Stuff," *Albuquerque Tribune,* August 11, 1994.

2. United States Air Force, *The Roswell Report: Fact versus Fiction in the New Mexico Desert* (Washington, D.C.: U.S. Government Printing Office, 1995). The twenty-three-page executive summary, released on September 8, 1994, was dated July 1994.

3. United States General Accounting Office, *Results of a Search for Records Concerning the 1947 Crash Near Roswell, New Mexico,* GAO/NSIAD-95-187 (Washington, D.C.: GAO, July 1995); "Schiff Receives, Releases Roswell Report," press release from the office of U.S. Congressman Steve Schiff, July 28, 1995.

4. Philip J. Klass, *The Real Roswell Crashed-Saucer Coverup* (Amherst, N.Y.: Prometheus Books, 1997), pp. 165–69.

EPILOGUE

"OUR REVELS NOW ARE ENDED..."

The Roswell that once seemed to so many, including myself, a UFO case overflowing with solid evidence and the exciting prospect of indisputable physical proof of alien visitation is no more. Like Shakespeare's "cloud-capped towers," it has dissolved, and in its place we find an interesting footnote to the Cold War and some fascinating science and technology history. But even though an "insubstantial pageant," Roswell offers lessons I hope I have learned and that others on both sides of the UFO belief divide may benefit from.

Belief is no substitute for critical thinking. It is one thing to be motivated by a hunch, a dream that something might be so. It is another thing altogether to allow hunches and dreams to becloud thinking, permit accommodation of contradiction and falsehood, and undermine common sense. When pursuing controversial quests, the courage of one's convictions can be the armor that makes it possible to resist the slings and arrows of one's detractors and triumph. However, it is all too easily transformed into a Maginot Line of intellectual arrogance that blinds us to evidence and logic that defies that which we want so much to believe—or disbelieve.

This pitfall is a threat to "pro-UFOlogist" and skeptic alike. Unrecognized certitudes close the door to knowledge. We must continually check our premises, our frames of reference to be sure we are not proceeding from either "They must be, therefore they are!" or "They can't be, therefore they aren't!" The will to believe cuts both ways.

When I began looking into Roswell, I was quite sure that, while I hoped there was a crashed flying saucer at the end of the road, I was approaching the case with true objectivity, a hopeful agnostic willing to follow the facts wherever they might lead and accept it if my hope was dashed. In reality, lurking in the back of my mind was an unstated conviction that there *was* a crashed saucer. Thus, despite my years of experience in intelligence, politics, the machinations of the nation's capital, and, for heaven's sake, ufology, I clung to that hope/conviction long after it should have been discarded. I ignored inconvenient facts, rationalized clues that certain persons were dissembling, dreamed up unlikely scenarios to keep my hope alive.

Part of the problem was the seeming richness of the evidence. What I missed, and what I fear others continue to miss, is that the case for Roswell is a classic example of

222

the triumph of quantity over quality. The advocates of the crashed-saucer tale, wittingly or not, simply shovel everything that seems to support their views into the box labeled "Evidence" and say, "See? Look at all this stuff. We *must* be right." Never mind the contradictions. Never mind the lack of independent supporting fact. Never mind the blatant absurdities. There is so much here, there has to be something to at least some of it, and if this or that witness or bit of data proves bogus, well, there are plenty more of both where they came from.

Those who are looking for reasons to believe have no difficulty at all finding "evidence" that convinces them. All the rest becomes convenient backdrop, "Oh, yeah? Well, then, what about . . . ?" props. This is greatly facilitated by the repeated tellings of the story on television and its incorporation into popular culture. Practically everyone has heard of Roswell, and those who have even a passing interest "know" what happened. "The baseless fabric of this vision," Roswell the legend, has assumed a greater measure of perceived reality than Roswell the objective reality.

In no small degree, Roswell is a microcosm of ufology today. We, all of us, from one end of the ufological spectrum to the other, can learn a lot from it. Or not.

"Our revels now are ended," our "insubstantial pageant faded." Time now to pursue dreams and hopes with feet firmly planted on the ground and eyes on the skies—taking great care about where we step.

JESSE A. MARCEL SR., DECEMBER 8, 1979, AND WALTER HAUT, JULY 11, 1990

O n December 8, 1979, *National Enquirer* reporter Bob Pratt interviewed Roswell incident principal Jesse A. Marcel Sr. at his home in Houma, Louisiana. An article based in part on this interview appeared in the *Enquirer* on February 28, 1980. The interview in its entirety appears here as transcribed by Pratt from his interview tapes a day or two after he met with Marcel. I have changed Pratt's text only to correct typographical errors, capitalization, and the like, to fully state Pratt's questions, which he set down in short form in his transcript, and by adding a limited amount of bracketed material to provided clarification. Marcel's words are exactly as transcribed by Pratt.

Following the Pratt-Marcel interview is an illuminating excerpt from another interview, this one with Walter Haut and captured on videotape, supplemented with an important historical elaboration from the official history of the 509th Bomb Group and Roswell Army Air Field.

Pratt: Tell me something about your background.

Marcel: [I] entered the U.S. Army Air Force in April 1942, was an aide to General Hap Arnold. [Marcel's official military personnel file includes no record of this, and the dates of his assignments completely preclude it.] Entered as second lieutenant. He [Arnold?] decided I should go to intelligence school, [for which there were] lengthy and strenuous exams. [I went to] Air Intelligence School, Harrisburg, Pennsylvania, under CO [commanding officer] Colonel Egmont Koenig. Was in school— first combat intelligence and [then] kept on in photo intelligence, since I had done a lot of cartographic work and interpreting aerial photographs. I used both combat intel[ligence] and photo intel in my work. He [Koenig] elected to retain me there as an instructor—one year, three months.

[I] applied for overseas duty, combat. Was sent to South Pacific, New Guinea, assigned as squadron intelligence officer. I had flying experience before going in service—started flying in 1928—so being in [the] air was not foreign to me. Did lot of flying, combat flying, [in] B-24s [four-engine heavy bombers]. From squadron, [I] was elevated to group intelligence officer until sent [me] back to the States just before A Bomb was dropped on Japan. [They] sent me back to take radar navigation course at Langley Field [Virginia]—was there when bomb was dropped and war ended.

[I] was [then] reassigned to Eighth Air Force—

Pratt: Headquarters was at Colorado Springs—

Marcel: [I] reported for duty there but following day transferred to Roswell [Army Air Field], New Mexico—which became Walker Air Force Base, immediately after end of war [Roswell AAF became Roswell AFB and then Walker AFB in fall 1947]—[the] 509th Bomb Wing [Group], I was intelligence officer for bomb wing.

Pratt: What was your rank?

Marcel: Major. [I] stayed there until October 1947. The 509th was the only A Bomb group in world. The first project I was sent on was an atom test on Bikini in 1946, came back to Roswell until latter part of 1947, when [I was] sent to Washington. [According to his personnel file, Marcel remained at Roswell AAF until August 16, 1948.]

[I was] in service for eight and a half years [and] had been in the Louisiana National Guard and the Texas Guard also. It became very difficult for me to get out of service, but I felt I had a duty to my family. [According to his file, Marcel was granted a family hardship release from active duty on September 19, 1950.] I was assigned to [the] Special Weapons Program, collecting air samples throughout the world and [getting them] analyzed. In fact, when we finally detected there had been a [Soviet] nuclear explosion, we—I had to write [a] report on it. In fact, I wrote the very report President Truman read on the air declaring that Russia had exploded an atomic device. This was after I left [the] 509th. I got out [of the air force] in 1950, latter part of 1950. [Note: Truman did not make a broadcast announcement about the Soviet bomb test. The White House issued a written statement.]

Pratt: What was your rank then?

Marcel: After this flying saucer thing came about in 1947, I was given a promotion to lieutenant colonel, in December 1947. [According to Marcel's file, this was a reserve promotion, which *he* applied for on October 29, 1947. It had nothing to do with the "flying saucer thing," and Marcel's active-duty rank remained major.]

Pratt: When did you learn you had been promoted?

Marcel: After I got out of the service. They kept me so busy I never even looked at my personal files. I was released from active duty as a lieutenant colonel. [Actually, according to his file, Marcel was informed of his promotion by a letter dated November 20, 1947, and he signed the oath accepting the promotion on December 1, 1947.]

Pratt: Was the flying you did before the war part of your work?

Marcel: Private pilot. [Marcel's file, including his 1942 application for appointment as an army air corps officer, lacks any mention of this and includes his "Reserve Officer Career Brief," dated November 20, 1947, which lists his flying experience as "NONE."]

Pratt: What work did you do before the war?

Marcel: I was a cartographer, mapmaker. Worked for U.S. Engineers and Shell Oil Company. I was working for Shell Oil Company as a photographer when the war began. All my map making for the Engineers and Shell Oil Company was derived from aerial photographs.

[I had] no degree then—got one later, six different schools. I speak French and English, understand several others but don't speak them. After war, [I] worked in electronics, repairing radios and TVs, since I had been a ham [radio] operator all these years. [I'm] retired now, [with my] wife. [My] son [is] a doctor in Helena, Montana. He's also a seismologist.

Pratt: When did you find the debris in New Mexico?

Marcel: I don't remember the exact date. It was in July 1947. How it all started—I was in my office. I went to the officers' club for lunch and was sitting having lunch when I got a call from the sheriff [George Wilcox] from Roswell, and he wanted to talk to me. He said, "There's a man here, a rancher who came to town to sell his wool—he'd just sheared his sheep—and he told me something that's weird. And you ought to know about this."

And I said, "Well, I'm all ears." He said, "This man's name is Brazelle [Brazel]. He said he found something on his ranch that crashed, either the day before or a few days before, and he doesn't know what it is." He [the sheriff] said, "This might be well worth your while to investigate this since I know you're the intelligence officer of the base."

So I said, "Well, fine." So I said, "Where can I meet him?" He said, "Well he's going to leave here about three-thirty or four o'clock, but he's in my office now, if you want to come and talk to him now. He'll be here waiting for you."

And he was, and he told me about it. Well, he got me interested, so I went back— I said [to Brazel], "You wait here." I said, "I have to go back to the base." So I talked to my CO [base and 509th Bomb Group commander Col. William H. Blanchard] about that. [I asked] what was his advice. He said, "My advice is you better get in that car." He said, "How much of that stuff is there, there?" I said, "Well, the way the man talks, quite a bit." He said, "Well, you have three CIC agents working for you—"

Pratt: "CIC"?

Marcel: That's Counter Intelligence [Corps] agents. See, my main job there was to clear the personnel through the Atomic Energy Commission to be stationed at that base— military personnel. I had five officers and about twenty enlisted typists working for me, with an office going like mine [sic] all the time. With [plus] those three CIC agents. They would do the investigating—Whenever we had to investigate somebody, I gave that job to them, and they'd turn in their reports in to my office and we'd write the reports.

Well, to come back to this. So I talked to Colonel Blanchard and he said take whatever you need with you, but go. So I got one of my agents named Cabot [Capt. Sheridan W. Cavitt], who, incidentally, we've never been able to find, since I don't know his first name. I didn't keep any paperwork on CIC agents. They didn't "belong" to me. So—but I had three of them.

So I took him [Cavitt]. He drove a jeep carryall. I drove my staff car, and we took off cross country behind this pickup truck this rancher [Brazel] had. He didn't follow any roads going out. This was an eighty square mile ranch, he told me. It was big. So we got to his place at dusk.

It was too late to do anything, so we spent the night there in that little—his— shack, and the following morning we got up and took off.

He took us to that place, and we started picking up fragments, which was foreign to me. I'd never seen anything like that. I didn't know what we were picking up. I still don't know. As of this day, I still don't know what it was. And I brought as much of it back to the base as I could and— Well, some ingenious young GI thought he'd try to put a few pieces together and see if he could match something. I don't think he ever matched two pieces. It was so fragmented. It was strewn over a wide area, I guess maybe three-quarters of a mile long and a few hundred feet wide. So we loaded up and we came back to the base.

In the meantime, we had an eager-beaver public relations officer [Walter Haut]— he found out about it—he calls AP [Associated Press] about it. Then that's when it really hit the fan—I don't mind using that expression. I probably got telephone calls from everywhere. News reporters were trying to come in to talk to me, but I had nothing for them. I couldn't tell them anything. I didn't have anything to talk about.

They wanted to see the stuff, which I couldn't show them.

So my CO [Blanchard], early the next morning, sent me to Carswell [Air Force Base, which in July 1947 was still Fort Worth Army Air Field] to stop over and talk to [Brigadier] General [Roger M.] Ramey [commander of the Eighth Air Force]. [I took] all the stuff in a B-29 [four-engine heavy bomber]. My CO told me to go ahead and fly it to Wright-Patterson air field [the adjacent Wright AAF and Patterson AAF in July 1947] in Ohio, but when I got to Carswell [Fort Worth AAF], General Ramey wasn't there, but they had a lot of news reporters and a slew of microphones that wanted to talk to me, but I couldn't say anything. I couldn't say anything until I talked to the general. I had to go under his orders. And he [General Ramey] said [Marcel chuckles—Pratt], "Well, just don't say anything." So I said, "General, Colonel Blanchard told me to get this stuff to Wright-Patterson. And he said, "You leave it right here. We'll take care of it from here." And that was the end of it—that was the end of my part in it. I still don't know what I picked up.

Pratt: Did they keep the B-29?

Marcel: No, no. It [the material] was transferred to a transport. The general told me, "You go back to Roswell. You're more needed there." He said, "You've got a big job there, what you're doing is important. This, there'll be nothing—"

Pratt: What was the rancher's name?

Marcel: Brazelle [Brazel], don't know his first name.

Pratt: Where is the ranch in relation to Roswell?

Marcel: North of the test sites and, I would say sixty miles northwest of Roswell.

Pratt: What was the sheriff's name?

Marcel: I don't recall it right now [it was George Wilcox]. He was sheriff of the county Roswell was in [Chaves].

Pratt: What kind of a ranch was it?

Marcel: Cattle and sheep.

Pratt: The next morning he took you out to this place?

Marcel: Yes. In fact, he saddled two horses. I never rode a horse in my life, and I said, "You two ride the horses." Cabot [Cavitt] was an odd— He was from west Texas. He was at home on a horse.

So they took off. We went up there, and we loaded all this stuff in the carryall, and we got through kind of late. But I wasn't satisfied. I went back. I told Cabot [Cavitt], "You drive this vehicle back to the base, and I'll go back out there and pick up as much as I can put in the car.

Pratt: What was the terrain like?

Marcel: Very flat. It's all very arid. You had tumbleweeds. It was adequate for a sheep ranch, for grazing. I didn't pay too much attention to that because my interest went another way.

Pratt: When you got out there, what did you actually see—bits of metal or what?

Marcel: I saw— Well, we found some metal, small bits of metal, but mostly we found some material that's hard to describe. I'd never seen anything like that, and I still don't know what it was. We picked it up anyway. One thing, one thing—

Pratt: It was something manufactured?

Marcel: Oh, it definitely was. But one thing I do remember, I recall that very distinctly. I wanted to see some of this stuff burn, but all I had—I had a cigarette lighter, since I'm a heavy smoker anyway. I lit the cigarette lighter to some of this stuff, and it didn't burn.

Pratt: Were there any markings?

Marcel: Yes, there were. Something undecipherable. I've never seen anything like that myself. Oh, I call them hieroglyphics myself. I don't know whether they were ever deciphered or not.

Pratt: There were some markings, though?

Marcel: Oh, yes—little members, small members, solid members that you could not bend or break, but it didn't look like metal. It looked more like wood.

Pratt: How big?

Marcel: They varied in size. They were, as I can recall, perhaps three-eighths of an inch by one-quarter of an inch thick, and just about all sizes. None of them were very long.

Pratt: How large was the biggest?

Marcel: I would say about three feet.

Pratt: How heavy?

Marcel: Weightless. You couldn't even tell you had it in your hands—just like you handle balsa wood.

Pratt: The piece three or four feet long—was it wide or what?

Marcel: Oh, no. It was a solid member, rectangular members, just like you get a square stick [here Marcel drew a sketch—Pratt]. Varied lengths, and along the length of some of those they had little markings, two-color markings as I recall—like Chinese writing to me. Nothing you could make any sense out of.

Pratt: Was everything in this shape, long and slender?

Marcel: All the solid members were that way. There was other stuff there that looked very much like parchment, that, again, didn't burn. Obviously—I surmise, I'm not—I was acquainted with just about every method of weather observation devices used by the military, and I couldn't recognize any of that as being weather observation devices.

Pratt: You've been flying since 1928, twenty years when this happened. Was this part of any aircraft that you recognize?

Marcel: No, it could not have been part of an aircraft.

Pratt: Nor part of a weather balloon or experimental balloon?

Marcel: I couldn't see that it could be, no. For one thing, if it had been a balloon, like the parts that we picked up, it would not have been porous. It was porous.

Pratt: Any jagged or broken ends or the like?

Marcel: No. As far as I can recall, they were clean. See, I had so little time to spend on this—I had other duties to perform. I brought the stuff over here, my CO saw it, my staff saw it, and then the following day my CO told me to take it to Wright-Patterson.

Pratt: Why there?

Marcel: For analysis. They wanted to see what it was.

Pratt: What was the agency at Wright-Pat?

Marcel: Air Force analysis laboratories, I think.

Pratt: How many pieces were there?

Marcel: It might have been hundreds. I don't recall. It's been so long since I handled all this stuff. I'd just about dismissed the whole thing from my mind.

Pratt: When you went out there that morning, you could see this stuff scattered for quite a ways in the distance?

Marcel: Lord, yes, about as far as you could see—three-quarters [of a] mile long and two hundred to three hundred feet wide. I['ll] tell you what I surmised. One thing I did notice—nothing actually hit the ground, bounced on the ground. It was something that must have exploded above ground and fell. And I learned later that, farther west, towards Carrizozo, they found something like that, too. That I don't know anything about. [It was] the same period of time, sixty to eighty miles west of there.

Pratt: Ranchers found something similar out there?

Marcel: I think it was discovered by some surveyor out there. [Marcel is probably referring to the Barney Barnett story, about which previous interviewers told him.]

Pratt: Did you pick up all the parts?

Marcel: I did not cover the entire area. [We] picked up as much as we could carry and some was left there.

Pratt: Was it grouped or bunched together, or was it scattered?

Marcel: Scattered all over—just like you'd explode something above the ground and [it would] just fall to the ground.

One thing I was impressed with was that it was obvious you could just about determine which direction it came from and which direction it was heading. It was traveling from northeast to southwest. It was in that pattern. You could tell where it started and where it ended by how it thinned out. Although I did not cover the entire area this stuff was in, I could tell that it was thicker where we first started looking, and it was thinning out as we went southwest.

Pratt: What was the length of the shortest pieces?

Marcel: Four or five inches. It was [as if it were from] something of some greater area that had been together.

Pratt: Were there clean breaks or obvious breaks?

Marcel: I don't recall that. Nothing seemed torn. It's pretty difficult to assimilate in your own mind just what it was because I wasn't with it that long. It's like you handle a hot potato—you want to get rid of it.

Pratt: Had the rancher been in that area recently before finding this?

Marcel: I faintly remember he told me he had heard an explosion at night and the following day he went out there in that direction and he saw that stuff.

Pratt: Of course, we didn't have artificial satellites in 1947—

Marcel: No.

Pratt: We had missiles, though, didn't we?

Marcel: Oh, yes.

Pratt: This obviously was no rocket?

Marcel: Oh, no. Unh, unh. I've seen rockets. I've seen rockets sent up at the White Sands testing grounds. It definitely was not part of an aircraft, nor a missile or rocket.

Pratt: Strange, isn't it?

Marcel: Yes, it is. It's bewildering. The one thing that I kept wondering—why no publicity was given about that by the Air Force. They probably got something they wanted to sit on. That's my opinion.

There had been a lot of reports about flying saucers in that area. In fact, I'm not sure—I wouldn't swear to this, but one night about eleven-thirty—I lived in town—the provost marshal called me and said, "You better come out here in a hurry." He wouldn't elaborate on the telephone what it was. So I got in my car and put my foot on the accelerator and [got] going as fast as I could go, and it was a straight road. Something caught my attention. It was a formation of lights moving from north to south. But it was so—I mean, we had nothing that traveled that fast anyway. I knew that. We had no aircraft that traveled at that speed, because it was visible only maybe three or four seconds from overhead to the horizon. They were bright lights flying a perfect vee formation. And I hesitated to open my mouth about that because I knew nobody would believe me, but two or three days later some GI said, "I saw something in the skies the other night." And he described exactly what I'd seen.

Pratt: Was this before the debris incident?

Marcel: Just slightly before. Anyway, I figure there's some credence to this UFO business. I believe in it. Even my son, Jesse [Dr. Jesse A. Marcel], one afternoon—he has two little boys and a girl, and the boys were with him—he was going into town and— They live on a little crooked road up the side of a mountain, and one of the boys said, "Dad, look at that!" My son stopped the car and looked up there and he saw a shiny circular object that all of a sudden took off like nobody's business.

Pratt: Tell me about Cabot's [Cavitt's] jeep carryall.

Marcel: It's slightly larger than a pickup truck, with a covered body. And we loaded the back end of that up with material and then I went back and loaded my car up.

Pratt: And there was a lot left?

Marcel: Oh, lord, yes. Yes, we picked up a very minor portion of it.

Pratt: You put all this on the B-29 and were going to take all the material to Wright—

Marcel: All we had.

Pratt: And you never heard back anything more from General Ramey or—

Marcel: Nothing at all.

Pratt: —or Wright Field?

Marcel: Nothing at all.

Pratt: Do you know if Blanchard did?

Marcel: That I wouldn't know. I rather doubt that he did, because if he had heard something about it, he would have told me. And he never mentioned anything. [But see the note following this transcript.*]

Pratt: How long did you stay at Roswell after that?

Marcel: [Until] latter part of 1947. [Actually, August 1948.]

Pratt: Where did you go then?

Marcel: Transferred to Washington, D.C. I was given an office with a title about that long [held hands apart—Pratt]. I was in the Selective Service building next to the State House [Department?] on E Street.

Pratt: What do you think this thing was?

Marcel: Well, as far as I know, or can surmise, it— I was pretty well acquainted with most of the things that were in the air at the time, not only from my own military aircraft but also in a lot of foreign countries, and I still believe it was nothing that came from earth. It came to earth, but not from earth. The biggest mistake I ever made—of course I couldn't—was not to keep a piece of it. But in all fairness to my work and the service, I couldn't.

Pratt: You had three thousand hours as a pilot—

Marcel: Right, [and] eight thousand hours [total] flying time.

Pratt: What medals were you awarded?

Marcel: I have five air medals because I shot down five enemy aircraft in combat. [Marcel's file shows he was awarded two air medals, both for accumulated flight time in combat. The file includes nothing about any shootdowns of enemy aircraft.]

Pratt: From a B-24?

Marcel: Yes, from the waist gun of a B-24 in the South Pacific. And I was given a bronze star for the work I did re-teaching personnel that came to fly combat, they were greenhorns that came out of the States. I had charge of that. I was given a bronze star for that. I've got commendations—even got one from the U.S. Navy—[from the] Air Force intelligence office, for the A Bomb tests in South Pacific, Kwajalein.

Pratt: You were all hand-picked officers.

Marcel: Right. [I've been] around the world five times, been in sixty-eight countries. [I have] a degree in nuclear physics, bachelor's, at—completed work at George Washington University in Washington[, D. C.]. [I] attended LSU [Louisiana State University], Houston, University of Wisconsin, New York University, Ohio State, [unintelligible—Pratt], and GW. [Marcel's military file indicates he had a year or year and a half of noncredit studies at LSU before the war. There is no record, in his file or at GWU, of him even attending GWU, let alone being awarded a degree.]

Pratt: Were you ever told not to talk about this?

Marcel: You don't have to be told, you just know. I couldn't jeopardize my part of the service and be criticized for what I said.

Pratt: The base public relations man [Walter Haut] called the Associated Press, and so on. Was the idea that a flying saucer had crashed?

Marcel: I don't know. I didn't talk to him or read what he said. I've heard contradicting reports on this. I had heard this PR man had called the press without consulting the CO, and later I heard the CO had authorized him to do that. But I haven't verified that.

Pratt: How many combat missions did you go on?

Marcel: I had a total of 468 hours of combat time, was intelligence officer for bomb wing, flew as a pilot, waist gunner and bombardier at different times. I got shot down one time, my third mission, out of Port Moresby.

Pratt: Did everyone survive?

Marcel: All but one crashed into a mountain. I bailed out just before we made landfall, I guess a quarter of a mile inland. Our engines gave out [on our] B-24. I bailed out at eight thousand feet, and I fell six thousand feet before I got my 'chute open. I was lucky to get it open—malfunction. Good thing I had a chest pack. My backpack wouldn't work, and I went to work on my chest pack. I wasn't taking any chances, and it paid off.

On July 11, 1990, Fred Whiting of the Fund for UFO research conducted a videotaped interview with Walter Haut in which this exchange took place:

Whiting: Did the colonel [Blanchard] say anything about this incident shortly after General Ramey's statement? For instance, in [a] staff meeting?

Haut: In the next staff meeting, which was about a week later—I believe we held them at that time every Monday—he made some comment about our agenda, what we were going to talk about. I believe after those comments he made some statement to the effect, "We sure messed up on that one last week. As a matter of fact," he said, "that outfit that was sending those balloons up were here on our station. They were from White Sands, and they were checking the upper atmosphere winds from east to west."

Of course, this could not have transpired the week after the incident, because Blanchard was on leave. However, the "Visitors and Executive Calendar" for the period September 3-15, 1947, in the "Combined History, 509th Bomb Group and Roswell Army Air Field, 1 September 1947 Through 30 September 1947," includes this entry for September 10: "Mr. Peoples, Mr. Hackman and First Lieutenant Thompson from Air Materiel Command arrived on the field to inspect Air Materiel Command installations and to confer with Lt. Colonel Briley."

James Peoples was the Project Mogul chief scientist. Clearly, he and his party were visiting Roswell AAF to make sure the just-renewed New York University/Project Mogul activities at Alamogordo Army Air Base would not lead to any further misunderstandings. Lt. Col. Joe Briley, in July 1947 a bomb squadron commander and in September the 509th group operations officer, is one of the witnesses whom Kevin Randle and Donald Schmitt have cited as offering testimony supportive of the crashed-saucer scenario.

APPENDIX B

EXCERPTS FROM PROJECT 93

(New York University Constant-Level Balloon Project)
Technical Report Number 1

This appendix presents facsimile excerpts from a New York University report to Project Mogul dated April 1, 1948. Included are the report title page, a numbered Mogul-service flight summary table, and a schematic diagram of Flight 5, launched June 5, 1947, the day after Flight 4, which became the Roswell "crashed saucer." I am grateful to Professor C. B. Moore, for providing me with this and other material on the project. As an NYU graduate student, Professor Moore served as the project engineer.

TECHNICAL REPORT NO. 1

Balloon Group, Constant Level Balloon Project

New York University

Covering the period Nov. 1, 1946 to Jan. 1, 1948

CONSTANT LEVEL BALLOON

Research Division, Project No. 93

Prepared in Accordance with Provisions of Contract
W2S–099–ac–241, between
Watson Laboratories, Red Bank, New Jersey
and
New York University

Prepared by: Charles B. Moore, James R. Smith, and
Seymour Goldstein

Approved by: Charles S. Schneider, Project Director
and
Prof. Athelstan F. Spilhaus
Director of Research

Research Division, College of Engineering, New York University.

April 1, 1948

New York 53, New York

TABLE XII

SUMMARY OF NYU CONSTANT-LEVEL BALLOON FLIGHTS

FLIGHT NUMBER	DATE AND RELEASE TIME	LOCATION	DESCRIPTION OF BALLOONS	WEIGHT	MANUFACTURER OF EQUIPMENT	TOTAL WEIGHT OF BALLOON INCLUDING BALLAST	DESCRIPTION OF ALTITUDE CONTROL	BALLAST WEIGHT	FREE LIFT	BALLOON LIFT	RADIOSONDE RECEPTION	TRACKING	AIRCRAFT OBSERVATION	FLIGHT DURATION	G-TERM CONSTANT	MAXIMUM CONSTANT LEVELS REL	AIRCRAFT LAND AND SITE	CRITIQUE
A	20 Nov. 1946 1036 EST	NYU, N.Y.	2 - 350 gram meteorological	0.7 kg	72.2 m Radiosonde	1.8 kg	None	0	Not known	Not known	of	of	of	70 min.	4 min. ± 1000'	Max. 21000' Const. 20000'	of	Balloon ballasting load. Free lift from 350 gram cutter clipped balloon. Successful cutting free of lifter balloon. Balloon did not level off.
B	16 Dec. 1946 1219 EST	NYU, N.Y.	2 - 350 gram meteorological	0.7 kg	72.2 m Radiosonde	1.8 kg	None	0	Not known	Not known	of	Theodolite of	of	31 min.	6 min. ± 1070'	Max. 15600' Const. 15000'	of	Balloon ballasting load. Free lift from 350 gram meteorological balloon. Successful cutting free of lifter balloon. Balloon did not level off.
1	3 April 1947 1018 MST	Bethlehem Pennsylvania	14 - 350 gram meteorological balloons, long cosmic ray train	4.9 kg	72.2 m Radiosonde Dead ballast	13.0 kg	2 cans of ballast to be dropped on descent	4.9 kg	Not known	Not known	of with recorder of with recorder	Theodolite of	of	115 min.	None	Max. 4000'	of	Failure due to poor rigging, poor launching technique. Lifter balloons 10 main balloons. Train rose until some balloons burst then descended rapidly.
5	5 June 1947 1017 MST	Alamogordo New Mexico	28 - 350 gram meteorological balloons, long cosmic ray train	10.5 kg	72.2 m Radiosonde Data gear Dead ballast Liquid ballast	18.4 kg	Balloons to cut off above 60000' 1 kg used and 1 kg liquid to fall under 31000'	10.0 kg	4.9 kg	34.3 kg	10% without recorder	Theodolite of	of R-17	248 min.	24 min. ± 200'	Max. 36000' Const. 31000'	100% E. of Roswell N.M.	First successful flight carrying a heavy load. 3 lifter balloons, 36 main balloons.
6	7 June 1947 0900 MST	Alamogordo New Mexico	28 - 350 gram meteorological balloons, long cosmic ray train	8.8 kg	72.2 m Radiosonde. Ball. acsembly. Ballast assembly	20.3 kg	Balloon to cut off above 60000' 1 kg and 1 kg liquid to fall under 31000'	10 kg	1.9	30.5 kg	93% without recorder	Theodolite of	of R-17	146 min.	None	Max. 18000'	of	Flight successful. Altitude control damaged on launching. 4 lifter balloons. 24 main balloons.
7	8 July 1947 0501 MST	Alamogordo New Mexico	20 - 350 gram meteorological balloons in 2 hollow cluster	7.0 kg	74.5 m Radiosonde Ballast assembly	35.7 kg	4 gear inflated balloons, 10 kg lead shot to fall under 31000'	10 kg	10.5 kg	36.3 kg	60% without recorder	Theodolite 100%	100% C-54	418 min.	147 min. ± 5000'	Max. 49500' Const. 35000'	25% (1 balloon) lost east	Best flight thought possible with flimsy neoprene balloons. 4 lifter balloons. 16 main balloons.
8	5 July 1947 0903 MST	Alamogordo New Mexico	10 Gen. Mills 3' .001 polyethylene	4.8 kg	74.5 m Radiosonde Ballast assembly	18.7 kg	Drthblur, compass field, fixed lead 140 gm/hr	3 kg	3.1 kg	30.8 kg	100% with recorder	Theodolite 35% Radar lost 55%	lost 15% C-15	395 min.	54 min. ± 1000'	Max. 18500' Const. 18000'	of	First non-extendible balloon flight. Due to the low polyethylene the altitude control was extended. Moreover, flight above a confined stability of non-extendible balloons. Loss of lift due to balloon leakage 1000 gm/hr.
10	5 July 1947 0943 MST	Alamogordo New Mexico	1 M.S. Smith 15' .008" polyethylene	16.8 kg	74.5 m Radiosonde Ballast assembly	16.8 kg	Drthblur Compass field	3 kg	3.4 kg	23.3 kg	55% with. with recorder	Theodolite 60 min.	of	Over 331 min.	130 min. ± 300 min. ± 2100'	Max. 13100' Const. 9000'	of	Successful flight with altitude control working. Balloon reported over Albuquerque, near Four Corners, Colorado, after 3½ hours. Theodolite turned out of transmission balloon due to convection currents over desert. Balloon diffusion 10 gm/hr.

TABLE III

• SUMMARY OF NEW CONSTANT-LEVEL BALLOON FLIGHTS •

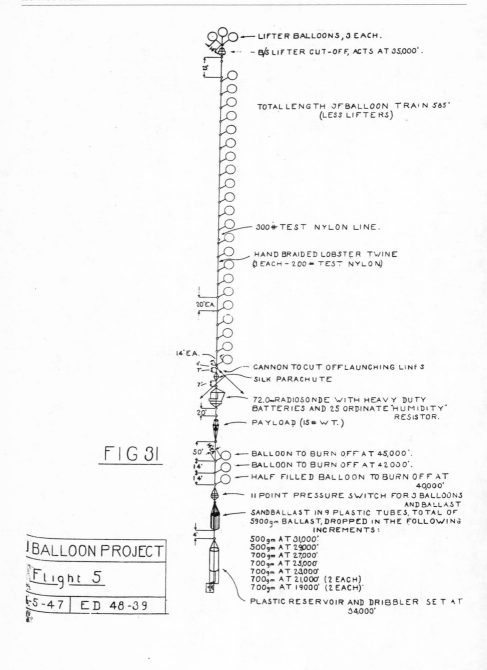

LIFTER BALLOONS, 3 EACH.

B/S LIFTER CUT-OFF, ACTS AT 35,000'.

TOTAL LENGTH OF BALLOON TRAIN 585'
(LESS LIFTERS)

300# TEST NYLON LINE.

HAND BRAIDED LOBSTER TWINE
(3 EACH - 200# TEST NYLON)

20' EA.

14' EA.

CANNON TO CUT OFF LAUNCHING LINES

SILK PARACHUTE

72.0-RADIOSONDE WITH HEAVY DUTY
BATTERIES AND 25 ORDINATE "HUMIDITY"
RESISTOR.

PAYLOAD (15# WT.)

FIG 31

BALLOON TO BURN OFF AT 45,000'.

BALLOON TO BURN OFF AT 42,000'.

HALF FILLED BALLOON TO BURN OFF AT
40,000'

II POINT PRESSURE SWITCH FOR 3 BALLOONS
AND BALLAST

SANDBALLAST IN 9 PLASTIC TUBES, TOTAL OF
5900gm BALLAST, DROPPED IN THE FOLLOWING
INCREMENTS:

500gm AT 31,000'
500gm AT 29,000'
700gm AT 27,000'
700gm AT 25,000'
700gm AT 23,000'
700gm AT 21,000' (2 EACH)
700gm AT 19000' (2 EACH)

PLASTIC RESERVOIR AND DRIBBLER SET AT
34,000'

BALLOON PROJECT

Flight 5

6-5-47 | ED 48-39

APPENDIX C

FBI TELETYPE MESSAGE, JULY 8, 1947, CONCERNING THE ROSWELL "DISC"

At 6:17 P.M. local time on the evening of July 8, 1947, the Dallas office of the Federal Bureau of Investigation sent a Teletype message to the bureau's headquarters and its Cincinnati office concerning the "flying disc" found near Roswell. This message, in which Maj. Edwin Kirton's last name is misspelled "Curtan," transmits the army air forces' description of what was found and states the material is "being transported to Wright Field by special plane for examination." The message provides convincing evidence that at least some of the Roswell debris was sent to Wright Field despite official denials. It also makes clear the debris was not from a weather balloon. Some have interpreted it as also proving the Roswell object was a flying saucer. However, considered in context, the message's rather sketchy description is more suggestive of materials from a New York University Mogul service flight.

(Note: this refers to the
" Roswell Incident ")

FLI DALLAS   7-8-47   6-17 PM

DIRECTOR AND SAC, CINCINNATI   URGENT

FLYING DISC, INFORMATION CONCERNING. MAJOR CURTAN, HEADQUARTERS
EIGHTH AIR FORCE, TELEPHONICALLY ADVISED THIS OFFICE THAT AN OBJECT
PURPORTING TO BE A FLYING DISC WAS RE COVERED NEAR ROSWELL, NEW
MEXICO, THIS DATE._ THE DISC IS HEXAGONAL IN SHAPE AND WAS SUSPENDED
FROM A BALLON BY CABLE, WHICH BALLON WAS APPROXIMATELY TWENTY
FEET IN DIAMETER. MAJOR CURTAN FURTHER ADVISED THAT THE OBJECT
FOUND RESEMBLES A HIGH ALTITUDE WEATHER BALLOON WITH A RADAR
REFLECTOR, BUT THAT TELEPHONIC CONVERSATION BETWEEN THEIR OFFICE
AND WRIGHT FIELD HAD NOT BORNE OUT THIS BELIEF. DISC AND
BALLOON BEING TRANSPORTED TO WRIGHT FIELD BY SPECIAL PLANE FOR EXAMIN
INFORMATION PROVIDED THIS OFFICE BECAUSE OF NATIONAL INTEREST IN CASE
FACT AND FACT THAT NATIONAL BROADCASTING COMPANY, ASSOCIATED PRESS, A
OTHERS ATTEMPTING TO BREAK STORY OF LOCATION OF DISC TODAY. MAJOR
CURTAN ADVISED WOULD REQUEST WRIGHT FIELD TO ADVISE CINCINNATI
OFFICE RESULTS OF EXAMINATION. NO FURTHER INVESTIGATION BEING
CONDUCTED.

                WYLY
END   RECORDED

CXXXX ACK IN ORDER   EX-23

UA 9½ FBI CI MJW

DPI H8

8-3C PM O

C-22 PM OK FBI WASH DC MH

AUTHOR'S SKETCHES AND NOTES FROM MAY 17, 1993, INTERVIEW WITH FRANK J. KAUFMANN

On May 17, 1993, I interviewed Frank J. Kaufmann about his alleged role in the Roswell affair. During the interview, Kaufmann made a number of crude sketches—of the alien beings he said he saw at the crash site, their craft and its features, and so on—and showed me a strange envelope that contained a folded paper representation of the alien craft. (Kaufmann's sketch of the craft and the bit of origami in no way resemble each other.) During the interview, I copied Kaufmann's sketches as closely as possible in my notebook. Afterward, I made annotated drawings of the paper craft and envelope from memory on a facing page. Facsimiles of these "masterworks" are reproduced in this appendix.

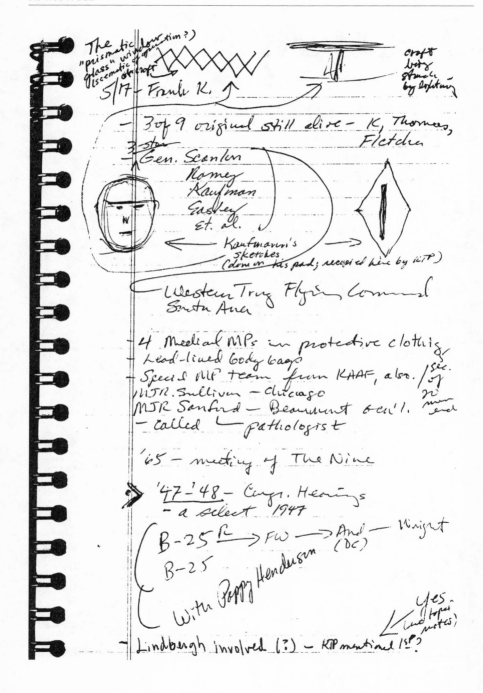

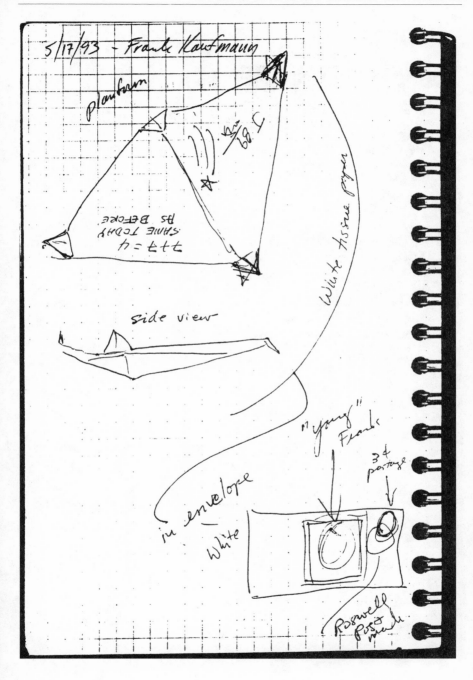

APPENDIX E

UNITED PRESS ASSOCIATION BROADCAST WIRE TRANSMISSIONS, JULY 8, 1947

T he news wires carried numerous stories and other communications about Roswell on the afternoon and early evening of July 8, 1947. This appendix presents facsimiles of a number of such transmissions which appeared on the United Press broadcast wire.

Among other things, they confirm Roswell AAF did *not* distribute a written press release on the Brazel discovery. I am indebted to Frank Joyce for providing this material. Joyce, in July 1947 an announcer with Roswell's Radio KGFL and a UP stringer, saved the stories as they came in on KGFL's UP terminal.

DXR 54

    MORE FLYING DISC (DXR53)

-O-

THE INTELLIGENCE OFFICE REPORTS THAT ⊥T GAINED POSSESSION   HE "DIS:" THROUGH THE COOPERATION OF A ROSWELL RANCHER AND SHERIFF GEORGE WILSON OF ROSWELL.

THE DISC LANDED ON A RANCH NEAR ROSWELL SOMETIME LAST WEEK. NOT HAVING PHONE FACILITIES, THE RANCHER, WHOSE NAME HAS NOT YET BEEN OBTAINED, STORED THE DISC UNTIL SUCH TIME AS HE WAS ABLE TO CONTACT THE ROSWELL SHERIFF'S OFFICE.

THE SHERIFF'S OFFICE IN TURN NOTIFIED A MAJOR OF THE 509TH INTELLIGENCE OFFICE.

ACTION WAS TAKEN IMMEDIATELY AND THE DISC WAS PICKED UP AT THE RANCHER'S HOME AND TAKEN TO THE ROSWELL AIR BASE. FOLLOWING EXAMINATION, THE DISC WAS FLOWN BY INTELLIGENCE OFFICERS IN A SUPER-FORTRESS TO AN UNDISCLOSED "HIGHER HEADQUARTERS."

THE AIR BASE HAS REFUSED TO GIVE DETAILS OF CONSTRUCTION OF THE DISC OR OF ITS APPEARANCE.

RESIDENTS NEAR THE RANCH ON WHICH THE DISC WAS FOUND REPORTED SEEING A STRANGE BLUE LIGHT SEVERAL DAYS AGO ABOUT THREE O'CLOCK IN THE MORNING.

J241P 7/8

DXR 55

    A BULLETIN FROM THE UNITED PRESS

BECKLEY, WEST VIRGINIA---AN OFFICIAL OF UNITED MINE WORKERS DISTRICT 29 IN WEST VIRGINIA SAYS THAT SIX SOUTHERN COAL OPERATORS HAVE SIGNED

FRR3

(SUB)

ROSWELL, NEW MEXICO---THE INTELLIGENCE OFFICE OF THE 509TH BOMB
GROUP OF THE ROSWELL ARMY AIR BASE REPORTS THAT IT HAS RECEOVERED A
"FLYING DISC" AND THAT IT IS BEING FLOWN IN A SUPERFORTRESS TO
"HIGHER HEADQUARTERS" FOR STUDY.

.ARMY OFFICIALS AT THE ROSWELL BASE WILL NOT DISCLOSE THE LOCATION
OF THE "HIGHER HEADQUARTERS."

SHERIFF GEORGE WILCOX (CORRECT) OF ROSWELL WAYS THAT THE DISC WAS
FOUND ABOUT THREE WEEKS AGO BY A RANCHER BY THE NAME OF W. W. BRIZELL
ON THE FOSTER RANCH NEAR CORONA, ABOUT 75 MILES NORTHWEST OF ROSWELL
NEAR THE CENTER OF NEW MEXICO.

SHERIFF WILCOX SAYS THE RANCHER DOES NOT HAVE A TELEPHONE, AND
THAT HE DID NOT REPORT FINDING THE DISC UNTIL DAY BEFORE YESTERDAY.
SHERIFF WILCOX SAYS THAT BRIZELL SAID HE DIDN'T KNOW WHAT
IT WAS, BUT THAT AT FIRST IT APPEARED TO BE A WEATHER METER.

HOWEVER, OFFICIALS AT THE ROSWELL ARMY AIR BASE WERE NOTIFIED,
AND AN OFFICER AND AN ENLISTED MAN CAME TO THE SHERIFF'S.OFFICE
TO CLAIM THE OBJECT.

SHERIFF WILCOX QUOTES BRIZELL AS SAYING THAT "IT MORE OR LESS
SEEMED LIKE TINFOIL." WILCOX SAYS THAT BRIZELL SAID THAT THE DIXC
WAS BROKEN SOME, APPARENTLY FROM THE FALL. THE SHERIFF SAYS THAT BRIZELL
DESCRIBED THE OBJECT ABOUT AS LARGE AS A SAFE IN THE SHERIFF'S
OFFICE. HE ADDED THAT THE SAFE WAS ABOUT THREE AND ONE-HALF BY FOUR
FEE.

-0-

(DXR

WILL HV ANOTHER ADD IN ABT 5 OR 10 MINWS.)

V7/3..

DESCRIBED THE OBJECT ABOUT AS LARGE AS A SAFE IN THE SHERIFF'S
OFFICE. HE ADDED THAT THE SAFE WAS ABOUT THREE AND ONE-HALF BY FOUR
FEE.

   -0-

  (DXR

     WILL HV ANOTHER ADD IN ABT 5 OR 10 MINWS.)

                              V7/8..

316P SPLIT 20 MINS DXR

SXR - IXR - HOLD FOR ONE
                   HCR

S AGR

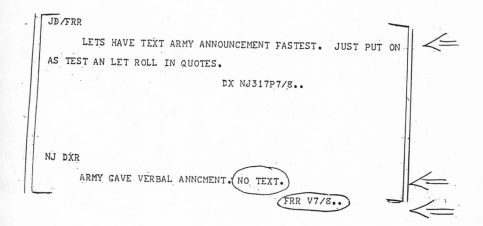

JD/FRR

     LETS HAVE TEXT ARMY ANNOUNCEMENT FASTEST. JUST PUT ON
AS TEST AN LET ROLL IN QUOTES.

                     DX NJ317P7/8..

NJ DXR

     ARMY GAVE VERBAL ANNCMENT. NO TEXT.

                    FRR V7/8..

FRR8

EEDITORS: PLEASE SUB FOR 5TH PGH AND REMAINDER OF FRRE8

-0-

HOWEVER, OFFICIALS AT THE ROSWELL ARMY AIR BASE WERE NOTIFIED IMMEDIATELY BY THE SHERIFF'S OFFICE. MAJOR JESSE A. MARCEL--- INTELLIGENCE OFFICER OT THE ROSWELL BASE---AND AN ENLISTED MAN THEN CHECKED WITH THE SHERIFF.

SHERIFF WILCOX QUOTED BRIZELL AS SAYING THAT "IT MORE OR LESS SEEMED LIKE TINFOIL." WILCOX SAID THAT BRIZELL RELATED THAT THE DISC WAS BROKEN SOMEWHAT---APPARENTLY FROM THE FALL. THE SHERIFF SAID THAT BRIZELL DESCRIBED THE OBJECT ABOUT AS LARGE AS A SAFE IN THE SHERIFF'S OFFICE. HE ADDED THAT THE SAFE WAS ABOUT THREE AND ONE-HALF BY FOUR FEET.

BRIZELL DID NOT BRING THE OBJECT TO THE SHERIFF'S OFFICE, BUT MERELY DROVE THE 75 MILES FROM THE RANCH TO ROSWELL TO REPORT HIS FINDING. SHERIFF WILCOX SAID THAT MAJOR MARCEL LEFT SHORTLY AFTER RECEIVING THE REPORT FOR THE AREA WHERE THE DISC WAS FOUND.

MEANWHILE, A REPORT FROM CARRIZOZO, NEW MEXICO, SAID THAT A DISC WAS FOUND 35 MILES SOUTHEAST OF CORONA. THE REPORT---WHICH WAS NOT SUBSTANTIATED---MERELY SAID THAT IT WAS "A RUBBER SUBSTANCE AND TINFOIL ENCASED." HOWEVER, IT WAS PRESUMED TO BE THE SAME, AS THE ONE REPORTED TO ROSWELL.

REPORTS FROM THE ROSWELL BASE SAID THAT MAJOR MARCEL WAS AT EIGHTH ARMY HEADQUARTERS IN FORT WORTH, TEXAS, BUT THAT "HE MIGHT BE ON HIS WAY BACK TO ROSWELL BY PLANE NOW." HOWEVER, OFFICIALS AT THE ROSWELL BASE SAY THEY KNOW NOTHING ABOUT THE DISC OR ITS DESCRIPTIONG, OR WHERE THE "HIGHER HEADQUARTERS" WHERE IT REPORTEDLY WAS TAKEN ARE LOCATED.

V342P7/8..

509th BOMB GROUP HEADQUARTERS MORNING REPORT, JULY 9, 1947

American military units are required to maintain daily records—morning reports—of the status of their personnel, including their departure on and return from leave. This appendix presents a facsimile of the July 9, 1947, morning report (with the continuation sheet of the report of July 8, 1947) for the 509th Bomb Group headquarters organization. The July 9 report reveals that, on July 9, group commander Col. William H. Blanchard commenced a twenty-one-day leave and Roswell AAF executive officer Lt. Col. Robert I. Barrowclough returned from a thirty-day leave. This document was located in the files of the National Personnel Records Center. I am grateful to researcher Joseph Stefula for providing me with a copy.

CONTINUATION
MORNING REPORT ... 5 ... July ... 7

Hq 50 th Bomb Gp (VH) ... AC

RAAFld, Rosw.l Nw Mexico

 sta Base (A) Comp (A) Dy 50K

1

PAGE OF PAGES

U S ARMY THRU ADV OR DCU

MORNING REPORT 7

Hq 50 th Bomb Group (..) AC

RAAFld, Roswell NM ..AAW

ANDRY FRED A : ... ...
Dy to reli ... ...
sion Army Aisory Grou wintire ...
Par 4 SO 110 Hq this sta ...

BLANCHARD WILLIA H (AC) ... 3 Col 106
Dy to Lv (Ordinary 21 ..s) ; Par 2 SO 7..
Hq Eighth Air Force

BARROW TOUGH ... T (AC)03 ... Col 100
Lv (Ordinary 30 days) to D

WOOD HAROLD H (AC) J-Ouli.. ... aj 1035
Lv (Ordinary 20 days) to D

ANDRON LEC A (AC) 0725097 Capt. 1028
Lv (Ordinary 8 days) to Dy
ENLISTED MEN

Medcalf Irving L RA6..73½ T Sgt 502
Asgd & Jd fron 393 omb Sq this sta, Par
24 SO 132 Hq this sta Dy 50C

1	1				1
6	6	5			
6	5	11	9		2
12	3	15	9	1	5
20	3	23	1	5/2	
3		3	2		1
1	18	50	11	5	9

	12	12			1
	4	4	3		1
	7	7	6	1	
	6	6	4	1	1
	7	7	4		
	7	7	1	1	
	1	1	1		
	44	44			1

I CERTIFY THAT THIS MORNING REPORT IS CORRECT

William C... ... JT
..t Air Corps

U S ARMY THRU ADV OR DCU

9 July 1947

APPENDIX G

NEW YORK UNIVERSITY FLIGHT 4 GROUND TRACK, JUNE 4, 1947

Utilizing U.S. Weather Bureau winds-aloft records and data from New York University Mogul service Flights 5 and 6, Professor C. B. Moore reconstructed the likely course followed by Flight 4 on its way into history as the Roswell "crashed saucer." Flight 5 was launched on June 5, 1947, and Flight 6 on June 7. The chart in this appendix shows the actual ground tracks of Flights 5 and 6 and the reconstructed track of Flight 4.

While Professor Moore is careful to explain that the reconstructed Flight 4 route is only a possible track, he and a number of colleagues who have examined the data and Moore's calculations have no doubt that the weather conditions do not preclude Flight 4 as the "culprit" and in fact positively allow for it. I am grateful to Professor Moore for providing this chart to me.

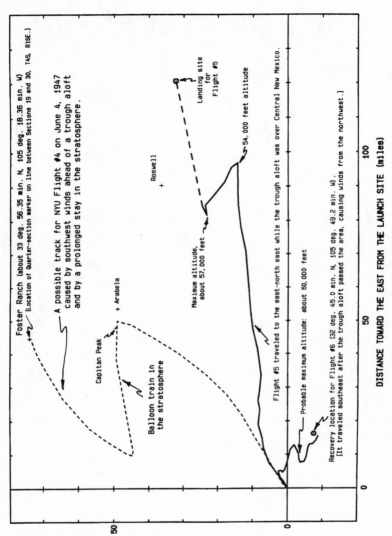

Figure 17. A possible ground track for NYU Flight #4 plotted on the tracks for Flights #5 and #6
(The plot for Flight #5 was taken without change from Figure 32 in NYU Balloon Project Technical Report #1,
but the data for Flight #6 have azimuth and height corrections to make them fit the recovery location.

APPENDIX H

ROSWELL WITNESS AFFIDAVITS

O n the order of thirty-five Roswell-related affidavits are on file with the Fund for UFO Research, and others are on file with the Center for UFO Studies. These were obtained through the efforts of Don Berliner, Stanton T. Friedman, Kevin D. Randle, Donald R. Schmitt, Frederic L. Whiting, and myself. Affidavits of twenty-eight witnesses and alleged witnesses (ten obtained from the signers by myself) are included in this appendix, arranged in alphabetical order. Two affidavits signed by the late Jim Ragsdale, one on January 27, 1993, and the other on April 15, 1995, are included to show how Ragsdale's account "evolved" as time passed and incentives changed.

These documents provide invaluable insight into the rich mix of tantalizing material confronting a researcher attempting to get at the actual facts about Roswell. They should also forcefully bring home to the reader how difficult it can be to sort fact from fiction, sincere attempt to help and faulty memory from dissembling, and how easy it is for the will to believe to influence the process.

AFFIDAVIT

(1) My name is Glenn Dennis.

(2) My address is: ███████████████████████████████

(3) I am ( ) employed as: _____ ( ) retired.

(4) In July 1947, I was a mortician, working for the Ballard Funeral Home in Roswell, which had a contract to provide mortuary services for the Roswell Army Air Field. One afternoon, around 1:15 or 1:30, I received a call from the base mortuary officer who asked what was the smallest size hermetically sealed casket that we had in stock. He said, "We need to know this in case something comes up in the future." He asked how long it would take to get one, and I assured him I could get one for him the following day. He said he would call back if they needed one.

(5) About 45 minutes to an hour later, he called back and asked me to describe the preparation for bodies that had been lying out on the desert for a period of time. Before I could answer, he said he specifically wanted to know what effect the preparation procedures would have on the body's chemical compounds, blood and tissues. I explained that our chemicals were mainly strong solutions of formaldehyde and water, and that the procedure would probably alter the body's chemical composition. I offered to come out to the base to assist with any problem he might have, but he reiterated that the information was for future use. I suggested that if he had such a situation that I would try to freeze the body in dry ice for storage and transportation.

(6) Approximately a hour or an hour and 15 minutes later, I got a call to transport a serviceman who had a laceration on his head and perhaps a fractured nose. I gave him first aid and drove him out to the base. I got there around 5:00 PM.

(7) Although I was a civilian, I usually had free access on the base because they knew me. I drove the ambulance around to the back of the base infirmary and parked it next to another ambulance. The door was open and inside I saw some wreckage. There were several pieces which looked like the bottom of a canoe, about three feet in length. It resembled stainless steel with a purple hue, as if it had been exposed to high temperature. There was some strange-looking writing on the material resembling Egyptian hieroglyphics. Also, there were two MPs present.

(8) I checked the airman in and went to the staff lounge to have a Coke. I intended to look for a nurse, a 2nd Lieutenant, who had been commissioned about three months earlier right out of college. She was 23 years of age at the time (I was 22). I saw her coming out of one of the examining rooms with a cloth over her mouth. She said, "My gosh, get out of here or you're going to be in a lot of trouble." She went into another door where a Captain stood. He asked me who I was and what I was doing here. I told him, and he instructed me to stay there. I said, "It looks like you've got a crash; would you like me to get ready?" He told me to stay right there. Then two MPs came up and began to escort me out of the infirmary. They said they had orders to follow me out to the funeral home.

(9) We got about 10 or 15 feet when I heard a voice say, "We're not through with that SOB. Bring him back." There was another Captain, a redhead with the meanest-looking eyes I had ever seen, who said, "You did not see anything, there was no crash here, and if you say anything you could get into a lot of trouble." I said, "Hey look mister, I'm a civilian and you can't do a damn thing to me." He said, "Yes we can; somebody will be picking your bones out of the sand." There was a black Sergeant with a pad in his hand who said, "He would make good dog food for our dogs." The Captain said, "Get the SOB out." The MPs followed me back to the funeral home.

(10) The next day, I tried to call the nurse to see what was going on. About 11:00 AM, she called the funeral home and said, "I need to talk to you." We agreed to meet at the officers club. She was very upset. She said, "Before I talk to you, you have to give me a sacred oath that you will never mention my name, because I could get into a lot of trouble." I agreed.

(11) She said she had gone to get supplies in a room where two doctors were performing a preliminary autopsy. The doctors said they needed her to take notes during the procedure. She said she had never smelled anything so horrible in her life, and the sight was the most gruesome she had ever seen. She said, "This was something no one has ever seen." As she spoke, I was concerned that she might go into shock.

(12) She drew me a diagram of the bodies, including an arm with a hand that had only four fingers; the doctors noted that on the end of the fingers were little pads resembling suction cups. She said the head was disproportionately large for the body; the eyes were deeply set; the skulls were flexible; the nose was concave with only two orifices; the mouth was a fine slit, and the doctors said there was heavy cartilage instead of teeth. The ears were only small orifices with flaps. They had no hair, and the skin was black--perhaps due to exposure in the sun. She gave me the drawings.

(13) There were three bodies; two were very mangled and dismembered, as if destroyed by predators; one was fairly intact. They were three-and-a-half to four feet tall. She told me the doctors said: "This isn't anything we've ever seen before; there's nothing in the medical textbooks like this." She said she and the doctors became ill. They had to turn off the air conditioning and were afraid the smell would go through the hospital. They had to move the operation to an airplane hangar.

(14) I drove her back to the officers' barracks. The next day I called the hospital to see how she was, and they said she wasn't available. I tried to get her for several days, and finally got one of the nurses who said the Lieutenant had been transferred out with some other personnel. About 10 days to two weeks later, I got a letter from her with an APO number. She indicated we could discuss the incident by letter in the future. I wrote back to her and about two weeks later the letter came back marked "Return To Sender--DECEASED." Later, one of the nurses at the base said the rumor was that she and five other nurses had been on a training mission and had been killed in a plane crash.

(15) Sheriff George Wilcox and my father were very close friends. The Sheriff went to my folks' house the morning after the events at the base and said to my father, "I don't know what kind of trouble Glenn's in, but you tell

your son that he doesn't know anything and hasn't seen anything at the base." He added, "They want you and your wife's name, and they want your and your children's addresses." My father immediately drove to the funeral home and asked me what kind of trouble I was in. He related the conversation with Sheriff Wilcox, and so I told him about the events of the previous day. He is the only person to whom I have told this story until recently.

(16) I had filed away the sketches the nurse gave me that day. Recently, at the request of a researcher, I tried to locate my personal files at the funeral home, but they had all been destroyed.

(17) I have not been paid or given anything of value to make this statement, which is the truth to the best of my recollection.

_____
(Signature)

8-7-91
_____
(Date)

Signature witnessed by:

_____
(Name)   WALTER G. HAUT

AFFIDAVIT

(1) My name is Thomas Jefferson DuBose.

(2) My address is: ████████████████████████████

(3) I retired from the U.S. Air Force in 1959 with the rank of Brigadier General.

(4) In July 1947, I was stationed at Fort Worth Army Air Field [later Carswell Air Force Base] in Fort Worth, Texas. I served as Chief of Staff to Major General Roger Ramey, Commander, Eighth Air Force. I had the rank of Colonel.

(5) In early July, I received a phone call from Maj. Gen. Clements McMullen, Deputy Commander, Strategic Air Command. He asked what we knew about the object which had been recovered outside Roswell, New Mexico, as reported by the press. I called Col. William Blanchard, Commander of the Roswell Army Air Field and directed him to send the material in a sealed container to me at Fort Worth. I so informed Gen. McMullen.

(6) After the plane from Roswell arrived with the material, I asked the Base Commander, Col. Al Clark, to take possession of the material and to personally transport it in a B-26 to Gen. McMullen in Washington, D.C. I notified Gen. McMullen, and he told me he would send the material by personal courier on his plane to Benjamin Chidlaw, Commanding General of the Air Materiel Command at Wright Field [later Wright Patterson AFB]. The entire operation was conducted under the strictest secrecy.

(7) The material shown in the photographs taken in Maj. Gen. Ramey's office was a weather balloon. The weather balloon explanation for the material was a cover story to divert the attention of the press.

(8) I have not been paid or given anything of value to make this statement, which is the truth to the best of my recollection.

_____
(Signature)

_____
(Date)

Signature witnessed by:

_____
(Name)

Notary Public
State of Florida
County of Orange

Notary Public, State of Florida
My Commission Expires Dec. 2, 1998
Bonded Thru Troy Fain - Insurance Inc.

AFFIDAVIT OF BARBARA DUGGER

(1) My name is Barbara Dugger.

(2) My address is:

(3) I am employed by:

(4) My grandmother was Inez Wilcox, and my grandfather was George Wilcox, who was the Sheriff in Chaves County, New Mexico, in 1947. I lived with my grandmother while I was teaching at the New Mexico Military Institute. I was 24 years old at the time.

(5) One evening, while we were watching a TV program about space, my grandmother told me that in the 1940s, there was a spacecraft--a flying saucer--that crashed outside Roswell. She told me not to tell anybody, because when the event occurred, "the military police came to the jailhouse and told George and I that if we ever told anything about the incident, not only would we be killed, but our entire family would be killed." I said, "Did you believe them?" She said, "What do you think? They meant it, Barbara-- they were not kidding." She didn't remember the names of those involved, however, she said it was Air Force personnel who threatened them. She never told anyone else in my family about the event, even my mother, Elizabeth Tulk.

(6) She said someone had come to Roswell and told him about this incident. My grandfather went out there to the site; it was in the evening. There was a big burned area, and he saw debris. He also saw four "space beings." One of the little men was alive. Their heads were large. They wore suits like silk.

(7) After he returned to his office, my grandfather got phone calls from all over the world--including England. MPs came to the jail. A lot of people came in and out of the jail at the time.

(8) She said the event shocked him. He never wanted to be sheriff again after that. Grandmother ran for sheriff and was defeated. She wrote an article about the event right after it happened to see if anyone else knew anything about it.

(9) My grandmother was a very loyal citizen of the United States, and she thought it was in the best interest of the country not to talk about the event. However, if she said it happened, it happened. Her state of mind was excellent at the time of this conversation. She was working in real estate. Grandfather had passed away by this time from hardening of the arteries. Grandmother passed away at age of 93.

(10) I have not been paid or given anything of value to make this statement, which is the truth to the best of my recollection.

Barbara Dugger
(Signature

_2-24-95_
(Date)

Signature witnessed by:

Veronica Garcia

AFFIDAVIT

(1) My name is Mary ~~Catherine~~ *KATHRYN* Goode.

(2) My address is: ▇▇▇▇▇▇▇▇▇▇▇▇▇▇▇▇

(3) I am employed as: ▇▇▇▇▇▇▇▇▇▇▇▇▇▇ .

(4) My father was Oliver W. Henderson. When I was growing up, he and I would often spend evenings looking at the stars. On one occasion, I asked him what he was looking for. He said, "I'm looking for flying saucers. They're real, you know."

(5) In 1981, during a visit to my parents' home, my father showed me a newspaper article which described the crash of a UFO and the recovery of alien bodies outside Roswell, New Mexico. He told me that he saw the crashed craft and the alien bodies described in the article, and that he had flown the wreckage to Ohio. He described the alien beings as small and pale, with slanted eyes and large heads. He said they were humanoid-looking, but different from us. I think he said there were three bodies.

(6) He said the matter had been top secret and that he was not supposed to discuss it with anyone, but that he felt it was all right to tell me because it was in the newspaper.

(7) I have not been paid or given anything of value to make this statement, which is the truth to the best of my recollection.

Mary K. Goode
(Signature)

August 14, 1991
(Date)

Signature witnessed by:

Robyn L. Christl
(Name)

```
ROBYN L. CHRISTL
Notary Public — Nevada
Douglas County
My Appointment Expires Aug. 23, 1992
```

AFFIDAVIT
L. M. Hall

(1)   My name is L. M. Hall.

(2)   My address is ▓▓▓▓▓▓▓▓▓▓▓▓▓▓▓▓▓▓▓▓▓▓

(3)   I am ~~employed as~~: _Retired_ . ( ) I am retired.

(4)   I came to Roswell, New Mexico, in 1943, while serving in the Army Air Force. I was a military policeman and investigator at Roswell Army Air Field (RAAF). In 1946, after being discharged from the service, I joined the Roswell Police Department, and in 1964 I was appointed chief of police, serving for 14 and a half years. I am now a member of the Roswell City Council.

(5)   In 1947, I was a motorcycle officer, with patrol duty on South Main Street, between town and RAAF. I and other police officers would often take our breaks in the small lounge at the Ballard Funeral Home at 910 South Main, where Glenn Dennis worked. I had gotten to know Glenn when I was a base MP because he made ambulance calls to the base under a contract Ballard's had, so I would sometimes have coffee with him if he was at work when I stopped in.

(6)   One day in July 1947, I was at Ballard's on a break, and Glenn and I were in the driveway "batting the breeze." I was sitting on my motorcycle, and Glenn stood nearby. He remarked, "I had a funny call from the base. They wanted to know if we had several baby caskets." Then he started laughing and said, "I asked what for, and they said they wanted to bury [or ship] those aliens," something to that effect. I thought it was one of those "gotcha" jokes, so I didn't bite. He never said anything else about it, and I didn't either.

(7)   I believe our conversation took place a couple of days after the stories about a crashed flying saucer appeared in the Roswell papers.

(8)   I have not been paid or given or promised anything of value to make this statement, which is the truth to the best of my recollection.

L. M. Hall
L. M. Hall
_____   9-15-93
(Signature and Printed Name)   (Date)

Signature witnessed by:

No One present to witness JR4

_____   _____
(Signature and Printed Name)   (Date)

yes I knew Dan Dwyer

AFFIDAVIT

(1) My name is Walter Haut. ████████████████████

(2) My address is: ███ .

(3) I am retired.

(4) In July 1947, I was stationed at the Roswell Army Air base, serving as the base Public Information Officer. At approximately 9:30 AM on July 8, I received a call from Col. William Blanchard, the base commander, who said he had in his possession a flying saucer or parts thereof. He said it came from a ranch northwest of Roswell, and that the base Intelligence Officer, Major Jesse Marcel, was going to fly the material to Fort Worth.

(5) Col. Blanchard told me to write a news release about the operation and to deliver it to both newspapers and the two radio stations in Roswell. He felt that he wanted the local media to have the first opportunity to have the story. I went first to KGFL, then to KSWS, then to the *Daily Record* and finally to the *Morning Dispatch*.

(6) The next day, I read in the newspaper that General Roger Ramey in Forth Worth had said the object was a weather balloon.

(7) I believe Col. Blanchard saw the material, because he sounded positive about what the material was. There is no chance that he would have mistaken it for a weather balloon. Neither is there any chance that Major Marcel would have been mistaken.

(8) In 1980, Jesse Marcel told me that the material photographed in Gen. Ramey's office was not the material he had recovered.

(9) I am convinced that the material recovered was some type of craft from outer space.

(10) I have not been paid nor given anything of value to make this statement, and it is the truth to the best of my recollection.

_____
(Signature)

5-14-93
_____
(Date)

Signature witnessed by:

_____
(Name)

AFFIDAVIT

(1) My name is Sappho Henderson.

(2) My address is: ▬▬▬▬▬▬▬▬▬▬▬▬▬▬▬▬▬

(3) I am retired.

(4) My husband was Oliver Wendell Henderson, who was called "Pappy," because he was older than the other ~~enlisted men~~ *PILOTS* in his squadron during World War II and had prematurely gray hair. We met during World War II, when he flew with the 446th Bomb Squadron; he flew B-24s and had 30 missions over Germany, for which he received two Distinguished Flying Crosses and the Air Medal with Four Oak Leaf Clusters.

(5) After the war, he returned home and was sent to Galveston Air Force Base, then transferred to Pueblo AFB, and then sent to Roswell (later Walker AFB), where we stayed for 13 years.

(6) While he was stationed at Roswell, he ran the "Green Hornet Airline," which involved flying C-54s and C-47s, carrying VIPs, scientists and materials from Roswell to the Pacific during the atom bomb tests. He had to have a Top Secret clearance for this responsibility. After separating from the service, he operated a construction business in Roswell. He died on March 25, 1986.

(7) In 1980 or 1981, he picked up a newspaper at a grocery store where we were living in San Diego. One article described the crash of a UFO outside Roswell, with the bodies of aliens discovered beside the craft. He pointed out the article to me and said, "I want you to read this article, because it's a true story. I'm the pilot who flew the wreckage of the UFO to Dayton, Ohio. I guess now that they're putting it in the paper, I can tell you about this. I wanted to tell you for years." Pappy never discussed his work because of his security clearance.

(8) He described the beings as small with large heads for their size. He said the material that their suits were made of was different than anything he had ever seen. He said they looked strange. I believe he mentioned that the bodies had been packed in dry ice to preserve them. He was not aware of the book [*The Roswell Incident*] that had been published about this event at the time he told me this.

(9) I have not been paid or given anything of value to make this statement, which is the truth to the best of my recollection.

[signature: Sappho Henderson]
(Signature)

[handwritten: PERSONA APPEARED MRS. SAPPHO HENDERSON]

[handwritten: July 9, 1991]
(Date)

Subscribed and sworn to before me this

Signature witnessed by:

9th day of July, 19 91.

[signature: Steve Goode]
(Name)

[signature] Notary Public
In and for the County of Los Angeles State of California

AFFIDAVIT
Jason Kellahin

(1)   My name is Jason Kellahin.

(2)   My address is ████████████████████████

(3)   ~~I am employed as:~~ Was a Practing attorny and (X) I am retired.

(4)   I am a native of Roswell, New Mexico, where, at the age of 12, I started working for the *Roswell Morning Dispatch*, sweeping out the back shop after school. Shortly before World War II, I was named editor of the paper. After the war, I became an Associated Press (AP) reporter, later going to law school and entering into practice in 1951. In July 1947 I was a reporter in the AP's Albuquerque bureau.

(5)   On July 8, 1947, someone in Roswell called our bureau with the news that the Roswell Army Air Field (RAAF) had announced the Army had "captured" a flying saucer on a ranch in Lincoln County. Although I may have taken the call, I do not remember doing so. The story was put on the wire, and AP headquarters in New York ordered our bureau chief to send someone to get more information. He sent me and, because he thought there might be a photo opportunity, our wire technician and photographer, R. (Robin) D. Adair. We took our portable wirephoto machine with us.

(6)   Our first stop was the Foster ranch, where the discovery had been made. At the ranch house, we found William "Mac" Brazel, his wife, and his small son. It was Brazel who made the find in a pasture some distance from the house. He was not happy about the attention he was getting and the people traipsing around his place. He said if he ever found anything again, he would not tell anyone unless it was a bomb.

(7)   Brazel took Adair and me to the pasture where he made his discovery. When we arrived, there were three or four uniformed Army officers searching some higher ground about a quarter to a half mile away. Apparently, they had been there for some time.

(8)   There was quite a lot of debris on the site—pieces of silver colored fabric, perhaps aluminized cloth. Some of the pieces had sticks attached to them. I thought they might be the remains of a high-altitude balloon package, but I did not see anything, pieces of rubber or the like, that looked like it could have been part of the balloon itself. The way the material was distributed, it looked as though whatever it was from came apart as it moved along through the air.

(9)   After looking at the material, I walked over to the military men. They said they were from RAAF and were just looking around to see what they could find. They said they were going back to Roswell and would talk with me

JK.
9-20-93

further there. They had a very casual attitude and did not seem at all disturbed that the press was there. They made no attempt to run us off.

(9)   Adair and I, Brazel, and the Army men then drove down to Roswell, traveling separately. Late that afternoon or early evening, we met at the offices of the *Roswell Daily Record*, the city's afternoon newspaper. The military men waited on the sidewalk out front, while I and a *Record* reporter named Skeritt interviewed Brazel and Adair took his picture. (Adair also took photos of Brazel and the debris at the ranch, but these were never used.) Walter E. Whitmore, owner of KGFL, one of Roswell's two radio stations, was also present during the interview. Whitmore did his best to maneuver Brazel away from the rest of the press.

(10)   After interviewing Brazel, I spoke with the military people outside and then went over to see Sheriff George Wilcox, whom I knew well. Wilcox said the military indicated to him it would be best if he did not say anything. I then phoned in my story to the AP office in Albuquerque. The next morning, Adair transmitted his photos on the portable wirephoto equipment.

(11)   I have not been paid or given or promised anything of value to make this statement, which is the truth to the best of my recollection.

JASON KELLAHIN

Jason Kellahin   Sept. 20, 1993
(Signature and Printed Name)   (Date)

Signature witnessed by:

Michele Guadagnole   Sept 20 1997
(Signature and Printed Name)   (Date)

My Commission Expires June 9th 1997

AFFIDAVIT

(1) My name is John Kromschroeder, DDS.

(2) My address is:

(3) I am retired from the field of dentistry.

(4) I met Oliver W. "Pappy" Henderson in 1962 or 1963. I learned that we shared an interest in metallurgy. We participated in several joint business ventures.

(5) In 1977, which was the 30th anniversary of Roswell event, Henderson told me about the Roswell incident. He said he transported wreckage and alien bodies to Wright Field in Dayton, Ohio. He described the wreckage as "spacecraft garbage." He said "the passengers suffered their death." He described the beings as small.

(6) Approximately one year later, Henderson produced a piece of metal taken from the craft. I gave it a good thorough looking at and decided that it was an alloy that we are not familiar with. It was a gray lustrous metal resembling aluminum, but lighter in weight and much stiffer.

(7) I have not been paid or given anything of value to make this statement, which is the truth to the best of my recollection.

(Signature)

(Date) May, 1991

Signature witnessed by:

(Name)

Lcdr   US Navy (Ret)

AFFIDAVIT
Arthur R. McQuiddy

(1)   My name is Arthur R. McQuiddy.

(2)   My address is ███████████████████████

(3)   I am employed as:_____, ( ) I am retired.

(4)   In July 1947, I was editor of the *Roswell Morning Dispatch*, one of the two newspapers here at the time. In 1948, I left the paper to become public relations director of the New Mexico Oil and Gas Association and later joined U.S. Steel as director of media relations. About eleven years ago I returned to Roswell after retiring as senior vice president for corporate relations at International Harvester.

(5)   Just before noon one day early in July 1947, Walter Haut, the public relations officer at Roswell Army Air Field (RAAF), brought a press release to me in the *Dispatch* office. The release said a crashed flying saucer had been found, taken to RAAF, and sent on to another base.

(6)   Haut had been to the two local radio stations, KGFL and KSWS, before coming to the *Dispatch*, so I gave him a bad time about that. Haut said the base policy was to rotate who got releases first to make sure everyone got a fair shake. We were a morning paper, so our edition for that day had long since hit the street, but I was disappointed at not being able to break the story on the Associated Press wire. George Walsh, the program manager at KSWS, had already moved the story on AP.

(7)   Not long after Haut left, a call came from RAAF. The caller said the release was incorrect, that what had been thought to be the wreckage of a flying saucer was actually the remains of a radiosonde balloon. However, the AP wire story had gotten the world's attention. I spent the rest of the afternoon taking long distance calls from overseas news editors. I remember calls from Rome, London, Paris, and Hong Kong.

(8)   Colonel William H. ("Butch") Blanchard, commander of RAAF and its 509th Bomb Group, was a good friend of mine. We often got together for a drink and off the record discussions of base-town relations and the like. After the flying saucer incident, I tried several times to get Blanchard to tell me the real story, but he repeatedly refused to talk about it.

(9)   About three or four months after the event, when we were a bit more "relaxed" that usual, I tried again. Blanchard reluctantly admitted he had authorized the press release. Then, as best I remember, he said, "I will tell you this and nothing more. The stuff I saw, I've never seen anyplace else in

my life." That was all he would say, and he never told me anything else about the matter.

(10)   I have not been paid or given or promised anything of value to make this statement, which is the truth to the best of my recollection.

_____   _Oct. 19 1993_

(Signature and Printed Name)   (Date)

A. R. McQuiddy
Signature witnessed by:

_____   _10-19-93_

(Signature and Printed Name)   (Date)

Charlotte Y. Gipson

AFFIDAVIT

(1) My name is Jesse A. Marcel, M.D.

(2) My address is: ████████████████████████

(3) I am a physician, and I have served in the National Guard since 1978; I am a certified crash investigator and helicopter pilot.

(4) In July 1947, I was eleven years old and lived in Roswell, New Mexico, where my father, Major Jesse Marcel, was stationed at the Roswell Army Air Field, serving as the base Intelligence Officer.

(5) One night, I was awakened by my father in the middle of the night. He was very excited about some debris he had picked up in the desert. The material filled up his 1942 Buick. He brought some of the material into the house, and we spread it out on the kitchen floor.

(6) There were three categories of debris: a thick, foil-like metallic gray substance; a brittle, brownish-black plastic-like material, like Bakelite; and there were fragments of what appeared to be I-beams.

(7) On the inner surface of the I-beam, there appeared to be a type of writing. This writing was a purple-violet hue, and it had an embossed appearance. The figures were composed of curved, geometric shapes. It had no resemblance to Russian, Japanese or any other foreign language. It resembled hieroglyphics, but it had no animal-like characters.

(8) My father said the debris was recovered from a crash site northwest of Roswell. He felt it was very unusual and may have mentioned the words "flying saucer" in connection with the material. He was certain it was not from a weather balloon.

(9) I have not been paid or given anything of value to make this statement, which is the truth to the best of my recollection.

_____
(Signature)

_____
(Date)

Signature witnessed by:

_____
(Name)

AFFIDAVIT
Bud Payne

(1)   My name is Bud Payne.

(2)   My address is ▮▮▮▮▮▮▮▮▮▮▮▮▮▮▮▮▮▮

(3)   I am employed as: *PRORATE JUDGE*   . (✓ I am retired.

(4)   I am now a Lincoln County, New Mexico, ~~magistrate~~ *PROBATE* judge and have been a Lincoln County commissioner, both elected offices. In 1947, I was a rancher and a neighbor of William "Mac" Brazel. Our ranch adjoined the Foster place, which Mac managed.

(5)   When I heard about the flying saucer coming down on the Foster ranch a few days after it happened in early July 1947, I decided to see if I could get a piece of the thing. The site where the saucer came down was about two or two and a half miles east of the east boundary of our pasture. I drove over there in a pickup truck.

(6)   Before I reached the site, I was stopped by two soldiers sitting in an Army truck parked beside the ranch road I was on. They were in field uniforms, and they may have been armed, wearing pistols. There were more vehicles and soldiers on higher ground beyond where I had been stopped.

(7)   I told the two soldiers who stopped me I was going to where the flying saucer came down. They said, "We know where you're going, but you can't go in there." I said, "Well, all I want is a little piece of that material." They said, "We know what you want, but there's the road you came up. You go back down that road." They were nice, jolly old boys. They did not threaten me, but they had their instructions to turn everybody back.

(8)   I have not been paid or given or promised anything of value to make this statement, which is the truth to the best of my recollection.

J.O."BUD"

_____   9/14/93
(Signature and Printed Name)   **(Date)**

Signature witnessed by:

STATE OF NEW MEXICO
COUNTY OF LINCOLN
_____   09/14/93
(Signature and Printed Name)   **(Date)**
Notary Public - Loree Vallejos

My Commission expires: 05-23-94

AFFIDAVIT

(1) My name is Robert R. Porter.

(2) My address is: ███████████████████████████

(3) I am (X) retired ( ) employed as:_____

(4) In July 1947, I was a Master Sergeant in the U.S. Army Air Force, stationed at Roswell, New Mexico. I was a flight engineer. My job entailed taking care of the engines in flight, maintaining weight and balance, and I was responsible for fuel management. We mostly flew B-29s.

(5) On this occasion, I was a member of the crew which flew parts of what we were told was a flying saucer to Fort Worth. The people on board included: Lt. Col. Payne Jennings, the Deputy Commander of the base; Lt. Col. Robert I. Barrowclough; Maj. Herb Wunderlich; and Maj. Jesse Marcel. Capt. William E. Anderson said it was from a flying saucer. After we arrived, the material was transferred to a B-25. I was told they were going to Wright Field in Dayton, Ohio.

(6) I was involved in loading the B-29 with the material, which was wrapped in packages with wrapping paper. One of the pieces was triangle-shaped, about 2 1/2 feet across the bottom. The rest were in small packages, about the size of a shoe box. The brown paper was held with tape.

(7) The material was extremely lightweight. When I picked it up, it was just like picking up an empty package. We loaded the triangle-shaped package and three shoe box-sized packages into the plane. All of the packages could have fit into the trunk of a car.

(8) After we landed at Fort Worth, Col. Jennings told us to take care of maintenance of the plane and that after a guard was posted, we could eat lunch. When we came back from lunch, they told us they had transferred the material to a B-25. They told us the material was a weather balloon, but I'm certain it wasn't a weather balloon. I think the government should let the people know what's going on.

(9) I have not been paid or given anything of value to make this statement, which is the truth to the best of my recollection.

Robert R. Porter -
(Signature)

June 7, 1991
(Date)

Signature witnessed by:

Ruth N. Ford 6/7/91
(Name)

AFFIDAVIT

(1) My name is Loretta Proctor.

(2) My address is:

(3) I am retired.

(4) In July 1947, my neighbor William W. "Mac" Brazel came to my ranch and showed my husband and me a piece of material he said came from a large pile of debris on the property he managed. The piece he brought was brown in color, similar to plastic. He and my husband tried to cut and burn the object, but they weren't successful. It was extremely light in weight. I had never seen anything like it before.

(5) "Mac" said the other material on the property looked like aluminum foil. It was very flexible and wouldn't crush or burn. There was also something he described as tape which had printing on it. The color of the printing was a kind of purple. He said it wasn't Japanese writing; from the way he described it, it sounded like it resembled hieroglyphics.

(6) Some time later, my husband, my brother and one of his friends saw "Mac" in Roswell, surrounded by soldiers. He walked right by them, without speaking a word. The Army kept him five or six days. When he got back, he said that the Army told him the object he found was a weather balloon. "If I see another one," he said, "I won't report it." He was upset about them keeping him from home that long. He wouldn't talk about it after he got back.

(7) "Mac" Brazel was a good neighbor, usually pretty friendly. He was not the kind of person who would tell a lie or create a hoax. He knew what weather balloons were like, because he had found them before.

(8) The piece of material I saw did not resemble anything from a weather balloon. I had seen weather balloons before. I had never seen anything like this.

(9) I have not been paid or given anything of value to make this statement. It is the truth, to the best of my recollection.

Loretta Procter.
(Signature)

May 5- 1991
(Date)

Signature witnessed by:

Alma Hobbs
(Name)

AFFIDAVIT

TO WHOM IT MAY CONCERN:

On a night during July, 1947, I, James Ragsdale, was in the company
of a woman in an area approximately forty (40) miles northwest of
Roswell, New Mexico, during a severe lightning storm. I and my
companion observed a bright flash and what appeared to be a bright
light source moving toward the southeast. Later, at sunrise, driving
in that direction, I and my companion came upon a ravine near a bluff
that was covered with pieces of unusual wreckage, remains of a damaged
craft and a number of smaller bodied beings outside the craft. While
observing the scene, I and my companion watched as a military convoy
arrived and secured the scene. As a result of the convoy's appearance
we quickly fled the area.

I hereby swear the aforementioned account is accurate and true to the
best of my knowledge and recollection.

James Ragsdale
James Ragsdale

STATE OF NEW MEXICO)
)ss
County of Chaves   )

    The foregoing instrument was acknowledged before me this 27TH
day of JANUARY, 1993, by JAMES RAGSDALE.

My Commission expires:
   11-7-96

                              Notary Public

MY NAME IS JIM RAGSDALE, FORMERLY OF 702 NORTH GREENWOOD, ROSWELL, N.M. AND I AM MAKING THE FOLLOWING INFORMATION AVAILABLE TO CLARIFY ANY AND ALL PORTIONS OF MY INVOLVEMENT IN THE UFO INCIDENT OCCURING IN 1947. EVERYTHING CONTAINED HEREIN IS THE RESULT OF MY PERSONAL OBSERVATION AND NOT FROM ANY SECONDARY SOURCE.

AT THAT DATE I WAS EMPLOYED BY AN OIL CO, LIVING IN CARLSBAD, N. M. AND MY TYPE OF WORK WAS TRANSIT HAULING, OPERATING ALL TYPES OF HEAVY EQUIPMENT RELATED TO OIL FIELD DEVELOPMENT. OVER THE LONG JULY 4TH WEEKEND, I HAD 7 OR 8 DAYS THAT I DID NOT REPORT FOR WORK. IT WAS ON THIS WEEKEND, MY FRIEND AND I SPENT SEVERAL DAYS IN THE PINE LODGE AREA, WEST OF ROSWELL.

AT THAT TIME THE PINE LODGE WAS A FAVORITE SPOT FOR ALL OF THE AREA RANCHERS AND OTHERS FROM ALL OVER SOUTHEAST NEW MEXICO, FOR THEY ALWAYS HAD A DANCE ON SATURDAY NIGHTS DURING THE SUMMER MONTHS. I HAD BEEN AT PINE LODGE ON MANY OCCASIONS DURING THE TIME BEFORE 1947.

MY FRIEND AND I HAD A PICKUP TRUCK ON THIS WEEKEND, SLEEPING IN THE BACK, WITH COVERS AND A TARPAULIN (TARP) COVERING THE BACK OF THE TRUCK. IT WAS ABOUT 11:00 PM, THE WEATHER WAS PERFECT, AND WE WERE LOOKING UP AT THE STARS. A STORM WAS IN THE WEST, WITH LIGHTNING, BUT FAR AWAY ENOUGH WE COULDN'T HEAR THE THUNDER.

SUDDENLY, A TREMENDOUS FLASH OCCURED, SEVERAL MILES TO THE NORTH, WITH IT BEING AS BRIGHT AS A FLAME FROM A WELDER'S ARC. IT WAS HUGE, BUT FAR ENOUGH AWAY WE COULDN'T HEAR IT IMMEDIATELY. THEN THE OBJECT STARTED IN OUR DIRECTION AND SOON WE COULD HEAR THE NOISE IT WAS MAKING. THE ONLY WAY TO COMPARE THE NOISE IT WAS MAKING COMING OUR DIRECTION, AND UNTIL IT HIT THE SIDE OF THE MOUNTAIN, WAS IT WAS LIKE THE SOUND OF A JET MOTOR NOW USED ON TAKE OFFS BY LARGE JET AIR LINERS. WE WERE FRIGHTENED AND DIDN'T KNOW IF IT WOULD MISS US. THE OBJECT PASSED THROUGH THE TREES NOT MORE THAN 60 YARDS FROM OUR TRUCK, AND STRUCK THE MOUNTAIN AT A POINT A FEW YARDS FARTHER FROM WHERE WE WERE IN THE TRUCK.

AFTER A LITTLE BIT WE TOOK FLASHLIGHTS AND WENT TO THE SITE OF THE IMPACT AND SPENT CONSIDERABLE TIME LOOKING ALL AROUND.

THE CRAFT SPLIT OPEN ON IMPACT AND HAD STRUCK LARGE BOULDERS IN THE AREA SOME AS LARGE AS AN AUTOMOBILE. THE CRAFT HAD SLID DOWN BETWEEN BOULDERS OF THIS SIZE, BUT WAS EASILY APPROACHED. WHEN WE LOOKED INTO THE CRAFT, WE SAW FOUR BODIES OF A TYPE WE HAD NEVER SEEN BEFORE, AND ALL WERE DEAD. THE INTERIOR OF THE CRAFT HAD THE EQUIVALENT OF A DASH BOARD WITH VARIOUS INSTRUMENTS AND WRITING OF SOME SORT I HAVE NEVER SEEN BEFORE OR SINCE.

IN ADDITION TO THE WRECKAGE ON THE INSIDE OF THE CRAFT, THERE WAS LOTS OF MATERIAL OF THE TYPE REPORTED ON THE SITE OF THE "CRASH" NEAR CORONA. THIS MATERIAL WAS ON THE OUTSIDE AND SCATTERED ALL OVER THE SIDE OF THE MOUNTAIN, DESCRIBED LATER AS WEATHER BALLON MATERIAL.

THE BODIES OF THE OCCUPANTS WERE ALL ABOUT FOUR FEET OR LESS TALL, WITH STRANGE LOOKING ARMS, LEGS AND FINGERS. THEY WERE DRESSED IN A SILVER TYPE UNIFORM AND WEARING A TIGHT HELMET OF SOME TYPE. THIS IS POSITIVE BECAUSE I TRIED TO REMOVE ONE OF THE HELMETS, BUT WAS UNABLE TO DO SO. THEIR EYES WERE LARGE, OVAL IN SHAPE, AND DID NOT RESEMBLE ANYTHING OF A HUMAN NATURE.

WE DECIDED TO RETURN TO OUR PICKUP UNTIL DAYLIGHT SO WE COULD BETTER SEE THE SITE, HOWEVER THERE WAS VERY LITTLE SLEEP UNTIL IT WAS DAYLIGHT. WHEN WE RETURNED WE FILLED TWO LARGE GUNNY SACKS WITH THE MATERIAL, AND IT WAS WITH US WHEN WE LEFT THE SITE.

DURING THE EARLY DAYLIGHT HOURS WE INSPECTED THE MATERIAL USED IN THE CRAFT AND THE PIECES RESULTING FROM THE CRASH. IT WASN'T A RIGID METAL, BUT EVEN THOUGH BEING THICK WAS FLEXIBLE UP TO A POINT. YOU COULD BEND IT AND IT WOULD COME RIGHT BACK TO IT'S ORIGINAL SHAPE. THIS WAS ALSO TRUE OF THE LIGHTER MATERIAL SCATTERED ALL OVER THE MOUNTAIN THAT LOOKED LIKE TIN FOIL AND WOULD GO BACK TO IT'S ORIGINAL SHAPE WHEN CRUMPLED IN YOUR HAND. THE MATERIAL OF THE CRAFT ITSELF HAD A SORT OF BRONZE-GRAY COLOR. THERE WERE NO RIVITES, SEAMS OR INDICATION OF HOW IT HAD BEEN CONSTRUCTED. THE CRAFT WAS ABOUT 20' IN DIAMETER + HAD A DOME IN THE MIDDLE, NO WINDOWS WERE SEEN. IT WASN'T TOO LONG AFTER WE WERE LOOKING AT THE TOTAL AREA, WE HEARD WHAT WE BELIEVED WAS TRUCKS AND HEAVY EQUIPMENT COMING OUR WAY, SO WE LEFT AND WERE NOT THERE WHEN WHAT EVER IT WAS ARRIVED.

THIS MATERIAL WAS WITH US LATER IN THE DAY WHEN WE STOPPED AT THE BLUE MOON TAVERN, JUST SOUTH OF ROSWELL, A FAVORITE PLACE FOR TRUCKERS GOING THROUGH THE AREA AND I SHOWED THE MATERIAL TO SEVERAL OF MY FRIENDS. HOWEVER, AS FAR AS I KNOW, ALL OF THEM ARE DEAD.

UNEXPLAINED TO THIS DAY IS THE DISAPPEARANCE OF THE MATERIAL. MY FRIEND HAD SOME IN HER VEHICLE WHEN SHE WAS KILLED HITTING A BRIDGE, AND IT WAS GONE WHEN THE WRECKAGE WAS BROUGH IN TO TOWN. MY TRUCK AND TRAILER WAS STOLEN FROM MY HOME, AGAIN WITH MATERIAL IN THE TRUCK, NEVER TO BE HEARD FROM ANYWHERE. MY HOME WAS BROKEN INTO, COMPLETELY RANSACKED, AND ALL THAT WAS TAKEN WAS THE MATERIAL, A GUN AND VERY LITTLE ELSE OF VALUE.

THE IMPACT SITE IS EXACT AND CAN BE DESCRIBED AS: A SIGN POST ON THE PINE LODGE ROAD INDICATES "53 MILES TO ROSWELL". NEAR THIS SIGN IS A ROAD GOING SOUTH TOWARD PINE LODGE (THE LODGE BUILDING WAS BURNED DOWN SEVERAL YEARS AGO) AND THE TURN OFF TO ARABELLA LEADS EAST AND SOUTH. 2 OR 3 MILES DOWN THIS ROAD TOWARDS ARABELLA IS THE SITE OF OUR PICKUP THAT NIGHT AND NEARBY THE IMPACT SITE. THIS AREA IS NEAR THE MOUNTAIN INDICATED AS "BOY SCOUT MOUNTAIN."

James R Ragsdale
JAMES R. RAGSDALE

State of Oklahoma
County of Logan

Subscribed and sworn to before me this 15th day of April, 1995.

Hockey Weaver
Notary Public

My commission expires 12-8-98

AFFIDAVIT OF GEORGE "JUD" ROBERTS

(1) My name is George "Jud" Roberts.

(2) My address is: ████████████████████████████

(3) I am (X) retired ( ) employed as: _____.

(4) In July 1947, I was a minority stockholder and manager of KGFL Radio in Roswell, New Mexico. We did an interview with W.W. "Mac" Brazel, the rancher who found some debris on his property. We hid him out at the home of the station owner, W.E. Whitmore, Sr., and recorded the interview on a wire recorder.

(5) The next morning, I got a call from someone in Washington, D.C. It may have been someone in the office of Clinton Anderson or Dennis Chavez. This person said, "We understand that you have some information, and we want to assure you that if you release it, it's very possible that your station's license will be in jeopardy, so we suggest that you not do it." The person indicated that we might lose our license in as quickly as three days. I made the decision not to release the story.

(6) I made an attempt to go out to the crash site to see it for myself, but I was turned back by a military person who said we were in a restricted area.

(7) At that time, there was quite a clamp on any discussion concerning this event. We just decided for Walter Haut's sake that we should sit tight and not say anything, even though in our own minds, we had some question about the validity of the weather balloon explanation. Weather balloons were launched about a block from our station every day. We didn't accept the official explanation, but we had no evidence to the contrary.

(8) I have not been paid or given anything of value to make this statement, which is the truth to the best of my recollection.

George F. "Jud" Roberts
(Signature)

_13/30/91_
(Date)

Signature witnessed by:
SIGNATURE GUARANTEED
SUNWEST BANK OF ROSWELL, N.E.
(Name) ROSWELL, NEW MEXICO
BY _Nancy Montgomery_
Assistant Cashier

(1) My name is Frankie Rowe.

(2) My address is:

(3) In July 1947, my father was a fire fighter with the Roswell,
New Mexico Fire Department. He returned one night, telling the
family that he had been on a fire run to the north of Roswell.
There he encountered the wreck of some kind of craft and the
bodies of the alien flight crew.

(4) In early July 1947, I was in the fire house waiting for my
father to take me home. A State Trooper arrived and displayed a
piece of metallic debris that he said he'd picked up on the crash
site. It was a dull gray and about the thickness of aluminum
foil. When wadded into ball, it would unfold itself. The fire
fighters were unable to cut it or burn it.

(5) A few days later, several military personnel visited the
house, telling my younger brothers and sisters to wait outside.
My mother and I were told to sit at the dining room table where I
was questioned about the piece of metal I had seen. I was told
that if I ever talked about it, I could be taken out into the
desert never to return, or that my mother and father would be
taken to "Orchard Park", a former POW camp.

(6) I have not been paid or given anything of value to make this
statement, which is the truth to the best of my recollection.

Frankie M. Rowe
(Signature)

_1-22-93_
(Date)

Signature witnessed by:

(Name) STATE OF NEW MEXICO, COUNTY OF CURRY ss.
Subscribed and sworn to before me this ____22nd____ day
of ___November___, 19_93_
Keeth Wallum Notary Public
My commission expires:
____12-11-94____

AFFIDAVIT
Bessie Brazel Schreiber

(1)   My name is Bessie Brazel Schreiber.

(2)   My address is [redacted]

(3)   I am employed as: _____ , ☑ I am retired.
        Mack Bel.

(4)   William W. "Mac" Brazel was my father. In 1947, when I was 14, he was the manager of the Foster Ranch in Lincoln County, New Mexico, near Corona. Our family had a home in Tularosa, where my mother, my younger brother Vernon, and I lived during the school year. The three of us spent summers on the Foster place with dad.

(5)   In July 1947, right around the Fourth, dad found a lot of debris scattered over a pasture some distance from the house we lived in on the ranch. None of us was riding with him when he found the material, and I do not remember anyone else being with him. He told us about it when he came in at the end of the day.

(6)   Dad was concerned because the debris was near a surface-water stock tank. He thought having it blowing around would scare the sheep and they would not water. So, a day or two later, he, Vernon, and I went to the site to pick up the material. We went on horseback and took several feed sacks to collect the debris. I do not recall just how far the site was from the house, but the ride out there took some time.

(7)   There was a lot of debris scattered sparsely over an area that seems to me now to have been about the size of a football field. There may have been additional material spread out more widely by the wind, which was blowing quite strongly.

(8)   The debris looked like pieces of a large balloon which had burst. The pieces were small, the largest I remember measuring about the same as the diameter of a basketball. Most of it was a kind of double-sided material, foil-like on one side and rubber-like on the other. Both sides were grayish silver in color, the foil more silvery than the rubber. Sticks, like kite sticks, were attached to some of the pieces with a whitish tape. The tape was about two or three inches wide and had flower-like designs on it. The "flowers" were faint, a variety of pastel colors, and reminded me of Japanese paintings in which the flowers are not all connected. I do not recall any other types of material or markings, nor do I remember seeing gouges in the ground or any other signs that anything may have hit the ground hard.

(9)   The foil-rubber material could not be torn like ordinary aluminum foil can be torn. I do not recall anything else about the strength or other properties of what we picked up.

Bel.
9-22-93

(10)   We spent several hours collecting the debris and putting it in sacks. I believe we filled about three sacks, and we took them back to the ranch house. We speculated a bit about what the material could be. I remember dad saying, "Oh, it's just a bunch of garbage."

(11)   Soon after, dad went to Roswell to order winter feed. It was on this trip that he told the sheriff what he had found. I think we all went into town with him, but I am not certain about this, as he made two or three trips to Roswell about that time, and we did not go on all of them. (In those days, it was an all-day trip, leaving very early in the morning and returning after dark.) I am quite sure it was no more than a day trip, and I do not remember dad taking any overnight or longer trips away from the ranch around that time.

(12)   Within a day or two, several military people came to the ranch. There may have been as many as 15 of them. One or two officers spoke with dad and mom, while the rest waited. No one spoke with Vernon and me. Since I seem to recall that the military were on the ranch most of a day, they may have gone out to where we picked up the material. I am not sure about this, one way or the other, but I do remember they took the sacks of debris with them.

(13)   Although it is certainly possible, I do not recall anyone finding any more of the material later. Dad's comment on the whole business was, "They made one hell of a hullabaloo out of nothing."

(14)   I have not been paid or given or promised anything of value to make this statement, which is the truth to the best of my recollection.

BESSIE I. BRAZEL SchREiBER

Bessie I. Brazel Schreiber   _Sept. 22, 1993_
(Signature and Printed Name)   **(Date)**

Signature witnessed by:

Pamela J. Carey
Pamela J. Carey   _9-22-93_
(Signature and Printed Name)   **(Date)**

```
       PAMELA J. CAREY
       NOTARY PUBLIC
     STATE OF WASHINGTON
       COMMISSION EXPIRES
         AUGUST 1 1994
```

AFFIDAVIT

(1) My name is Robert Shirkey.

(2) My address is: ████████████████████████

(3) I am ( ) retired ( ) employed as _____.

(4) In July 1947, I was stationed at the Roswell Army Air Field with the rank of 1st Lieutenant. I served as the assistant flight safety officer and was assigned to base operations for the 509th Bomb Group.

(5) During that period, the call came in to have a B-29 ready to go as soon as possible. Its destination was to be Fort Worth, on orders from the base commander, Col. Blanchard. I was in the Operations Office when Col. Blanchard arrived. He asked if the aircraft was ready. When he was told it was, Blanchard waved to somebody, and approximately five people came in the front door, down the hallway and on to the ramp to climb into the airplane, carrying parts of what I heard was the crashed flying saucer.

(6) At this time, I asked Col. Blanchard to turn sideways so I could see what was going on. I saw them carrying what appeared to be pieces of metal; there was one piece that was 18 x 24 inches, brushed stainless steel in color. I also saw what was described by another witness as an I-beam and markings. The plane took off for Fort Worth; Major Marcel was on the flight.

(7) Several days later, a B-25 was scheduled to take something to Ft. Worth. This was the second flight during this period: the third was a B-29 piloted by Oliver W. "Pappy" Henderson directly to Wright Patterson.

(8) I learned later that a Sergeant and some airmen went to the crash site and swept up everything, including bodies. The bodies were laid out in Hanger 84. Henderson's flight contained all that material.

(9) All of those involved--the Sergeant of the Guards, all of the crewmen, and myself--were shipped out to different bases within two weeks.

(10) I have not been paid or given anything of value to make this statement, and it is the truth to the best of my recollection.

Robert J Shirkey
(Signature)

30 April 1991
(Date)

Signature witnessed by:

Luse V Sandoval
(Name)
My Commission Expires:
03/13/93

REF: #9 : I HAVE LEARNED SINCE MAKING THE STATEMENT #9, THAT, WHILE I WAS AWARE OF SEVERAL PEOPLE BEING "SHIPPED OUT" ON CHANGE OF STATION, NOT EVERYONE ACTUALLY WERE THAT MAY HAVE BEEN INVOLVED, WITH THE INCIDENT AFTERMATH.

AFFIDAVIT
Lydia A. Sleppy

(1)   My name is Lydia A. Sleppy.

(2)   ██

(3)   I am employed as:_____, (X) I am retired. *9-30-77 from*
        State of California, Dept. Parks & Recreation

(4)   In 1947, worked at KOAT Radio in Albuquerque, New Mexico. My
duties included operating the station's teletype machine, which received news
and allowed us to send stories to the ABC and Mutual networks, with which
KOAT was affiliated.

(5)   In early July 1947, I received a call from John McBoyle, general
manager and part-owner of KSWS Radio in Roswell, New Mexico, which was
associated with KOAT. I do not remember the exact date, but it definitely was
a weekday (I never worked weekends) and almost certainly after the Fourth of
July. The call came in before noon.

(6)   McBoyle said he had something hot for the network. I asked Karl
Lambertz, our program director and acting manager (KOAT owner and
manager Merle Tucker was out of town), to be present in my office while I
took the story from McBoyle and put it on the teletype. Using the teletype, I
alerted ABC News headquarters in Hollywood to expect an important story,
and Mr. Lambertz stood behind me while I typed.

(7)   To the best of my recollection, McBoyle said, "There's been one of those
flying saucer things crash down here north of Roswell." He said he had been
in a coffee shop on his morning break when a local rancher, "Mac" Brazel,
came in and said he had discovered the object some time ago while he was out
riding on the range, and that he had towed it in and stored it underneath a
shelter on his property. Brazel offered to take McBoyle to the ranch to see the
object. McBoyle described it as "a big crumpled dishpan."

(8)   As I typed McBoyle's story, a bell rang on the teletype, indicating an
interruption. The machine then printed a message something to this effect:
"THIS IS THE FBI. YOU WILL IMMEDIATELY CEASE ALL COMMUNICATION."
Whatever the precise words were, I definitely remember the message was
from the FBI and that it directed me to stop transmitting. I told McBoyle the
teletype had been cut off and took the rest of his story in shorthand, but we
never put it on the wire because we had been scooped by the papers.

(9)   I never again discussed the matter with McBoyle, but the next day, he
told Mr. Lambertz the military had isolated the area where the saucer was
found and was keeping the press out. He told Lambertz he saw planes come in
from Wright Field, Ohio, to take the thing away. He also said they claimed

7/14/93   *[signature]*

they were going to take it to one place, but the planes went to another. Either they were supposed to have gone to Texas but went to Wright Field or vice versa.

(10)   I have not been paid or given or promised anything of value to make this statement, which is the truth to the best of my recollection.

_Lydia A. Clarkep_____   _9-14-93_____
(Signature and Printed Name)   (Date)
LYDIA H SLEPPY

Signature witnessed by:

_Ada A Somers_____   _9/14/93_____
(Signature and Printed Name)   (Date)
ADA A SOMERS

STATEMENT OF ROBERT A. SLUSHER

(1) My name is Robert A. Slusher.

(2) My address is: ██████████████████████████.

(3) I am (✓) retired ( ) employed by: _____.

(4) I was stationed at the Roswell Army Air Field from 1946 -
1952. On July 9, 1947, I boarded a B-29 which taxied to the bomb
area on the base to get a crate, which we loaded into the forward
bomb bay. Four armed MPs guarded the crate, which was
approximately four feet high, five feet wide, and 12 feet long.
We departed Roswell at approximately 4:00 PM for Fort Worth
[later Carswell AFB]. Maj. Edgar Skelley was the flight
operations officer.

(5) The flight to Ft. Worth was at a low level, about 4-5,000
feet. Usually, we flew at 25,000 feet, and the cabin is
pressurized. We had to fly at a low level because of the MPs in
the bomb bay.

(6) On arrival at Fort Worth, we were met by six people,
including three MPs. They took possession of the crate. The
crate was loaded on to a flatbed weapons carrier and hauled off.
Their MPs accompanied the crate. One officer present was a
major, the other a 1st lieutenant. The sixth person was an
undertaker who had been a classmate of a crewman on our flight,
Lt. Felix Martucci. Major Marcel came up to our plane in a jeep
and got on board. We were at Ft. Worth about 30 minutes before
returning to Roswell.

(7) The return flight was above 20,000 feet, and the cabin was
pressurized. After returning to Roswell, we realized that what
was in the crate was classified. There were rumors that they had
carried debris from a crash. Whether there were any bodies, I
don't know. The crate had been specially made; it had no
markings.

(8) We brought Maj. Jesse Marcel back on the flight. Capt.
Frederick Ewing was the pilot; the co-pilot was Lt. Edgar Izard.
Sgt. David Tyner was the engineer: the navigator was James
Eubanks; others involved were T/Sgt. Arthur Osepchook and Corp.
Thaddeus D. Love. The MPs also came back with us.
* *S:d E Eng Lt Elmer Landry flew on this flight* ✱
(9) The flight was unusual in that we flew there, dropped the
cargo and returned immediately. It was a hurried flight;
normally we knew the day before there would be a flight. The
round trip took approximately three hours, 15 minutes. It was
still light when we returned to Roswell. Lt. Martucci said, "We
made history."

(10) I have not been paid or given anything of value to make
this statement, which is the truth to the best of my
recollection.

R.A. Slusher
(Signature)

May 23, 93
(Date)

Signature witnessed by:

_X_____ _5/23/93_
(Name) Karl T. Pflock

AFFIDAVIT

(1) My name is Robert E. Smith.

(2) My address is: ███████████████████████

(3) I am (X) retired ( ) employed by_____.

(4) In July 1947, I was stationed at the Roswell Army Air Field as a member of the 1st Air Transport Unit. I worked in the cargo outfit with C-54s. My involvement in the Roswell incident was to help load crates of debris on to the aircraft. We all became aware of the event when we went to the hangar on the east side of the ramp. Our people had to re-measure the ~~aircraft on the inside~~ to accommodate the ~~crates~~ they were making for this material. All I saw was a little piece of material. The piece of debris I saw was two-to-three inches square. It was jagged. When you crumpled it up, it then laid back out; and when it did, it kind of crackled, making a sound like cellophane, and it crackled when it was let out. There were no creases. One of our people put it in his pocket.

[margin annotations: CENTER, AIRCRAFT]

(5) The largest piece was roughly 20 feet long; four-to-five feet high, four-to-five feet wide. The rest were two-to-three feet long, two feet square or smaller. The sergeant who had the piece of material said that was the material in the crates. There were words stenciled on the crates, but I don't remember what they were; however, the word "section" appeared on most of the crates. The entire loading took at least six, perhaps eight hours. Lunch was brought to us, which was unusual. The crates were brought to us on flatbed dollies, which also was unusual.

(6) A lot of people began coming in all of a sudden because of the official investigation. Somebody said it was a plane crash; but we heard from a man in Roswell that it was not a plane crash but it was something else, a strange object. Officially, we were told it was a crashed plane, but crashed planes usually were taken to the salvage yard, not flown out. I don't think it was an experimental plane, because not too many people in that area were experimenting with planes--the didn't have the money to.

(7) We were taken to the hangar to load crates. There was a lot of farm dirt on the hangar floor. We loaded it on flatbeds and dollies; each crate had to be checked as to width and height. We had to know which crates went on to which plane. We loaded crates on to three or four C-54s. It took the better part of the day to load the planes. One crate took up the entire plane; it wasn't that heavy, but it was a large volume.

(8) This would have involved [Oliver W.] "Pappy" Henderson's crew. I remember seeing Tech Sgt. Harbell Ellzey and Sgt. T/Sgt. Edward Bretherton and S/Sgt. William Fortner; Elszey was on "Pappy's" crew.

(9) We weren't supposed to know the destination, but we were told they were headed north. Wright Field at that time was closed down for modernization; therefore, I would deduce that the next safest place was Los Alamos, the most secret base available and still under the Manhattan Project. There were armed guards present during the loading of the planes, which was unusual. There was

no way to get to the ramp except through armed guards. There were MPs on the outer skirts, and our personnel were between them and the planes.

(10) There were a lot of people in plainclothes all over the place; they were "inspectors," but they were strangers on the base. When challenged, they replied that they were here on project so-and-so and flashed a card, which was different than a military ID card.

(11) There was another indication that something serious was going on: several nights before this, when we were coming back to Roswell, a convoy of trucks covered with canvas passed us. The truck convoy had red lights and sirens. When they got to the gate, they headed over to this hangar on the east end, which was rather unusual.

(12) I have a distant cousin who was in the Secret Service named Raymond deVinney. In the early 1970s, at a family reunion, he told me that he was at Roswell at this time, more or less as a representative of President Truman. He saw me and recognized me, but he didn't speak. He said the material most likely was taken to Los Alamos. He said there were several people with him at the time, but he didn't mention any names. He passed away in 1975.

(13) A lot of the people involved in the event believe that they should go to their deathbeds without telling anything about it. We were told: "This is a hot shipment; keep quiet about it." This wasn't unusual for us--there were a lot of times we were told that.

(14) I'm convinced that what we loaded was a UFO that got into mechanical problems. Even with the most intelligent people, things go wrong.

(15) I have not been paid or given anything of value to make this statement, which is the truth to the best of my recollection.

Robert Earl Smith
(Signature)

_10/10/91_
(Date)

Signature witnessed by:

Pagon M. Short
(Name)

> PAGON M. SHORT
> Notary Public
> STATE OF TEXAS
> My Comm. Exp. 05/31/93

AFFIDAVIT
Sally Strickland Tadolini

(1)   My name is Sally Strickland Tadolini.

(2)   My address is ▇▇▇▇▇▇▇▇▇▇▇▇▇▇▇▇▇

(3)   I am employed as: ▇▇▇▇▇▇▇▇▇▇▇▇▇( ) I am retired.

(4)   In July 1947, I was nine years old and lived with my parents, Lyman and Marian Strickland, and my two brothers on our ranch in Lincoln County, New Mexico. The neighboring ranch was the Foster place, which was managed by William W. ("Mac") Brazel. His house was about 10 miles from ours.

(5)   I remember my parents talking about Mac Brazel finding a lot of unusual debris in one of his pastures and that there was a great deal of excitement about it among the neighbors. I recall the adults at first thought it was some kind of newfangled weather balloon, then deciding, no, there was no way it could be anything like that. I also recall that, later, the neighbors talked about how badly Mac Brazel had been treated, and that when he came back to the ranch, he never again wanted to talk about what he had found.

(6)   A week or so after all the excitement, Mac's son Bill, who was quite a bit older and married, stopped by our house. He had someone with him, and while I am not absolutely certain. I think it was his brother Vernon, who was my age. We—my father, brothers, myself, and possibly my mother—sat at the kitchen table with them. Bill showed us a piece of the thing his father had found, and he asked us not to say anything about it.

am not certain that he was married at that time.
SJ

(7)   What Bill showed us was a piece of what I still think of as fabric. It was something like aluminum foil, something like satin, something like well-tanned leather in its toughness, yet it was not precisely like any of one of those materials. While I do not recall this with certainty, I think the fabric measured about four by eight or ten inches. Its edges, which were smooth, were not exactly parallel, and its shape was roughly trapezoidal. It was about the thickness of very fine kidskin glove leather and a dull metallic grayish silver, one side slightly darker than the other. I do not remember it having any design or embossing on it.

(8)   Bill passed it around, and we all felt of it. I did a lot of sewing, so the feel made a great impression on me. It felt like no fabric I have touched before or since. It was very silky or satiny, with the same texture on both sides. Yet when I crumpled it in my hands, the feel was like that you notice when you crumple a leather glove in your hand. When it was released, it sprang back into its original shape, quickly flattening out with no wrinkles. I did this several times, as did the others. I remember some of the others stretching it between their hands and "popping" it, but I do not think anyone tried to cut or tear it.

SJ 9/27/93

(9) While all I saw was the piece of fabric, I remember hearing discussions about what must have been part of the frame, which was said to be somehow very different. I also remember Mac Brazel referring to—and I think these were his exact words—"all that junk all over out there." These recollections make me think there must have been more than just a lot of fabric there.

(10) I have not been paid or given or promised anything of value to make this statement, which is the truth to the best of my recollection.

Sallye Strickland Tadolini

_____ 9/27/93
(Signature and Printed Name)   (Date)

Signature witnessed by:

_____ 10-27-93
(Signature and Printed Name)   (Date)
          Elizabeth Deganhart   My commission expires
                                        06-04-94

AFFIDAVIT

(1) My name is Elizabeth Tulk.

(2) My address is: █████████████████

(3) I am retired.

(4) In July 1947, I visited my parents in Roswell, New Mexico. On the day my husband and I arrived, there were jeeps and some Air Force people at the county jail.

(5) My husband, Jay, went in to see my father. He asked, "What's going on, George?" My father said, "Well, we had this man come in saying there was this flying saucer and brought him a piece of it; he said it looked like burned grass out there [where the material was found]."

(6) My mother wouldn't talk about the event for years. However, as the years went along, my mother would say, "Remember the time we had the flying saucer in Roswell?" I know of an article she wrote that said, "We do not to this day know whether it was a flying saucer, because they told my husband not to say a word." When the Air Force came and picked up the piece, she said they reprimanded him not to discuss the event. The article was submitted to *Readers Digest* and delivered to the Roswell Historical Society in 1980.

(7) I have not been paid or given anything of value to make this statement. It is the truth to the best of my recollection.

Elizabeth Tulk
(Signature)

April 22, 1991
(Date)

Signature witnessed by:

Christine Tulk
(Name)

AFFIDAVIT
David N. Wagnon

(1)   My name is David N. Wagnon.

(2)   My address is ████████████████████████████.

(3)   I am employed as: _Toxicologist_____. ✓ I am retired.   *Semi-*

(4)   I arrived in Roswell, New Mexico, in April 1946 as an enlisted member of the U.S. Army Air Force. I served at Roswell Army Air Field (RAAF) for two years, assigned to Squadron "M," the medical unit, as a technician in the base hospital laboratory. After leaving the service, I earned undergraduate and graduate degrees in science, taught high school, and was a school principal and drug education consultant. In July 1947, I was 19 and a private first class.

(5)   I do not recall anything about a crashed flying saucer incident during the time I was stationed at RAAF, but I do remember an Army nurse named Naomi Self, who was assigned to the base hospital. She was small, attractive, in her twenties, and, I believe, a brunette. I seem to recall Miss Self was transferred from RAAF while I was still stationed there, but I am not at all certain about this.

(6)   Miss Self's name really stuck with me because it is somewhat unusual and she was dating the local Red Cross representative, who was quite a bit older, probably in his late forties. I do not remember the man's name, but do recall he had an office in town and was always hanging around Squadron "M" and the emergency room.

(7)   There were rumors about Miss Self having a D&C (dilatation and curettage) in the base hospital, the tissue being sent off (probably to Brooke Army Medical Center in San Antonio, Texas), and the biopsy report coming back with some indication of fetal tissue. There was a lot of speculation about this in the squadron.

(8)   I have not been paid or given or promised anything of value to make this statement, which is the truth to the best of my recollection.

David N. Wagnon _____   _November 15, 1993_
(Signature and Printed Name)   (Date)

DAVID N. WAGNON
Signature witnessed by: SUBSCRIBED AND SWORN TO BEFORE ME
                           THIS 15 DAY OF Nov. 19 93
                           _____
                                  NOTARY PUBLIC

LISA C Dotson _____
(Signature and Printed Name)   (Date)

AFFIDAVIT
George Walsh

(1)   My name is George Walsh.

(2)   My address is ▮▮▮▮▮▮▮▮▮▮▮▮▮▮▮▮▮▮▮

(3)   I am employed as:_____. (✓) I am retired.

(4)   In 1947, I was program manager of KSWS, one of two radio stations in Roswell, New Mexico. I left KSWS and Roswell in 1951, and in 1952 I joined CBS, where, among other on-air roles, I was the announcer for "Gun Smoke." I was with CBS for 38 years, retiring in 1980. *(handwritten: GW 34)* *(handwritten: 1986. GW)*

(5)   One day in July 1947, about mid-day, I received a telephone call at KSWS from Lieutenant Walter Haut, the public information officer at Roswell Army Air Field (RAAF). It was his custom to phone us with news items. He said he had a release for me, which he read and I took down in longhand. The gist of the release was that the wreckage of a flying saucer had been recovered by RAAF personnel on a ranch north of Roswell. Chaves County Sheriff George Wilcox had contacted RAAF after a rancher told him about finding the material.

(6)   Naturally, I was astounded. I fired several questions at Haut about the nature and origin of the wreckage (was the thing manmade? Was it American made? Etc.). Haut, who acted as though he considered the matter quite routine, said he could not answer my queries and stuck to the release. I asked what the Army was going to do with the wreckage. Haut said it was to be flown to Washington, D.C., via Fort Worth, where several senior Eighth Air Force officers were to be picked up. I asked what kind of aircraft was to be used, and I think he said a B-25, which prompted me to suggest the wreckage must not be too large. Haut told me to stop asking so many questions.

(7)   I immediately put the story on the air as a bulletin. I then went to my office and called the Associated Press bureau in Albuquerque (our teletype machine did not have a transmit capability). Jason Kellahin, who had been editor of the *Roswell Morning Dispatch*, was on the desk and answered the phone. I then went into the back room where our teletype was and saw the story coming over the wire. AP Albuquerque had broken into the national wire, quoting Walter Haut and naming me as the source.

(8)   All afternoon, I tried to call Sheriff Wilcox for more information, but could never get through to him. Apparently he was swamped with calls about the story, as was I. Media people called me from all over the world, including London and Tokyo. This continued until as late as midnight, well after the story had been killed by an announcement from the Army that what had been found was a weather balloon. Word of this explanation came to us on the AP

wire. To my knowledge, other than two calls from Walter Haut, KSWS was never directly contacted by the military about the matter.

(9)   Sometime that same afternoon, Haut called for the second time. He was quite indignant. "What the hell did you do?" he asked. I told him. He then said he had not been able to make a call out of his office since his initial conversation with me. He also said, "I got a call from the War Department that told me to shut up." This was very unusual, so I asked if the department had given him a correction or another contact to provide the media. He told me his orders were to, quote, shut up, unquote.

(10)   I have not been paid or given or promised anything of value to make this statement, which is the truth to the best of my recollection.

_____   _____
(Signature and Printed Name)   (Date)
        GEORGE R. WALSH   Sept. 13, 1993
Signature witnessed by:

_____   _____
(Signature and Printed Name)   (Date)
        CHRISTINE   D. YEE   Sept 13. 1993

AFFIDAVIT
William M. Woody

(1)   My name is William M. Woody.

(2)   My address is [redacted]

(3)   I am employed as:_____. ( ) I am retired.

W.M.W. 14

(4)   In 1947 I was 12 years old and living with my family on our farm, located south of Roswell, New Mexico, and east of what was then Roswell Army Air Field. I still live on that farm.

N.M.W 3°South of

(5)   One hot night during the summer of 1947, probably in early July, my father and I were outside on the farm. It was well after sundown and quite dark. Suddenly, the sky lit up. When we looked up to see where the light was coming from, we saw a large, very bright object in the southwestern sky, moving rapidly northward.

(6)   The object had the bright white intensity of a blow torch, and had a long, flame-like tail, with colors like a blow-torch flame fading down into a pale red. Most of the tail was this pale red color. The tail was very long, equal to about 10 diameters of a full moon.

(7)   We watched the object travel all the way across the sky until it disappeared below the northern horizon. It was moving fast, but not as fast as a meteor, and we had it in view for what seemed like 20 to 30 seconds. Its brightness and colors did not change during the whole time, and it definitely went out of sight below the horizon, rather than winking out like a meteor does. My father thought it was a big meteorite and was convinced it had fallen to earth about 40 miles north of Roswell, probably just southwest of the intersection of U.S. Highway 285 and the Corona road (State Highway 247).

(8)   My father knew the territory, all its roads, and many of the people very well, so two or three days later (definitely not the next day), he decided to look for the object. He took me with him in our old flatbed truck. We headed north through Roswell on U.S. 285. About 19 miles north of town, where the highway crosses the Macho Draw, we saw at least one uniformed soldier stationed beside the road. As we drove along, we saw more sentries and Army vehicles. They were stationed at all places—ranch roads, crossroads, etc.—where there was access to leave the highway and drive east or west, and they were armed, some with rifles, others with sidearms. I do not remember seeing any military activity on the ranchland beyond the highway right of way.

(9)   We stopped at one sentry post, and my father asked a soldier what was going on. The soldier, who's attitude was very nice, just said his orders were not to let anyone leave 285 and go into the countryside.

N.M.W 9-28-93

(10)   As we drove north, we saw that the Corona road (State 247), which runs west from Highway 285, was blocked by soldiers. We went on as far as Ramon, about nine miles north of the 247 intersection. There were sentries there, too. At Ramon we turned around and headed south and home.

(11)   I remember my father saying he thought the Army was looking for something it had tracked on its way down. He may have gotten this from the soldier he spoke with during our drive up 285, but I am not sure.

(12)   I also recall that two neighbors, both now dead, stopped by and told my father they had seen the same object we had seen. One said others in his family had seen it, too. There were also many rumors about flying saucers that summer, and I recall the weather balloon story, explaining away the report of a flying saucer crash near Corona. This seemed reasonable to us at the time.

(13)   I have not been paid or given or promised anything of value to make this statement, which is the truth to the best of my recollection.

William M Woody

_William M. Woody_____   _9-28-93_
(Signature and Printed Name)   (Date)

Signature witnessed by:

Tracy L. Callaway

_Tracy L. Callaway_____   _9·28·93_
(Signature and Printed Name)   (Date)

Expires April 20, 1997

AFFIDAVIT
Earl L. Zimmerman

(1)   My name is Earl L. Zimmerman.

(2)   My address is ███████████████████████

(3)   I am employed as:_____. ☑ I am retired.

(4)   During World War II, I served in the Army Air Force as an aircraft radio operator. After the war ended, I left the service, but reenlisted a short time later, reporting to Roswell Army Air Field (RAAF), New Mexico, in or or about March 1947. There I served in the base radio shack as a high-speed code transmission radio operator. In early 1949, I was transferred to the Office of Special Investigations and assigned to District 17 headquarters at Kirtland Air Force Base in Albuquerque.

(5)   While stationed at RAAF, I moonlighted as a bartender in the base officers' club. During the summer of 1947, I heard many rumors about flying saucers in the club and around the base, including something about investigating the discovery of one under the guise of a plane crash investigation. At about this time, I saw Eighth Air Force commander General Roger Ramey in the O club more than once. On a couple of these occasions, he had Charles Lindbergh with him, and I heard they were on the base because of the flying saucer business. There was no publicity about Lindbergh's visits, and I was very surprised to see him in the club. I think he came to Roswell with Ramey, and I seem to recall that on one of these occasions Ramey had flown in from Puerto Rico

(6)   At about the same time, I learned that an officer not stationed at the base, a big man whom I saw in the club a number of times, was a Counter Intelligence Corps (CIC) agent. I do not recall how I learned the man was with CIC, but on one occasion when this officer was in the club, I called him to the attention of Colonel William H. Blanchard, the base commander. Blanchard was unaware that this CIC agent was on his base, so he went over and introduced himself. Later, Blanchard told me there was no problem.

(7)   In early 1949, after being transferred to OSI in Albuquerque, I worked with Dr. Lincoln LaPaz of the University of New Mexico on an extended project at the university's research station on top of Sandia Peak. We were told the Air Force was concerned about "something" being in the night sky over Los Alamos, and we took 15-minute exposures of the sky with a four by five Speed Graphic camera. We worked in three-man, one-week shifts, and Dr. LaPaz was in charge.

(8)   During this project, which lasted for several months, I got to know Dr. LaPaz very well. When I mentioned to him I had been stationed in Roswell

during 1947, he told me he had been involved in the investigation of the thing found in the Roswell area that summer. He did not discuss the case in any detail, but he did say he went out with two agents and interviewed sheepherders, ranchers, and others. They told these witnesses they were investigating an aircraft accident. I seem to recall LaPaz also saying they found an area where the surface of the earth had been turned a light blue and wondering if lightning could cause such an effect.

(10)   I have not been paid or given or promised anything of value to make this statement, which is the truth to the best of my recollection.

EARL L. ZIMMERMAN

Earl Zimmerman _____   _Nov 2, 93_
(Signature and Printed Name)   (Date)

Signature witnessed by:

Beverly J. Maggard _____   _11-2-93_
(Signature and Printed Name)   (Date)

APPENDIX I

THE FORMERLY CLASSIFIED RECORD—REAL AND BOGUS, OCTOBER 1947— NOVEMBER 1948

This appendix presents in chronological order five examples of the authentic formerly classified record concerning UFOs and one clever forgery based upon one of the genuine documents. These documents clearly show that while flying saucers were of great concern to senior U.S. Air Force officials, Roswell did not enter into the picture. They also demonstrate that while physical evidence was on everyone's mind, it was the lack thereof that was bothering them.

The forged document is the artfully edited and created version of the Schulgen draft intelligence collection memorandum package discussed in chapter 15.

DEPARTMENT OF THE AIR FORCE—SECRET   AFOIR-CO/Lt Col Garrett/mcb/4544
                                      28 Oct 47

Intelligence Requirements on Flying Saucer Type Aircraft

Hq, USAF - AFOIR

30 OCT 1947
Lt Col Garrett/mcb/4544

CSGID
Attn: Plans and
Collection Branch

1. It is requested that a Collection Memorandum, similar to the attached draft, be issued to the addressees indicated thereon. This is in accordance with conversation between Lt. Colonel Smith and Lt. Colonel Garrett.

2. It will be appreciated if, at the time this Memorandum is reproduced, ten (10) additional copies could be run off and sent to the Directorate of Intelligence, Air Intelligence Requirements Division, Collection Branch, for file purposes.

FOR THE SECRETARY OF THE AIR FORCE:

2 Incls.
  1. Intelligence
     Requirements
  2. Draft of Collec-
     tion Memorandum

GEO. F. SCHULGEN
Brigadier General, U.S.A.
Chief, Air Intelligence Requirements Div.
Office of Ass't. Chief of Air Staff-2

AAF
30 OCT 1947
AAG - MAIL BRANCH

PRM   11681

OFFICE SYMBOL	1. AFOIR-CO	2. AFOIR	3.	4.	5.
	Col Taylor 3rd				
	Lt Col Garrett	Geo. F. Schulgen Brig. Gen., USA			

Genuine October 30, 1947, Secret draft intelligence collection memorandum package prepared for the signature of Brig. Gen. George F. Schulgen, Chief, Air Intelligence Requirements Division of the Office of the Assistant Chief of Staff of the Air Force for Intelligence.

SECRET

DRAFT OF COLLECTION MEMORANDUM

OBJECT

1. This Memo sets forth the current intelligence requirements in the field of Flying Saucer type aircraft.

GENERAL

1. An alleged "Flying Saucer" type aircraft or object in flight, approximating the shape of a disc, has been reported by many observers from widely scattered places, such as the United States, Alaska, Canada, Hungary, the Island of Guam, and Japan. This object has been reported by many competent observers, including USAF rated officers. Sightings have been made from the ground as well as from the air.

2. Commonly reported features that are very significant and which may aid in the investigation are as follows:

   a. Relatively flat bottom with extreme light-reflecting ability.

   b. Absence of sound except for an occasional roar when operating under super performance conditions.

   c. Extreme maneuverability and apparent ability to almost hover.

   d. A plan form approximating that of an oval or disc with a dome shape on the top surface.

   e. The absence of an exhaust trail except in a few instances when it was reported to have a bluish color, like a Diesel exhaust, which persisted for approximately one hour. Other reports indicated a brownish smoke trail that could be the results of a special catalyst or chemical agent for extra power.

   f. The ability to quickly disappear by high speed or by complete disintegration.

   g. The ability to suddenly appear without warning as if from an extremely high altitude.

   h. The size most reported approximated that of a C-54 or Constellation type aircraft.

   i. The ability to group together very quickly in a tight formation when more than one aircraft are together.

   j. Evasive action ability indicates possibility of being manually operated, or possibly by electronic or remote control devices.

   k. Under certain power conditions, the craft seems to have the ability to cut a clear path through clouds -- width of path estimated to be approximately one-half mile. Only one incident indicated this phenomenon.

SECRET

SECRET

3. The first sightings in the U.S. were reported around the middle of May. The last reported sighting took place in Toronto, Canada, 14 September. The greatest activity in the U.S. was during the last week of June and the first week of July.

4. This strange object, or phenomenon, may be considered, in view of certain observations, as long-range aircraft capable of a high rate of climb, high cruising speed (possibly sub-sonic at all times) and highly maneuverable and capable of being flown in very tight formation. For the purpose of analysis and evaluation of the so-called "flying saucer" phenomenon, the object sighted is being assumed to be a manned aircraft, of Russian origin, and based on the perspective thinking and actual accomplishments of the Germans.

5. There is also a possibility that the Horten brothers' perspective thinking may have inspired this type of aircraft - particularly the "Parabola", which has a crescent plan form. Records show that only a glider version was built of this type aircraft. It is reported to have been built in Heilegenberg, Germany, but was destroyed by fire before having ever been flown. The Horten brothers' latest trend of perspective thinking was definitely toward aircraft configurations of low aspect ratio. The younger brother, Riemar, stated that the "Parabola" configuration would have the least induced drag - which is a very significant statement. The theory supporting this statement should be obtained if possible.

6. The German High Command indicated a definite interest in the Horten type of flying wing and were about to embark on a rigorous campaign to develop such aircraft toward the end of the war. A Horten design, known as the IX, which was designated as the Go-8-229 and Go-P-60 (night fighter) was to be manufactured by the Gotha Plant. It is reported that a contract for fifty such aircraft was planned, but only three or four were built. This plant is now in the hands of the Russians. A recent report indicates that the Russians are now planning to build a fleet of 1,800 Horten VIII (six engine pusher) type flying wing aircraft. The wing span is 131 feet. The sweepback angle is 30 degrees. The Russian version is reported to be jet propelled.

REQUIREMENTS

1. Requirements appear at Inclosure No. 1.

SPECIAL INSTRUCTIONS

Control No. A-1917

DISTRIBUTION

1. To MA's England, France, Sweden, Finland, USSR, Turkey, Greece, Iran, China, Norway, Philippines, and to Commander-in-Chief, Far East, and Commanding General, United States Air Forces in Europe, through Commanding General, EUCOM.

SECRET

~~SECRET~~

INCLOSURE NO. 1

1. Research and Development *X091.4 Byplex* *X201-10c*

   a. What German scientists had a better-than-average knowledge of the Horten brothers' work and perspective thinking; where are these scientists now located, and what is their present activity? Should be contacted and interrogated.

   b. What Russian factories are building the Horten VIII design?

   c. Why are the Russians building 1,800 of the Horten VIII design?

   d. What is their contemplated tactical purpose?

   e. What is the present activity of the Horten brothers, Walter and Riemar?

   f. What is known of the whereabouts of the entire Horten family, particularly the sister? All should be contacted and interrogated regarding any contemplated plans or perspective thinking of the Horten brothers, and any interest shown by the Russians to develop their aircraft.

   g. Are any efforts being made to develop the Horten "Parabola" or modify this configuration to approximate an oval or disc?

   h. What is the Horten perspective thinking on internal controls or controls that are effective mainly by streams of air or gas originating from within the aircraft to supplant conventional external surface controls?

2. Control

   For any aircraft whose shape approximates that of an oval, disc, or saucer, information regarding the following items is requested:

   a. Boundary layer control method by suction, blowing, or a combination of both.

   b. Special controls for effective maneuverability at very slow speeds or extremely high altitudes.

   c. Openings either in the leading edge top and bottom surfaces that are employed chiefly to accomplish boundary layer control or for the purpose of reducing the induced drag. Any openings in the leading edge should be reported and described as to shape, size, etc. This investigation is significant to justify a disc shape configuration for long-range application.

~~SECRET~~

SECRET

d. Approximate airfoil shape in the center and near the tips.

e. Front view and rear view shape.

3. Items of Construction

   a. Type of material, whether metal, ferrous, non-ferrous; or non-metallic.

   b. Composite or sandwich construction utilizing various combinations of metals, plastics, and perhaps balsa wood.

   c. Unusual fabrication methods to achieve extreme light weight and structural stability particularly in connection with great capacity for fuel storage.

4. Items of Arrangement

   a. Special provisions such as retractable domes to provide unusual observation for the pilot or crew members.

   b. Crew number and accomodation facilities.

   c. Pressurized cabin equipment.

   d. High altitude or high speed escapement methods.

   e. Methods of pressurization or supercharging from auxillary units or from the prime power plant.

   f. Provisions for towing - especially with short fixed bar, and for re-fueling in flight.

   g. Provisions for assisted take off application.

   h. Bomb bay provisions, such as dimensions, approximate location, and unusual features regarding the opening and closing of the doors.

5. Landing Gear

   a. Indicate type of landing gear - whether conventional, tricycle, multiple wheel, etc.

   b. Retractable, and jettison features for hand gear.

   c. Provisions for takeoff from ice, snow, or water.

   d. Skid arrangements for either takeoff or landing.

SECRET

SECRET

6. Power Plant

    a. Information is needed regarding the propulsion system used in the aircraft. Possible types of engines that could be employed include:

        (1) Reciprocating (piston type) engine or gas turbine. Either or both of these could be used to drive propellers of conventional or special design, rotating vanes, ducted fans, or compressors.

        (2) Jet propulsion engines including turbo jets, rockets, ramjets, pulse jets, or a combination of all four.

        (3) Nuclear propulsion (atomic energy). Atomic energy engines would probably be unlike any familiar type of engine, although atomic energy might be employed in combination with any of the above types.

           Aircraft would be characterized by lack of fuel systems and fuel storage place.

    b. The power plant would likely be an integral part of the aircraft and could possibly not be distinguished as an item separate from the aircraft. If jet propulsion is used, large air handling capacity, characterized by a large air inlet and large exhaust nozzle, should be evident. The size of entrance and exit areas would be of interest. It is possible that the propulsive jet is governed or influenced for control of the aircraft. The presence of vanes or control surfaces in the exhaust or methods of changing the direction of the jet should be observed.

    c. Information desired on the propulsion systems pertains to the following items:

        (1) Type of power plant or power plants.

        (2) General description.

        (3) Rating (thrust, horsepower, or air flow)

        (4) Type of fuel.

        (5) Catalytic agents for super-performance or normal crusing power.

SECRET

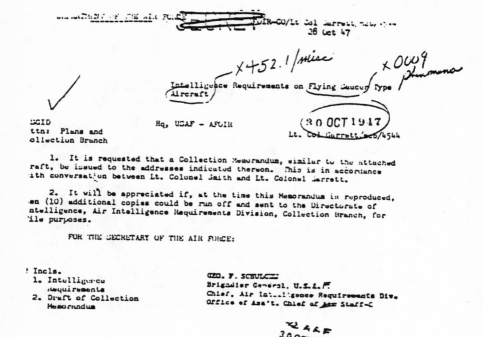

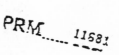

Fraudulent version of the October 30, 1947, Schulgen draft memorandum package made available to UFO researcher Bruce Maccabee by Roswell author William L. Moore in the mid-1980s.

DRAFT OF COLLECTION MEMORANDUM

OBJECT

1. This Memo sets forth the current intelligence requirements in the field of Flying Saucer type aircraft.

GENERAL

1. An alleged "Flying Saucer" type aircraft or object in flight, approximating the shape of a disc, has been reported by many observers from widely scattered places, such as the United States, Alaska, Canada, Hungary, the Island of Guam, and Japan. This object has been reported by many competent observers, including USAF rated officers. Sightings have been made from the ground as well as from the air.

2. Commonly reported features that are very significant and which may aid in the investigation are as follows:

    a. Relatively flat bottom with extreme light-reflecting ability.

    b. Absence of sound except for an occasional roar when operating under super performance conditions.

    c. Extreme maneuverability and apparent ability to almost hover.

    d. A plan form approximating that of an oval or disc with a dome shape on the top surface.

    e. The absence of an exhaust trail except in a few instances when it was reported to have a bluish color, like a Diesel exhaust, which persisted for approximately one hour. Other reports indicated a brownish smoke trail that could be the results of a special catalyst or chemical agent for extra power.

    f. The ability to quickly disappear by high speed or by complete disintegration.

    g. The ability to suddenly appear without warning as if from an extremely high altitude.

    h. The size most reported approximated that of a C-54 or Constellation type aircraft.

    i. The ability to group together very quickly in a tight formation when more than one aircraft are together.

    j. Evasive action ability indicates possibility of being manually operated, or possibly by electronic or remote control devices.

    k. Under certain power conditions, the craft seems to have the ability to cut a clear path through clouds — width of path estimated to be approximately one-half mile. Only one incident indicated this phenomenon.

3. The first sightings in the U.S. were reported around the middle of May. The last reported sightings took place in Toronto, Canada, 14 September. The greatest activity in the U.S. was during the last week of June and the first week of July.

4. This strange object, or phenomenon, may be considered, in view of certain observations, as long-range aircraft capable of a high rate of climb, high cruising speed and highly maneuverable and capable of being flown in very tight formation. For the purpose of analysis and evaluation of these so-called "flying saucers" the object sighted is being assumed to be a manned craft of unknown origin. While there remains the possibility of Russian manufacture, based on the perspective thinking and actual accomplishments of the Germans, it is the considered opinion of some elements that the object may in fact represent an interplanetary craft of some kind.

5. There is also a possibility that the Horton brothers' perspective thinking may have inspired this type of aircraft - particularly the "Parabola", which has a crescent plan form. Records show only that a glider version was built of this type aircraft. It is reported to have been built in Heilegenberg, Germany, but was destroyed by fire before having ever been flown. The Horton brothers' latest trend of perspective thinking was definitely toward aircraft configurations of low aspect ratio. The younger brother, Riemar, stated that the "Parabola" configuration would have the least induced drag - which is a very significant statement. The theory supporting this statement should be obtained if possible.

6. The German High Command indicated a definite interest in the Horton type of flying wing and were about to embark on a rigorous campaign to develop such aircraft during the end of the war. A Horton design, known as the IX, which was designated as the Go-8-229 and Go-P-60 (night fighter) was to be manufactured by the Gotha Plant. It is reported that a contract for fifty such aircraft was planned, but only three or four were built. This plant is now in the hands of the Russians.

REQUIREMENTS

    1. Requirements appear at Inclosure No. 1.

SPECIAL INSTRUCTIONS

        Control No. A-1917

DISTRIBUTION

    1. To MA's England, France, Sweden, Finland, USSR, Turkey, Greece, Iran, China, Norway, Philippines, and to Commander-in-Chief, Far East, and Commanding General, United States Air Forces in Europe, through Commanding General, EUCOM.

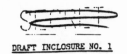

DRAFT INCLOSURE NO. 1

1. Research and Development

   a. What German scientists had a better-than-average knowledge of the Horten brothers' work and perspective thinking; where are these scientists now located, and what is their present activity? These should be contacted and interrogated.

   b. What is the present activity of the Horten brothers, Walter and Riemar?

   c. What is known of the whereabouts of the entire Horten family, particularly the sister? All should be contacted and interrogated regarding any contemplated plans or perspective thinking of the Horten brothers, and any interest shown by the Russians to develop their aircraft.

   d. Are any efforts being made to develop the Horten "Parabola" or modify this configuration to approximate an oval or disc?

   e. What is the Horten perspective thinking on internal controls or controls that are effective mainly by streams of air or gas originating from within the aircraft to supplant conventional external surface controls?

2. Control

   For any aircraft whose shape approximates that of an oval, disc, or saucer, information reagrding the following items is requested:

   a. Boundary layer control method by suction, blowing, or a combination of both.

   b. Special controls for effective maneuverability at very slow speeds or extremely high altitudes.

   c. Openings in either the leading edge top and bottom surfaces that are employed chiefly to accomplish boundary layer control or for the purpose of reducing the induced drag. Any openings in the leading edge should be reported and described as to shape, size, etc. This investigation is significant to justify a disc shape configuration for long-range application.

   d. Approximate airfoil shape in the center and near the tips.

   e. Front view and rear view shape.

3. Items of Construction

   a. Type of material, whether metal, ferrous, non-ferrous. or non-metallic.

   b. Composite or sandwich construction utilizing various combinations of metals, metallic foils, plastics, and perhaps balsa wood or similar material.

   c. Unusual fabrication methods to achieve extreme light weight and structural stability.

4. Items of Arrangement

   a. Special provisions such as retractable domes to provide unusual observation for the pilot or crew members.

   b. Crew number and accomodation facilities.

   c. Pressurized cabin equipment.

   d. High altitude or high speed escapement methods.

   e. Methods of pressurization or supercharging from auxillary units or from the prime power plant.

   f. Provisions for towing - especially with short fixed bar, and for re-fueling in flight.

   g. Provisions for assisted take off application.

   h. Unusual features or provisions regarding the opening and closing of the doors.

   i. Bomb bay provisions, such as dimensions and approximate location.

5. Landing Gear

   a. Indicate type of landing gear - whether conventional, tricycle, multiple wheel, etc., or of an unconventional type such as tripod or skid.

   b. Retractable, and jettison features for hand gear.

   c. Provisions for takeoff from ice, snow, sand or water.

6. Power Plant

   a. Information is needed regarding the propulsion system used in the aircraft. Possible types of engines that could be employed include:

      (1) Reciprocating (piston type) engine or gas turbine. Either or both of these could be used to drive propellers of conventional or special design, rotating vanes, ducted fans, or compressors.

      (2) Jet propulsion engines including turbo jets, rockets, ramjets, pulse jets, or a combination of all four.

      (3) Nuclear propulsion (atomic energy). Atomic energy engines would probably be unlike any familiar type of engine, although atomic energy might be employed in combination with any of the above types.

      Aircraft would be characterized by lack of fuel systems and fuel storage space.

   The presence of an unconventional or unusual type of propulsion system cannot be ruled out and should be considered of great interest.

b. The power plant would likely be an integral part of the aircraft and could possibly not be distinguished as an item separate from the aircraft. If jet propulsion is used, large air handling capacity, characterized by a large air inlet and large exhaust nozzle, should be evident. The size of entrance and exit areas would be of interest. It is possible that the propulsive jet is governed or influenced for control of the aircraft. The presence of vanes or control surfaces in the exhaust or methods of changing the direction of the jet should be observed.

c. Information desired on the propulsion systems pertains to the following items:

(1) Type of power plant or power plants.

(2) General description.

(3) Rating (thrust, horsepower, or air flow).

(4) Type of fuel, or, conversely, lack of visible fuel supply.

(5) Catalytic agents for super-performance or normal cruising power.

SCIENTIFIC ADVISORY BOARD CONFERENCE HELD 17 - 18 MARCH 1948, ROOM SE-869, THE PENTAGON, WASHINGTON, D. C., DR. THEODORE VON KARMAN, CHAIRMAN, PRESIDED. (Conference Convened at 9:00 A.M. and Adjourned at 5:45 P.M. 17 March)

GENERAL CRAIGIE: Gentlemen, may I have your attention, please? We will start our meeting of the Scientific Advisory Board. General Vandenberg will say a few words on behalf of General Spaatz. General Vandenberg.

GENERAL VANDENBERG: Gentlemen, the Chief, as you know, is unavoidably detained at the moment on a project, and asked me to come down and express to you his appreciation for your serving on this Board. He asked me to again state his appreciation and the fact that he feels that it is most important, as I am sure you all agree, that the Scientific end of the business get tied up properly with the military. With world conditions the way they are today, I am sure you all realize as we do that there is a possibility that we may need some expediting of our various scientific resources. I think that at this time the meeting of the Board and the discussions that you will have these few days is of more importance than perhaps it has been at any time since the last war.

Once again, on behalf of General Spaatz, I would like to thank you very much for your attendance and I hope we will have a good meeting. Thank you very much.

GENERAL CRAIGIE: Gentlemen, I would like to add a word of welcome to the Board as a whole, and to Dr. Von Karman in particular, whom we are all very happy to see back in this Country again.

Selected pages from the Secret transcript of the March 17–18, 1948, meeting of the U.S. Air Force Scientific Advisory Board. Col. Howard M. McCoy, Air Materiel Command intelligence chief, discusses an item of recently captured equipment, the establishment of Project Sign to investigate flying saucer reports, and physical evidence of the reality of flying saucers.

COLONEL McCOY [extracts from pp. 77–78 of transcript]:

We only have one recent item of captured equipment, which is a Russian IL-7 aircraft, which crash-landed in Korea a few months ago. We first found out about it in the New York Times. (Laughter) We had our requirements and shipping directions and everything into the theater, through this Headquarters, before they had even

- 77 - **UNCLASSIFIED**

initiated—because of the red tape—the notification of the existence of that piece of equipment. I might add, we have gone over that with a fine-toothed comb. It may be interesting to know it is a type air craft very similar to our P-47, about the same characteristics. It has all the latest and modern innovations of a propeller internal combustion craft.

● ● ●

We have a new project—Project SIGN—which may surprise you as a development from the so-called mass hysteria of the past Summer when we had all the unidentified flying objects or discs. This can't be laughed off. We have over 300 reports which haven't been publicized in the papers from very competent personnel, in many instances—men as capable as Dr. K. D. Wood, and practically all Air Force, Airline people with broad experience. We are running down every report. I can't even tell you how much we would give to have one of those crash in an area so that we could recover whatever they are.

- 78 - **UNCLASSIFIED**

AFOIN-4 (Rev 5 Dec 47) COVER SHEET 2-516

IS. Cont. #

a. RECORD OF BASIC CORRESPONDENCE OR REQUEST

b. CLASSIFICATION: TOP SECRET

| FROM: AFOAI | DATE: 19 Aug 4 |
| | TYPE: Memo for D/I |

SUMMARY:

Progress on Study "Pattern of Tactics of Flying Objects & Probability of Existence."

SUSPENSE

DATE 1 Oct. 48

ASGD BY Col Mussett

DATE RECEIVED DIR/INT Originated, OIN. 27 July 48

NO. OIN - 8540

c. AFOAI: **SPECIAL INSTRUCTIONS – REMARKS**

For completion of final study, per para. 3 of attached Memo.

DATE _____

NO. 5

AFOIN/Col Mussett

USE OTHER SIDE THIS SHEET FOR ADDITIONAL REMARKS

d.

TO DOWN	BR.	TO UP		TO DOWN	DIV.	TO UP		TO DOWN	DIR/INT	TO UP
	OIP-PP								ASST EXEC	
	OIP-FL				AFOIP					
	ADMIN									
	OIR-CO								ASST EXEC	
	OIR-DD									
	OIR-AA				AFOIR					
	OIR-CH								EXECUTIVE X	
	OIR-RC									
	OAI-OA								DIR/INT X	
	OAI-DA								12 Oct	
X	OAI-AE	Out	X		AFOAI	X				
	OAI-AF									
	OAI-SV									
	OCI-IS							DECLASSIFIED		
	OCI-RR				AFOCI			Authority NND 813055		
	OCI-CI							RARS, Date		

X Action
✓ Coordination

e. DATE REC'D BR ____ ACTION ASGD TO ____ DATE 27 July '48 SIGNED ____ DATE 11 Nov 48

f. DISPATCH ____ FILE ____
DISPATCHED BY ____ TO ____
DATE DISPATCHED ____

8-8477,AF

Top Secret October 11, 1948, memorandum from Col. Brooke E. Allen, Chief, Air Estimates Branch of air force intelligence, to Maj. Gen. Charles P. Cabell, air force director of intelligence. Colonel Allen discusses the reality and elusive nature of flying saucers.

g. 10:

SPECIAL INSTRUCTIONS - REMARKS (Continued)

AFOAI

Report attached

Restrict

DATE 11 October '48

NO. 6

1. Report on "Flying Saucers" attached per Gen. Cabell's request.

2. A total of five copies of this study are available for distribution and it is request that OAI be notified of distribution required.

(Lt col Ferill)

Date 11 OCT 48

No. 7

h. TO:

DATE _____

NO. _____

8-3477, AF

I OP SECRET

2-3931
T.S. Cont. #
D.L—Hq. USA¹

MEMORANDUM FOR RECORD

PROBLEM:

1. To transmit completed study, "Analysis of Flying Object Incidents in the U.S."

FACTS AND DISCUSSION:

2. Air Intelligence Division Memorandum, dated 6 August 1948, subject: "Flying Saucers", required that a study be made by the Defensive Air Branch to examine the pattern of tactics of reported flying saucers and develop conclusions as to their probability. Lt. Col. R. N. Smith, Air Estimates Branch, was designated as monitoring officer, and to assist in the preparation of the final report.

3. An interim report on the progress of the study was submitted 11 August 1948, and outlined the methods of analysis being utilized in the preparation of the required study and the methods suggested to Project "Sign" personnel at Headquarters, Air Materiel Command, for pursuing flying object phenomena to the end that positive identification might be achieved.

ACTION:

4. Study completed and forwarded to Air Estimates Branch for final distribution.

DECLASSIFIED
Authority NND 813055
BY   NARS, Date

TOP SECRET

TOP SECRET

2 - 3931

T.S. Cont. #
DI—Hq. USAF

11 October 1948

MEMORANDUM FOR CHIEF, AIR INTELLIGENCE DIVISION

SUBJECT: Analysis of Flying Object Incidents in the U. S.

    1. As directed by Cover Sheet, dated 27 July 1948,
subject "Pattern of Flying Saucers," a study was commenced
to determine the tactics of flying objects and the probability of their existence.

    2. The attached study "Analysis of Flying Object
Incidents in the United States," has been compiled in an
attempt to answer the questions.

    3. An exhaustive study was made of all information
pertinent to the subject in this Division and the Intelligence Division of Air Materiel Command. Opinions of both
aeronautical engineers and well qualified intelligence
specialists have been solicited in an endeavor to consider
all possible aspects of the questions.

    4. Because the subject matter is of such an elusive
nature, this study is presented as a preliminary report to
be reconsidered when information on hand warrants it.

    5. Tentative conclusions have been drawn and are as
follows:

        a. It must be accepted that some type of flying
objects have been observed, although their identification
and origin are not discernable. In the interest of national
defense it would be unwise to overlook the possibility that
some of these objects may be of foreign origin.

        b. Assuming that the objects might eventually be
identified as foreign or foreign-sponsored devices, the
possible reason for their appearance over the U. S. requires

consideration. Several possible explanations appear noteworthy, viz:

>   1. To negate U.S. confidence in the atom bomb
> as the most advanced and decisive weapon in warfare.
>   2. To perform photographic reconnaissance
> missions.
>   3. To test U.S. air defenses.
>   4. To conduct familiarization flights over U.S.
> territory.

   6. It is recommended that distribution of this study be
limited to the Air Staff.

                              BROOKE E. ALLEN
                              Colonel, U.S.A.F.
                              Chief, Air Estimates Branch

DECLASSIFIED PER EXECUTIVE ORDER 12356, Section 3.3, NND 863511

By _WGLewis_ NARA, Date _8/13/86_ .

-214

DEPARTMENT OF THE AIR FORCE
HEADQUARTERS UNITED STATES AIR FORCE
WASHINGTON

3 NOV 1948

SUBJECT: Flying Object Incidents in the United States

TO: Commanding General, Air Materiel Command
          Wright-Patterson Air Force Base
          Dayton, Ohio

1. By letter dated 30 December 1947 from the Director of
Research and Development, Headquarters USAF, your Headquarters
was required to establish Project "SIGN".

2. The conclusion appears inescapable that some type of
flying object has been observed. Identification and the origin
of these objects is not discernible to this Headquarters. It is
imperative, therefore, that efforts to determine whether these
objects are of domestic or foreign origin must be increased until
conclusive evidence is obtained. The needs of national defense
require such evidence in order that appropriate countermeasures
may be taken.

3. In addition to the imperative need for evidence to permit
countermeasures, is the necessity of informing the public as to
the status of the problem. To date there has been too little data
to present to the public. The press, however, is about to take it
into its own hands and demand to be told what we do or do not know
about the situation. Silence on our part will not long be accept-
able.

4. Request immediate information as to your conclusions to
date and your recommendations as to the information to be given
to the press. Your recommendation is requested also as to
whether that information should be offered to the press or withheld until it is actively sought by the press.

        BY COMMAND OF THE CHIEF OF STAFF:

C. P. Cabell
Major General, USAF
Director of Intelligence, Office of
Deputy Chief of Staff, Operations

m-72017

Secret November 3, 1948, request from chief of air force intelligence Maj. Gen. Charles P.
Cabell to the Air Materiel Command for immediate information as to AMC conclusions on flying
saucers; Secret November 8, 1948, response to General Cabell, signed by Howard M. McCoy,
chief of AMC intelligence.

See TS-2-3931
(F Cover Sheet ~~SECRET~~   8 Nov 48
F MR of basic

Basic ltr fr Hq USAF, 3 Nov 48 to CG, AMC, "Flying Object Incidents in
the United States"

1st Ind   MCIAT/ABD/amb

Hq AMC, Wright-Patterson Air Force Base, Dayton, Ohio. 8 Nov 48

TO: Chief of Staff, United States Air Force, Washington 25, D. C., ATTN:
AFOIR

1. In attempting to arrive at conclusions as to the nature of unidentified flying object incidents in the United States, this Command has made
a study of approximately 180 such incidents. Data derived from initial reports have been supplemented by further information obtained from check
lists submitted by mail, from interrogations of other field agencies, and
by personal investigation by personnel of this Command in the case of incidents that seem to indicate the possibility of obtaining particularly
significant information.

2. The objects described fall into the following general classification groups, according to shape or physical configuration:

a. Flat disc of circular or approximately circular shape.

b. Torpedo or cigar shaped aircraft, with no wings or fins visible
in flight.

c. Spherical or balloon shaped objects.

d. Balls of light with no apparent form attached.

3. Some of the objects sighted have definitely been identified, upon
further investigation, as weather or upper air scientific balloons of some
type. A great many of the round or balloon shaped objects indicated in
paragraph 2c above are probably of the same nature, although in most cases,
definite confirmation of that fact has been impossible to obtain.

4. Some of the objects have been identified as being astro-physical
in nature. For example, in daylight sightings, the planet Venus has been
reported as a round, silvery object at extremely high altitude. Action is
being taken to obtain the services of a prominent astro-physicist as a consultant, to study all of the incidents to determine whether some can be
identified as meteors, planets or other manifestations of astral bodies.

5. Arrangements for accomplishing a study of the psychological problems
involved in this project are being made in coordination with the Aero-Medical
Laboratory at this Headquarters. The possibility that some of the sightings
are hallucinations, optical illusions or even deliberate hoaxes has been considered.

File - 6 Jan 48
Maj Jones   *F/C*   2

DECLASSIFIED PER EXECUTIVE ORDER 12356, Section 3.3, NND 86351

By ____WGLewis____

____NARA, Date 8/13/86____.

~~SECRET~~

1st Ind
Basic ltr fr Hq USAF, 3 Nov 48 to CG, AMC, "Flying Object Incidents in
the United States?"

6. Although explanation of many of the incidents can be obtained from
the investigations described above, there remains a certain number of reports for which no reasonable everyday explanation is available. So far,
no physical evidence of the existence of the unidentified sightings has
been obtained. Prominent scientists, including Dr. Irving Langmuir of the
General Electric Company, have been interviewed to determine whether they
could advance any reasonable explanation for characteristics exhibited by
the objects sighted. In an early interview, Dr. Langmuir indicated that
these incidents could be explained, but insufficient data were available
at that time on which to base definite conclusions. It is planned to have
another interview with Dr. Langmuir in the near future to review all the
data now available, and it is hoped that he will be able to present some
opinion as to the nature of many of the unidentified objects, particularly
those described as "balls of light."

7. All information that has been made available to this Headquarters
indicates that the discs, the cigar shaped objects, and the "balls of light"
are not of domestic origin. Engineering investigation indicates that disc
or wingless aircraft could support themselves in flight by aerodynamic means.
It is probable that the problems of stability and control could also be
solved for such aircraft. However, according to current aerodynamic theory
in this country, aircraft with such configurations would have relatively
poor climb, altitude and range characteristics with power plants now in
use.

8. The possibility that the reported objects are vehicles from another
planet has not been ignored. However, tangible evidence to support conclusions about such a possibility are completely lacking. The occurrence
of incidents in relation to the approach to the earth of the planets Mercury,
Venus and Mars have been plotted. A periodic variation in the frequency of
incidents, which appears to have some relation to the planet approach curves,
is noted, but it may be purely a coincidence.

9. Reference is made to "The Books of Charles Fort" with an introduction by Tiffany Thayer, published 1941, by Henry Holt & Co., New York, N. Y.
It appears that similar phenomena have been noted and reported for the past
century or more.

10. In view of the above, the following conclusions are drawn:

a. In the majority of cases reported, observers have actually
sighted some type of flying object which they cannot classify as an aircraft within the limits of their personal experience.

3

T-73017

DECLASSIFIED PER·EXECUTIVE ORDER 12356, Section 3.3, NND 863511

By ___WGLewis___ NARA, Date 8/13/86 .

SECRET

1st Ind

Basic ltr fr Hq USAF, 3 Nov 48 to CG, AMC, "Flying Object Incidents in the United States"

b. There is as yet no conclusive proof that unidentified flying objects, other than those which are known to be balloons, are real aircraft.

c. Although it is obvious that some types of flying objects have been sighted, the exact nature of those objects cannot be established until physical evidence, such as that which would result from a crash, has been obtained.

11. It is not considered advisable to present to the press information on those objects which we cannot yet identify or about which we cannot present any reasonable conclusions. In the event that they insist on some kind of a statement, it is suggested that they be informed that many of the objects sighted have been identified as weather balloons or astral bodies, and that investigation is being pursued to determine reasonable explanations for the others.

12. A report, summarizing the results obtained from analysis of the data and a technical investigation of the engineering aspects of the objects described, is nearly complete, and a copy will be forwarded to your Headquarters in the near future.

FOR THE COMMANDING GENERAL:

H. M. McCOY
Colonel, USAF
Chief, Intelligence Department

Index

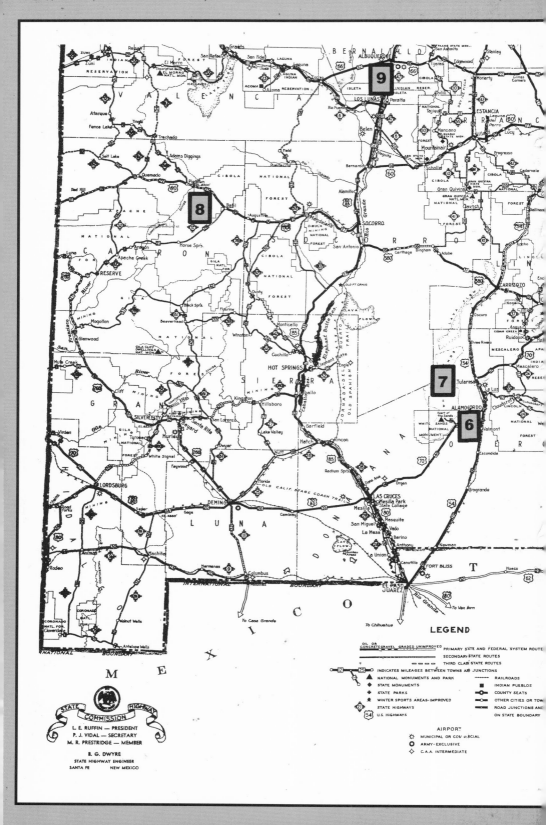